MKSAP® 16

Medical Knowledge Self-Assessment Program®

Nephrology

D0731218

Welcome to the Nephrology section of MKSAP 16!

Here, you will find updated information on the clinical evaluation of kidney function, fluids and electrolytes, acid-base disorders, hypertension, chronic tubulointerstitial disorders, glomerular diseases, genetic disorders and kidney disease, acute kidney injury, kidney stones, the kidney in pregnancy, and chronic kidney disease. All of these topics are uniquely focused on the needs of generalists and subspecialists *outside* of nephrology.

The publication of the 16th edition of Medical Knowledge Self-Assessment Program heralds a significant event, culminating 2 years of effort by dozens of leading subspecialists across the United States. Our authoring committees have strived to help internists succeed in Maintenance of Certification, right up to preparing for the MOC examination, and to get residents ready for the certifying examination. MKSAP 16 also helps you update your medical knowledge and elevates standards of self-learning by allowing you to assess your knowledge with 1,200 all-new multiple-choice questions, including 108 in Nephrology.

MKSAP began more than 40 years ago. The American Board of Internal Medicine's examination blueprint and gaps between actual and preferred practices inform creation of the content. The questions, refined through rigorous face-to-face meetings, are among the best in medicine. A psychometric analysis of the items sharpens our educational focus on weaknesses in practice. To meet diverse learning styles, we offer MKSAP 16 online and in downloadable apps for PCs, tablets, laptops, and smartphones. We are also introducing the following:

High-Value Care Recommendations: The Nephrology section starts with several recommendations based on the important concept of health care value (balancing clinical benefit with costs and harms) to address the needs of trainees, practicing physicians, and patients. These recommendations are part of a major initiative that has been undertaken by the American College of Physicians, in collaboration with other organizations.

Content for Hospitalists: This material, highlighted in blue and labeled with the familiar hospital icon (H), directly addresses the learning needs of the increasing number of physicians who work in the hospital setting. MKSAP 16 Digital will allow you to customize quizzes based on hospitalist-only questions to help you prepare for the Hospital Medicine Maintenance of Certification Examination.

We hope you enjoy and benefit from MKSAP 16. Please feel free to send us any comments to mksap_editors@acponline.org or visit us at the MKSAP Resource Site (mksap.acponline.org) to find out how we can help you study, earn CME, accumulate MOC points, and stay up to date. I know I speak on behalf of ACP staff members and our authoring committees when I say we are honored to have attracted your interest and participation.

Sincerely,

Patrick Alguire, MD, FACP
Editor-in-Chief
Senior Vice President
Medical Education Division
American College of Physicians

Nephrology

Committee

Gerald A. Hladik, MD, Editor[1]
Doc J. Thurston Distinguished Professor of Medicine
University of North Carolina Kidney Center
Training Program Director, Division of Nephrology
The University of North Carolina at Chapel Hill
Chapel Hill, North Carolina

Virginia U. Collier, MD, MACP, Associate Editor[2]
Hugh R. Sharp, Jr. Chair of Medicine
Christiana Care Health System
Newark, Delaware
Professor of Medicine
Jefferson Medical College of Thomas Jefferson University
Philadelphia, Pennsylvania

Gabriel Contreras, MD, MPH[2]
Professor of Clinical Medicine
University of Miami
Miller School of Medicine
Division of Nephrology and Hypertension
Miami, Florida

Melanie Hoenig, MD[1]
Assistant Professor
Harvard Medical School
Renal Division
Beth Israel Deaconess Hospital
Joslin Clinic
Boston, Massachusetts

James Paparello, MD[2]
Associate Professor
Department of Medicine, Nephrology
Northwestern University
Chicago, Illinois

Raymond R. Townsend, MD[2]
Professor of Medicine
Department of Medicine, Renal Division
Perelman School of Medicine
University of Pennsylvania
Philadelphia, Pennsylvania

Suzanne Watnick, MD[1]
Associate Professor of Medicine
Training Program Director, Nephrology
Division of Nephrology and Hypertension
Portland VA Medical Center and

Oregon Health and Science University
Portland, Oregon

Editor-in-Chief

Patrick C. Alguire, MD, FACP[1]
Senior Vice President, Medical Education
American College of Physicians
Philadelphia, Pennsylvania

Deputy Editor-in-Chief

Philip A. Masters, MD, FACP[1]
Senior Medical Associate for Content Development
American College of Physicians
Philadelphia, Pennsylvania

Senior Medical Associate for Content Development

Cynthia D. Smith, MD, FACP[2]
American College of Physicians
Philadelphia, Pennsylvania

Nephrology Clinical Editor

Virginia U. Collier, MD, MACP[2]

Nephrology Reviewers

Robert J. Anderson, MD, MACP[1]
Pieter Cohen, MD, FACP[1]
Frantz Duffoo, MD, FACP[1]
Robert T. Means, Jr., MD, FACP[2]
Ileana L. Piña, MD, MPH[2]
Steven Ricanati, MD, FACP[1]
Mark D. Siegel, MD, FACP[2]

Nephrology Reviewer Representing the American Society for Clinical Pharmacology & Therapeutics

Carol Collins, MD[1]

Nephrology ACP Editorial Staff

Megan Zborowski[1], Staff Editor
Sean McKinney[1], Director, Self-Assessment Programs
Margaret Wells[1], Managing Editor
Linnea Donnarumma[1], Assistant Editor

ACP Principal Staff

Patrick C. Alguire, MD, FACP[1]
Senior Vice President, Medical Education

D. Theresa Kanya, MBA[1]
Vice President, Medical Education

Sean McKinney[1]
Director, Self-Assessment Programs

Margaret Wells[1]
Managing Editor

Valerie Dangovetsky[1]
Program Administrator

Becky Krumm[1]
Senior Staff Editor

Ellen McDonald, PhD[1]
Senior Staff Editor

Katie Idell[1]
Senior Staff Editor

Randy Hendrickson[1]
Production Administrator/Editor

Megan Zborowski[1]
Staff Editor

Linnea Donnarumma[1]
Assistant Editor

John Haefele[1]
Assistant Editor

Developed by the American College of Physicians

---

1. Has no relationships with any entity producing, marketing, re-selling, or distributing health care goods or services consumed by, or used on, patients.

2. Has disclosed relationships with entities producing, marketing, re-selling, or distributing health care goods or services consumed by, or used on, patients. See below.

Conflicts of Interest

The following committee members, reviewers, and ACP staff members have disclosed relationships with commercial companies:

Virginia U. Collier, MD, MACP
Stock Options/Holdings
Celgene, Pfizer, Merck, Schering-Plough, Abbott, Johnson and Johnson, Medtronic, McKesson, Amgen

Gabriel Contreras, MD, MPH
Speakers Bureau
Roche

Robert T. Means, Jr., MD
Consultantship
Beckman Coulter

James Paparello, MD
Other
Medtronic

Ileana L. Piña, MD
Employment
Case Western Reserve University
Research Grants/Contracts
NIH
Consultantship
FDA, GE HealthCare, Solvay
Speakers Bureau
AstraZeneca, Novartis, Otuska

Mark D. Siegel, MD, FACP
Research Grants/Contracts
Altor Bioscience, Bristol-Myers Squibb, Pfizer
Consultantship
Siemens

Cynthia D. Smith, MD, FACP
Stock Options/Holdings
Merck and Company

Raymond R. Townsend, MD
Consultantship
Pfizer, Novartis, Nicox, Medtronic
Speakers Bureau
ASN, ASH
Research Grants/Contracts
NIH

Acknowledgments

The American College of Physicians (ACP) gratefully acknowledges the special contributions to the development and production of the 16th edition of the Medical Knowledge Self-Assessment Program® (MKSAP® 16) made by the following people:

Graphic Services: Michael Ripca (Technical Administrator/Graphic Designer) and Willie-Fetchko Graphic Design (Graphic Designer).

Production/Systems: Dan Hoffmann (Director, Web Services & Systems Development), Neil Kohl (Senior Architect), and Scott Hurd (Senior Systems Analyst/Developer).

MKSAP 16 Digital: Under the direction of Steven Spadt, Vice President, ACP Digital Products & Services, the digital version of MKSAP 16 was developed within the ACP's Digital Product Development Department, led by Brian Sweigard (Director). Other members of the team included Sean O'Donnell (Senior Architect), Dan Barron (Senior Systems Analyst/Developer), Chris Forrest (Senior Software Developer/Design Lead), Jon Laing (Senior Web Application Developer), Brad Lord (Senior Web Developer), John McKnight (Senior Web Developer), and Nate Pershall (Senior Web Developer).

The College also wishes to acknowledge that many other persons, too numerous to mention, have contributed to the production of this program. Without their dedicated efforts, this program would not have been possible.

Introducing the MKSAP Resource Site (mksap.acponline.org)

The MKSAP Resource Site (mksap.acponline.org) is a continually updated site that provides links to MKSAP 16 online answer sheets for print subscribers; access to MKSAP 16 Digital, Board Basics® 3, and MKSAP 16 Updates; the latest details on Continuing Medical Education (CME) and Maintenance of Certification (MOC) in the United States, Canada, and Australia; errata; and other new information.

ABIM Maintenance of Certification

Check the MKSAP Resource Site (mksap.acponline.org) for the latest information on how MKSAP tests can be used to apply to the American Board of Internal Medicine for Maintenance of Certification (MOC) points.

RCPSC Maintenance of Certification

In Canada, MKSAP 16 is an Accredited Self-Assessment Program (Section 3) as defined by the Maintenance of Certification Program of The Royal College of Physicians and Surgeons of Canada (RCPSC) and approved by the Canadian Society of Internal Medicine on December 9, 2011. Approval of Part A sections of MKSAP 16 extends from July 31, 2012, until July 31, 2015. Approval of Part B sections of MKSAP 16 extends from December 31, 2012, to December 31, 2015. Fellows of the Royal College may earn three credits per hour for participating in MKSAP 16 under Section 3. MKSAP 16 will enable Fellows to earn up to 75% of their required 400 credits during the 5-year MOC cycle. A Fellow can achieve this 75% level by earning 100 of the maximum of 174 *AMA PRA Category 1 Credits*™ available in MKSAP 16. MKSAP 16 also meets multiple CanMEDS Roles for RCPSC MOC, including that of Medical Expert, Communicator, Collaborator, Manager, Health Advocate, Scholar, and Professional. For information on how to apply MKSAP 16 CME credits to RCPSC MOC, visit the MKSAP Resource Site at mksap.acponline.org.

The Royal Australasian College of Physicians CPD Program

In Australia, MKSAP 16 is a Category 3 program that may be used by Fellows of The Royal Australasian College of Physicians (RACP) to meet mandatory CPD points. Two CPD credits are awarded for each of the 174 *AMA PRA Category 1 Credits*™ available in MKSAP 16. More information about using MKSAP 16 for this purpose is available at the MKSAP Resource Site at mksap.acponline.org and at www.racp.edu.au. CPD credits earned through MKSAP 16 should be reported at the MyCPD site at www.racp.edu.au/mycpd.

Continuing Medical Education

The American College of Physicians is accredited by the Accreditation Council for Continuing Medical Education (ACCME) to provide continuing medical education for physicians.

The American College of Physicians designates this enduring material, MKSAP 16, for a maximum of 174 *AMA PRA Category 1 Credits*™. Physicians should claim only the credit commensurate with the extent of their participation in the activity.

Up to 16 *AMA PRA Category 1 Credits*™ are available from December 31, 2012, to December 31, 2015, for the MKSAP 16 Nephrology section.

Learning Objectives

The learning objectives of MKSAP 16 are to:
- Close gaps between actual care in your practice and preferred standards of care, based on best evidence
- Diagnose disease states that are less common and sometimes overlooked and confusing
- Improve management of comorbid conditions that can complicate patient care
- Determine when to refer patients for surgery or care by subspecialists
- Pass the ABIM Certification Examination
- Pass the ABIM Maintenance of Certification Examination

Target Audience

- General internists and primary care physicians
- Subspecialists who need to remain up-to-date in internal medicine
- Residents preparing for the certifying examination in internal medicine
- Physicians preparing for maintenance of certification in internal medicine (recertification)

Earn "Same-Day" CME Credits Online

For the first time, print subscribers can enter their answers online to earn CME credits in 24 hours or less. You can submit your answers using online answer sheets that are provided at mksap.acponline.org, where a record of your MKSAP 16 credits will be available. To earn CME credits, you need to answer all of the questions in a test and earn a score of at least 50% correct (number of correct answers divided by the total number of questions). Take any of the following approaches:

1. Use the printed answer sheet at the back of this book to record your answers. Go to mksap.acponline.org, access the appropriate online answer sheet, transcribe your answers, and submit your test for same-day CME credits. There is no additional fee for this service.

2. Go to mksap.acponline.org, access the appropriate online answer sheet, directly enter your answers, and submit your test for same-day CME credits. There is no additional fee for this service.

3. Pay a $10 processing fee per answer sheet and submit the printed answer sheet at the back of this book by mail or fax, as instructed on the answer sheet. Make sure you calculate your score and fax the answer sheet to 215-351-2799 or mail the answer sheet to Member and Customer Service, American College of Physicians, 190 N. Independence Mall West, Philadelphia, PA 19106-1572, using the courtesy envelope provided in your MKSAP 16 slipcase. You will need your 10-digit order number and 8-digit ACP ID number, which are printed on your packing slip. Please allow 4 to 6 weeks for your score report to be emailed back to you. Be sure to include your email address for a response.

If you do not have a 10-digit order number and 8-digit ACP ID number or if you need help creating a username and password to access the MKSAP 16 online answer sheets, go to mksap.acponline.org or email custserv@acponline.org.

Disclosure Policy

It is the policy of the American College of Physicians (ACP) to ensure balance, independence, objectivity, and scientific rigor in all of its educational activities. To this end, and consistent with the policies of the ACP and the Accreditation Council for Continuing Medical Education (ACCME), contributors to all ACP continuing medical education activities are required to disclose all relevant financial relationships with any entity producing, marketing, re-selling, or distributing health care goods or services consumed by, or used on, patients. Contributors are required to use generic names in the discussion of therapeutic options and are required to identify any unapproved, off-label, or investigative use of commercial products or devices. Where a trade name is used, all available trade names for the same product type are also included. If trade-name products manufactured by companies with whom contributors have relationships are discussed, contributors are asked to provide evidence-based citations in support of the discussion. The information is reviewed by the committee responsible for producing this text. If necessary, adjustments to topics or contributors' roles in content development are made to balance the discussion. Further, all readers of this text are asked to evaluate the content for evidence of commercial bias and send any relevant comments to mksap_editors@acponline.org so that future decisions about content and contributors can be made in light of this information.

Resolution of Conflicts

To resolve all conflicts of interest and influences of vested interests, the ACP precluded members of the content-creation committee from deciding on any content issues that involved generic or trade-name products associated with proprietary entities with which these committee members had relationships. In addition, content was based on best evidence and updated clinical care guidelines, when such evidence and guidelines were available. Contributors' disclosure information can be found with the list of contributors' names and those of ACP principal staff listed in the beginning of this book.

Hospital-Based Medicine

For the convenience of subscribers who provide care in hospital settings, content that is specific to the hospital setting has been highlighted in blue. Hospital icons (H) highlight where the hospital-only content begins, continues over more than one page, and ends.

Educational Disclaimer

The editors and publisher of MKSAP 16 recognize that the development of new material offers many opportunities for error. Despite our best efforts, some errors may persist in print. Drug dosage schedules are, we believe, accurate and in accordance with current standards. Readers are advised, however, to ensure that the recommended dosages in MKSAP 16 concur with the information provided in the product information material. This is especially important in cases of new, infrequently used, or highly toxic drugs. Application of the information in MKSAP 16 remains the professional responsibility of the practitioner.

The primary purpose of MKSAP 16 is educational. Information presented, as well as publications, technologies, products, and/or services discussed, is intended to inform subscribers about the knowledge, techniques, and experiences of the contributors. A diversity of professional opinion exists, and the views of the contributors are their own and not those of the ACP. Inclusion of any material in the program does not constitute endorsement or recommendation by the ACP. The ACP does not warrant the safety, reliability, accuracy, completeness, or usefulness of and disclaims any and all liability for damages and claims that may result from the use of information, publications, technologies, products, and/or services discussed in this program.

Publisher's Information

Unauthorized Use of This Book Is Against the Law

The ACP will consider granting an individual permission to reproduce only limited portions of this publication for his or her own exclusive use. Send requests in writing to MKSAP® Permissions, American College of Physicians, 190 N. Independence Mall West, Philadelphia, PA 19106-1572, or email your request to mksap_editors@acponline.org.

MKSAP 16 ISBN: 978-1-938245-00-8
(Nephrology) ISBN: 978-1-938245-10-7

Printed in the United States of America.

For order information in the U.S. or Canada call 800-523-1546, extension 2600. All other countries call 215-351-2600. Fax inquiries to 215-351-2799 or email to custserv@acponline.org.

Errata and Norm Tables

Errata for MKSAP 16 will be available through the MKSAP Resource Site at mksap.acponline.org as new information becomes known to the editors.

MKSAP 16 Performance Interpretation Guidelines with Norm Tables, available July 31, 2013, will reflect the knowledge of physicians who have completed the self-assessment tests before the program was published. These physicians took the tests without being able to refer to the syllabus, answers, and critiques. For your convenience, the tables are available in a printable PDF file through the MKSAP Resource Site at mksap.acponline.org.

Table of Contents

Nephrology High-Value Care Recommendations

The American College of Physicians, in collaboration with multiple other organizations, is embarking on a national initiative to promote awareness about the importance of stewardship of health care resources. The goals are to improve health care outcomes by providing care of proven benefit and reducing costs by avoiding unnecessary and even harmful interventions. The initiative comprises several programs that integrate the important concept of health care value (balancing clinical benefit with costs and harms) for a given intervention into various educational materials to address the needs of trainees, practicing physicians, and patients.

To integrate discussion of high-value, cost-conscious care into MKSAP 16, we have created recommendations based on the medical knowledge content that we feel meet the below definition of high-value care and bring us closer to our goal of improving patient outcomes while conserving finite resources.

High-Value Care Recommendation: A recommendation to choose diagnostic and management strategies for patients in specific clinical situations that balances clinical benefit with cost and harms with the goal of improving patient outcomes.

Below are the High-Value Care Recommendations for the Nephrology section of MKSAP 16.

- Kidney ultrasonography is safe, not dependent upon kidney function, noninvasive, and relatively inexpensive and may be used to diagnose urinary tract obstruction, cysts, and mass lesions as well as to assess kidney size and cortical thickness (see Item 90).
- Although home blood pressure monitors are usually not reimbursed by insurers, their relatively low cost (usually less than $100) and reasonable accuracy have made them attractive components to the management of hypertension.
- There is wide variability in the cost of antihypertensive medications; newer and more expensive agents have not been shown to be significantly safer or more effective than many older, well-established medications that are available in generic form.
- Fixed combinations of antihypertensive medications offer less dosing flexibility and are often substantially more expensive than prescribing the component medications independently.
- Lifestyle modifications, including weight loss, reduction of dietary sodium intake, aerobic physical activity of at least 30 minutes a day at least three times a week, and a reduction in alcohol consumption, are a relatively cost-effective way to reduce high blood pressure (see Item 6 and Item 102).
- Only consider evaluating for secondary causes of hypertension when there is onset at a young age, no family history, no risk factors, rapid onset of significant hypertension, abrupt change in blood pressure in a patient with previously good control, or a concomitant endocrine abnormality (see Item 43, Item 58, Item 62, Item 91, and Item 107).
- The benefit of ultrafiltration for fluid removal over adequately dosed diuretics is unproved, especially when the risk of the procedure (central line placement) and increased hypotension are considered.
- Rasburicase is considerably more expensive than allopurinol and is therefore used primarily in patients with high risk for tumor lysis syndrome or if excessively high uric acid levels occur in the context of chemotherapy (see Item 3).
- Plain abdominal radiography has no role in the acute diagnosis of kidney stones (see Item 21 and Item 75).
- Cinacalcet is currently the only calcimimetic agent available; this agent is very expensive, and its role in patients with chronic kidney disease has not yet been defined (see Item 42).
- There is no role for the routine measurement of erythropoietin levels in patients with chronic kidney disease (see Item 105).
- Hospice services are infrequently utilized for patients with end-stage kidney disease who choose to avoid or withdraw from dialysis but would be a potential benefit.

Clinical Evaluation of Kidney Function

Glomerular Filtration Rate

Glomerular filtration rate (GFR) is the parameter most frequently used to assess kidney function and monitor disease progression. GFR can be estimated by mathematical equations based on the serum creatinine level or, in special circumstances, by methods such as creatinine clearance measurement or radionuclide kidney clearance scanning.

Estimation of Glomerular Filtration Rate

Serum Indicators of Kidney Function

Measurement of the serum creatinine level has historically been used to evaluate kidney function. The relationship between GFR and serum creatinine is not linear, but inversely proportional (**Figure 1**). A 50% reduction in GFR results in a doubling of the serum creatinine level once steady state conditions are attained. At high levels of GFR, small changes in the serum creatinine level may reflect large changes in GFR. At low levels of GFR, large changes in the serum creatinine level reflect relatively smaller changes in GFR. In patients who become functionally anephric (for

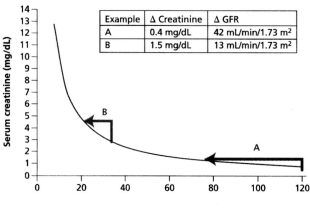

Example	Δ Creatinine	Δ GFR
A	0.4 mg/dL	42 mL/min/1.73 m²
B	1.5 mg/dL	13 mL/min/1.73 m²

FIGURE 1. The relationship between serum creatinine and glomerular filtration rate. Example A illustrates that a small increase in the serum creatinine level in the reference range (in this case, 0.8 to 1.2 mg/dL [70.7-106 micromoles/L]) reflects a relatively large change in GFR (120 to 78 mL/min/1.73 m²). Example B illustrates that a relatively greater increase in the serum creatinine level (in the high range of 3.0 to 4.5 mg/dL [265-398 micromoles/L]) reflects a proportionately smaller change in GFR (35 to 22 mL/min/1.73 m²). GFR = glomerular filtration rate.

example, from profound acute kidney injury), the serum creatinine level typically increases 1.0 to 1.5 mg/dL (88.4-133 micromoles/L) per day.

Although serum creatinine is one of the most commonly used markers of GFR, it is an imperfect measure of kidney function. Reduction of muscle mass, as seen in amputees and patients with malnutrition or muscle wasting, can result in a lower serum creatinine level without a corresponding change in GFR. Younger persons, men, and black persons often have higher muscle mass and higher serum creatinine levels at a given level of GFR compared with older persons with decreased muscle mass. Patients with advanced liver disease produce lower levels of precursors of serum creatinine and often have muscle wasting, with a correspondingly lower serum creatinine level at a particular level of GFR. Finally, serum creatinine overestimates kidney function in elderly persons, especially women.

Certain medications, including cimetidine and trimethoprim, block tubular secretion of creatinine and result in a higher serum creatinine level without a change in GFR. The nephrotic syndrome is associated with increased tubular secretion of creatinine, leading to overestimation of GFR. The colorimetric assay for serum creatinine cross-reacts with cefoxitin, flucytosine, and acetoacetate, leading to falsely high values. Elevated bilirubin levels interfere with the colorimetric assay, resulting in falsely low values of serum creatinine.

Serum cystatin C is an alternative marker of GFR that is less influenced by age, gender, muscle mass, and body weight compared with serum creatinine. Serum cystatin C is more sensitive in identifying milder decrements in kidney function than serum creatinine. Serum levels, however, are affected by thyroid status, inflammation, diabetic status, and corticosteroid use. The clinical utility of serum cystatin C remains to be established, and it is not clear whether serum cystatin C will replace the serum creatinine level as a marker of GFR.

Blood urea nitrogen (BUN) is derived from the metabolism of proteins. Although widely used, BUN concentration is a poor marker of kidney function for several reasons: it is not produced at a constant rate; it is reabsorbed along the tubules; and alterations in kidney blood flow markedly influence tubular reabsorption and excretion. BUN should not be used in isolation to predict kidney function. Urea clearances significantly underestimate GFR but may be useful in estimating GFR when it is less than 15 mL/min/1.73 m². **Table 1** outlines several factors unrelated to the kidney that can affect BUN and serum creatinine levels.

TABLE 1.	Factors Altering Blood Urea Nitrogen and Serum Creatinine Levels Independent of Kidney Function	
	Decreased	**Increased**
Blood urea nitrogen	Muscle wasting; protein malnutrition; cirrhosis	Poor kidney perfusion (volume depletion, chronic heart failure, cirrhosis); gastrointestinal bleeding; hyperalimentation; hypercatabolic states
Serum creatinine	Decreased muscle mass; cirrhosis	Tubular secretion blocked (trimethoprim, cimetidine); interference of assay (ketones, bilirubin, flucytosine, cephalosporins); overproduction (creatine ingestion, rhabdomyolysis, sustained exercise)

Methods for Estimating Glomerular Filtration Rate

The National Kidney Foundation Kidney Disease Outcomes Quality Initiative (NKF KDOQI) recommends the use of mathematical equations to estimate GFR (**Table 2**). These equations should only be used when the serum creatinine level has been stable for at least 24 to 48 hours.

The Modification of Diet in Renal Disease (MDRD) study equation has been validated in multiple populations with chronic kidney disease (CKD); however, this equation frequently underestimates GFR when it is greater than 60 mL/min/1.73 m². The Chronic Kidney Disease Epidemiology (CKD-EPI) Collaboration equation performs better at higher (normal) values of GFR.

Accurate estimation of GFR is important for appropriate adjustment of drug dosing, particularly in the elderly population and in patients with kidney disease. Historically, drug dosing guidelines were developed based on the estimated creatinine clearance derived from the Cockcroft-Gault equation. This equation takes into account lean body weight, age, and gender. Simulation studies show a high concordance rate between the estimates via the Cockcroft-Gault and MDRD study equations for drug dosing.

Most clinical laboratories employ the MDRD study equation to estimate GFR, and higher levels of GFR are reported as ">60 mL/min/1.73 m²." This practice raises concern because physicians may ignore other signs or symptoms of CKD, such as proteinuria, after erroneously assuming that the GFR is normal. Conversely, the benefits of labeling a patient with a stable GFR around 55 mL/min/1.73 m² (apart from guiding appropriate drug dosing) as having stage 3 CKD when there are no other signs of kidney disease remain unclear.

Estimation equations are less accurate when there are extremes in age and weight, in the setting of pregnancy, and in patients who have undergone amputation or have underlying cirrhosis. In these circumstances, a 24-hour urine collection for creatinine clearance should be used to estimate GFR. Because creatinine is secreted by renal tubules, creatinine clearance overestimates GFR. Inaccuracies arise with over- or undercollection of urine. Observed creatinine excretion can be compared with expected excretion to assess the accuracy of the sample. The expected excretion of creatinine is 20 to 25 mg/kg/24 h (177-221 mmol/kg/24 h) for men and 15 to 20 mg/kg/24 h (133-177 mmol/kg/24 h) for women.

GFR can be measured very precisely using radionuclide kidney clearance scanning, which measures clearance of radiolabeled iothalamate or diethylenetriamine pentaacetic acid (DTPA). The complexity and cost of these methods limit use in clinical practice, but they may be of value when there is a need to precisely measure GFR.

KEY POINTS

- Most clinical laboratories employ the Modification of Diet in Renal Disease study equation to estimate the glomerular filtration rate (GFR), and higher levels of GFR are often reported as ">60 mL/min/1.73 m²."

- Observed creatinine excretion can be compared with expected excretion to assess the accuracy of a 24-hour urine collection.

- Glomerular filtration rate can be measured very precisely using radionuclide kidney clearance scanning.

Interpretation of the Urinalysis

Dipstick analysis and microscopic examination of the urine are indicated in the clinical evaluation of kidney function for both acute and chronic kidney disease (**Table 3, on page 4**). The sample is best collected without contamination, which requires a "clean catch" midstream collection or a bladder catheterization. The specimen should ideally be examined within 1 hour of being produced to minimize the breakdown of formed elements.

Urine Dipstick

Specific Gravity

Specific gravity is the ratio of the weight of urine to an equal quantity of the weight of water. The typical range is 1.005 to 1.030 but can vary depending on hydration status and the capacity of an individual's kidneys to maximally dilute and concentrate the urine. **Table 4 (on page 4)** illustrates the approximate urine osmolality that corresponds to a given value of urine specific gravity.

pH

Ingestion of a typical high-protein American diet results in consumption of a high "acid-ash" content and the need to

TABLE 2. Methods for Estimating Kidney Function

Method	Considerations	Application
Modification of Diet in Renal Disease (MDRD) Study Equation[a]		
$GFR = 175 \times (Scr)^{-1.154} \times (age)^{-0.203} \times 0.742$ (if female) or $\times 1.212$ (if black)	Most accurate when eGFR is 15-60 mL/min/1.73 m^2	Chronic kidney disease when GFR is 15-60 mL/min/1.73 m^2
	Underestimates GFR when GFR >60 mL/min/1.73 m^2	
	Less accurate in populations with normal or near normal GFR, extremes of age and weight, amputees, in pregnancy, and cirrhosis	
Chronic Kidney Disease Epidemiology (CKD-EPI) Collaboration Study Equation[a]		
$GFR = 141 \times min(Scr/K,1)^{\alpha} \times max(Scr/K,1)^{-1.209} \times 0.993^{age} \times 1.018$ (if female) $\times 1.159$ (if black)[b]	Superior to CGE and MDRD equations in patients with eGFR <60 mL/min/1.73 m^2	More accurate than MDRD equation in elderly population
Cockcroft-Gault Equation (CGE)		
$CrCl = \dfrac{(140 - age) \times (weight\ in\ kg) \times (0.85\ if\ female)}{(72 \times Scr)}$	Most accurate when eGFR is 15-60 mL/min/1.73 m^2	Improved accuracy when age is <65 years
	Underestimates GFR in obesity	
	Overestimates GFR when BMI <25	
Creatinine Clearance		
$\dfrac{Ucr\ (mg/dL) \times 24\text{-}hour\ urine\ volume\ (mL/24\ h)}{Scr\ (mg/dL) \times 1440\ (min/24\ h)}$	Overestimates GFR 10%-20%	Use in pregnancy, extremes of age and weight, amputees, and cirrhosis
	Incomplete or excessive 24-hour urine collections limit accuracy	
Serum Cystatin C		
	Levels are affected by thyroid status, inflammation, and corticosteroids	More accurate in elderly population and patients with cirrhosis
Radionuclide Kidney Clearance Scanning		
Iothalamate GFR scan Diethylenetriamine pentaacetic acid (DTPA) GFR scan	Most precise method and expensive	Kidney donor evaluation if GFR is borderline for donation; research; prediction of GFR following nephrectomy

CrCl = creatinine clearance; eGFR = estimated glomerular filtration rate; GFR = glomerular filtration rate; Scr = serum creatinine (mg/dL); Ucr = urine creatinine (mg/dL).

[a]Mathematical equations recommended by the National Kidney Foundation Kidney Disease Outcomes Quality Initiative for estimation of GFR.

[b]K is 0.7 for women and 0.9 for men; α is -0.329 for women and -0.411 for men; min = the minimum of Scr/K or 1; max = the maximum of Scr/K or 1.

excrete the acid load, primarily via the kidneys. The urine in this case is relatively more acidic, ranging from 5.0 to 6.0. An alkaline pH of 7.0 or greater can occur in strict vegetarians, patients with distal renal tubular acidosis, or those with infections caused by urease-splitting organisms, including *Proteus* and *Pseudomonas* species.

Albumin
Albumin is the predominant protein detected on urine dipstick. The urine dipstick detects albumin excretion graded as trace (5-30 mg/dL), 1+ (30 mg/dL), 2+ (100 mg/dL), 3+ (300 mg/dL), and 4+ (>1000 mg/dL). Highly alkaline urine specimens can produce false-positive results.

The sulfosalicylic acid (SSA) test is a simple bedside test that can be used to detect the presence of albumin and other proteins such as urine light chains. Recent exposure to radiocontrast can result in false-positive results. The diagnosis of myeloma cast nephropathy should be raised in patients with acute kidney injury when the urine dipstick reads negative or trace for protein but shows increased positivity for protein by the SSA test, reflecting the presence of urine light chains or immunoglobulins not detected by the urine dipstick.

TABLE 3. Findings on Urinalysis

	Reference Range	Comments
Dipstick		
Specific gravity	1.005-1.030	Low with dilute urine; high with concentrated urine or hypertonic product excretion such as contrast dye
pH	5.0-6.5	Elevated with low acid ingestion, inability to excrete acid load (renal tubular acidosis), urease-splitting organisms
Blood	None	False positives with myoglobin or intravascular hemolysis
Albumin	None to trace	Most dipsticks detect primarily albumin but not other proteins; trace positive can be normal in a concentrated specimen
Glucose	None	Positive when plasma glucose level exceeds 180 mg/dL (10.0 mmol/L)
Ketones	None	Positive for acetoacetic acid, not acetone or β-hydroxybutyrate
Nitrites	None	Detects nitrite converted from dietary nitrate by bacteria; normally, no nitrites are present in urine
Leukocyte esterase	None	Detects the presence of leukocytes in the urine; positive test requires at least 3 leukocytes/hpf
Microscopy		
Erythrocytes	0-3/hpf	Urine microscopy should be performed to evaluate erythrocyte morphology
Leukocytes	0-3/hpf	Lower levels can be abnormal
Casts	None or hyaline	Hyaline casts are indicative of poor kidney perfusion but can be benign or reversible; other casts are indicative of intrinsic injury
Crystals	None	Most common include calcium oxalate, calcium phosphate, uric acid, and struvite; occur when urine is supersaturated with a specific substance

TABLE 4. Relationship Between Urine Specific Gravity and Urine Osmolality[a]

	Maximally Dilute		Isosmotic	Concentrated	Maximally Concentrated
Urine osmolality (mosm/kg H_2O)	50-100	200	300	600-900	1200
Urine specific gravity	1.002	1.005	1.010	1.020	1.030

[a]These correlations are not valid when solutes such as glucose or radiocontrast, which disproportionately increase the specific gravity relative to osmolality, are present in the urine.

Glucose

Glycosuria typically occurs when the plasma glucose concentration is greater than 180 to 200 mg/dL (10.0-11.1 mmol/L). Proximal tubular dysfunction, such as that observed in proximal renal tubular acidosis, may result in glycosuria in the absence of hyperglycemia.

Ketones

Ketones are associated with diabetic ketoacidosis, salicylate toxicity, isopropyl alcohol poisoning, and states of starvation such as alcoholic ketoacidosis. Because the urine dipstick detects acetoacetate but not β-hydroxybutyrate, ketotic patients with β-hydroxybutyrate as the only ketone body do not display a positive urine dipstick for ketones; this scenario may occur in patients with alcoholic ketoacidosis. Drugs such as captopril or levodopa have sulfhydryl groups that can result in a false-positive urine dipstick for ketones.

Blood

The urine dipstick detects both free hemoglobin and intact erythrocytes via peroxidase activity. One to three erythrocytes/hpf are usually required for positive results.

Other substances with peroxidase activity can cause false-positive reactions, including myoglobin, bacteria expressing peroxidase activity, hypochlorite, rifampin, chloroquine, and certain forms of iodine. Ascorbic acid can cause a false-negative result. Urine myoglobin levels can be measured to confirm myoglobinuria in patients with rhabdomyolysis.

Leukocyte Esterase and Nitrites

Leukocyte esterase is an enzyme present in leukocytes. When approximately 3 leukocytes/hpf are present in the urine, the urine dipstick is usually positive for leukocyte esterase. Nitrites result from the conversion of nitrates to nitrites, which occur in urinary tract infections (UTIs) caused by gram-negative organisms, including *Escherichia coli*, *Klebsiella pneumoniae*, and *Proteus* and *Pseudomonas* species. False-negative results for nitrites can occur in the setting of a UTI when the infecting organism is gram-positive, such as *Enterococcus* species. The presence of both leukocyte esterase and nitrites on urine dipstick is highly suggestive of a UTI; the absence of both has a high negative predictive value for a UTI.

Bilirubin

Conjugated bilirubin is not usually present in the urine of patients with normal serum bilirubin levels. The presence of conjugated bilirubin is suggestive of severe liver disease or obstructive jaundice. False-positive results occur with chlorpromazine, and false-negative results occur with ascorbic acid.

Urobilinogen

Urobilinogen is produced in the gut from the metabolism of bilirubin and is then reabsorbed and excreted in the urine. A positive urine dipstick for urobilinogen usually results from hemolytic anemia or hepatic necrosis but not from obstructive causes.

KEY POINTS

- Albumin is the predominant protein that is detected on urine dipstick.
- The presence of both leukocyte esterase and nitrites on urine dipstick is highly suggestive of a urinary tract infection (UTI); the absence of both has a high negative predictive value for a UTI.

Urine Microscopy

Microscopic assessment of the urine sediment is indicated for patients with abnormalities on urine dipstick, acute kidney injury, suspicion for glomerulonephritis, or newly diagnosed CKD. Cells, casts, and crystals are possible findings in a patient with kidney disease.

Leukocytes

Pyuria refers to excess leukocytes in the urine and is defined as 4 or more leukocytes/hpf. The most common cause of pyuria is a UTI. Sterile pyuria refers to the presence of leukocytes in the urine in the setting of a negative urine culture. *Mycobacterium tuberculosis* infection is an important infectious cause of sterile pyuria. Acute interstitial nephritis is often caused by antibiotics, NSAIDs, or proton pump inhibitors and is associated with sterile pyuria and low-grade proteinuria. Kidney stones and kidney transplant rejection can also cause sterile pyuria.

Eosinophils

Urine eosinophils are visualized via Wright or Hansel stains. The presence of eosinophils in the urine can be indicative of an allergic reaction, atheroembolic disease, rapidly progressive glomerulonephritis, small-vessel vasculitis, UTI, prostatic disease, or parasitic infections. Poor sensitivity and specificity limit the utility of assays for urine eosinophils in the diagnosis of interstitial nephritis.

Erythrocytes

Erythrocytes in the urine can originate at any location along the genitourinary tract, from the glomerulus to the urethra. Assessment of erythrocyte morphology is a key component in the evaluation of hematuria (see Clinical Evaluation of Hematuria). Isomorphic erythrocytes are of the same size and shape and usually arise from a urologic process such as a tumor, stone, or infection. Conversely, dysmorphic erythrocytes demonstrate varying sizes and shapes. Acanthocytes, one form of dysmorphic erythrocytes, are characterized by vesicle-shaped protrusions (**Figure 2**). Although some types of dysmorphic erythrocytes can be caused by pH or osmolality shifts, this is not true of acanthocytes. Acanthocytes and erythrocyte casts are most commonly present in glomerulonephritis but occasionally can be seen in severe interstitial nephritis and acute tubular necrosis. Such findings on microscopy should prompt an assessment for proteinuria and impaired kidney function.

Microscopic hematuria can be variously defined as the presence of 2 to 4 erythrocytes/hpf in a spun urine sediment, with lower cut-off values corresponding to increased sensitivity but decreased specificity. There is no lower limit that can exclude significant pathology, and the reference range needs to be interpreted within the clinical context. For example, 3 erythrocytes/hpf has greater significance in a patient with a long history of smoking at increased risk for urothelial malignancy.

Casts

Urine casts consist of a matrix comprised of Tamm-Horsfall mucoprotein, which may contain cells, cellular debris, or

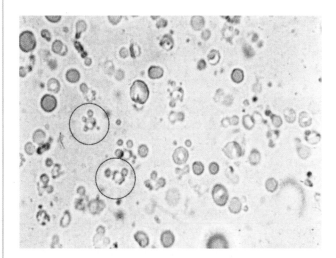

FIGURE 2. Urine microscopy demonstrating acanthocytes, indicated in the red circles. Acanthocytes, one form of dysmorphic erythrocytes, are characterized by vesicle-shaped protrusions.

Courtesy of J. Charles Jennette, MD.

lipoprotein droplets. Casts are formed within the tubular lumen and are therefore cylindrical, conforming to the shape of the tubule. Documentation of particular types of casts is instrumental in the diagnostic evaluation of acute and chronic kidney disease. Hypovolemia may lead to low urine flow rates and the presence of hyaline casts composed of Tamm-Horsfall mucoprotein alone. Tubular injury may lead to deposition of pigmented epithelial tubular debris in the proteinaceous matrix of the cast, with the formation of pigmented granular (muddy brown) casts. Erythrocyte casts are found primarily in patients with glomerulonephritis. Tubulointerstitial inflammation of the kidney, including pyelonephritis, can lead to the formation of leukocyte casts.

Crystals

Table 5 highlights the crystals commonly observed in the urine, along with morphology and associated conditions.

Certain medications, including sulfa drugs, calcium carbonate, intravenous acyclovir, and indinavir, can also result in crystals in the urine.

Measurement of Albumin and Protein Excretion

Protein detected by urine dipstick or by the SSA test should always be quantified, and the NKF KDOQI recommends measurement of the urine protein–creatinine ratio on randomly obtained samples to quantify proteinuria (**Table 6**). This ratio correlates with daily protein excretion. A ratio of 2 mg/mg, for example, indicates a daily protein excretion of approximately 2 grams per 1.73 m^2 per day. A ratio of less than 0.2 mg/mg is considered normal. Nephrotic-range proteinuria is defined as a urine protein–creatinine ratio greater than 3.5 mg/mg, and, when comprised of albumin, is indicative of underlying glomerular disease. A urine

TABLE 5. Urine Crystals

Type	Morphology/Shape	Associated Conditions
Calcium oxalate	Envelope Dumbbell Needle	Hypercalciuria Hyperoxaluria Calcium oxalate stones Ethylene glycol poisoning
Calcium phosphate	Prism Needle Star-like clumps	Distal renal tubular acidosis Urine pH above 6.5 Tumor lysis syndrome Acute phosphate nephropathy
Uric acid	Rhomboid Needle Rosette	Diabetes mellitus Obesity Gout Hyperuricemia Tumor lysis syndrome Urine pH below 6.0
Magnesium ammonium phosphate (struvite)	Coffin-lid	Chronic urinary tract infection with urease-producing organisms
Cystine	Hexagonal	Cystinuria

TABLE 6. National Kidney Foundation Kidney Disease Outcomes Quality Initiative Definitions of Proteinuria and Albuminuria

	Urine Collection Method	Normal	Microalbuminuria	Albuminuria or Clinical Proteinuria
Total Protein	24-Hour excretion (varies with method)	<300 mg/24 h	–	>300 mg/24 h
	Spot urine dipstick	<30 mg/dL	–	>30 mg/dL
	Spot urine protein–creatinine ratio (varies with method)	<0.2 mg/mg	–	>0.2 mg/mg
Albumin	24-Hour excretion	<30 mg/24 h	30-300 mg/24 h	>300 mg/24 h
	Spot urine albumin-specific dipstick	<3 mg/dL	>3 mg/dL	–
	Spot urine albumin–creatinine ratio	<30 mg/g	30-300 mg/g	>300 mg/g

Modified from American Journal of Kidney Diseases. 39(2 Suppl 1). K/DOQI clinical practice guidelines for chronic kidney disease: evaluation, classification, and stratification. Part 4: Definition and classification of stages of chronic kidney disease. S46-S75. [PMID: 11904577] Copyright 2002, with permission from Elsevier.

protein–creatinine ratio less than 2 mg/mg may indicate either tubulointerstitial disease or glomerular disease. At least two samples on different days should be collected to confirm the diagnosis of proteinuria.

Proteinuria is most commonly comprised of albumin, but other proteins, including kidney-derived low-molecular-weight proteins, monoclonal immunoglobulins and light chains, myoglobin, and hemoglobin, may be present. If monoclonal immunoglobulins are found, it is important to further characterize the proteinuria using urine immunofixation. Low-molecular-weight proteinuria is more common in tubulointerstitial disease, whereas a predominance of albuminuria favors a glomerular process.

The American Diabetes Association (ADA) recommends annual testing to assess urine albumin excretion by measuring the urine albumin–creatinine ratio in patients with type 1 diabetes mellitus of 5 years' duration and in all patients with type 2 diabetes starting at the time of diagnosis. Microalbuminuria is defined by the ADA as a urine albumin–creatinine ratio of 30 to 300 mg/g; diagnosis requires an elevated urine albumin–creatinine ratio on two of three random samples obtained over 6 months.

Patients at increased risk for kidney disease, particularly those with diabetes or hypertension, should be screened for proteinuria. Quantitation of urine protein excretion is important to assess prognosis and cardiovascular risk and to follow response to therapy. Patients with diabetes and microalbuminuria, for example, are at increased risk for progression and cardiovascular disease. Use of ACE inhibitors or angiotensin receptor blockers in patients with proteinuric kidney disease or in diabetic patients with microalbuminuria delays progression of kidney disease, underscoring the importance of early detection.

Transient proteinuria is common and is associated with febrile illnesses or rigorous exercise and requires no further evaluation. Orthostatic proteinuria occurs when proteinuria increases during the day and decreases at night when the patient is recumbent; this benign condition, more common in adolescents, can be assessed via a split urine collection. This test should be obtained in patients younger than 30 years of age who have persistent proteinuria.

Clinical Evaluation of Hematuria

Hematuria may be a sign of a life-threatening process and thus merits careful clinical evaluation (**Figure 3**). More than 3 erythrocytes/hpf constitutes hematuria and is a common finding on urinalysis. The most common causes are kidney stones and UTIs. A single episode in older patients or those at risk should prompt a full evaluation of the upper and lower urinary tract. In low-risk patients who are younger than 40 years old, a repeat urinalysis should be performed to establish hematuria.

Gross hematuria is more commonly associated with malignancy than microscopic hematuria. Red-colored urine is more common with urinary tract bleeding, whereas brown- or tea-colored urine is more common in glomerulonephritis.

Careful examination of the urine sediment is indicated to document erythrocyte morphology and whether there are concurrent erythrocyte casts. Erythrocytes with normal morphometry on urine microscopy are associated with urologic causes of hematuria, whereas dysmorphic erythrocytes or acanthocytes are associated with nephrologic causes of hematuria, usually of glomerular origin (see Erythrocytes).

The presence of hematuria should raise suspicion for genitourinary tract malignancies in patients with risk factors. The U.S. Preventive Services Task Force currently does not recommend screening urinalysis for asymptomatic adults for purposes of bladder cancer screening. Recent evidence, however, demonstrated an adjusted hazard ratio of 18.5 for the development of end-stage kidney disease in patients found to have microscopic hematuria in a large unselected cohort of adolescents and young adults followed for 21 years, raising the question whether routine screening with urine dipstick should be recommended in adolescents and adults.

Risk factors for urologic malignancy or features of systemic vasculitis should be sought in the medical history. Risk factors for bladder cancer include smoking, male gender, and age over 40 years. The presence of isomorphic hematuria in this setting warrants cystoscopy and upper urinary tract imaging. Conversely, the presence of acanthocytes, erythrocyte casts, and proteinuria warrants prompt nephrologic consultation for possible kidney biopsy.

Urinary tract imaging is important in the evaluation of hematuria to identify or exclude specific causes. The choice of imaging modality for evaluating the upper urinary tract depends on the risk factor profile of a given patient and the estimated GFR (**Table 7, on page 9**). CT urography is the test of choice for high-risk patients with well-preserved GFR. MR urography may be helpful when the estimated GFR is in the range of 30 to 60 mL/min/1.73 m². Ultrasonography is warranted in patients less than 40 years old with no risk factors for urologic malignancy. Noncontrast abdominal helical CT is indicated when there is suspicion for nephrolithiasis. Intravenous pyelography has low sensitivity for urologic tumors or stones and is no longer recommended. In patients who have hematuria with a negative upper urinary tract evaluation, visualization of the lower urinary tract is typically accomplished by cystoscopy to assess for lower ureteral, bladder, or urethral causes. Cytologic studies may also be indicated for detecting possible malignancies not identified on imaging or direct visualization.

Urologic follow-up for patients with an initial negative evaluation for isomorphic hematuria is guided by risk factors, with more aggressive surveillance for those with increased risk for urologic malignancy. The choice of studies and optimal timing have yet to be determined. The American Urological Association opinion-based protocol is outlined in Figure 3.

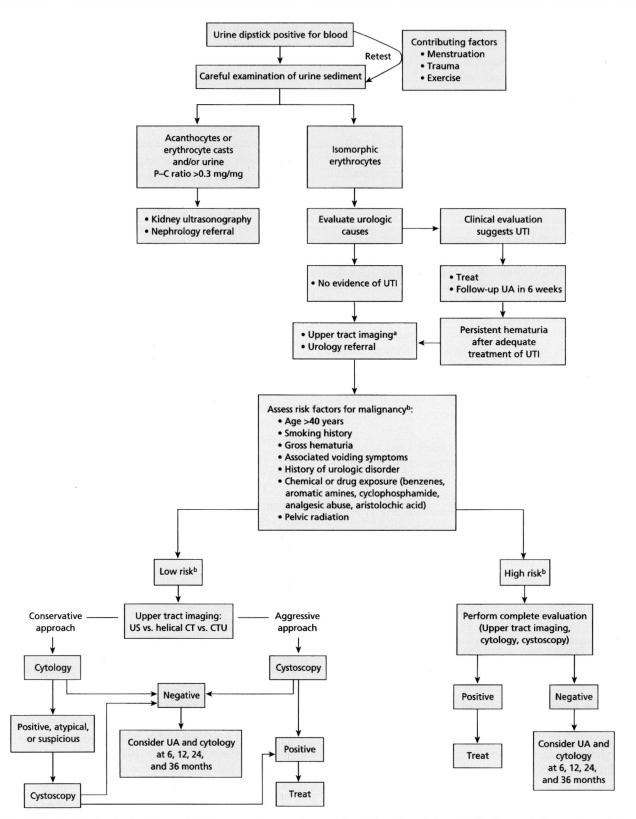

FIGURE 3. The clinical evaluation of hematuria. CTU = computed tomography urography; eGFR = estimated glomerular filtration rate; P–C = protein–creatinine; UA = urinalysis; US = ultrasonography; UTI = urinary tract infection.

aSee Table 7 for imaging studies used in the evaluation of hematuria.

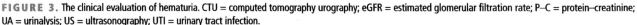

bModified with permission from Urology. 57(4). Grossfeld GD, Litwin MS, Wolf JS, et al. Evaluation of asymptomatic microscopic hematuria in adults: the American Urological Association best practice policy–part II: patient evaluation, cytology, voided markers, imaging, cystoscopy, nephrology evaluation, and follow-up. 604-610. 2001, [PMID: 11306357] with permission from Elsevier.

TABLE 7.	Imaging Used in the Evaluation of Hematuria	
Study	**Advantages**	**Disadvantages**
CT urography (CTU)	High sensitivity (100%) and specificity (97%)	High radiation dose ($2 \times$ IVP) Risk of CIN Contraindicated in pregnancy
MR urography	Useful in eGFR range of 30-60 mL/min/1.73 m^2	Contraindicated when eGFR <30 mL/min/1.73 m^2 (gadolinium) Less sensitive than CTU for smaller cancers and stones
Ultrasonography	No contrast No radiation exposure Useful in setting of pregnancy Lower cost	Limited sensitivity, especially for lesions <2 cm
Intravenous pyelography (IVP)	Less radiation than CTU	Risk of CIN Low sensitivity (40%-65%)

CIN = contrast-induced nephropathy; eGFR = estimated glomerular filtration rate.

Hematuria in patients with an underlying bleeding diathesis or on anticoagulation requires evaluation and should not be attributed to the coagulopathy until other causes are excluded.

KEY POINTS

- Microscopic assessment of the urine sediment is indicated for patients with abnormalities on urine dipstick, acute kidney injury, suspicion for glomerulonephritis, or newly diagnosed chronic kidney disease.
- The most common cause of pyuria is a urinary tract infection.
- Isomorphic erythrocytes are of the same size and shape and usually arise from a urologic process such as a tumor, stone, or infection.
- Acanthocytes and erythrocyte casts are most commonly present in glomerulonephritis but occasionally can be seen in severe interstitial nephritis and acute tubular necrosis.
- The most common causes of hematuria are kidney stones and urinary tract infections, but the presence of hematuria should raise suspicion for genitourinary tract malignancies in patients with risk factors.

Imaging Studies

Assessment of kidney disease often includes imaging of the kidneys and urinary tract. Kidney ultrasonography is safe, not dependent upon kidney function, noninvasive, and relatively inexpensive. Because it does not require contrast, ultrasonography does not place patients at risk for contrast-induced nephropathy. This is often the first imaging study used to evaluate the structure of the upper genitourinary tract. Ultrasonography can be used to diagnose urinary tract obstruction, cysts, and mass lesions as well as to assess kidney size and cortical thickness. Doppler ultrasonography can detect renal artery stenosis when performed by experienced technicians.

Abdominal CT with contrast offers better resolution and characterization of kidney mass lesions or cysts than ultrasonography; however, contrast can be harmful to patients with an estimated GFR of less than 60 mL/min/1.73 m^2. CT urography is the test of choice for the evaluation of urologic bleeding in patients at high risk for bladder cancer with an estimated GFR above 60 mL/min/1.73 m^2.

Noncontrast abdominal helical CT is more accurate than ultrasonography in identifying nephrolithiasis and may be more useful in obese patients in whom technical problems may arise during general ultrasonography. Plain abdominal radiography of the kidneys, ureters, and bladder (KUB) can identify non-uric acid–containing kidney stones, although CT offers greater contrast resolution to detect nephrolithiasis.

MRI of the kidneys can accurately identify mass lesions and cysts. Gadolinium enhancement can be useful to determine whether a mass lesion has malignant features. MR angiography, which usually employs gadolinium, is useful in the diagnosis of renal artery stenosis. Gadolinium, however, has been associated with nephrogenic systemic fibrosis in patients with stage 4 and stage 5 CKD, acute kidney injury, and in patients following kidney and liver transplantation and should be avoided in these populations.

Radionuclide kidney clearance scanning is the gold standard for quantifying GFR and renal plasma flow. These studies are very accurate and are useful in the evaluation of renal plasma flow and function of transplanted kidneys, the assessment of the functional significance of renovascular disease, the presurgical assessment of kidney function before nephrectomy, and the functional significance of hydronephrosis in patients with possible urinary tract obstruction.

KEY POINTS

- Because it does not require contrast, ultrasonography does not place patients at risk for contrast-induced nephropathy and is often the first imaging study used to evaluate the structure of the upper genitourinary tract.
- MRI of the kidneys can accurately identify mass lesions and cysts.
- Radionuclide kidney clearance scanning is the gold standard for quantifying the glomerular filtration rate and renal plasma flow.

Kidney Biopsy

In patients with kidney disease, a kidney biopsy provides tissue that can be used for diagnosis, prognosis, treatment, and surveillance. Indications include suspected glomerular pathology such as glomerulonephritis and the nephrotic syndrome, acute kidney injury of unclear cause, and kidney transplant dysfunction. Biopsies are usually performed under direct visualization with ultrasonographic or CT guidance.

Contraindications include bleeding diatheses, active infection of the genitourinary system, hydronephrosis, atrophic kidneys, and uncontrolled hypertension. Relative contraindications include a solitary kidney, severe anemia, and chronic anticoagulation. Risks include pain within the first few days after biopsy; gross hematuria that can result in urinary obstruction; bleeding with the need for transfusion in approximately 5% of patients; potential nephrectomy in less than 0.3% of patients; and death in less than 0.1%.

KEY POINTS

- Indications for kidney biopsy include suspected glomerular pathology such as glomerulonephritis and the nephrotic syndrome, acute kidney injury of unclear cause, and kidney transplant dysfunction.
- Contraindications to kidney biopsy include bleeding diatheses, active infection of the genitourinary system, hydronephrosis, atrophic kidneys, and uncontrolled hypertension.

Fluids and Electrolytes

Osmolality and Tonicity

Under normal physiologic conditions, plasma osmolality is determined by the concentration of sodium and its accompanying anions; plasma glucose; and blood urea nitrogen (BUN).

Osmolality can be directly measured with an osmometer or calculated using the following equation:

$$\text{Plasma Osmolality (mosm/kg } H_2O) = 2 \times \text{Serum Sodium (meq/L)} + \text{Plasma Glucose (mg/dL)}/18 + \text{BUN (mg/dL)}/2.8$$

The serum osmolal gap is the difference between the measured and calculated plasma osmolality; a value greater than 10 mosm/kg H_2O is considered elevated and reflects the presence of unmeasured solutes.

Under conditions of normal health, the effective osmolality is maintained in the range of 275 to 295 mosm/kg H_2O. Effective osmolality is tightly regulated, thereby maintaining constant intracellular volume. Changes in effective osmolality are sensed by osmoreceptors near the hypothalamus. A 1% to 2% increase in effective osmolality causes release of antidiuretic hormone ([ADH]; also known as arginine vasopressin), which results in increased reabsorption of water in the collecting ducts. Physiologic, non-osmotic release of ADH also occurs in response to true hypovolemia. Nonphysiologic ADH secretion causes the syndrome of inappropriate antidiuretic hormone secretion (SIADH).

KEY POINTS

- A serum osmolal gap greater than 10 mosm/kg H_2O is considered elevated and reflects the presence of unmeasured solutes.

Disorders of Serum Sodium
Hyponatremia

Hyponatremia is defined as a serum sodium concentration less than 135 meq/L (135 mmol/L). It may occur with increased, normal, or decreased plasma osmolality (**Figure 4** and **Figure 5, on page 12**).

Causes
Pseudohyponatremia

Pseudohyponatremia is a laboratory artifact that may be observed in patients with hyperglobulinemia or severe hyperlipidemia. Although this artifact is now less common with the use of ion-specific electrodes, it remains a problem in laboratories using indirect potentiometry to assess the amount of sodium in a specific sample volume; an increase in the solid phase of a specimen displaces and decreases the effective volume analyzed for sodium content, leading to reporting of an artificially low serum sodium level. Visible lipemia is usually present with hyperlipidemia-associated pseudohyponatremia but may be absent in patients with high levels of cholestasis-associated lipoprotein-X. Measured osmolality is normal in pseudohyponatremia; the increased osmolal gap cannot be accounted for by an increase in glucose, BUN, or other solutes such as mannitol, sorbitol, or glycine.

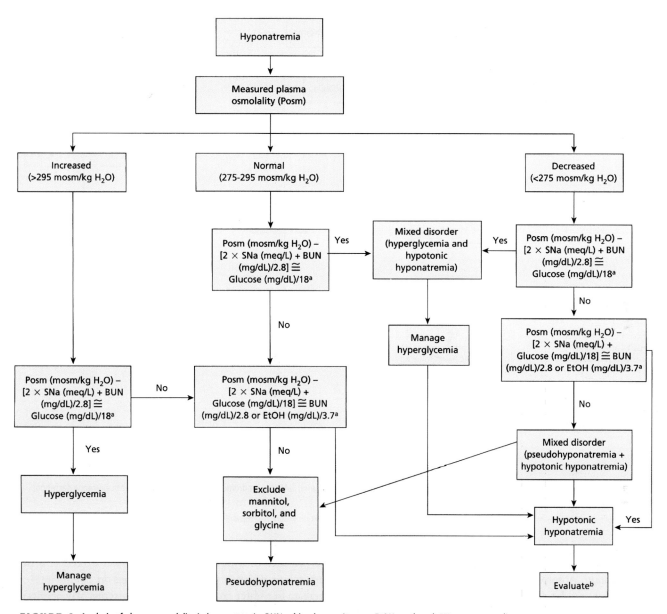

FIGURE 4. Analysis of plasma osmolality in hyponatremia. BUN = blood urea nitrogen; EtOH = ethanol; SNa = serum sodium.

[a]Difference may vary by approximately 5 mosm/kg H$_2$O due to unmeasured osmoles that are normally present in the serum.

[b]See Figure 5 for the evaluation of hypotonic hyponatremia.

Hypotonic Hyponatremia

Hypotonic hyponatremia is the most common form of hyponatremia. It may occur in patients with normal, increased, or decreased extracellular fluid (ECF) volumes. Measured plasma osmolality is usually low but may be normal or increased in the presence of elevated BUN, glucose, or an exogenous solute such as alcohol.

Hypertonic Hyponatremia

Hypertonic hyponatremia is caused by marked hyperglycemia or exogenously administered solutes such as mannitol or sucrose. Hyperglycemia causes the translocation of water from

the intracellular to the ECF compartment, which results in a decrease in the serum sodium level by approximately 1.6 meq/L (1.6 mmol/L) for every 100 mg/dL (5.6 mmol/L) increase in the plasma glucose above 100 mg/dL (5.6 mmol/L).

Isosmotic Hyponatremia

Isosmotic hyponatremia may occur as a result of pseudohyponatremia or when two or more disorders are present simultaneously. For example, a patient with hyponatremia due to SIADH who subsequently develops hyperglycemia will have a normal measured plasma osmolality when the increase in osmolality resulting from increased glucose counterbalances the initial

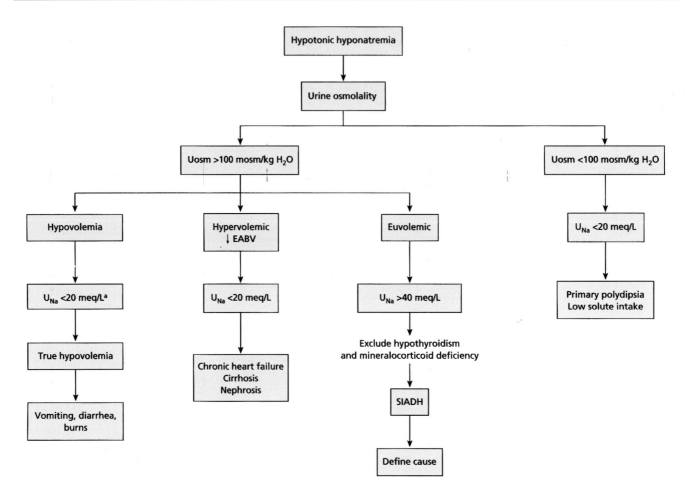

FIGURE 5. Evaluation of hypotonic hyponatremia. EABV = effective arterial blood volume; SIADH = syndrome of inappropriate antidiuretic hormone secretion; U_{Na} = urine sodium concentration; Uosm = urine osmolality.

aExceptions include diuretic therapy, mineralocorticoid deficiency, cerebral salt wasting, osmotic diuresis, and salt wasting nephropathy.

decrement in osmolality that resulted from SIADH-associated water retention. Absorption of isosmotic irrigating solutions such as glycine or sorbitol also can cause isosmotic hyponatremia.

Evaluation

The first step in the evaluation of hyponatremia is to check plasma osmolality (see Figure 4). If pseudohyponatremia is suspected, plasma osmolality will be normal, and documentation of elevated levels of cholesterol, triglycerides, or serum total protein will lend support to the diagnosis. The plasma sodium concentration is normal in pseudohyponatremia when measured with blood gas analyzers equipped with direct potentiometry.

The cause of hypotonic hyponatremia can be established by patient history, volume status, urine osmolality, and urine sodium level (see Figure 5).

Hypotonic Hyponatremia with an Appropriately Low Urine Osmolality

Patients with primary polydipsia and hyponatremia typically present with urine osmolality less than 100 mosm/kg H_2O in

the presence of hypotonicity. Because water excretion is in part solute dependent, severe limitations in solute intake decrease free water excretion, and hyponatremia may develop in this setting with only modest increases in fluid intake. This syndrome is termed *beer potomania* when observed in patients with chronic alcohol abuse and low solute intake.

Hypotonic Hyponatremia with an Inappropriately High Urine Osmolality

Urine osmolality greater than 100 mosm/kg H_2O in the setting of hypotonic hyponatremia reflects non-osmotic ADH secretion due to true hypovolemia, decreased effective arterial blood volume (EABV), or nonphysiologic ADH release. Total body water and ECF volume are increased in SIADH; however, this increase cannot be detected clinically by physical examination, principally because two thirds of the excess water is retained in the intracellular fluid compartment. Increased ECF volume leads to increased sodium excretion resulting from increased kidney perfusion and decreased sodium uptake in the proximal nephron.

Consequently, the urine sodium concentration is greater than 40 meq/L (40 mmol/L) when dietary sodium intake is adequate (>80 meq/d).

Reset osmostat is a syndrome that may occur in patients with quadriplegia, tuberculosis, advanced age, pregnancy, and psychiatric disorders. These patients can be distinguished from those with SIADH by documenting excretion of dilute urine following a water load. Stability of the serum sodium under conditions of variable fluid intake is a clue to the diagnosis.

It is often difficult to differentiate between mild hypovolemia with appropriate osmotically stimulated ADH release and SIADH by physical examination and urinary indices, particularly when solute intake is decreased and urine sodium values are equivocal. Clinical history and interpretation of serum and urine levels of urea and uric acid may help in the diagnostic evaluation (**Table 8**). An increase in the serum sodium concentration after infusion of 1 liter of normal saline favors a diagnosis of hypovolemia but should only be attempted in asymptomatic patients when the diagnosis remains uncertain. Hypothyroidism and adrenal insufficiency should be excluded in patients with euvolemic hyponatremia. **Table 9** summarizes the causes of SIADH.

Patients with hyponatremia secondary to non-osmotic ADH secretion include those with true hypovolemia as well as patients with decreased EABV who have heart failure, the nephrotic syndrome, or cirrhosis. The urine sodium concentration is usually less than 20 meq/L (20 mmol/L) in this setting. Exceptions include patients on active diuretic therapy or those with kidney sodium wasting as may occur

TABLE 8. Serum and Urinary Indices in the Syndrome of Inappropriate Antidiuretic Hormone Secretion and Hypovolemia

Favors SIADH
Urine sodium >40 meq/L (40 mmol/L)
FE_{Na} >1%
Serum uric acid <4 mg/dL (0.24 mmol/L)
FE_{UA} >10%
BUN <10 mg/dL (3.6 mmol/L)
FE_{UN} >50%
Favors Hypovolemia
Urine sodium <20 meq/L (20 mmol/L)
FE_{Na} <1%
Serum uric acid >6 mg/dL (0.35 mmol/L)
FE_{UA} <10%
BUN >15 mg/dL (5.4 mmol/L)
FE_{UN} <35%

BUN = blood urea nitrogen; FE_{Na} = fractional excretion of sodium; FE_{UA} = fractional excretion of uric acid; FE_{UN} = fractional excretion of urea; SIADH = syndrome of inappropriate antidiuretic hormone secretion.

TABLE 9. Causes of the Syndrome of Inappropriate Antidiuretic Hormone Secretion

Central nervous system disorders
  Hemorrhage[a]
  Infections
  Inflammatory disorders
  Guillain-Barré syndrome
  Multiple sclerosis
  Mass lesions[a]

Drugs
  3,4-Methylenedioxymethamphetamine (also known as ecstasy)[a]
  Antipsychotic medications
  Carbamazepine
  Chlorpropamide
  Clofibrate
  Cyclooxygenase-2 inhibitors[a]
  Cyclophosphamide
  Desmopressin[a]
  Ifosfamide
  Nicotine
  NSAIDs[a]
  Opiates[a]
  Phenothiazines
  Selective serotonin reuptake inhibitors[a]
  Serotonin norepinephrine reuptake inhibitors[a]
  Tricyclic antidepressants
  Vasopressin[a]
  Vincristine

Endurance exercise

Familial disorders

Infections
  HIV infection
  Rocky Mountain spotted fever

Postoperative setting
  Anesthesia[a]
  Nausea[a]
  Pain[a]

Pulmonary disorders
  Infections[a]
  Inflammatory disorders
  Positive pressure mechanical ventilation[a]
  Respiratory failure

Tumors
  Gastrointestinal tract tumors
  Genitourinary tract tumors
  Lymphomas
  Respiratory tract tumors[a]
  Sarcomas
  Small cell carcinoma[a]
  Thymomas

[a]Most common causes.

H CONT. in mineralocorticoid deficiency, cerebral salt wasting, chronic kidney disease (CKD), or following cisplatin chemotherapy. Cerebral salt wasting is a syndrome of hypotonic hyponatremia that may complicate subarachnoid hemorrhage or neurosurgery. Increased levels of B-type natriuretic peptide result in kidney sodium wasting and hypovolemic hyponatremia.

Clinical Presentation

Acute hyponatremia is defined as the onset of hypotonicity in less than 24 hours. Risk factors include postoperative administration of hypotonic fluids, the use of thiazide diuretics, the use of the illicit drug 3,4-methylene-dioxymethamphetamine (also known as ecstasy), overhydration associated with extreme exercise, and primary polydipsia. Increased neuronal cell volume may result in neurologic symptoms and the high mortality seen in patients with severe hypotonic hyponatremia.

Patients with symptomatic hyponatremia may initially have nonspecific symptoms such as nausea, fatigue, and headache. Cerebral edema most commonly occurs in patients in whom the serum sodium level decreases by more than 10 meq/L (10 mmol/L) over 1 to 3 days. As cerebral edema worsens, symptoms may progress to obtundation, seizures, coma, hypoxia, and respiratory arrest.

Chronic hyponatremia develops over 72 hours or more, and patients are less likely to have symptomatic cerebral edema. Chronic hypotonicity stimulates extrusion of intracellular solutes and leads to a reduction in cell volume toward normal. Overly rapid correction of hyponatremia in these patients is more likely to induce osmotic demyelination syndrome (see Treatment, Osmotic Demyelination Syndrome). Many patients with chronic hyponatremia develop superimposed acute symptomatic hyponatremia in the setting of acute illness such as concomitant hypovolemia.

Recent evidence suggests that patients with mild degrees of chronic hyponatremia (serum sodium level of 125-135 meq/L [125-135 mmol/L]) without overt symptoms of cerebral edema may have subtle neurocognitive deficits that can only be detected with careful neurocognitive and functional testing. These patients have an increased risk of falls, hip fracture, and osteoporosis. The benefits of implementing measures to correct the serum sodium level to greater than 135 meq/L (135 mmol/L) in these patients remain an area of investigation. **H**

KEY POINTS

- Patients with symptomatic hyponatremia may initially have nonspecific symptoms such as nausea, fatigue, and headache.
- As cerebral edema worsens in patients with symptomatic hyponatremia, symptoms may progress to obtundation, seizures, coma, hypoxia, and respiratory arrest.

Treatment

Treatment of patients with hyponatremia depends on the cause as well as the presence and severity of symptoms.

Symptomatic Hyponatremia

Patients with symptoms of cerebral edema merit more rapid correction. Symptomatic patients with SIADH warrant treatment with hypertonic saline, whereas patients with hyponatremia secondary to true hypovolemia can be treated with normal saline. The safety of vasopressin receptor antagonists (vaptans) in symptomatic patients has yet to be validated. These agents are contraindicated in patients with hypovolemic hyponatremia. Treatment should continue until symptoms resolve, and serum sodium correction should not exceed 10 meq/L (10 mmol/L) within the first 24 hours or 18 meq/L (18 mmol/L) within the first 48 hours. Recent evidence suggests that acutely increasing the serum sodium concentration by 4 to 6 meq/L (4-6 mmol/L) within the first 24 hours is sufficient for most patients with symptomatic hyponatremia. Patients with acute hypotonic hyponatremia complicated by seizures or coma should be treated with 100 mL or 2 mL/kg bolus infusions of 3% saline, which can be repeated up to two times if needed.

Close monitoring of the serum sodium level at least every 2 to 4 hours is indicated during the initial phase of therapy. Patients with SIADH and highly concentrated urine may develop worsening hyponatremia with infusion of normal saline due to excretion of urine with increased tonicity relative to serum ("desalination") and retention of infused water; therefore, 3% saline is preferred for treatment of symptomatic patients with SIADH. Patients with hyponatremia due to volume depletion or SIADH often exhibit water diuresis during therapy, which can result in overly rapid correction. Correction of concurrent hypokalemia may also induce overly rapid correction. When this occurs, the serum sodium concentration can be corrected back to the target level with use of 5% dextrose in water and/or desmopressin.

Osmotic Demyelination Syndrome

Correction of acute hyponatremia that exceeds 10 meq/L (10 mmol/L) within the first 24 hours and 18 meq/L (18 mmol/L) within the first 48 hours of therapy has been associated with onset of the osmotic demyelination syndrome (ODS). These values should be considered upper limits of correction rather than goals of therapy. Clinical features of ODS include progressive quadriparesis, speech and swallowing disorders, coma, and "locked-in" syndrome. Neurologic deficits are often irreversible; therefore, preventive measures are essential.

Asymptomatic Hyponatremia

Treatment of patients with asymptomatic hyponatremia depends on the underlying cause (**Table 10**). Fluid restriction is essential in patients with SIADH or hypervolemic

TABLE 10. Management of Asymptomatic Hypotonic Hyponatremia

Etiology	Management
True hypovolemia	Correct etiology of hypovolemia
	Isotonic saline
Syndrome of inappropriate antidiuretic hormone secretion (SIADH)	Treat underlying cause
	Discontinue offending drugs
	Fluid restriction
	Furosemide
	Demeclocycline
	Vasopressin receptor antagonists (vaptans)
	Ensure adequate solute and protein intake
Hypervolemic hyponatremia (chronic heart failure, cirrhosis, nephrosis)	Treat underlying cause
	Fluid and sodium restriction
	Furosemide
	Vasopressin receptor antagonists (vaptans)

hyponatremia. Total intake, including both oral and intravenous, must be less than total output (including insensible losses) in order to cause a rise in the serum sodium level.

Hypertonic hyponatremia due to hyperglycemia will correct as plasma glucose levels fall with insulin therapy, leading to movement of water back into the intracellular compartment. No further intervention for hyponatremia per se is warranted for pseudohyponatremia, and hyperlipidemia and hyperproteinemia should be evaluated and treated as indicated. **H**

KEY POINTS

- Hypertonic saline is indicated for symptomatic patients who have the syndrome of inappropriate antidiuretic hormone secretion.

- Patients with hyponatremia secondary to true hypovolemia can be treated with normal saline.

- Recent evidence suggests that acutely increasing the serum sodium concentration by 4 to 6 meq/L (4-6 mmol/L) over the first 24 hours is sufficient for most patients with symptomatic hyponatremia.

- Fluid restriction is essential in patients with asymptomatic hyponatremia who have the syndrome of inappropriate antidiuretic hormone secretion or hypervolemic hyponatremia.

Hypernatremia

Hypernatremia is defined as a serum sodium concentration greater than 145 meq/L (145 mmol/L). Hypernatremia is a common disorder in critically ill patients and is associated with high morbidity and mortality. The cause can usually be ascertained from evaluating the history and volume status, in conjunction with determination of the urine volume and urine osmolality (**Table 11**).

Causes

Inadequate Water Intake
Thirst and water intake protect against the development of hypernatremia. Failure to adequately replace water loss is the most common cause of hypernatremia. Hypernatremia is often observed in elderly patients or infants with impaired mentation or functional impairment that precludes access to water. Hypothalamic lesions may interfere with the thirst response, resulting in marked hypernatremia.

Hypotonic Fluid and Pure Water Loss
Urinary and gastrointestinal fluid losses are usually hypotonic, causing a rise in the serum sodium concentration in the absence of compensatory fluid intake. Gastrointestinal losses, diuretic therapy, and osmotic diuresis cause hypernatremia in association with hypovolemia.

Patients with diabetes insipidus are typically able to replace urinary water losses by drinking, and the serum sodium level is usually only slightly increased unless water intake is impaired. Causes of diabetes insipidus include decreased release of ADH (central diabetes insipidus); ADH resistance (nephrogenic diabetes insipidus); and metabolism of ADH by circulating vasopressinase (gestational diabetes insipidus) (**Table 12**). Adipsic diabetes insipidus results in severe hypernatremia in patients with central nervous system lesions involving both the posterior pituitary gland and hypothalamic thirst center.

Assessment of Polyuria
Polyuria in adults is defined by an increase in urine volume above 3 L/24 h and is often accompanied by hypernatremia. The differential diagnosis of polyuria includes diabetes insipidus, primary polydipsia (which, unlike other causes of polyuria, results in hyponatremia), and osmotic diuresis.

TABLE 11. Causes and Clinical Findings in Hypernatremia			
Cause	**Volume Status**	**Urine Volume**	**Urine Osmolality (mosm/kg H$_2$O)**
Hypotonic Fluid Loss			
Gastrointestinal losses (vomiting, nasogastric suction, diarrhea)	Hypovolemic	Decreased	>600
Diuretics (except osmotic diuretics)	Hypovolemic	Variable	~150
Osmotic diuresis (hyperglycemia; urea [high protein diet or enteral feeding, relief of urinary tract obstruction, recovery phase of acute tubular necrosis])	Hypovolemic	Increased	>300
Pure Water Loss			
Insensible water losses (skin, respiratory tract) that are not replaced (impaired mentation, stroke, hypothalamic lesion, functional impairment limiting access to fluids)	Normal	Decreased	>600
Diabetes insipidus	Normal	Increased	<200
Hypertonic Fluid Gain			
Administration or ingestion of sodium chloride, hypertonic saline, or sodium bicarbonate	Hypervolemic	Increased	>300

TABLE 12. Causes of Diabetes Insipidus
Central diabetes insipidus
Autoimmune hypophysitis (idiopathic)[a]
Malignancy (metastatic or primary)[a]
Neurosurgery[a]
Trauma
Infiltration (sarcoidosis, histiocytosis X, lymphocytic hypophysitis, granulomatosis with polyangiitis [also known as Wegener granulomatosis], IgG4 disease)[a]
Following correction of supraventricular tachycardia
Hypoxic encephalopathy
Anorexia nervosa
Sheehan syndrome
Familial
Nephrogenic diabetes insipidus
Lithium[a]
Other medications (demeclocycline, cidofovir, foscarnet, didanosine, amphotericin B, ifosfamide, ofloxacin)[a]
Electrolyte disorders (hypercalcemia, hypokalemia)[a]
Sickle cell nephropathy
Urinary tract infection
Amyloidosis
Sjögren syndrome
Nephronophthisis
Cystinosis
Gestational diabetes insipidus (placental vasopressinase)
[a]Most common causes.

Patients with central diabetes insipidus are more likely to present with abrupt onset of polyuria.

Urine osmolality during osmotic diuresis is usually greater than 300 mosm/kg H$_2$O, whereas it usually is less than 200 mosm/kg H$_2$O in diabetes insipidus and primary polydipsia. Urine osmolality occasionally rises above 200 mosm/kg H$_2$O in hypovolemic patients with partial central diabetes insipidus. The serum sodium concentration is typically less than 138 meq/L (138 mmol/L) in primary polydipsia and greater than 142 meq/L (142 mmol/L) in diabetes insipidus. Water deprivation testing demonstrates an increase in urine osmolality to approximately 600 mosm/kg H$_2$O in primary polydipsia. Urine osmolality remains less than 200 mosm/kg H$_2$O in patients with diabetes insipidus with water deprivation. Administration of desmopressin results in a rise in urine osmolality to approximately 600 mosm/kg H$_2$O in central diabetes insipidus and in gestational diabetes insipidus but not in nephrogenic diabetes insipidus. Unlike ADH, desmopressin is not metabolized by pregnancy-related vasopressinase.

Treatment

Patients with circulatory collapse should initially be treated with sufficient isotonic saline to correct organ hypoperfusion. Isotonic saline boluses should be avoided in the absence of shock given the risk of associated cerebral edema, and hypotonic solutions such as 5% Dextrose in water are preferred. Hypernatremia should be corrected at a rate no more than 10 meq/L (10 mmol/L) per day to avoid cerebral edema. The water deficit can be estimated by the following equation:

$$\text{Total Body Water } [0.6 \text{ in Men and } 0.5 \text{ in Women} \times \text{Body Weight (kg)}] \times [(\text{Serum Sodium}/140 \text{ [or target serum sodium]}) - 1]$$

This equation does not account for urinary, gastrointestinal, and insensible losses; it is also inaccurate because of the error inherent in estimating total body water. Furthermore, this calculation estimates the water deficit relative to total body sodium and only represents the amount of free water needed to correct the hypernatremia and not the total body volume deficit. The serum sodium concentration should therefore be monitored carefully during correction.

A patient with a serum sodium level of 160 meq/L (160 mmol/L) weighing approximately 70 kg (154 lb) presenting with hypotension and circulatory shock, for example, should receive bolus therapy with isotonic saline until shock is resolved. Therapy is then directed toward correcting the hyponatremia based on estimating the water deficit (Total Body Water = 0.5 × 70 kg = 35 L; water deficit necessary to correct serum sodium to 150 meq/L = 35 L × [160/150 – 1] = 2.33 L). 5% Dextrose in water could then be infused at a rate of approximately 100 mL/h over the first 24 hours, measuring the serum sodium every 3 to 4 hours to permit appropriate adjustment of the infusion rate.

Polyuria caused by central or gestational diabetes insipidus is treated with intranasal desmopressin. Thiazide diuretics increase proximal sodium and water reabsorption and can be employed to decrease urine volume in nephrogenic diabetes insipidus.

If possible, lithium should be discontinued in patients with severe nephrogenic diabetes insipidus, particularly when associated with progressive lithium-related interstitial kidney disease. If lithium must be continued, amiloride (which blocks uptake into apical sodium channels in the collecting duct epithelium) can be used to limit tubular uptake and toxicity. Careful monitoring of lithium levels is warranted when diuretics are used, because hypovolemia increases proximal lithium reabsorption, thereby increasing serum lithium levels. **H**

KEY POINTS

- Causes of hypernatremia include hypotonic fluid loss, pure water loss, diabetes insipidus, and hypertonic fluid gain.
- Gastrointestinal losses, diuretic therapy, and osmotic diuresis cause hypernatremia in association with hypovolemia.
- Hypernatremia should be corrected at a rate no more than 10 meq/L (10 mmol/L) per day to avoid cerebral edema.

Disorders of Serum Potassium
Hypokalemia

Hypokalemia is defined as a serum potassium concentration less than 3.5 meq/L (3.5 mmol/L). The differential diagnosis includes cellular redistribution, kidney or gastrointestinal tract losses, and decreased intake. Hypokalemia manifests with abnormal skeletal and cardiac muscle cell function related to alterations in action potential generation or changes in renal tubular cell function (**Table 13**). Symptoms generally do not occur until the serum potassium concentration decreases to less than 3 meq/L (3 mmol/L).

TABLE 13. Clinical Manifestations of Hypokalemia
Cardiac
Arrhythmias
Premature atrial beats
Atrial tachycardia
Sinus bradycardia
Atrioventricular block
Junctional tachycardia
Premature ventricular beats
Ventricular tachycardia
Ventricular fibrillation
Electrocardiographic changes
Depressed ST segment
Decreased T wave amplitude
Increased U wave amplitude
Skeletal muscle
Muscle cramps
Ascending muscle weakness
Respiratory muscle weakness
Paralysis
Rhabdomyolysis
Smooth muscle dysfunction and ileus
Glucose intolerance
Kidney
Increased ammoniagenesis and alkalosis
Impaired urinary concentration
Hypokalemic nephropathy

Evaluation

The evaluation of hypokalemia begins with a thorough history. Diuretics are the most common cause of hypokalemia. Assessment of factors that alter the cellular distribution of serum potassium should then be considered (**Figure 6**).

Pseudohypokalemia, a laboratory artifact caused by intracellular uptake of serum potassium in patients with marked leukocytosis, is a diagnostic consideration in patients with myeloproliferative disorders. β_2-Agonists, epinephrine, insulin, vitamin B_{12} repletion, and systemic alkalosis also can result in increased intracellular uptake of serum potassium, as can toxicity due to barium, chloroquine, quetiapine, and risperidone. Hypokalemic periodic paralysis is a rare syndrome that presents with acute episodic muscle weakness, often following a high carbohydrate meal or strenuous exercise. Hypokalemic periodic paralysis presents as either a familial syndrome or as an acquired form due to interferon therapy or thyrotoxicosis. Persons of Asian or Mexican descent are at increased risk for this syndrome.

After excluding conditions that cause cellular redistribution, the diagnosis of hypokalemia is established by history

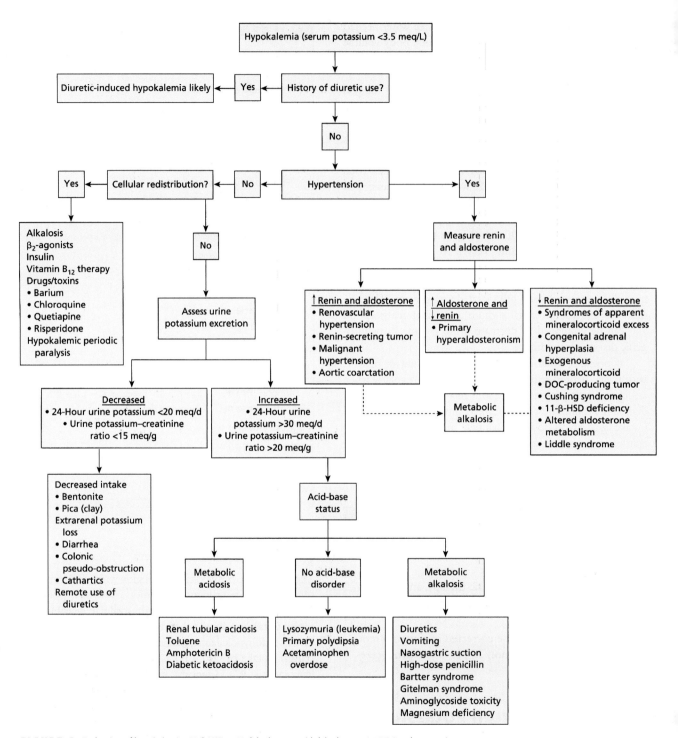

FIGURE 6. Evaluation of hypokalemia. 11-β-HSD = 11-β-hydroxysteroid-dehydrogenase; DOC = deoxycorticosterone.

and assessment of urine potassium excretion, blood pressure, and acid-base status. Urine potassium excretion is determined by the amount of potassium secreted in the cortical collecting duct (CCD). Aldosterone, enhanced lumen-negative voltage, and increased tubular flow and sodium delivery to the CCD increase urine potassium excretion.

Potassium depletion due to gastrointestinal losses decreases kidney potassium excretion to levels less than 20 meq/L (20 mmol/L) per day. In hypokalemic patients, a 24-hour urine potassium excretion above 30 meq/L (30 mmol/L) per day suggests ongoing urine potassium losses. Random values of urine potassium can be used to assess the kidney response to hypokalemia but must be corrected for the degree of urinary concentration. This can be achieved by calculating the urine potassium–creatinine ratio, which when expressed in meq/g creatinine, is derived from the following equation:

$$\text{Urine Potassium–Creatinine Ratio (meq/g)} =$$
$$\text{Urine Potassium (meq/L)} \times 100\ [(\text{mg} \times \text{L})/(\text{dL} \times \text{g})] \div$$
$$\text{Urine Creatinine (mg/dL)}$$

A urine potassium–creatinine ratio above 20 meq/g is characteristic of kidney potassium wasting, whereas a value below 15 meq/g reflects cellular redistribution, decreased intake, or extrarenal potassium loss. Patients with kidney potassium wasting can be divided into those with or without hypertension. Plasma renin activity and aldosterone levels are then used to differentiate causes of hypokalemia associated with hypertension. The cause of hypokalemia in patients with normal or low blood pressure is diagnosed based on acid-base status and urine sodium and chloride levels (see Figure 6).

Hypokalemia commonly occurs with concomitant metabolic alkalosis. Diuretics, vomiting, and nasogastric suction are frequent causes that are also associated with urine potassium loss. Bartter and Gitelman syndromes are congenital disorders presenting with hypokalemic metabolic alkalosis resulting from abnormalities in the loop diuretic–sensitive sodium-potassium-chloride cotransporter in the thick ascending limb and the thiazide diuretic–sensitive sodium-chloride cotransporter in the distal tubule. Aminoglycosides such as gentamicin, when given for prolonged courses, can induce a Bartter-like syndrome resulting from activation of the calcium-sensing receptor in the thick ascending limb, thereby inhibiting the sodium-potassium-chloride cotransporter in the thick ascending limb.

Treatment

A decrease in the serum potassium concentration from 4 to 3 meq/L (4 to 3 mmol/L) is associated with a potassium deficit of approximately 100 meq when there is no change in cellular distribution. However, a linear relationship between the serum potassium concentration and the total body potassium deficit is not observed below serum levels of 3 meq/L (3 mmol/L), and careful monitoring of the serum potassium concentration during repletion is therefore indicated to avoid iatrogenic hyperkalemia.

Patients with large potassium deficits, particularly when associated with cardiac or skeletal muscle dysfunction, should be treated with intravenous potassium chloride at a maximum rate of 20 meq/h infused at a concentration no greater than 40 meq/L (40 mmol/L). Addition of sodium bicarbonate and/or glucose to intravenous solutions, which cause increased intracellular uptake of potassium, should be avoided during initial therapy of symptomatic hypokalemia.

Oral supplementation is appropriate for asymptomatic patients or for those with mild symptoms. Potassium citrate can be used for patients with concomitant metabolic acidosis due to renal tubular acidosis. Potassium-sparing diuretics are helpful for patients with conditions associated with chronic kidney potassium wasting but should be avoided when there is concomitant metabolic acidosis. Magnesium depletion frequently accompanies hypokalemia, and correction of magnesium deficits may limit urine potassium loss. **H**

KEY POINTS

- Hypokalemia manifests with abnormal skeletal and cardiac muscle cell function related to alterations in action potential generation or changes in renal tubular cell function.

- Diuretics are the most common cause of hypokalemia.

- In patients with hypokalemia, a urine potassium–creatinine ratio above 20 meq/g is characteristic of kidney potassium wasting, whereas a value below 15 meq/g reflects cellular redistribution, decreased intake, or extrarenal potassium loss.

- Patients with large potassium deficits, particularly when associated with cardiac or skeletal muscle dysfunction, should be treated with intravenous potassium chloride at a maximum rate of 20 meq/h infused at a concentration no greater than 40 meq/L (40 mmol/L).

Hyperkalemia

Hyperkalemia is defined as a serum potassium concentration greater than 5 meq/L (5 mmol/L). Risk factors include underlying acute or chronic kidney disease and decreased renin-angiotensin-aldosterone activity. Clinical manifestations include ascending muscle weakness, electrocardiogram (ECG) changes, and life-threatening cardiac arrhythmias and paralysis when the hyperkalemia is severe.

Evaluation

The initial goal is to establish whether hyperkalemia is life-threatening through the history and physical examination and analysis of the ECG. As the serum potassium level rises, the ECG most commonly reveals peaked T waves with a shortened QT interval initially, followed by an increased PR interval and QRS duration, decreased P wave amplitude, and eventually a sinoventricular pattern heralding ventricular standstill. The presence of ECG changes warrants emergency therapy (see Treatment).

The initial evaluation of hyperkalemia also includes assessment for cellular redistribution (**Figure 7**). In the absence of symptoms or ECG changes, pseudohyperkalemia should be considered. Severe leukocytosis (leukocyte count >120,000/microliters [120 × 10⁹/L]) and thrombocytosis

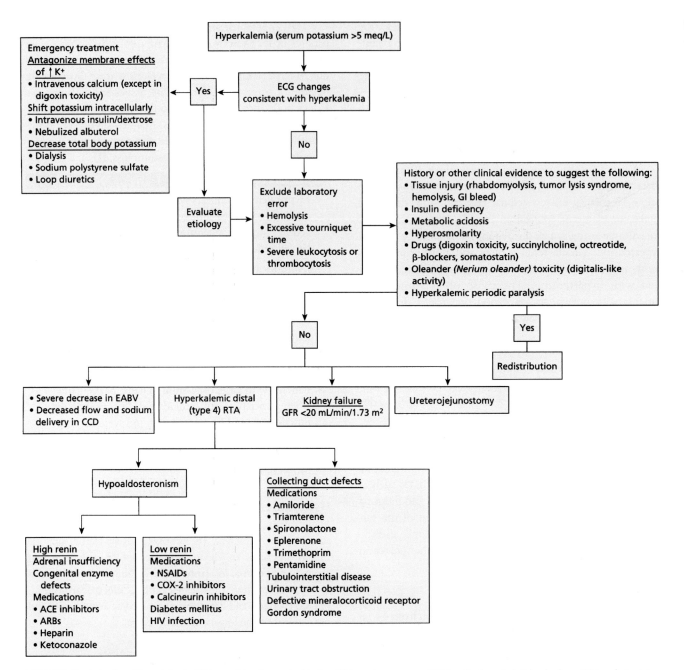

FIGURE 7. Evaluation of hyperkalemia. ARB = angiotensin receptor blocker; COX = cyclooxygenase; EABV = effective arterial blood volume; ECG = electrocardiography; GFR = glomerular filtration rate; GI = gastrointestinal; K = potassium; RTA = renal tubular acidosis.

(platelet count >600,000/microliters [600 × 10⁹/L]) can result in the release of intracellular potassium in serum specimens. The diagnosis of pseudohyperkalemia due to thrombocytosis is established by documenting a simultaneous normal plasma (heparinized sample) potassium level. Pseudohyperkalemia related to leukocytosis is diagnosed by repeating a serum potassium measurement in a sample carefully transported to the laboratory without agitation immediately following phlebotomy. Measurement of whole blood

potassium in uncentrifuged specimens using ion-specific electrodes also confirms the diagnosis.

Hyperkalemia may also occur as a result of mechanical trauma or a prolonged tourniquet time during venipuncture, and a serum potassium measurement should be repeated in asymptomatic patients with no apparent risk factors for hyperkalemia or ECG changes.

Due to increased release of aldosterone and resultant enhanced kidney potassium excretion, the serum potassium concentration remains in the normal range in healthy adults with potassium intake as high as 280 meq/d (280 mmol/d), well above the average daily intake of 70 meq (70 mmol) in a typical Western diet. Dietary intake of potassium contributes to the pathogenesis of hyperkalemia only in patients with a kidney defect in potassium secretion, usually resulting from a defect in the renin-angiotensin-aldosterone system or a glomerular filtration rate (GFR) less than 20 mL/min/1.73 m². Hyperkalemia that occurs above this level of GFR indicates that there is a defect in potassium secretion in the CCD (see Figure 7).

The capacity of the kidney to excrete potassium in the setting of hyperkalemia can be evaluated by calculating the transtubular potassium gradient (TTKG), which estimates the ratio of the potassium level in the CCD to that in the peritubular capillary. The TTKG is calculated by the following equation:

TTKG = [Urine Potassium ÷ (Urine Osmolality/ Plasma Osmolality)] ÷ Serum Potassium

The TTKG should be greater than 10 in hyperkalemia under normal physiologic conditions. A TTKG less than 10 in a hyperkalemic patient indicates a kidney defect in potassium excretion.

Various drugs interfere directly or indirectly with CCD potassium secretion. Blockade of the renin-angiotensin-aldosterone system with drugs, particularly use of combination therapy such as an ACE inhibitor and spironolactone in CKD, frequently induces hyperkalemia. Hyporeninemic hypoaldosteronism most commonly occurs in patients with long-standing diabetes mellitus or HIV infection. Injury to the CCD epithelium because of chronic tubulointerstitial disease, sickle cell nephropathy, or urinary tract obstruction impairs potassium secretion and leads to hyperkalemia. Factors resulting in decreased mineralocorticoid activity, including congenital or acquired adrenal insufficiency as well as inherited mineralocorticoid receptor defects, may be associated with hyperkalemia. Hyperkalemia may also develop as a complication of ureterojejunostomy because of increased absorption of urine potassium in the jejunal bypass limb.

Treatment

Patients with symptomatic hyperkalemia or those with a rapidly rising serum potassium level and/or ECG manifestations should receive prompt treatment under continuous cardiac monitoring. Intravenous calcium chloride or calcium gluconate antagonizes the depolarization effects of hyperkalemia and should be administered every 5 minutes until ECG changes resolve. Intravenous calcium is contraindicated in patients with digoxin toxicity, because it potentiates adverse electrophysiologic effects. Treatment directed toward increasing intracellular uptake of potassium should then be initiated. Intravenous insulin (with intravenous glucose when the plasma glucose level is <250 mg/dL [13.9 mmol/L]) is the most efficient intervention that enhances intracellular potassium uptake. This effect begins within 10 minutes and is sustained

for 4 to 6 hours. High-dose nebulized albuterol (10-20 mg) is additive to the action of insulin, with a peak effect at 90 minutes. Sodium bicarbonate may be used to treat hyperkalemia when complicated by metabolic acidosis but has minimal efficacy in patients with end-stage kidney disease.

The use of intravenous calcium, insulin, sodium bicarbonate, and nebulized albuterol is only a temporizing measure. Definitive therapy must include measures that decrease total body potassium. Sodium polystyrene sulfate in sorbitol has historically been used to decrease total body potassium in patients with hyperkalemia. However, preparations containing sorbitol have been implicated in gastrointestinal necrosis and bleeding; therefore, use of the sorbitol-free preparation is preferred. Hemodialysis is indicated when hyperkalemia is severe, particularly in patients with severe kidney failure.

Mild to moderate hyperkalemia can often be controlled through dietary potassium restriction to less than 2500 mg/d. Hypovolemia and urinary tract obstruction, when present, should be corrected. Contributing medications such as NSAIDs and cyclooxygenase-2 inhibitors should be strictly avoided. Medications that inhibit the activity of the renin-angiotensin-aldosterone system such as ACE inhibitors or spironolactone may require dose reduction or discontinuation when the serum potassium level remains above 5.5 meq/L (5.5 mmol/L). Patients with a GFR less than 30 mL/min/1.73 m² require closer monitoring of the serum potassium level (every 7 to 10 days after initiating or increasing the dose of renin-angiotensin-aldosterone system inhibitors such as ACE inhibitors). Loop diuretics can be used to promote decreased total body potassium in patients with CKD or chronic heart failure.

KEY POINTS

- Clinical manifestations of hyperkalemia include ascending muscle weakness, electrocardiogram changes, and life-threatening cardiac arrhythmias and paralysis when the hyperkalemia is severe.

- Dietary intake of potassium contributes to the pathogenesis of hyperkalemia only in patients with a kidney defect in potassium secretion, usually resulting from a defect in the renin-angiotensin-aldosterone system or a glomerular filtration rate less than 20 mL/min/1.73 m².

- Intravenous insulin (with intravenous glucose when the plasma glucose level is <250 mg/dL [13.9 mmol/L]) is the most efficient intervention that enhances intracellular potassium uptake.

- Mild to moderate hyperkalemia can often be controlled through dietary potassium restriction to less than 2500 mg/d.

- Medications that inhibit the activity of the renin-angiotensin-aldosterone system may require dose reduction or discontinuation when the serum potassium level remains above 5.5 meq/L (5.5 mmol/L).

Disorders of Serum Phosphate

Hypophosphatemia

Hypophosphatemia is defined as a serum phosphate concentration less than 2.5 mg/dL (0.81 mmol/L) and is most common in patients with a history of chronic alcohol use, critical illness, and malnutrition. Most patients with hypophosphatemia are asymptomatic, but symptoms of weakness may manifest at levels less than 2 mg/dL (0.65 mmol/L). Serum phosphate levels less than 1 mg/dL (0.32 mmol/L) may result in respiratory muscle weakness, hemolysis, and rhabdomyolysis.

Evaluation

The causes of hypophosphatemia are summarized in **Table 14**. In most cases, the cause is evident from the history. If the diagnosis remains unclear, urine phosphate excretion can be assessed by obtaining a 24-hour urine phosphate excretion or by calculating the fractional excretion of phosphate from a random urine specimen.

When hypophosphatemia is due to increased cellular uptake or extrarenal phosphate loss, the 24-hour urine phosphate excretion is less than 100 mg/dL (32.3 mmol/L) and the fractional excretion of phosphate is less than 5%.

Treatment

Hypophosphatemia usually resolves with treatment of the underlying cause. Phosphate supplementation is indicated for symptomatic patients and for those with chronic phosphate

---

TABLE 14. Causes of Hypophosphatemia

Kidney phosphate wasting
  Acetaminophen poisoning
  Vitamin D deficiency or resistance
  Hyperparathyroidism
  Osmotic diuresis
  Oncogenic osteomalacia
  Kidney transplantation
  Proximal (type 2) renal tubular acidosis (Fanconi syndrome)
    Tenofovir
    Ifosfamide
  Hypophosphatemic rickets
Chronic diarrhea
Decreased absorption
  Vitamin D deficiency or resistance
  Phosphate binders and antacids
Decreased intake
Intracellular uptake
  Refeeding syndrome
  Treatment of diabetic ketoacidosis with insulin
  Parathyroidectomy (hungry bone syndrome)
  Respiratory alkalosis

---

wasting. Oral phosphate supplementation is preferred because of the risk of hypocalcemia and acute kidney injury associated with intravenous phosphate infusions. Intravenous phosphate supplementation is indicated for symptomatic patients with serum phosphate levels less than 1 mg/dL (0.32 mmol/L). Serum phosphate and calcium levels should be monitored every 6 hours during intravenous therapy, and doses of phosphate should be restricted to 80 mmol over 12 hours.

Hyperphosphatemia

Hyperphosphatemia is defined as a serum phosphate concentration greater than 4.5 mg/dL (1.45 mmol/L). Hyperphosphatemia most commonly occurs in patients with advanced CKD but may also occur when there is increased cell turnover, cell injury, or exogenous phosphate administration. The cause is usually apparent from the clinical history. Patients with CKD are treated with phosphate binders taken with meals to limit intestinal absorption of phosphate. Patients with acute phosphate nephropathy or tumor lysis syndrome with severe hyperphosphatemia (serum phosphate >10 mg/dL [3.23 mmol/L]) and concomitant oliguria may warrant initiation of hemodialysis.

KEY POINTS

- Hypophosphatemia is most common in patients with a history of chronic alcohol use, critical illness, and malnutrition.
- Serum phosphate levels less than 2 mg/dL (0.65 mmol/L) may cause symptomatic weakness, and levels less than 1 mg/dL (0.32 mmol/L) may result in respiratory muscle weakness, hemolysis, and rhabdomyolysis.
- Intravenous phosphate supplementation is indicated for symptomatic patients with serum phosphate levels less than 1 mg/dL (0.32 mmol/L).

Acid-Base Disorders

General Approach

Because of the importance of maintaining a stable metabolic milieu, the systemic pH is carefully controlled through both renal and respiratory mechanisms. Disturbances in acid-base balance lead to predictable responses that serve to limit the magnitude of change of blood pH. The cause of acid-base disturbances is often apparent by examining data from an arterial blood gas study (pH and P_{CO_2}) and venous electrolyte measurement (primarily serum bicarbonate) in the context of a given clinical situation.

Primary acid-base disorders are classified as respiratory or metabolic. Respiratory acidosis is defined as an arterial P_{CO_2} above the normal range, with a value below normal representing respiratory alkalosis. Metabolic acidosis is defined as a serum bicarbonate level below the normal range, with a value above normal representing metabolic alkalosis.

Analysis involves identification of the likely dominant acid-base disorder, followed by an assessment of the secondary, compensatory response. The expected compensatory responses to primary acid-base disturbances are listed in **Table 15**. When measured values fall outside the range of the predicted secondary response, a mixed acid-base disorder is present; multiple acid-base disturbances may coexist in a single patient. The correct diagnosis of respiratory acid-base disorders, particularly when associated with a second disorder, often requires correlation with the clinical history.

Metabolic Acidosis

Metabolic acidosis occurs when there is loss of serum bicarbonate, decreased excretion of acid, imbalance between production and consumption of endogenous acids, or ingestion or intravenous administration of exogenous acids.

Evaluation

When metabolic acidosis is present, it should be further characterized by analysis of the anion gap. The anion gap is useful in assessing whether the decreased serum bicarbonate is due to the presence of an additional unmeasured acid (such as lactate or an ingested acid) that will raise the anion gap, or a loss or lack of production of serum bicarbonate in which the serum chloride increases to maintain electroneutrality, in which case the anion gap is normal. Based on this analysis, a metabolic acidosis is classified as being either an *increased anion gap* or a *normal anion gap* metabolic acidosis. The anion gap is calculated from the following equation:

Anion Gap = Serum Sodium (meq/L) − [Serum Chloride (meq/L) + Serum Bicarbonate (meq/L)]

The normal reference range for the anion gap is approximately 8 to 10 meq/L ± 2 meq/L (8-10 mmol/L ± 2 mmol/L), which may vary among laboratories and individuals. Because albumin is an unmeasured anion, changes in the serum albumin level can affect the magnitude of the expected anion gap. For every 1 g/dL (10 g/L) decrease in serum albumin, for example, the expected or "normal" anion gap falls by approximately 2.3 meq/L (2.3 mmol/L). The presence of unmeasured cations such as cationic light chains also decreases the anion gap. **H**

KEY POINTS

- Metabolic acidosis occurs when there is loss of serum bicarbonate, decreased excretion of acid, imbalance between production and consumption of endogenous acids, or ingestion or intravenous administration of exogenous acids.

  The anion gap is used to characterize the nature of a metabolic acidosis.

  The presence of a low serum albumin level or unmeasured cations such as cationic light chains results in a decreased anion gap.

Classification

Mixed Metabolic Disorders

Additional analysis is required when an increased anion gap metabolic acidosis is present to determine whether the serum bicarbonate level was normal before the development of the acidosis or if there was a preexisting metabolic abnormality before the acidosis creating the anion gap occurred. This is done by calculating the corrected bicarbonate based on the change in the anion gap (termed the *delta anion gap* or *delta gap*), which estimates the serum bicarbonate level

TABLE 15. Compensation in Acid-Base Disorders	
Condition	**Expected Compensation**
Metabolic acidosis	Acute: $P_{CO_2} = (1.5) [HCO_3] + 8$
	Chronic: $P_{CO_2} = [HCO_3] + 15$
	Failure of the P_{CO_2} to decrease to expected value = complicating respiratory acidosis; excessive decrease of the P_{CO_2} = complicating respiratory alkalosis
	Quick check: P_{CO_2} = value should approximate last two digits of pH
Metabolic alkalosis	For each ↑ 1 meq/L in $[HCO_3]$, P_{CO_2} ↑ 0.7 mm Hg
Respiratory acidosis	Acute: 1 meq/L ↑ $[HCO_3]$ for each 10 mm Hg ↑ in P_{CO_2}
	Chronic: 3.5 meq/L ↑ $[HCO_3]$ for each 10 mm Hg ↑ in P_{CO_2}
	Failure of the $[HCO_3]$ to increase to the expected value = complicating metabolic acidosis; excessive increase in $[HCO_3]$ = complicating metabolic alkalosis
Respiratory alkalosis	Acute: ↓ 2 meq/L $[HCO_3]$ for each 10 mm Hg ↓ in P_{CO_2}
	Chronic: 4-5 meq/L ↓ $[HCO_3]$ for each 10 mm Hg ↓ in P_{CO_2}
	Failure of the $[HCO_3]$ to decrease to the expected value = complicating metabolic alkalosis; excessive decrease in $[HCO_3]$ = complicating metabolic acidosis

CONT.

that existed in the absence of the increased anion gap acidosis. The corrected bicarbonate is calculated from the following equation:

$$\text{Corrected Bicarbonate} = 24 \text{ meq/L} - \Delta \text{ Anion Gap (meq/L)}$$

(in which Δ anion gap is the increase in the anion gap above normal)

If the measured bicarbonate is greater than the corrected bicarbonate, it suggests that a concomitant metabolic alkalosis may be present in addition to the increased anion gap metabolic acidosis. If the measured serum bicarbonate is less than the corrected bicarbonate, a concomitant normal anion gap metabolic acidosis is likely present in addition to the increased anion gap metabolic acidosis.

This approach is limited by the assumption that organic acids are buffered 1:1 by bicarbonate. Because buffering also occurs through intracellular uptake of protons, an increase in the measured bicarbonate to a level greater than the corrected bicarbonate may reflect intracellular buffering rather than metabolic alkalosis. The ratio of the change in anion gap to the change in bicarbonate can be used to account for the effect of intracellular buffering. A ratio of less than 1 may reflect the presence of concurrent normal anion gap metabolic acidosis, whereas a ratio of greater than 2 may indicate the presence of metabolic alkalosis.

Anion Gap Metabolic Acidosis

The differential diagnosis of increased anion gap metabolic acidosis is shown in **Table 16**.

Lactic Acidosis

Lactic acidosis, the most common form of increased anion gap metabolic acidosis, is defined as a serum lactate level greater than 4 mg/dL (0.44 mmol/L). Type A lactic acidosis occurs when tissue hypoperfusion is apparent, whereas type B lactic acidosis occurs in the absence of hypoperfusion. Lactic acidosis associated with acetaminophen toxicity is caused by direct hepatic injury as well as by a metabolite that uncouples oxidative phosphorylation. Lactic acidosis frequently accompanies severe asthma in which high doses of β_2-agonists and corticosteroids as well as respiratory alkalosis all contribute to increased lactic acid production.

Treatment of lactic acidosis is directed toward reversing or removing the underlying cause as well as supportive measures such as fluid resuscitation in patients with hypovolemic shock. Sodium bicarbonate therapy, targeting an arterial pH of approximately 7.2, should be considered when the arterial pH is less than 7.1, particularly in patients with cardiovascular compromise.

Propofol-Related Infusion Syndrome

Administration of intravenous propofol in doses exceeding 4 mg/kg/h for more than 48 hours can induce type B lactic

TABLE 16. Causes of Increased Anion Gap Metabolic Acidosis
Advanced acute and chronic kidney disease
Alcoholic ketoacidosis
Diabetic ketoacidosis
D-Lactic acidosis
Diethylene glycol poisoning
Ethylene glycol poisoning
Type A lactic acidosis (hypoperfusion or hypoxia)
Anemia (severe)
Carbon monoxide poisoning
Cardiogenic shock
Septic shock
Hemorrhagic shock
Hypoxia
Type B lactic acidosis (no hypoperfusion or hypoxia)
Medications or toxins
Acetaminophen poisoning
Cyanide
Ethylene glycol
Linezolid
Mangosteen juice
Metformin
Methanol
Nucleoside reverse transcriptase inhibitors (stavudine, didanosine)
Propylene glycol
Propofol
Salicylates
Thiamine deficiency
Systemic disease
Liver failure
Malignancy
Glucose 6-phosphatase dehydrogenase deficiency
Pyroglutamic acidosis
Salicylate toxicity

acidosis and a syndrome characterized by rhabdomyolysis, hyperlipidemia, and J-point elevation on electrocardiogram. Once recognized, propofol should be discontinued. Treatment is supportive, and hemodialysis may be required for severe acidosis and kidney failure.

D-Lactic Acidosis

Accumulation of the D-isomer of lactic acid can occur in patients with short-bowel syndrome following jejunoileal bypass or small-bowel resection. In these patients, excess carbohydrates that reach the colon are metabolized to D-lactate. Symptoms include intermittent confusion, slurred speech, and ataxia. This condition may be mistaken for a neurologic syndrome. Neurologic symptoms may be mediated by as yet unidentified toxins produced by bacteria in the colon rather than D-lactate. Laboratory studies show increased anion gap metabolic acidosis with normal serum lactate levels, because the D-isomer is not measured by conventional laboratory assays for lactate. Diagnosis should be considered in patients with an unexplained increased anion gap metabolic acidosis in the appropriate clinical context and is confirmed by specifically measuring D-lactate. Therapy consists of antibiotics directed toward bowel flora such as metronidazole or neomycin as well as restriction of dietary carbohydrates.

Diabetic Ketoacidosis

Diabetic ketoacidosis usually presents with an increased anion gap metabolic acidosis, but it may also present with normal anion gap metabolic acidosis in the absence of hypovolemia due to excretion of ketoacids in the urine. Insulin deficiency, increased catecholamines, and glucagon result in incomplete oxidation of fatty acids, which leads to the production of acetoacetate and β-hydroxybutyrate. The presence of ketoacids can be measured using the nitroprusside assay or by directly measuring serum assays for specific ketoacids. Because the nitroprusside assay detects only acetone and acetoacetate (and not the predominant ketoacid β-hydroxybutyrate), the results can be falsely negative in the presence of severe ketoacidosis.

Administration of insulin is critical in reversing the underlying cause, and intravenous fluids are indicated to correct volume deficits. Serum potassium levels need to be followed closely with careful repletion because patients are typically potassium depleted, and serum levels will fluctuate with correction of the serum pH. Sodium bicarbonate therapy to correct the metabolic acidosis is controversial because ketoacidosis will reverse with insulin administration, and sodium bicarbonate therapy may slow recovery or lead to a rebound metabolic alkalosis following recovery. Therefore, sodium bicarbonate therapy is generally reserved for patients with a pH less than 7.0, metabolic instability due to acidosis, or life-threatening hyperkalemia potentially corrected by sodium bicarbonate administration. Although phosphate depletion is common, there is no evidence that intravenous repletion is beneficial in the absence of severe symptoms, and resumption of oral intake is usually sufficient to correct the deficit.

Alcoholic Ketoacidosis

Alcoholic ketoacidosis presents with an increased anion gap metabolic acidosis and ketosis in patients with chronic ethanol abuse. It often follows a period of poor caloric intake. Nausea, vomiting, and hypovolemia are common. Increased levels of circulating catecholamines result in mobilization of fatty acids and ketoacidosis. The predominant ketoacid is β-hydroxybutyrate, thereby limiting the sensitivity of the nitroprusside assay.

Intravenous glucose administration or resumption of caloric intake reverses the ketoacidosis by stimulating insulin release, resulting in decreased fatty acid mobilization and decreased hepatic release of ketoacids. Hypovolemia, when present, should be corrected with intravenous normal saline.

Ethylene Glycol and Methanol Toxicity

Ethylene glycol and methanol poisoning are highly lethal intoxications that present with severe increased anion gap metabolic acidosis usually associated with an osmolal gap greater than 10 mosm/kg H_2O (see Fluids and Electrolytes, Osmolality and Tonicity). The acidosis is due to acid metabolites of the parent compound as well as lactic acidosis. The increase in the osmolal gap results from elevated levels of the parent alcohol; patients presenting after complete metabolism of the parent alcohol may have a normal osmolal gap. Simultaneous ingestion of ethylene glycol or methanol with ethanol may delay the onset of acidosis and symptoms because ethanol inhibits alcohol dehydrogenase, thereby limiting the breakdown of the parent alcohol to toxic metabolites. Clinical manifestations of ethylene glycol and methanol poisoning include inebriation early in the course to obtundation, seizures, coma, and cardiovascular collapse.

Patients with ethylene glycol toxicity may have flank pain or oliguria resulting from calcium oxalate precipitation in the renal tubules. Clinically, the calcium oxalate precipitation manifests as acute kidney injury often accompanied by hypocalcemia, nephrocalcinosis on abdominal radiograph, and calcium oxalate crystals in the urine sediment. Cardiovascular collapse and pulmonary edema may ensue.

Methanol toxicity may result in impaired vision that can progress to blindness, abdominal pain, and pancreatitis. Retinal toxicity is mediated by formic acid. Physical examination may demonstrate mydriasis or an afferent pupillary defect. Approximately 10% to 20% of patients who survive methanol poisoning have permanent visual impairment. Methanol can induce putaminal injury, and survivors may develop secondary parkinsonism.

Diagnosis of ethylene glycol and methanol toxicity is usually established on clinical grounds in patients with severe anion gap metabolic acidosis and increased osmolal gap. Serum levels are not rapidly available in most hospital laboratories, and treatment must be instituted before confirmatory levels are available. Increased anion gap acidosis associated with a serum bicarbonate level less than 10 meq/L (10 mmol/L) and an osmolal gap greater than 25 mosm/kg H_2O should raise suspicion for ethylene glycol or methanol poisoning. A normal osmolal gap, however, does not exclude the diagnosis.

Treatment includes supportive measures to optimize ventilation and organ perfusion. Fomepizole, a competitive inhibitor of alcohol dehydrogenase that prevents the formation of toxic acid metabolites, is indicated once the diagnosis is suspected. Hemodialysis should be initiated when there is significant high anion gap metabolic acidosis or evidence of end-organ injury such as kidney failure or neurologic symptoms. Acidemia is known to facilitate the cellular uptake of toxic metabolites, and sodium bicarbonate therapy should be administered to maintain the pH above 7.3 until hemodialysis can be initiated. Intravenous folic acid should be administered in suspected methanol poisoning, and pyridoxine and thiamine should be given in ethylene glycol poisoning to facilitate metabolism of the parent alcohol to nontoxic compounds.

Propylene Glycol Toxicity

Propylene glycol is a solvent used as a vehicle for numerous intravenously administered medications. Toxicity has been reported in association with the use of high-dose lorazepam. It is more likely to occur when propylene glycol levels exceed 25 mg/dL or when the osmolal gap is greater than 12 mosm/kg H_2O. Laboratory findings include increased anion gap metabolic acidosis and concomitant increased osmolal gap. The metabolic acidosis is principally due to L-lactic and D-lactic acidosis, the acid metabolites of propylene glycol. Acid-base status and plasma osmolality should be carefully monitored in patients receiving lorazepam at doses greater than 1 mg/kg/d. The syndrome is unlikely to develop if the 24-hour lorazepam dose is limited to less than 166 mg/d in adults.

Most patients improve with discontinuation of the intravenous infusion. Early initiation of hemodialysis is indicated for patients with kidney failure or severe metabolic acidosis. The use of fomepizole in propylene glycol toxicity is unproved, although theoretically it would inhibit generation of toxic metabolites.

Salicylate Toxicity

Ingestion of as little as 10 to 30 grams of aspirin in an adult can result in lethal salicylate toxicity. Toxicity can also develop from ingestion or mucocutaneous exposure to salicylate-containing preparations such as methyl salicylate (oil of wintergreen). Salicylate toxicity commonly presents with abnormalities in acid-base balance, the most common in adults being respiratory alkalosis, which occurs in response to stimulation of the medullary respiratory center. With more severe intoxication, increased anion gap metabolic acidosis develops both as a result of the salicylate anion and concomitant lactic and ketoacidosis.

Clinical manifestations are primarily due to intracellular toxicity of salicylic acid rather than acid-base abnormalities. Early manifestations include tinnitus, confusion, tachypnea, and, occasionally, low-grade fever. Nausea, vomiting, and resultant metabolic alkalosis may develop as a result of direct gastric mucosal toxicity as well as stimulation of medullary chemoreceptors. Neurologic dysfunction is mediated by salicylate-induced cellular toxicity and neuroglycopenia and manifests as mental status changes that can progress to cerebral edema and fatal brainstem herniation. Acute lung injury and noncardiogenic pulmonary edema have been reported in older adults, particularly in the setting of chronic salicylate exposure. Large ingestions may cause hepatic injury and impaired vitamin K metabolism, resulting in increases in the prothrombin time and INR.

Treatment of salicylate poisoning includes judicious volume expansion and sodium bicarbonate therapy to maintain the arterial pH between 7.45 and 7.6. Urine alkalinization also promotes urine excretion of salicylic acid, and sodium bicarbonate infusions should be adjusted to maintain urine pH above 7.5. Supplemental intravenous glucose, 100 mL of 50% dextrose in adults, should be provided when mental status changes are present to treat neuroglycopenia irrespective of the plasma glucose level. The serum salicylate level, arterial blood gases, and venous electrolytes should be monitored at least every 2 hours until clinical and laboratory manifestations and toxic drug levels resolve.

Intubation should be avoided whenever possible because of the risk of inducing a decrease in arterial pH, thereby enhancing intracellular salicylic acid uptake. Hypokalemia should be corrected, because it interferes with urine alkalinization. Indications for hemodialysis include impaired mental status, cerebral edema, serum salicylate levels above 80 mg/dL (5.8 mmol/L), severe metabolic acidosis, pulmonary edema, and kidney failure.

Pyroglutamic Acidosis

Pyroglutamic acidosis is a cause of increased anion gap acidosis in patients receiving therapeutic doses of acetaminophen on a chronic basis. Clinical manifestations are limited to mental status changes and increased anion gap acidosis. The syndrome most commonly occurs in patients with critical illness, poor nutrition, liver disease, or chronic kidney disease as well as in persons on a vegetarian diet. Chronic treatment with acetaminophen in these conditions can cause disruption of the γ-glutamyl cycle and accumulation of pyroglutamic acid (also called 5-oxoproline). Diagnosis can be confirmed by measuring urine levels of pyroglutamic acid. Treatment includes discontinuation of acetaminophen, volume expansion with isotonic saline and glucose, and possibly N-acetylcysteine to replace depleted glutathione stores.

Acidosis in Acute and Chronic Kidney Disease

Metabolic acidosis in patients with acute and chronic kidney disease is mediated by two mechanisms: decreased ammonia buffer synthesis when the glomerular filtration rate (GFR) decreases to less than 45 mL/min/1.73 m^2, causing normal anion gap metabolic acidosis; and retention of sulfates, phosphates, and organic acids when the GFR decreases below 15 mL/min/1.73 m^2, resulting in an increased anion gap metabolic acidosis. **H**

KEY POINTS

- Lactic acidosis, the most common form of increased anion gap metabolic acidosis, is defined as a serum lactate level greater than 4 mg/dL (0.44 mmol/L).

- Ethylene glycol and methanol poisoning are characterized by a severe increased anion gap metabolic acidosis associated with an osmolal gap greater than 10 mosm/kg H_2O.

- Fomepizole, an inhibitor of alcohol dehydrogenase that prevents the formation of toxic acid metabolites, is indicated for patients with ethylene glycol and methanol toxicity.

Normal Anion Gap Metabolic Acidosis

Normal anion gap metabolic acidosis may be due to failure of the kidney to excrete the daily fixed acid load, gastrointestinal loss of bicarbonate, diversion of urine through a gastrointestinal conduit, or retention of hydrogen ions derived from organic anions that are excreted in the urine as sodium salts. The cause is often apparent from the history. When the cause remains unclear, analysis of urine acid excretion may be helpful in making a specific diagnosis.

The normal kidney response to acidemia is characterized by an increase in urine ammonium excretion from a baseline of approximately 0.5 meq/kg/d to approximately 3 meq/kg/d. This response occurs in patients with a normal GFR in the absence of concomitant hyperkalemia over the course of 3 to 5 days. Thus, if urine ammonium excretion is elevated, the kidney response is appropriate and the cause of the acidosis is likely due to a non-kidney cause, whereas low urine excretion suggests a primary kidney defect. Because urine ammonium is not easily measured, two methods are used to estimate urine acid secretion: the urine anion gap and the urine osmolal gap.

The urine anion gap uses the urine sodium (Na^+), potassium (K^+), and chloride (Cl^-) concentration values and is defined as:

$$\text{Urine Anion Gap} = [Na^+] + [K^+] - [Cl^-]$$

If significant urine NH_{4+} is present, the urine anion gap will be negative because urine NH_{4+} is a positive ion and is not directly measured. If present, increased negatively charged ions (primarily Cl^-) will also be present in the urine in order to maintain electrical neutrality. As the negative ions are directly measured, and the known positive ions in the urine are subtracted from this measurement, the presence of more negative than positive ions in the urine (a negative anion gap) infers that another positively charged ion must be present, specifically NH_{4+}. Therefore, a negative urine anion gap indicates appropriate tubular ammonium excretion and acidification of the urine in the presence of a metabolic acidosis. Conversely, if the urine anion gap is 0 or positive, it is unlikely

that significant urine NH_{4+} is present, indicating that there has been an inadequate renal response to the acidosis.

If the urine osmolal gap is used, the urine ammonium may be estimated by dividing the urine osmolal gap by two:

$$\text{Urine Ammonium (meq/L)} \cong \text{Urine Osmolal Gap} \\ (\text{mosm/kg } H_2O)/2$$

$$\text{Urine Osmolal Gap} = \text{Measured Urine Osmolality} - \\ \text{Calculated Urine Osmolality}$$

$$\text{Calculated Urine Osmolality (mosm/kg } H_2O) = 2 \\ (\text{Urine Sodium [meq/L]} + \text{Urine Potassium [meq/L]}) + \\ \text{Urine Urea (mg/dL)/2.8} + \text{Urine Glucose} \\ (\text{mg/dL})/18$$

The urine osmolal gap is not an accurate marker of urine ammonium excretion when there is a urinary tract infection due to a urea-splitting organism or when a solute such as an alcohol or mannitol is present in the urine.

Patients with predominantly extrarenal loss of bicarbonate exhibit urine ammonium levels above 80 meq/L, whereas ammonium levels in individuals with a primary kidney defect remain less than 30 meq/L (**Figure 8**). In patients with metabolic acidosis due to renal tubular dysfunction, the various causes of renal tubular acidosis (RTA) may be defined and evaluated based on the serum potassium level and urine pH (**Figure 9, on page 29**).

Proximal (Type 2) Renal Tubular Acidosis

Metabolic acidosis in proximal (type 2) RTA is caused by a reduction of bicarbonate reabsorption in the proximal tubule, which initially leads to bicarbonaturia. Once a new steady state is established at a lower serum bicarbonate level, the urine is then devoid of bicarbonate and the urine pH is less than 5.5. Proximal RTA is rarely an isolated finding and is usually associated with Fanconi syndrome, which is characterized by other signs of proximal tubular dysfunction such as low-molecular-weight proteinuria, phosphaturia, or glycosuria (**Table 17**). Mild hypokalemia is usually present as a consequence of secondary hyperaldosteronism. 1α-Hydroxylase activity is often decreased, leading to 1,25-dihydroxy vitamin D deficiency, hypocalcemia, and osteomalacia. Distal urine acidification is preserved; therefore, urine pH is less than 5.5 in the presence of systemic acidemia.

In patients with proximal RTA, correction of the metabolic acidosis is usually difficult because of urine bicarbonate wasting that occurs with alkali therapy. The efficacy of alkali therapy may be enhanced through the addition of a thiazide diuretic, which enhances proximal bicarbonate absorption. When induced by a medication, discontinuation of the offending agent is indicated when possible.

Hypokalemic Distal (Type 1) Renal Tubular Acidosis

Hypokalemic distal (type 1) RTA is a defect in distal urine acidification related to a primary tubular disorder or to injury

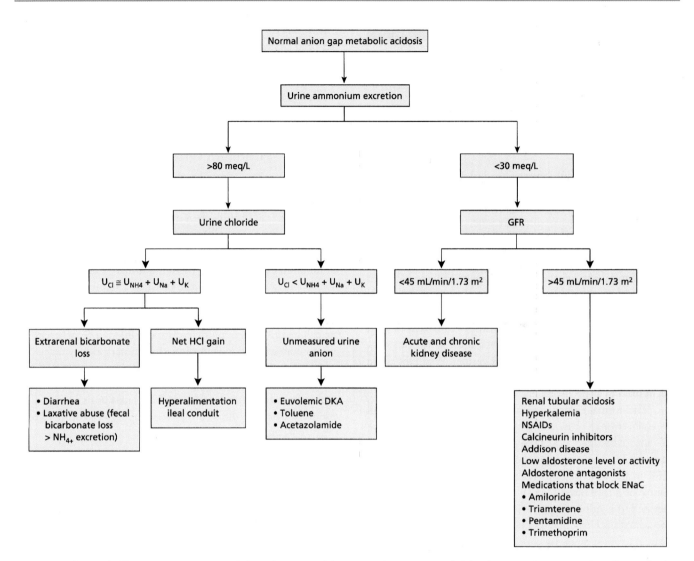

FIGURE 8. Evaluation of normal anion gap metabolic acidosis. DKA = diabetic ketoacidosis; ENaC = epithelial sodium channel on apical surface of principal cells in collecting duct; GFR = glomerular filtration rate; HCl = hydrochloric acid; NH_{4+} = ammonium; U_{Cl} = urine chloride concentration (meq/L); U_K = urine potassium concentration (meq/L); U_{Na} = urine sodium concentration (meq/L); U_{NH4} = ammonium concentration (meq/L).

TABLE 17. Causes of Proximal (Type 2) Renal Tubular Acidosis
Medications
Tenofovir
Ifosfamide
Amyloidosis
Multiple myeloma
Kidney transplantation
Heavy metal toxicity
Cadmium
Copper
Lead
Mercury
Cystinosis
Wilson disease

of the tubular epithelium, resulting in impaired excretion of hydrogen ions (**Table 18**). Decreased secretion of hydrogen ions leads to lumen-negative voltage, urine pH greater than 6.0, kidney potassium wasting, and hypokalemia. Calcium-phosphate kidney stones and nephrocalcinosis develop because of increased urine pH and decreased levels of urine citrate. Correction of the potassium deficit should precede correction of acidosis to avoid exacerbating hypokalemia. Acidosis should be corrected by the use of supplemental alkali in the form of potassium citrate at a dose of 1 meq/kg/d. Potassium-sparing diuretics are relatively contraindicated because of associated metabolic acidosis.

Hyperkalemic Distal (Type 4) Renal Tubular Acidosis
Hyperkalemic distal (type 4) RTA occurs in two distinct forms (see Figure 9). The first type, often associated with hypoaldosteronism, is characterized by urine pH less than 5.5.

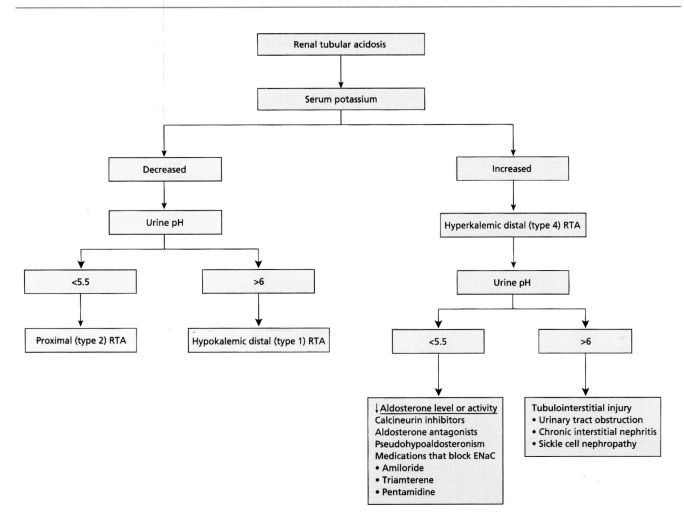

FIGURE 9. Evaluation of renal tubular acidosis. ENaC = epithelial sodium channel on apical surface of principal cells in collecting duct; RTA = renal tubular acidosis.

TABLE 18.	Causes of Hypokalemic Distal (Type 1) Renal Tubular Acidosis
Familial	
Autoimmune disorders	
Sjögren syndrome	
Systemic lupus erythematosus	
Rheumatoid arthritis	
Cirrhosis	
Medications	
Amphotericin B	
Ifosfamide	
Lithium	
Hypercalciuria	
Hyperglobulinemia	

Hyperkalemia results in impaired generation of ammonia and metabolic acidosis. Treatment of hyperkalemia in these patients corrects the acidosis. Management includes correcting the hyperkalemia, treating the underlying cause, and either reducing the dose or discontinuing contributing medications. Replacement of mineralocorticoids with fludrocortisone is indicated for patients with Addison disease. Dietary potassium restriction to approximately 2500 mg/d is a useful adjunct, and patients should be referred for dietary counseling.

The second type is associated with tubulointerstitial injury involving the collecting duct, as may occur in sickle cell nephropathy or urinary obstruction, which impairs urine acidification to a greater degree, resulting in urine pH levels above 6.0. Treatment of hyperkalemia in patients with these disorders does not correct the acidosis. Treatment includes relief of urinary obstruction when present, dietary potassium restriction, and sodium bicarbonate therapy to correct the serum potassium to approximately 23 meq/L (23 mmol/L).

Mixed Forms of Renal Tubular Acidosis

Defects in carbonic anhydrase result in combined proximal and distal RTA. An acquired form can develop in patients treated with topiramate, which inhibits carbonic anhydrase in the proximal and distal tubule. Topiramate is associated with an increased risk of calcium phosphate stones because of the high urine pH (greater than 6.0 despite acidemia) and hypocitraturia.

Metabolic Alkalosis

Metabolic alkalosis is caused by net loss of acid or retention of serum bicarbonate. Metabolic alkalosis can be classified as either occurring with normal extracellular fluid volume, hypovolemia, or decreased effective arterial blood volume (EABV) and increased extracellular fluid volume (heart failure, cirrhosis, nephrosis) or occurring with increased extracellular fluid volume and hypertension (**Figure 10**). Metabolic alkalosis, when associated with increased extracellular fluid volume and hypertension, is saline-resistant. Metabolic alkalosis associated with true hypovolemia responds to correction of the volume deficit with isotonic saline and is categorized as saline-responsive.

Urine sodium and chloride levels can help distinguish the various causes of metabolic alkalosis (see Figure 10). Metabolic alkalosis is commonly associated with increased

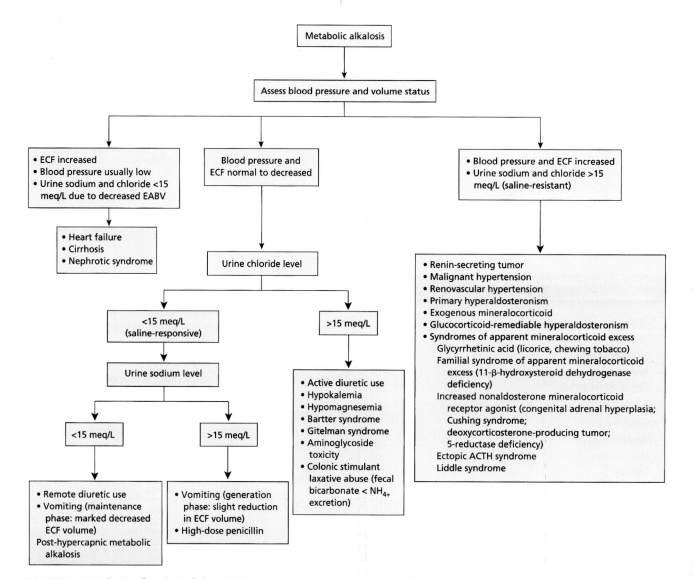

FIGURE 10. Evaluation of metabolic alkalosis. ACTH = adrenocorticotropic hormone; EABV = effective arterial blood volume; ECF = extracellular fluid; NH_{4+} = ammonium.

aldosterone or aldosterone-like activity and is usually accompanied by concomitant hypokalemia. The differential diagnosis of saline-responsive metabolic alkalosis includes vomiting, loss of gastric secretions through nasogastric suction, diuretic use, and post-hypercapnic alkalosis.

Treatment of saline-responsive metabolic alkalosis is directed toward correcting volume, sodium, chloride, and potassium deficits as well as reversing the underlying cause. Hypokalemia and symptomatic hypovolemia associated with diuretic-induced metabolic alkalosis are treated with potassium chloride supplementation and intravenous isotonic saline. Patients with severe metabolic alkalosis and symptomatic edema and decreased EABV as a consequence of severe chronic heart failure or cirrhosis can be treated with acetazolamide.

Bartter and Gitelman syndromes are rare inherited defects in kidney sodium and chloride handling that mimic the effects of loop and thiazide diuretics, respectively. Bartter syndrome typically presents in childhood, whereas Gitelman syndrome usually presents in late childhood or adulthood. Hypomagnesemia is frequently present. Symptoms include muscle cramps, postural hypotension, and weakness. Infusion of saline does not correct the alkalosis because of continued urine sodium and chloride losses. Laboratory abnormalities generally persist even with aggressive replacement of electrolytes; therefore, treatment should be directed toward ameliorating symptoms. Patients should be instructed to maintain a diet high in sodium and potassium. Amiloride is a useful adjunct for persistent symptomatic hypokalemia.

Metabolic alkalosis associated with hypertension results in increased urine sodium and chloride levels consequent to volume expansion and resultant decreased kidney sodium and chloride reabsorption. Diagnosis is established through measuring plasma renin and aldosterone levels. The most common form of saline-resistant metabolic alkalosis is primary hyperaldosteronism, which is characterized by increased aldosterone production, suppressed renin, and hypertension. Primary hyperaldosteronism may be due to either unilateral or bilateral adrenal gland hypersecretion of aldosterone (see MKSAP 16 Endocrinology and Metabolism). Therapy with aldosterone antagonists such as spironolactone can be used to control blood pressure and correct increased aldosterone production and hypokalemia. Patients with unilateral hypersecretion are candidates for unilateral adrenalectomy, especially when hypertension and metabolic abnormalities are resistant to medical therapy.

Syndromes of apparent mineralocorticoid excess present with hypertension and hypokalemic metabolic alkalosis and low plasma renin and aldosterone levels (**Figure 11**). **H**

KEY POINTS

- Saline-responsive metabolic alkalosis is characterized by true hypovolemia and responds to correction of the volume deficit with isotonic saline.
- Treatment of saline-responsive metabolic alkalosis is directed toward correcting volume, sodium, chloride, and potassium deficits as well as reversing the underlying cause.

Respiratory Acidosis

Respiratory acidosis usually results from decreased effective ventilation, leading to hypercapnia and retention of hydrogen ions. Respiratory acidosis can also result from intrinsic lung pathology or from processes that impede ventilation (**Table 19**).

Clinical Manifestations and Diagnosis

When severe, respiratory acidosis can impair mentation, increase cerebral blood flow, and result in cerebral edema, asterixis, decreased cardiac contractility, or cardiac arrhythmias. Neurologic effects of hypercapnia may decrease respiratory drive, further exacerbating the acidosis.

An elevation in the measured or expected arterial P_{CO_2} is the hallmark of respiratory acidosis and results in secondary hyperbicarbonatemia due to increased proximal bicarbonate reabsorption. In the first several hours, the serum bicarbonate level increases by 1 meq/L (1 mmol/L) for every 10 mm Hg (1.3 kPa) increase in P_{CO_2}. After 3 to 5 days, the serum bicarbonate level increases by 3.5 meq/L (3.5 mmol/L) for every 10 mm Hg (1.3 kPa) increase in P_{CO_2}.

TABLE 19. Causes of Respiratory Acidosis

Upper airway obstruction

Impaired pulmonary capillary CO_2 exchange
  Pulmonary parenchymal disease
  Obstructive lung disease
  Pulmonary edema
  Thromboembolic disease

Respiratory muscle weakness
  Muscle fatigue due to increased work of breathing
  Hypokalemia
  Hypophosphatemia
  Neuromuscular disease

Inadequate response of the medullary respiratory center
  Asthma
  Central hypoventilation syndrome
  Chronic obstructive lung disease

Suppression of the medullary respiratory center
  Hypercapnia
  Myxedema coma
  Central nervous system depressants

Increased tissue CO_2 production
  Extreme exercise
  Seizures
  Severe heart failure
  Hyperalimentation in mechanically ventilated patients

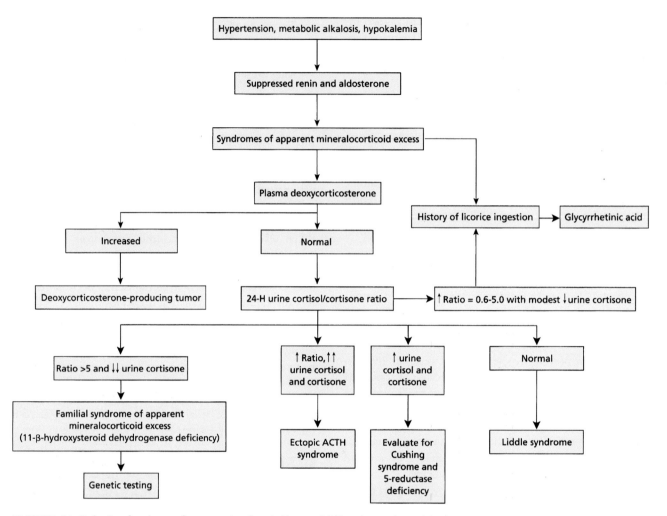

FIGURE 11. Evaluation of syndromes of apparent mineralocorticoid excess. ACTH = adrenocorticotropic hormone.

Treatment

Treatment of respiratory acidosis should initially focus on correcting hypoxia. Supplemental oxygen may decrease ventilatory drive in some patients with chronic respiratory acidosis, but this should not deter correction of hypoxia. Mechanical ventilation should be considered in patients in whom correction of hypoxia decreases the arterial pH to less than 7.2. When mechanical ventilation is required, the PCO_2 should be slowly decreased to minimize the magnitude of post-hypercapnic metabolic alkalosis, which will persist in the setting of hypovolemia. Infusion of isotonic saline and discontinuation of diuretics when possible may be necessary to correct the alkalosis. Patients with significant edema and persistent post-hypercapnic alkalosis can be treated with acetazolamide.

Respiratory Alkalosis

Respiratory alkalosis is a common acid-base disorder associated with a high mortality. Salicylate poisoning is the most important cause of respiratory alkalosis. Salicylate poisoning should be suspected in patients with mental status changes, tachypnea, and respiratory alkalosis often with concomitant increased anion gap metabolic acidosis (see Metabolic Acidosis, Anion Gap Metabolic Acidosis, Salicylate Toxicity). The causes of respiratory alkalosis are listed in **Table 20**.

Mixed respiratory alkalosis and lactic acidosis should raise suspicion for sepsis or severe liver disease. Respiratory alkalosis results in secondary hypobicarbonatemia due to decreased proximal tubular reabsorption of bicarbonate. The serum bicarbonate level decreases by 2 meq/L (2 mmol/L) in the first few hours and by 4 to 5 meq/L (4-5 mmol/L) after 3 to 5 days for every 10 mm Hg decrease in PCO_2. The anion gap is frequently increased as a result of increased albumin anionic charge and increased lactate production. Ionized calcium levels may fall due to increased binding of calcium to albumin.

Respiratory alkalosis is known to decrease cerebral blood flow, and hyperventilation can be employed in the treatment of cerebral edema. Symptoms of respiratory alkalosis include circumoral and extremity paresthesias and dizziness, which can progress to carpopedal spasm and tetany with more severe levels of alkalosis.

TABLE 20. Causes of Respiratory Alkalosis

Anxiety

Medications
  Salicylates
  Medroxyprogesterone
  Theophylline

Advanced liver disease

Sepsis

Hypoxia
  Cyanotic heart disease
  Chronic heart failure
  Pulmonary parenchymal disease
  High altitude exposure

Pregnancy

Subarachnoid hemorrhage

Thoracic stretch receptor stimulation
  Asthma
  Pulmonary fibrosis
  Pneumonia
  Pulmonary edema
  Pulmonary embolism

Management is directed toward identifying and treating the underlying cause. Anxiety-related respiratory alkalosis can be treated with a closed bag rebreathing system, which results in a rise in the P_{CO_2}. **H**

KEY POINTS

- An elevation in the measured or expected arterial P_{CO_2} is the hallmark of respiratory acidosis and results in secondary hyperbicarbonatemia due to increased proximal bicarbonate reabsorption.

- Treatment of respiratory acidosis should initially focus on correcting hypoxia; although supplemental oxygen may decrease ventilatory drive in some patients with chronic respiratory acidosis, this should not deter correction of hypoxia.

- The most important cause of respiratory alkalosis is salicylate poisoning, which should be suspected in patients with mental status changes, tachypnea, and respiratory alkalosis often with concomitant increased anion gap metabolic acidosis.

- Management of respiratory alkalosis is directed toward identifying and treating the underlying cause.

Hypertension

Epidemiology

Hypertension is a common finding among adults and is the greatest contributor to cardiovascular disease, premature death, and disability from cardiovascular diseases worldwide. Hypertension, along with coronary artery disease, accounts for most incident heart failure outcomes. Hypertension also is the leading cardiovascular risk factor for stroke as well as stroke recurrence.

Prevalence increases with age and is associated with numerous comorbidities, including diabetes mellitus and chronic kidney disease. Hypertension is controlled in approximately 50% of U.S. adults diagnosed with the condition, with control rates lower in younger (18-39 years of age) and Hispanic patients.

Associated Complications

End-Organ Damage
The principal target organs affected by hypertension are the brain, the heart wall and coronary circulation, and the kidneys. The mechanisms by which hypertension mediates damage to these organs involve changes in vessel walls and linings.

Brain
In the upright position, blood pressure is lower in the brain than in the heart or kidneys. The brain has an obligate blood flow requirement at all times. Consequently, the brain has a remarkable ability to regulate blood flow across a wide range of arterial pressures. Damage to the brain as a result of elevated blood pressure may lead to hemorrhage into brain tissue from rupture of tiny Charcot-Bouchard aneurysms, progressive narrowing and occlusion of small vessels resulting in lacunar infarction, promotion of major vessel (carotid, middle cerebral arteries) atherosclerosis with brain infarction, and dementia.

Heart
Because the heart generates the blood pressure through muscular contraction, elevated blood pressure levels function as a pathophysiologic stimulus to thickening of the heart muscle itself (left ventricular hypertrophy). To a certain degree, such adaptation is well tolerated, but as the heart wall thickens progressively, the subendocardial layers experience relative ischemia, potentially generating an arrhythmogenic focus or the development of pump failure. Hypertension also promotes atherosclerosis in the coronary artery circulation.

Kidney
The kidney, like the brain, is an extensive vascular bed. Although the kidneys represent less than 1% of body weight, they receive approximately 20% of the cardiac output. Dealing with this high level of blood flow requires an exquisite adaptation in the vascular resistance of the kidneys. This organ, like the brain, adapts well across a large range of blood pressure levels. Unlike the brain, the circulation to the kidney allows the mean arterial pressure to penetrate very deeply into the microcirculation of the kidney. As a result, the delicate

capillary structure in the glomerulus is at risk when there is a failure in the upstream autoregulation of vascular resistance.

Hypertension tends to accelerate the course of primary kidney disorders, including glomerulonephritis and diabetic nephropathy. Hypertension is the second most common cause of end-stage kidney disease in the United States.

Cardiovascular Risk

In isolation, elevated blood pressure is a modest but important component of overall cardiovascular risk. Numerous studies indicate that this risk from elevated blood pressure has no specific pressure-defined cut-off point. Additionally, elevated blood pressure levels enhance the cardiovascular risk of other factors, including diabetes, dyslipidemia, obesity, and cigarette smoking.

There are two basic ways in which elevated blood pressure contributes to cardiovascular risk. First, elevated blood pressure can result in heart wall thickening as an adaptation to the increased afterload as well as remodeling of the blood vessel wall in response to the elevated pressure, leading to vascular hypertrophy. The second way is through enhancement of proatherosclerotic influences. Elevated blood pressure levels interact specifically with increased cholesterol, diabetes, and a host of proinflammatory cytokines, contributing to the loss of vascular lumen patency. The unique susceptibility of the heart wall and the heart circulation to elevated blood pressure levels contributes to its prominence as the most commonly affected target organ of the hypertensive process.

KEY POINT

- Hypertension is the greatest contributor to cardiovascular disease, premature death, and disability from cardiovascular diseases worldwide.

Evaluation

The evaluation of a patient with high blood pressure is directed toward determining if the blood pressure is elevated as a secondary phenomenon, if there are other cardiovascular risk factors present, and if there is evidence of target organ damage.

History

Patient history can help determine the duration of blood pressure elevation and evaluate for symptoms that may indicate the presence of a provoking cause or clues to the presence of target organ damage. Several common over-the-counter and prescription drugs can influence blood pressure (**Table 21**). It is useful to ask about alternative or herbal medications, because patients may not consider them to have significant pharmacologic actions.

Physical Examination

Physical examination should focus on the target organs: the brain, heart, kidney, retina, and peripheral pulses. Neurologic damage from hypertension is evidenced by focal neurologic findings, such as gait or motor function impairment. Some

TABLE 21.	Over-The-Counter and Prescription Agents that Increase Blood Pressure	
Type	**Agent**	**Mechanism(s)**
OTC	Black licorice (European)	Mineralocorticoid activity enhancement; sodium retention
OTC	Ethanol	Adrenergic stimulation
OTC	NSAIDs	Sodium retention
Rx	Calcineurin inhibitors (e.g., cyclosporine)	Vasoconstriction; sodium retention
Rx	Selective serotonin or norepinephrine reuptake inhibitors	Adrenergic stimulation
Rx	Erythrocyte simulation agents (e.g., erythropoietins)	Vasoconstriction
Rx	Highly active antiretroviral therapies	Not clear
Rx	Sympathomimetics; appetite suppressants; decongestants; vigilance enhancers (e.g., amphetamines)	Vasoconstriction; sodium retention
Rx	Vascular endothelial growth factor antagonists (e.g., bevacizumab)	Vasoconstriction (endothelial dysfunction)
Rx	Corticosteroids (e.g., prednisone)	Sodium retention; weight gain
Rx	Oral contraceptives	Increased renin-angiotensin system activity; sodium retention
–	Caffeine	Adrenergic stimulation
–	Cocaine; 3,4-methylenedioxymethamphetamine (ecstasy); recreational drugs	Adrenergic stimulation

OTC = over the counter; Rx = prescription.

patients will have changes on central nervous system imaging, such as lacunar infarction or white matter disease, which are usually attributed to hypertension.

Changes in retinal arteriolar appearance can be used to classify blood pressure and to gauge the degree of target organ impairment. Hemorrhage, exudate, and cotton wool spots suggest advanced degrees of retinopathy secondary to hypertension.

On cardiac and pulmonary examinations, the presence of an S_4 heart sound, detection of left ventricular enlargement, and evidence of possible left ventricular failure may indicate cardiac end-organ damage from hypertension.

In patients with autosomal dominant polycystic kidney disease, enlarged kidneys may be palpable on physical examination; high blood pressure is a frequent component of this disorder. Auscultation of the renal circulation may reveal systolic or diastolic bruits, which may suggest potentially restricted renal arterial flow, a possible secondary cause of hypertension.

Adequacy of the large-vessel circulation to the lower extremities may be assessed by calculating the ratio of ankle and brachial systolic blood pressures (the ankle-brachial index); a ratio of less than 0.9 suggests circulatory disease.

Laboratory Studies

The initial laboratory evaluation of a patient with high blood pressure includes a complete blood count, electrolyte panel, fasting lipid profile, fasting glucose, an estimate of glomerular filtration rate, and a urinalysis. Elevated levels of hemoglobin or hematocrit reflect increased blood viscosity, which can contribute to elevated blood pressure. Reduced kidney function, manifested by a decrease in estimated glomerular filtration rate, is an indicator of target organ damage and may also implicate the kidney as a factor causing high blood pressure. Reductions in serum potassium concentration may be evidence of aldosterone excess. Elevated plasma glucose levels signal the presence, or a tendency toward, diabetes, which has substantial cardiovascular risk implications. The fasting lipid profile may show an atherogenic dyslipidemia. A urinalysis showing blood or protein can reflect target organ damage to the kidney or point to a kidney-related process contributing to blood pressure increase.

12-Lead electrocardiography (ECG) is needed to evaluate for cardiac changes associated with hypertension and to provide a baseline for comparison in the future to determine adequacy of blood pressure therapy. On ECG, cardiac damage from hypertension is manifested by left ventricular hypertrophy and possibly the presence of Q waves.

KEY POINTS

- The evaluation of a patient with elevated blood pressure should address the presence of secondary factors that increase blood pressure, other cardiovascular risk factors, and target organ damage.

Blood Pressure Measurement

Despite its critical importance as a vital sign, surprisingly few health care workers receive formal training in proper blood pressure measurement. Errors in positioning the patient, incorrect cuff size relative to arm circumference, and interferences such as recent caffeine intake or cigarette smoking contribute to variability in blood pressure measurement.

Office Measurement

Accuracy and reliability in measuring blood pressure in the clinic setting are of great importance (**Table 22**). Following a standard approach reduces the variability in blood pressure measurement. There is evidence that blood pressure measurements by physicians tend to be higher than by other health care personnel in the same patient in the same setting. Repeated measurements, possibly by different physicians, may be helpful in obtaining accurate data when making treatment decisions. The increasing use of devices that allow patients to have repeated blood pressure measurements without a health care worker present may obviate some of this variability. Additionally, obtaining clinical information from different sources, such as home blood pressure measurements, may be useful in better informing physicians about the true level of blood pressure or adequacy of treatment.

Ambulatory Blood Pressure Monitoring

Ambulatory blood pressure monitoring (ABPM) is an effective means of assessing blood pressure over 24 hours and away from a health care setting. ABPM typically takes blood pressure measurements every 15 to 20 minutes during daytime hours and every 30 to 60 minutes during the night. It is important to emphasize to the patient the need to complete

TABLE 22. Accurate Office Blood Pressure Measurement
Caffeine, exercise, and smoking should be avoided by the patient ≥30 minutes before measurement
The patient should be seated quietly for 5 minutes (in a chair, not the examination table) with feet on the floor
The patient's arm should be supported at heart level
The auscultatory method is preferred
Use the correct cuff size for accuracy (cuff bladder encircles at least 80% of the patient's arm)
Cuff should be inflated to an adequate pressure (approximately 20-30 mm Hg above the systolic pressure) to avoid measurement error from an auscultatory gap and then deflated at a rate of 2 mm Hg per second
Record systolic (onset of first sound) and diastolic (disappearance of sound) pressures
Average two or more measurements

Data from the U.S. Department of Health and Human Services. Seventh Report of the Joint National Committee on Prevention, Detection, Evaluation, and Treatment of High Blood Pressure. www.nhlbi.nih.gov/guidelines/hypertension/jnc7full.htm. Accessed June 8, 2012.

the diary correctly so that the hours of sleep can be incorporated into the ABPM report.

Research using ABPM increasingly shows that nighttime blood pressure measurements appear to provide the greatest information regarding cardiovascular risk. Cardiovascular risk is more closely associated with nighttime blood pressure levels than office-based measurement or those of the cumulative daytime hours (**Figure 12**). In addition, patients with the greatest variability in blood pressure during the 24 hours of monitoring are at greater risk of cardiovascular target organ damage.

Although ABPM is approved only for the indication of white coat hypertension, it is specifically used to diagnose both white coat hypertension and masked hypertension. **Figure 13** shows the permutations of clinic and ambulatory blood pressure monitoring (see Classification).

Electronic Blood Pressure Measurement

With the nearly complete disappearance of mercury-based blood pressure measurements, electronic devices are increasingly used to measure blood pressure. Most of these devices work on oscillometric principles. The cuff is inflated while electronically monitoring the brachial pulse and its disappearance. On deflation, sensors detect increasing amplitude in the brachial pulsation and measure the mean arterial pressure. From this value, the systolic and diastolic values are usually inferred. Typically, the systolic blood pressure reported by these devices is slightly lower than the real value as measured intra-arterially, and the diastolic blood pressure reads slightly higher than the intra-arterial pressure. Although the solid-state

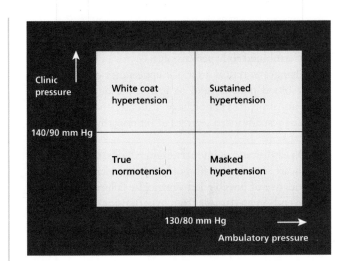

FIGURE 13. Classification of blood pressure when there may be discordance between clinic/office values and ABPM values. Blood pressures are dichotomized (either above or below 140/90 mm Hg clinic/office or above or below 130/80 mm Hg by ABPM). For example, if a patient has an office blood pressure of 150/94 mm Hg and an ABPM value of 142/88 mm Hg, the patient is in the category labeled "sustained hypertension." ABPM = ambulatory blood pressure monitoring.

technology in these devices maintains a reasonable degree of calibration over time, it is good clinical practice to periodically compare the results from these instruments with a device of known accuracy to ensure their precision and reliability. The accuracy of wrist and finger blood pressure monitors has not been well established. These devices in particular should be compared with a known, reliable instrument if they are to be

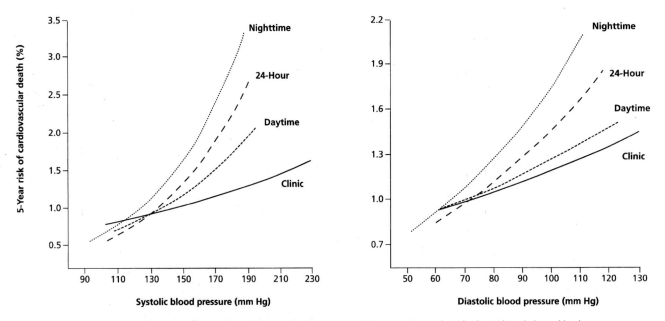

FIGURE 12. The relationships between office systolic and diastolic blood pressures and 5-year cardiovascular risk, alongside ambulatory blood pressure measurements shown as 24-hour averaged, daytime averaged, and nighttime averaged systolic and diastolic levels in 5292 subjects.

used in making treatment decisions. There is a substantial range in cost depending on the presence of memory, the ability to program for multiple blood pressure measurements, the ability to connect to the Internet for downloading data, and the presence of printing capabilities.

Home Blood Pressure Monitoring

Approximately 50% of patients with hypertension measure their blood pressure at home. Although blood pressure monitors are usually not reimbursed by insurers, their relatively low cost (usually less than $100) and reasonable accuracy have made them attractive components to the management of hypertension. Specific recommendations have been published detailing how to incorporate home pressure measurements into overall blood pressure care. For example, two measurements in the morning between 7 AM and 10 AM and two measurements in the evening between 7 PM and 10 PM for 7 consecutive days are recommended. Values from the first day are discarded, and the readings from the subsequent 6 days are averaged. If the average is less than 125/76 mm Hg, the patient is said to be not hypertensive, and drug treatment can be deferred. If the value exceeds 135/85 mm Hg, hypertension is likely present. For values falling between these two ranges (125-135/76-85 mm Hg), ABPM is recommended. If the 24-hour value is greater than 130/80 mm Hg, antihypertensive treatment is reasonable.

Other Settings for Electronic Blood Pressure Management

Internet-based blood pressure management protocols have been developed, sometimes termed "eBP." Patients with access to a computer with Internet connectivity are able to upload home blood pressure readings to a designated health care provider who reviews the data and coordinates communication between the patient and physician. This strategy is particularly useful in patients whose blood pressures are not at target when measured in the office setting; it also allows patients to more actively participate in their own care. Existing data suggest that achieving a target blood pressure level in patients with uncontrolled hypertension taking multiple medications is nearly twice as likely when enrolled in this type of program.

KEY POINTS

- Errors in positioning the patient, incorrect cuff size relative to arm circumference, and interferences such as recent caffeine intake or cigarette smoking contribute to variability in blood pressure measurement.
- Ambulatory blood pressure monitoring provides the best estimate of cardiovascular risk from hypertension, particularly when nighttime blood pressure measurements are considered.
- Electronic devices that measure blood pressure may report the systolic blood pressure as slightly lower than the real value as measured intra-arterially and the diastolic blood pressure as slightly higher than the intra-arterial pressure.

Classification

The Seventh Report of the Joint National Committee on Prevention, Detection, Evaluation, and Treatment of High Blood Pressure (JNC 7) guidelines remain the current U.S. standard for the evaluation, classification, and management of hypertension (**Table 23**). As of publication, the Eighth Report reflecting current research data is in progress. Blood pressure is classified utilizing both the systolic and diastolic components, and the categories are determined by the higher value of either the systolic or the diastolic blood pressure.

Classification of hypertension is based on an average of two or more seated blood pressure readings obtained more than 1 minute apart at two or more visits. It is important to check the blood pressure more than once during the same visit and to recheck this within several weeks to a month

TABLE 23. Classification of Hypertension		
Classification[a]	**Office Blood Pressure (mm Hg)**	**24-Hour ABPM (mm Hg)[b]**
Normal	<120/80	<125/75
Prehypertension	120-139/80-89	(125-130/75-80)
Stage 1 hypertension	140-159/90-99	>130/80
Stage 2 hypertension	≥160/100	–

ABPM = ambulatory blood pressure monitoring.

[a]When discordant values are found in the blood pressure values (for example, office blood pressure measurement of 136/94 mm Hg), the higher classification category of the two values (in this case, the diastolic value of 94 mm Hg) is used to classify the blood pressure (stage 1 hypertension in this example). Classification should use blood pressure data obtained in at least duplicate readings on at least two occasions.

[b]These are values averaged over the full 24 hours. The values inside the parentheses are inferred because ABPM is not used for the diagnosis of prehypertension. Once ABPM values exceed 130/80 mm Hg, they are not further parsed into stage 1 and 2.

Data from Chobanian AV, Bakris GL, Black HR, et al. Seventh Report of the Joint National Committee on Prevention, Detection, Evaluation, and Treatment of High Blood Pressure. Hypertension. 2003;42(6):1206-1252. [PMID: 14656957] and Kikuya M, Hansen TW, Thijs L, et al. Diagnostic thresholds for ambulatory blood pressure monitoring based on 10-year cardiovascular risk. Circulation. 2007;115(16):2145-2152. [PMID: 17420350]

(depending on the clinical severity) before acting on the information.

In a large meta-analysis encompassing more than 1 million patient years, it was found that the level of blood pressure below which no risk from blood pressure could be inferred was 115/75 mm Hg. This meta-analysis also established the current clinical dictum that for every increase in systolic pressure of 20 mm Hg or diastolic pressure of 10 mm Hg, cardiovascular risk doubles.

KEY POINTS

- The Seventh Report of the Joint National Committee on Prevention, Detection, Evaluation, and Treatment of High Blood Pressure guidelines define normal blood pressure as less than 120/80 mm Hg and hypertension as 140/90 mm Hg or higher.
- Classification of hypertension is based on an average of two or more seated blood pressure readings obtained more than 1 minute apart at two or more visits.

Prehypertension

The prehypertension category established by the JNC 7 designates a group at high risk for progression to hypertension, in whom lifestyle modifications may be preemptive (see Table 23). Studies such as the Trial of Preventing Hypertension (TROPHY) have shown that about two thirds of patients diagnosed as prehypertensive will develop stage 1 hypertension during 4 years of follow-up. This finding argues strongly for implementation of lifestyle modifications in this population. At present, there is no evidence that drug therapy, more extensive blood pressure monitoring, or further work are needed when managing prehypertension.

Essential Hypertension

Pathogenesis

The pathogenesis of essential hypertension remains poorly elucidated and likely results from the complex interaction of multiple factors. **Figure 14** illustrates a useful concept of how different physiologic processes work together to regulate the blood pressure. Given the crucial need to preserve organ blood flow, these processes are redundant and designed to overlap if failure of one occurs.

The pathogenic processes of essential hypertension can be divided into those based on genetic mechanisms and those in which environmental influences play a role. Isolated genetic mutations inherited in mendelian fashion probably account for less than 1% of hypertension. To date, single gene mutations found to influence blood pressure meaningfully are relatively few in number and almost all relate to mechanisms that govern sodium excretion by the kidney. Genetic studies underscore the primary importance of sodium handling in blood pressure control, as most single gene mutations that have a significant impact on blood pressure levels are in sodium-handling pathways. Recently, genetic influences are thought to be many in number (polygenic), with each accounting for only a fraction of increased blood pressure. Attempts to integrate these genetic polymorphisms into the different physiologic pathways known to influence blood pressure may help in the understanding of the roles that genes play in blood pressure control.

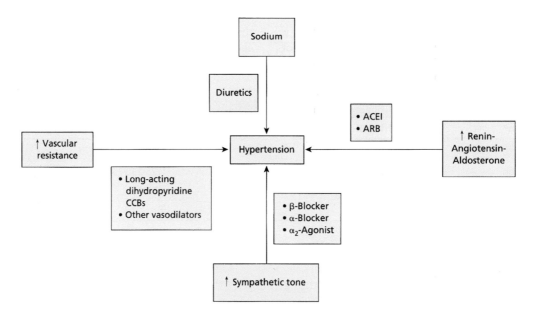

FIGURE 14. Schema for understanding major physiologic processes influencing blood pressure levels and main mechanistic pathways by which antihypertensive drugs work. ACEI = angiotensin-converting enzyme inhibitor; ARB = angiotensin receptor blocker; CCB = calcium channel blocker.

Complex environmental exposures also influence blood pressure levels. These include sodium intake, socioeconomic stress, cigarette smoking, various drug exposures, obesity, and the occurrence of comorbidities such as diabetes and chronic kidney disease (CKD), all of which alter the processes of normal blood pressure regulation.

Secondary forms of hypertension have been helpful in understanding the pathogenesis of elevated blood pressure (see Secondary Hypertension).

A substantial area of interest in the pathogenesis of hypertension relates to the relationship of the endothelium to the underlying vascular smooth muscle, which is represented as the "vascular resistance" component of Figure 14. The production and release of the vasodilator nitric oxide at the endothelial level plays a clear regulatory role on the underlying vascular smooth muscle tone. Abnormalities in nitric oxide generation or its inactivation by oxidative stresses underlie the findings of endothelial dysfunction, which is often found before the onset of hypertension.

Management
Blood Pressure Goals
According to the JNC 7, in the absence of comorbidities or compelling indications, the blood pressure goal in patients younger than 80 years is 140/90 mm Hg. For patients aged ≥80 years, the recommendation is a systolic blood pressure goal of less than 150 mm Hg based on the Hypertension in the Very Elderly Trial (HYVET) (see Special Populations, Older Patients). In patients with diabetes and most patients with CKD, the blood pressure goal set by the American Diabetes Association and the National Kidney Foundation remains at less than 130/80 mm Hg.

Strong evidence exists that treating systolic pressures ≥160 mm Hg in patients aged 60 years or older or diastolic values ≥90 mm Hg in those aged 30 years or older reduces cardiovascular outcomes (cardiovascular death, myocardial infarction, heart failure, fatal and nonfatal stroke). In those with isolated systolic blood pressure elevations between 140 and 159 mm Hg (inclusive) or in those younger than 30 years of age, there is scant evidence of benefit, although most guidelines support lifestyle modifications and initiation of drug therapy if systolic blood pressures greater than 140 mm Hg persist.

Lifestyle Modifications
Several nondrug approaches are useful in lowering blood pressure. The most effective measure to reduce blood pressure is weight loss if the patient is overweight. The second most effective measure is a reduction in salt (sodium chloride) intake, followed by an increase in aerobic physical activity of at least 30 minutes a day at least 3 days per week. Lastly, a reduction in alcohol consumption helps reduce blood pressure.

Other approaches, including potassium, magnesium, and calcium supplementation, fish oil, garlic usage, and green tea consumption, have had variable success in managing hypertension. Although they do not appear harmful, these approaches typically do not have robust data to recommend their widespread use in the management of prehypertension and hypertension.

Choosing an Antihypertensive Agent
Many patients with hypertension find it difficult to lose weight or to adjust their dietary intake and physical activity status to effectively control their blood pressure. Drug treatment is recommended when blood pressure remains above 140/90 mm Hg in patients younger than 80 years of age. In patients aged 80 years or older, a systolic blood pressure of 150 mm Hg is recommended as the threshold for treatment initiation. See **Table 24** for indications, contraindications, and side effects for antihypertensive agents. There is wide variability in the cost of antihypertensive medications; newer and more expensive agents have not been shown to be significantly safer or more effective than many older, well-established medications that are available in generic form.

A large, recent meta-analysis suggests that the five main classes of antihypertensive agents (ACE inhibitors, angiotensin receptor blockers [ARBs], β-blockers, calcium channel blockers, and diuretics), when used effectively to treat elevated blood pressure, can be relied upon to reduce target organ damage. Choosing an agent involves a decision-making process that takes into account the patient's demographics such as age and ethnicity, the cost of the drug, and the anticipated side-effect profile.

The chief mechanism of action of medications in each class of antihypertensive agents is interference at the point of at least one defined process in the control of blood pressure (see Figure 14). The usual response to monotherapy is a reduction in systolic pressure ranging from 12 to 15 mm Hg and diastolic pressure ranging from 8 to 10 mm Hg.

A few caveats about antihypertensive treatment have arisen in recent years. α-Blockers such as prazosin are not recommended as first-line therapy because they have not been shown to produce the cardiovascular benefit noted, for example, with diuretics. Secondly, β-blockers (particularly atenolol) given to older patients with hypertension do not produce as much reduction in stroke as other classes. It is not known if this concern also applies to newer β-blockers such as nebivolol or α-β blockers such as carvedilol. Finally, heart failure and stroke are the target organ damages most benefited by long-term antihypertensive therapy.

When single-agent treatment is initiated, most agents exert their effect at a given dose by 2 to 4 weeks. Consequently, follow-up visits for blood pressure assessment and possible drug titration are usually scheduled at 2- to 4-week intervals to assess adequacy of treatment.

Combination Therapy
In patients whose goal blood pressure requires reductions of systolic pressure more than 20 mm Hg and diastolic pressure

TABLE 24. Compelling Indications, Contraindications, and Side Effects for Antihypertensive Medications

Class of Medication	Compelling Indications	Contraindications	Side Effects
Thiazide diuretics	Heart failure; advanced age; volume-dependent hypertension; low-renin hypertension; systolic hypertension	Gout	Hypokalemia; hyperuricemia; glucose intolerance; hypercalcemia; impotence
Aldosterone antagonists	Primary hyperaldosteronism; resistant hypertension; sleep apnea	Reduced GFR; hyperkalemia	Hyperkalemia; increased creatinine level; painful gynecomastia; menstrual irregularities; gastrointestinal distress
ACE inhibitors	Heart failure; left ventricular dysfunction; proteinuria; diabetic nephropathy; chronic kidney disease; post–myocardial infarction	Pregnancy; hyperkalemia	Cough; angioedema; hyperkalemia; potential increased creatinine level in patients with bilateral renal artery stenosis; rash; loss of taste; leukopenia (captopril)
Angiotensin receptor blockers	Same as ACE inhibitors; useful when ACE inhibitors are not tolerated	Pregnancy; hyperkalemia	Angioedema (rare); hyperkalemia; potential increased creatinine level in patients with bilateral renal artery stenosis
Calcium channel blockers	Systolic hypertension; cyclosporine-induced hypertension; angina; coronary heart disease	Heart block (for nondihydropyridine calcium channel blockers verapamil and diltiazem)	Headache; flushing; gingival hyperplasia; edema; constipation
β-Blockers	Angina; heart failure; post–myocardial infarction; migraine; tachyarrhythmias	Asthma and COPD; heart block	Bronchospasm; bradycardia; heart failure; impaired peripheral circulation; insomnia; fatigue; decreased exercise tolerance; hypertriglyceridemia
α-Blockers	Prostatic hyperplasia	Orthostatic hypotension	Headache; drowsiness; fatigue; weakness; postural hypotension

GFR = glomerular filtration rate.

more than 10 mm Hg, current JNC 7 recommendations indicate that combination therapy can be used, which can shorten the time to achieve the blood pressure goal, increase the likelihood of achieving the goal, and reduce the number of visits needed for drug titrations.

Combination drug therapy is often more desirable than giving agents at maximum dose in stepwise fashion, because, in most cases, the majority of the antihypertensive effect is manifest at approximately half the manufacturer's maximum recommended dose, and increasing the dose to the maximum usually only produces a few millimeters of Hg more blood pressure reduction but risks greater side-effect occurrence.

Combination drug treatment approaches can be used to intervene in different blood pressure control processes (see Figure 14). Added benefit occurs when a known side effect of one class (for example, edema associated with calcium channel blockers) can be offset by the use of a class such as ACE inhibitors, which provide additional antihypertensive benefit (and offset the edema due to calcium channel blockers). Both the JNC 7 and the International Society for Hypertension in Blacks espouse the use of combination drug therapy approaches, which reduce the time needed to achieve control and improve the overall likelihood of achieving target blood pressure levels.

Until recently, no data supported superiority of one combination drug approach. However, the Avoiding Cardiovascular Events through Combination Therapy in Patients Living With Systolic Hypertension (ACCOMPLISH) trial demonstrated that despite identical blood pressure control, a regimen combining an ACE inhibitor with a calcium channel blocker was superior to a regimen of an ACE inhibitor with a diuretic in hypertensive patients at high cardiovascular risk.

Many fixed combinations of antihypertensive medications are available. Although these may be more convenient for patients who have achieved a stable, effective dose, they tend to offer less dosing flexibility and are often substantially more expensive than prescribing the component medications independently.

KEY POINTS

- Lifestyle modifications, including weight loss, reduction of dietary sodium intake, aerobic physical activity of at least 30 minutes a day at least three times a week, and a reduction in alcohol consumption, can help reduce high blood pressure.

- Drug treatment is recommended when blood pressure remains above 140/90 mm Hg in patients younger than 80 years of age; in those aged 80 years and older, a systolic blood pressure of 150 mm Hg is recommended as the threshold for treatment initiation.

- In patients whose goal blood pressure requires reductions of systolic pressure more than 20 mm Hg and diastolic pressure more than 10 mm Hg, combination therapy can be used, which can shorten the time to achieve the blood pressure goal, increase the likelihood of achieving the goal, and reduce the number of visits needed for drug titrations.

Secondary Hypertension

Secondary hypertension accounts for less than 10% of all forms of high blood pressure and typically emanate from the kidney (vascular and parenchymal origins) or the adrenal gland (cortex or medulla). Secondary hypertension is important to recognize, because it often points to specific mechanisms elevating blood pressure, which guide therapy.

Because most cases of elevated blood pressure are essential, most patients with hypertension do not require evaluation for an underlying cause. However, clinical factors that raise the possibility of secondary hypertension include onset at a young age in patients with no family history of hypertension or other risk factors, or a rapid onset of significant hypertension or an abrupt change in blood pressure in patients with previously well-controlled hypertension. Most commonly, resistant hypertension suggests a possible underlying contributing factor to the blood pressure elevation (see Resistant Hypertension). Additionally, any patient with other symptoms or findings associated with a possible secondary cause (such as an endocrine abnormality) may warrant further investigation.

Kidney Disease
Epidemiology
Kidney disease is the most common cause of secondary hypertension. Depending on the degree of functional kidney impairment, up to 90% of patients with advanced kidney failure or patients on dialysis have hypertension.

Pathophysiology
The processes by which impaired kidney function raises blood pressure are complex. Because the kidney is the primary regulator of sodium balance, disorders of sodium metabolism rank high among the pathogenic processes. The kidney also is a target organ of the hypertensive process, which makes adequate control of blood pressure in patients with hypertension associated with kidney failure essential.

Management
The first step in the management of hypertension in patients with CKD is to determine the presence or absence of proteinuria. When proteinuria is present, most guidelines recommend the use of either an ACE inhibitor or ARB, because these agents seem to have particular benefit for both proteinuria reduction and blood pressure control. The current target blood pressure level in patients with CKD is less than 130/80 mm Hg. When significant proteinuria is present (>500 mg/24 h), the target level is less than 125/75 mm Hg. In the absence of proteinuria, no specific antihypertensive agent class has proved to be superior in lowering blood pressure or reducing target organ damage.

When treating patients with CKD, it is common to see an increase in the serum creatinine level as blood pressure falls. In most cases, an increase of up to 25% is an acceptable trade-off for blood pressure control. When the serum creatinine level increases beyond this, for example, to levels two or three times baseline value, it is reasonable to reassess the aggressiveness of the diuretic regimen (if one is used) or to consider the possibility of bilateral renal arterial disease, particularly when patients are treated with an ACE inhibitor or ARB (see Renovascular Hypertension).

- Secondary hypertension accounts for less than 10% of all forms of high blood pressure and typically emanates from the kidney or the adrenal gland.

- Kidney disease is the most common cause of secondary hypertension; depending on the degree of functional kidney impairment, up to 90% of patients with advanced kidney failure or patients on dialysis have hypertension.

Renovascular Hypertension
Epidemiology
Renovascular hypertension is an increase in blood pressure due to significant narrowing of one or both of the renal arteries resulting in abnormal vasoregulatory responses by the kidney because of a perceived decrease in the adequacy of renal blood flow. True renovascular hypertension is found in only 1% to 2% of all patients with hypertension but may have a higher prevalence in those with known atherosclerotic vascular occlusive disease.

Pathophysiology
The renin-angiotensin system is activated when blood flow to the kidney is significantly reduced, with pathologic consequences such as renovascular hypertension occurring only when there is substantial luminal obstruction (>75%).

Narrowing of the renal arteries occurs either as part of generalized atherosclerosis or in the form of fibromuscular dysplasia. In the former, atherosclerotic risk factors are typically present, foremost among them being cigarette smoking,

CONT.

often with a modest impairment in kidney function. Fibromuscular dysplasia is more often found in younger patients, particularly women. Whereas atherosclerosis tends to affect the proximal portion of the renal artery, fibromuscular dysplasia is usually found more distally. Both forms of renovascular disease may be associated with midepigastric bruits. Unilateral renal lesions are thought to elevate blood pressure through renin-mediated mechanisms, whereas bilateral (or unilateral with a single functioning kidney) forms of vascular disease have a strong component of sodium excess in causing blood pressure elevation.

Renal artery stenosis is best demonstrated by angiography (conventional kidney angiography or CT of the renal arteries); however, these studies involve contrast, which may precipitate acute kidney injury in susceptible persons. Alternatives include MR angiography, often using gadolinium, or renal Doppler studies. In patients with reduced kidney function (<30 mL/min/1.73 m^2) in whom neither iodinated nor gadolinium contrast is desirable, a renal Doppler study is a reasonable screening consideration.

Management

Considerable debate exists on how to manage renovascular disease in patients with hypertension. In young patients with fibromuscular dysplasia, percutaneous transluminal kidney angioplasty is considered low risk and deemed the treatment of choice given the high likelihood of both technical success and meaningful blood pressure improvement.

The management of atherosclerotic renovascular disease is much more controversial. Several recent trials, including Angioplasty and Stenting for Renal Artery Lesions (ASTRAL) and Stent Placement in Patients with Atherosclerotic Renal Artery Stenosis and Impaired Renal Function (STAR), do not support an angioplasty intervention, although ongoing trials may provide further guidance regarding appropriate therapy. Current recommendations for the treatment of atherosclerotic renovascular disease support aggressive risk factor management (blood pressure control, antihyperlipidemic therapy, smoking cessation techniques), with angioplasty or surgical intervention reserved for those with refractory hypertension despite extensive treatment or progressive diminution in kidney function.

Patients with bilateral renal artery disease (or unilateral disease in a single functioning kidney) are at risk of a worsening of kidney function when treated with drugs that interfere with the renin-angiotensin system such as ACE inhibitors or ARBs. This is particularly true in the presence of aggressive diuretic use and should be suspected in those with known atherosclerotic vascular occlusive disease, especially when serum creatinine values rise much more than 25% from baseline.

Aldosterone Excess

Aldosterone excess may be present in up to 10% of patients with new-onset hypertension. Many patients found to have elevated serum aldosterone levels display normal serum potassium and bicarbonate levels. Diagnosis can be aided by a 24-hour urine collection for aldosterone, plasma renin activity measurement, and an imaging study. See MKSAP 16 Endocrinology and Metabolism for a detailed discussion of primary hyperaldosteronism.

Pheochromocytoma

Pheochromocytomas and paragangliomas increase blood pressure through secretion of norepinephrine and epinephrine. Diagnosis requires a high degree of suspicion, with confirmation of excess catecholamine production either by 24-hour urine collection for catecholamine and metanephrine excretion or by plasma metanephrine measurement. Definitive therapy for these tumors is surgical removal. See MKSAP 16 Endocrinology and Metabolism for a detailed discussion of pheochromocytoma. **H**

KEY POINTS

- Percutaneous transluminal kidney angioplasty is considered the treatment of choice for young patients with fibromuscular dysplasia.

- Current recommendations for the treatment of atherosclerotic renovascular disease support aggressive risk factor management (blood pressure control, antihyperlipidemia therapy, smoking cessation techniques), with angioplasty or surgical intervention reserved for those with refractory hypertension despite extensive treatment or progressive diminution in kidney function.

White Coat Hypertension

Patients with white coat hypertension have elevated blood pressure measurements in the office setting but normal measurements (for example, daytime blood pressure $<130/80$ mm Hg) outside the office, accompanied by the absence of target organ damage. ABPM is considered the gold standard for diagnosing white coat hypertension. Pharmacologic management of white coat hypertension has not been shown to reduce morbid events or produce cardiovascular benefit.

Masked Hypertension

Masked hypertension is characterized by blood pressure that is higher at home than in the office setting, which is confirmed by ambulatory blood pressures that are greater than 130/80 mm Hg despite office blood pressures of less than 140/90 mm Hg. There are no clear guidelines to pursue the diagnosis of masked hypertension; ABPM does not carry a formal indication for this diagnosis but may be useful in establishing this blood pressure pattern. An increasing number of studies suggest that the cardiovascular risk of masked hypertension approaches that of sustained hypertension.

Resistant Hypertension

Resistant hypertension occurs when blood pressure measurements consistently exceed the blood pressure goal despite taking three antihypertensive drugs (one of which is a diuretic). This occurs in approximately 10% to 15% of patients with hypertension. Evaluation includes confirmation that the blood pressure is truly high outside of the office, with verification that good technique, including correct cuff size, was used in blood pressure measurement. There should also be a search for factors that might potentially lead to suboptimal control, such as high salt intake or use of drugs such as NSAIDs, and consideration of potentially modifiable pathogenic factors, such as aldosterone excess and obstructive sleep apnea. Resistant hypertension is one of the most common reasons for referral to a hypertension specialist.

KEY POINTS

- Patients with white coat hypertension have elevated blood pressure measurements in the office setting but normal measurements outside the office.
- Ambulatory blood pressure monitoring is considered the gold standard for diagnosing white coat hypertension.
- Resistant hypertension is defined as blood pressure above goal despite the administration of three antihypertensive drugs, one of which is a diuretic.

Special Populations

Women

To date, women show similar blood pressure responses to men in randomized clinical trials. Before menopause, women have lower blood pressures than similarly aged men. This tends to reverse after menopause, and black women tend to have the highest blood pressures. In women of childbearing potential who have hypertension, ACE inhibitors and ARBs should be avoided because of the risk of fetal malformations. Women tend to develop hypokalemia more often when treated with diuretics and have a greater risk of hyponatremia when treated with thiazide diuretics.

Patients with Diabetes Mellitus

Patients with diabetes mellitus and hypertension are at substantial cardiovascular risk. Managing high blood pressure is an effective way to reduce this risk, but debate exists regarding goal blood pressure levels. The American Diabetes Association and the National Kidney Foundation currently recommend target blood pressure levels of less than 130/80 mm Hg, regardless of age. In the recently completed Action to Control Cardiovascular Risk in Diabetes (ACCORD) trial,

the intensive therapy group randomly assigned to the lower blood pressure goal (<120 mm Hg systolic) did not experience an improvement in the primary outcome despite systolic blood pressures that were 14 mm Hg lower than the values achieved in the standard therapy group. Stroke, however, was significantly reduced in the lower blood pressure goal group. On the other hand, the increased medication requirement to achieve the intensive therapy goal blood pressures resulted in more side effects, including worse kidney function.

Black Patients

Black patients tend to experience enhanced target organ damage at any level of blood pressure compared with most other groups, particularly white patients. The reasons for this are not clear, but the intense search for genetic predisposition continues to attract much attention. Cardiovascular complications are more frequent in black patients, and black patients are approximately fourfold more likely to experience end-stage kidney disease compared with white patients.

The African American Study of Kidney Disease and Hypertension (AASK), performed in black patients with long-standing hypertension and mild proteinuria, demonstrated that the ACE inhibitor ramipril was superior to the β-blocker metoprolol and the calcium channel blocker amlodipine in slowing kidney disease progression in black patients with impaired kidney function caused by hypertension.

Other recommendations for the management of high blood pressure in black patients were released in the International Society on Hypertension in Blacks (ISHIB) consensus statement. ISHIB defines treatment goals in black patients based upon either the *absence* of target organ damage (primary prevention), in which the blood pressure goal is less than 135/85 mm Hg, or the *presence* of target organ damage (secondary prevention), in which the blood pressure goal is less than 130/80 mm Hg.

Older Patients

The pattern of blood pressure elevation in older patients is typically characterized by a prominent systolic blood pressure. This relates in large part to the significant role of vascular stiffness in the blood pressure increases of older patients, which in addition to raising systolic pressure, also leads to a decline in the diastolic pressure. Clinical trials have documented the value of reducing elevated systolic pressures when they exceed 160 mm Hg. Although a target blood pressure of 140/90 mm Hg is generally accepted for most patients, there are less data on patients over the age of 80 years to guide therapy. The Hypertension in the Very Elderly Trial (HYVET) enrolled patients at least 80 years of age and used a target systolic blood pressure of 150 mm Hg. The trial demonstrated decreased mortality and heart failure with active drug therapy; therefore, treatment to this blood pressure goal appears reasonable for persons over age 80 years.

For patients who are aged 60 to 79 years, the 140/90 mm Hg blood pressure goal (in the absence of comorbidities such as diabetes, coronary artery disease, or CKD) remains reasonable if it can be achieved without significant side effects, particularly orthostatic hypotension, of which elderly patients are more prone to than other populations. Reducing a systolic blood pressure that is above 160 mm Hg systolic results in less stroke and less cardiovascular disease. There is concern regarding lowering an already low diastolic blood pressure in patients with existing coronary artery disease. In this regard, a "J-curve" is thought to exist, in which an *increase* in cardiovascular events occurs below a certain threshold of blood pressure. Current recommendations are to avoid lowering the diastolic blood pressure below 70 mm Hg in those with active coronary disease at any age.

KEY POINTS

- In women of childbearing potential who have hypertension, ACE inhibitors and angiotensin receptor blockers should be avoided because of the risk of fetal malformations.

- For patients with diabetes mellitus, current recommendations indicate a target blood pressure goal of less than 130/80 mm Hg.

- A target systolic blood pressure goal of 150 mm Hg or less appears reasonable for patients aged 80 years or older.

- Current recommendations are to avoid lowering the diastolic blood pressure below 70 mm Hg in those with active coronary disease at any age.

Chronic Tubulointerstitial Disorders

Pathophysiology and Epidemiology

Pathologic processes that affect the tubules and/or the interstitium of the kidney are termed *tubulointerstitial disorders*.

In their chronic form, these disorders develop over months to years from long-term exposures or systemic processes and are associated with a slow decline in kidney function. Glomerular and vascular renal lesions can be accompanied by secondary chronic tubulointerstitial nephritis. In contrast, acute interstitial nephritis develops over days to weeks and is associated with acute kidney injury.

Acute interstitial nephritis may evolve into chronic tubulointerstitial nephritis. Glomerular and vascular structures are subsequently involved, with fibrosis and scarring throughout the kidney. The degree of fibrosis is predictive of progression to end-stage kidney disease (ESKD), and 10% to 20% of incident ESKD is attributed to tubulointerstitial disease.

For further discussion of acute interstitial nephritis, see Acute Kidney Injury.

KEY POINTS

- Chronic tubulointerstitial disorders develop over months to years from long-term exposures or systemic processes and are associated with a slow decline in kidney function.

Clinical Manifestations

The pathophysiology of chronic tubulointerstitial disorders gives insight to the clinical manifestations of these diseases. Ongoing tubulointerstitial damage leads to the defects listed in **Table 25**.

Diagnosis and Evaluation

The clinical diagnosis of chronic tubulointerstitial disease is often one of exclusion. History and physical examination should address conditions that may be associated with this disorder. A careful review of medications is essential (**Table 26**).

Laboratory values can show anemia as a result of damage to the erythropoietin-producing cells in the kidney. Urinalysis can be bland or reveal sterile pyuria, with minimal hematuria. Urine protein excretion (usually low-molecular-weight protein rather than albumin) is typically less than 2 g/24 h. Kidney ultrasound can show small, atrophic kidneys consistent with

TABLE 25.	Clinical Manifestations of Chronic Tubulointerstitial Disorders
Abnormality[a]	**Cause**
Decline in glomerular filtration rate	Obstruction of tubules; damage to microvasculature; fibrosis and sclerosis of glomeruli
Proximal tubular damage (Fanconi syndrome)	Incomplete absorption and renal wasting of glucose, phosphates, bicarbonate, and amino acids
Non–anion gap metabolic acidosis	Proximal and distal renal tubular acidosis; decreased ammonia production
Isosthenuria and polyuria	Decreased concentrating and diluting ability
Proteinuria	Decreased tubular protein reabsorption (usually <2 g/24 h)
Hyperkalemia	Defect in potassium secretion (hyperkalemic distal renal tubular acidosis)

[a]The degree of these abnormalities depends on the extent and location of injury.

TABLE 26. Causes of Chronic Tubulointerstitial Disorders

Autoimmune disorders
  Anti–tubular basement membrane antibody-mediated tubulointerstitial nephritis
  Sarcoidosis
  Sjögren syndrome
  Systemic lupus erythematosus
  Tubulointerstitial nephritis with uveitis

Balkan endemic nephropathy

Heavy metal nephropathy
  Lead
  Cadmium
  Mercury

Hereditary tubulointerstitial nephritis
  Medullary cystic disease (type II is associated with hyperuricemia and gout)
  Mitochondrial disorders

Infection-related
  Polyoma BK virus (posttransplantation; most common following kidney transplantation)
  Brucellosis
  Cytomegalovirus
  Epstein-Barr virus
  Fungal infections
  Legionella species
  Mycobacterium tuberculosis
  Toxoplasmosis

Malignancy-related
  Leukemia
  Lymphoma
  Myeloma cast nephropathy
  Plasmacytomas

Medication-induced
  Analgesic nephropathy (highest toxicity with combination therapy)
  Calcineurin inhibitors (secondary tubulointerstitial injury consequent to arteriolopathy)
  Chinese herb nephropathy (aristolochic acid)
  Cyclooxygenase-2 inhibitors
  Lithium
  NSAIDs
  Prolonged exposure to any medication that can cause acute interstitial nephritis
    5-Aminosalicylates (e.g., mesalamine)
    Allopurinol
    Cephalosporins
    Fluoroquinolones
    H_2 blockers
    Indinavir
    Penicillins
    Proton pump inhibitors
    Rifampin
    Sulfonamides

Secondary tubulointerstitial injury due to glomerular and vascular disorders

Urinary tract obstruction

chronic kidney disease (CKD). Indications for biopsy include unclear etiology of disease, with potential for a change in therapy based on biopsy results.

KEY POINTS

- Chronic tubulointerstitial disease is suspected in patients who have slowly progressive chronic kidney disease associated with a relatively bland urine sediment and urine protein excretion that is typically less than 2 g/24 h.
- In patients with chronic tubulointerstitial disease, kidney ultrasound can show small, atrophic kidneys consistent with chronic kidney disease.

Causes

The causes of primary chronic tubulointerstitial disorders often lead to progressive CKD (see Table 26).

Immunologic Diseases
Sjögren Syndrome
Chronic tubulointerstitial disease occurs in 25% to 50% of patients with Sjögren syndrome and is typically seen within the first several years of the disease. Interstitial nephritis may precede the onset of extrarenal manifestations. A decreased glomerular filtration rate (GFR), urinary concentrating defects, and renal tubular acidosis are also common. Glomerular disease, such as membranous or membranoproliferative nephropathies, is less common and occurs later in the disease course. Corticosteroid therapy may improve the course of disease.

Sarcoidosis
Noncaseating granulomatous interstitial nephritis is the classic renal lesion of sarcoidosis, although tubulointerstitial nephritis without granulomas is also common. Other associated disorders can lead secondarily to chronic tubulointerstitial nephritis, including hypercalcemia, nephrocalcinosis, and nephrolithiasis from increased 1,25-dihydroxy vitamin D levels. Polyuria is common in these patients. Corticosteroid therapy can lead to renal recovery if viable tissue remains.

Systemic Lupus Erythematosus
Tubulointerstitial nephritis in patients with systemic lupus erythematosus most commonly occurs in conjunction with glomerular disease. In more than 50% of patients, biopsy specimens reveal immune complex deposits in tubular basement membranes. Tubulointerstitial disease without glomerular involvement is rare but displays clinical manifestations similar to those listed in Table 25. More extensive tubulointerstitial involvement is a poor prognostic marker. Therapy is aimed at treating the underlying glomerular lesions and other systemic manifestations of the disease.

Infectious Diseases
Infectious organisms are associated with tubulointerstitial nephritis via direct infiltration or a reactive systemic inflammatory response. Patients predisposed to infection-related tubulointerstitial damage include those with preexisting kidney disease (such as kidney transplant recipients) or those with impaired immune system function (such as patients on chemotherapy or chronic immunosuppressant medications or those with advanced HIV infection). Organisms include *Mycobacterium tuberculosis*, Epstein-Barr virus, cytomegalovirus, and polyoma BK virus (in kidney transplant recipients).

Malignancy
Malignancies associated with chronic tubulointerstitial nephritis include multiple myeloma and lymphoproliferative disorders. In multiple myeloma, kidney dysfunction is present in more than 50% of patients at the time of initial presentation. Myeloma cast nephropathy is common and is caused by precipitation of Bence-Jones protein with Tamm-Horsfall mucoprotein in the renal tubule acutely, which causes direct tubular toxicity, with multinucleated giant cells present in the tubular walls and interstitium. This leads to tubular obstruction and injury and acute kidney injury. Predisposing factors for kidney involvement in multiple myeloma include volume depletion and hypercalcemia. A more chronic process with tubular dysfunction associated with myeloma light chain deposition may occur over months to years and lead to proximal renal tubular acidosis and electrolyte and concentration abnormalities resembling the Fanconi syndrome. Therapy includes treatment of hypercalcemia, correction of volume depletion, and treatment of the underlying plasma cell dyscrasia (see Glomerular Diseases and Acute Kidney Injury).

Lymphomatous or leukemic infiltration is present in up to 50% of patients with lymphoproliferative disorders on postmortem examination. Patients present with non–nephrotic-range proteinuria, sterile pyuria, and kidneys that appear large on imaging studies. Therapy directed at the malignancy can lead to a decrease in kidney size and improvement in function.

Medications
Analgesics
A strong association exists between chronic tubulointerstitial nephritis and long-term use of combination analgesics such as aspirin, phenacetin, and caffeine. The incidence and prevalence of analgesic nephropathy have diminished over the past two decades, coinciding with the removal of phenacetin and other analgesic mixtures as over-the-counter pain relievers. Data suggest that there is an association between chronic daily acetaminophen use and CKD, although a causal relationship has not been established. The epidemiologic data supporting the association between analgesic nephropathy

and NSAIDs are not as robust; however, exposure to large quantities may result in CKD.

Studies suggest that nephrotoxicity is dose-dependent, with clinically evident disease appearing after chronic, high-dose use of NSAIDs for 5 or more years. There is a female predominance, and the kidney manifestations are nonspecific, including sterile pyuria, mild proteinuria, reduced GFR, and urinary concentrating defects. Hypertension and anemia are characteristic of patients with more advanced disease. Early diagnosis is important, because kidney function can stabilize or moderately improve if analgesics are discontinued before advanced disease occurs.

Analgesic nephropathy is associated with genitourinary tract malignancies, which develop in up to 10% of patients. In patients with analgesic nephropathy and hematuria, upper urinary tract imaging, urine cytology, and cystoscopy are recommended.

Calcineurin Inhibitors

Chronic use of calcineurin inhibitors such as cyclosporine or tacrolimus is associated with kidney disease, especially in transplant recipients and in those with autoimmune disorders. Chronic vasoconstriction causes kidney fibrosis and scarring as well as direct tubular and vascular toxicity. Toxicity is dose-dependent. Hyperkalemic distal renal tubular acidosis is common.

Lithium

Long-term lithium exposure can result in chronic tubulointerstitial nephritis. Repeated toxicity and high chronic lithium levels can result in worsening dysfunction. Other kidney manifestations include decreased GFR, partial nephrogenic diabetes insipidus, and incomplete distal renal tubular acidosis. Lithium is reabsorbed along the nephron at sites where sodium is reabsorbed, resulting in ubiquitous uptake along the renal tubules. Amiloride blocks lithium uptake at the epithelial sodium channel and attenuates nephrogenic diabetes insipidus. Discontinuation of lithium may reverse some of the underlying kidney damage and should be considered if a patient's underlying disorder is controlled with other medications.

Lead

Lead nephropathy is an underrecognized cause of chronic tubulointerstitial disorders. Lead is taken up by the proximal tubule, leading to direct toxic tubulointerstitial effects, including Fanconi syndrome, decreased urine uric acid excretion, and interstitial fibrosis. Patients who are hypertensive, are prone to (saturnine) gout, and have a decreased GFR should be asked about past lead exposure.

Serum lead levels are a poor marker for lead nephropathy, because more than 90% of body lead resides in the bone. Calcium disodium ethylenediaminetetraacetic acid (EDTA) mobilization testing with 24-hour urine lead excretion should be performed if lead toxicity is suspected. Levels of more than 600 micrograms (2.9 micromoles) in 24 hours are diagnostic.

Hyperuricemia

The association of hyperuricemia and CKD has been demonstrated; however, causality has neither been proved nor refuted. In one study of more than 21,000 persons, those with a serum uric acid level of 7.0 to 8.9 mg/dL (0.413-0.525 mmol/L) had double the risk of incident kidney disease, and those with levels of more than 9.0 mg/dL (0.531 mmol/L) had triple the risk. Some epidemiologic studies also have demonstrated hyperuricemia to be a marker of worse cardiovascular outcomes.

The kidney is the primary organ for uric acid excretion. With a pKa of 5.4, uric acid exists in its non-ionized form in acidic urine and exists as urate salts in the more alkaline environments of the interstitium and blood. Chronic urate nephropathy may result in tubulointerstitial nephritis from deposition of sodium urate crystals in the medullary interstitium. The chronic inflammatory response leads to interstitial fibrosis and CKD. Many patients believed to have urate nephropathy may have a form of hereditary interstitial kidney disease (type II medullary cystic disease).

Although allopurinol can be used to lower serum uric acid levels, it is unclear if treatment of asymptomatic hyperuricemia results in improved outcomes. If a patient has clinical gout and hyperuricemia, uric acid–lowering therapy should be more strongly considered.

Obstruction

Obstructive uropathy results from functional or structural obstruction to urinary flow anywhere along the urinary tract. Obstruction and reflux of urinary flow can result in an inflammatory response in the interstitium and eventual ischemic atrophy. The most common obstructive causes are benign prostatic hyperplasia in men and disorders of the reproductive system (including malignancy) in women. Prompt diagnosis via radiographic imaging studies is indicated to prevent the long-term sequelae of CKD. Obstruction that is present for more than 6 to 12 weeks typically results in irreversible damage.

KEY POINTS

- Patients predisposed to infection-related tubulointerstitial damage include those with preexisting kidney disease or those with impaired immune system function.

- Kidney manifestations of analgesic nephropathy include sterile pyuria, mild proteinuria, reduced glomerular filtration rate, and urinary concentrating defects.

- The most common obstructive causes of chronic tubulointerstitial diseases are benign prostatic hyperplasia in men and disorders of the reproductive system (including malignancy) in women.

Management

Rapid assessment and treatment of underlying causes of chronic tubulointerstitial disorders may slow down progression to ESKD or may result in some degree of reversibility. However, once chronic damage has occurred, significant reversibility is unlikely. Steps for practitioners to take include discontinuation of drugs and removal of exogenous toxins; diagnosing immunologic, infectious, or malignant disease; ensuring obstruction is not present; treating the underlying cause; and consideration for immunosuppressive therapy in consultation with a nephrologist.

KEY POINT

- Rapid assessment and treatment of underlying causes of chronic tubulointerstitial disorders may slow down progression to end-stage kidney disease or may result in some degree of reversibility.

Glomerular Diseases

Pathophysiology

The kidneys contain approximately two million ultrafiltration units known as nephrons, each comprised of two components: the glomerulus and the renal tubule. The glomerulus is the primary filtration unit of the kidney and is composed of a tuft of capillaries between the afferent and efferent arterioles of the renal circulation. The glomerular capillaries are supported by the mesangium, which is made of specialized mesangial cells and a surrounding structural matrix. The glomerular capillary has three distinct components: an inner layer of endothelial cells, the capillary basement membrane, and an outer layer of visceral epithelial cells known as podocytes, which wrap around the capillaries, leaving small slits (slit diaphragm) between these projections (foot processes). Together these components form a selective filtration barrier (**Figure 15**).

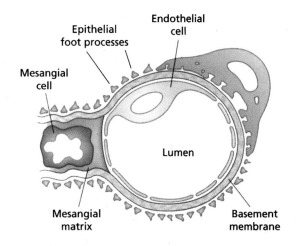

FIGURE 15. Normal glomerular capillary.

The glomerular capillary tufts are almost completely surrounded by a cup-like sac composed of a single layer of parietal epithelial cells called the Bowman's capsule that is continuous with the renal tubule. Filtrate from the glomerular capillaries is collected in this space and then passes to the renal tubule, which is the primary location for the processing of the glomerular filtrate.

Damage to the glomerulus may alter glomerular capillary permselectivity and result in proteinuria, the clinical hallmark of glomerular diseases. It also may alter the continuity of the filtration barrier, manifesting as glomerular hematuria. Extensive damage to glomeruli is associated with a progressive decline in the glomerular filtration rate (GFR), leading to advanced chronic kidney disease (CKD) and possibly end-stage kidney disease (ESKD).

Clinical Manifestations

Glomerular diseases are frequently characterized by different patterns of clinical presentation, including the nephrotic syndromes, in which significant leakage of plasma proteins is predominant, and the nephritic syndromes (also called glomerulonephritis), in which there is passage of both plasma proteins and cells (erythrocytes and leukocytes) from the glomerulus into the renal tubule. Because certain diseases tend to follow specific patterns, these characterizations may be useful in understanding the potential causes of a clinical kidney disorder. However, these classifications are not exclusive because some conditions may present with either pattern, others may have features of both, and some disorders may progress from one pattern to the other. Kidney biopsy is usually essential in making a correct diagnosis and guiding therapy.

Glomerular diseases may also be designated by their clinical time course. Rapidly progressive glomerulonephritis (RPGN) is a form of the nephritic syndrome characterized by the rapid loss of kidney function over weeks to months compared with other forms of glomerular disease, which may be more chronic or slowly progressive.

The Nephrotic Syndrome

The nephrotic syndrome is characterized by heavy proteinuria, defined as a urine protein–creatinine ratio of greater than 3.5 mg/mg or a timed urine protein collection of greater than 3.5 g/24 h. Hypoalbuminemia and edema are hallmark findings of the nephrotic syndrome. Other clinical manifestations, such as hyperlipidemia or coagulation abnormalities, are related to losses of proteins other than albumin or caused by increased protein synthesis (**Table 27**).

The Nephritic Syndrome

Compared with the nephrotic syndrome in which there is primarily protein leakage across the glomeruli, the nephritic syndrome involves injury to or inflammation within the glomerulus that allows the passage of protein, erythrocytes, and leukocytes into the renal tubule. The resulting damage may be associated

TABLE 27. Clinical Manifestations of Urine Protein Losses and Associated Altered Protein Synthesis in the Nephrotic Syndrome

Urine Protein Losses

Proteins	Clinical Manifestations
Albumin	Edema
High-density lipoprotein	Atherosclerosis
Heparan sulfate	Atherosclerosis
α1-Acid glycoprotein	Atherosclerosis
Complement component factor B	Infections
Immunoglobulin (IgG)	Infections
Antithrombin III; proteins S and C	Thrombosis
Coagulation factors IX, XI, and XII	Bleeding
Iron-binding protein	Anemia
Erythropoietin	Anemia
Vitamin D–binding proteins	Osteomalacia
Thyroid-binding protein and thyroxine	Hypothyroidism

Altered Protein Synthesis

Proteins	Clinical Manifestations
Insufficient synthesis of albumin	Hypoalbuminemia
Increased synthesis of apolipoprotein B; LDL cholesterol	Atherosclerosis
Increased synthesis of fibrinogen	Thrombosis
Increased synthesis of coagulation factors V, VII, VIII, and X	Thrombosis
Increased synthesis of α_2-globulins and β-globulins	Unknown
Increased synthesis of immunoglobulin IgM	Unknown

with decreased glomerular filtration, decreased kidney function, and abnormal blood pressure regulation. Thus, the nephritic syndrome is characterized by proteinuria, hematuria, pyuria, and, frequently, decreased kidney function and hypertension.

RPGN, a severe form of acute nephritis, is a nephrologic emergency characterized by a rapid decline in kidney function that can lead to advanced CKD and ESKD in weeks to months if untreated. The histologic correlate of RPGN is the crescent. Crescents develop in Bowman's space following glomerular capillary rupture with extravasation of inflammatory cells, macrophages, and fibrin resulting in parietal cell proliferation that takes on a characteristic crescent shape on microscopy. Prompt diagnosis and initiation of therapy in RPGN are essential to optimize clinical outcomes and decrease the risk of progression to ESKD.

KEY POINTS

- The nephrotic syndrome is characterized by heavy proteinuria (a urine protein–creatinine ratio >3.5 mg/mg); hypoalbuminemia, edema, and hyperlipidemia are common clinical findings.
- The nephritic syndrome is characterized by proteinuria, hematuria, pyuria, and, frequently, decreased kidney function and hypertension.

- Rapidly progressive glomerulonephritis is a nephrologic emergency characterized by a rapid decline in kidney function that can lead to advanced chronic kidney disease and end-stage kidney disease in weeks to months if untreated.

Conditions that Cause the Nephrotic Syndrome

Disorders presenting with the nephrotic syndrome may occur as a primary condition or may be a secondary manifestation of another disease process. **Table 28** lists the causes of the nephrotic syndrome.

Major Causes of the Nephrotic Syndrome with Kidney-Limited Disease

Focal Segmental Glomerulosclerosis
Epidemiology and Pathophysiology

Focal segmental glomerulosclerosis (FSGS) is the leading cause of primary nephrotic syndrome and is the most common primary glomerular disease leading to ESKD in the United States. FSGS may be primary, familial, or secondary to HIV infection (see HIV-Associated Nephropathy),

TABLE 28. Nondiabetic Causes of the Nephrotic Syndrome in Adults[a]

Condition	Frequency as a Cause of Primary Nephrotic Syndrome	Comments
Focal segmental glomerulosclerosis	36%-80%	Most common cause of primary nephrotic syndrome in the United States
		Predilection for black persons
		Five subtypes: not otherwise specified; perihilar variant; tip variant; cellular variant; collapsing variant (may be associated with HIV infection, heroin use, parvovirus infection, or pamidronate exposure)
		Familial forms
		Morbid obesity
		Decreased kidney mass (congenital kidney dysplasia, reflux nephropathy)
Membranous glomerulopathy	18%-41%	Primary form (most common worldwide): antiphospholipase A_2 receptor autoantibodies can be found in 75% of cases
		May be associated with or secondary to:
		Systemic lupus erythematosus
		Infections: hepatitis B and C virus infections; syphilis; malaria
		Medication exposure: penicillamine; NSAIDs; anti-TNF therapy; tiopronin
		Mercury or gold exposure
		Malignancies: bladder, breast, colon, lung, pancreas, prostate, stomach carcinoma; carcinoid; sarcomas; lymphomas; leukemias
		Thyroid disease
		Highest predilection for renal vein thrombosis among all causes of the nephrotic syndrome
Minimal change glomerulopathy	9%-16%	Most common cause of primary nephrotic syndrome in children
		May be associated with or secondary to:
		Atopic diseases
		Mononucleosis
		Malignancies: Hodgkin lymphoma and carcinomas
		Medication exposure: NSAIDs; interferon; pamidronate; lithium; rifampin
Fibrillary glomerulopathy	<1%	May be associated with malignancy
Immunotactoid glomerulopathy	<1%	May be associated with chronic lymphocytic leukemia or B-cell lymphomas
Amyloidosis	2%	AL (light chains) or AH (heavy chains) amyloidosis may be primary or associated with myeloma
		AA amyloidosis is usually associated with inflammatory conditions such as rheumatoid arthritis, familial Mediterranean fever, chronic infections, or malignancies
		Familial forms
Monoclonal immunoglobulin deposition disease	<1%	Frequently associated with multiple myeloma
Membranoproliferative glomerulonephritis[b]	25%-30%	May present with features of the nephrotic syndrome, the nephritic syndrome, or both

TNF = tumor necrosis factor.

[a]See Table 29 for the clinical stages of diabetic nephropathy.

[b]See Table 30 for causes of the nephritic syndrome.

morbid obesity, reflux nephropathy, and heroin use. Primary FSGS is postulated to be in part mediated by lymphocytes that release cytokines, leading to increased permeability and injury to the glomerular capillary bundle and podocytes.

Risk factors associated with progression of FSGS to ESKD include black race, proteinuria greater than 2 g/24 h, elevated serum creatinine levels, low GFR, BMI greater than 27, hypertension at onset, lack of remission, and relapse during follow-up.

Clinical Manifestations
Primary FSGS frequently presents as the nephrotic syndrome and is commonly accompanied by kidney failure, hematuria, and hypertension. FSGS may also present as asymptomatic subnephrotic proteinuria. Progressive CKD is common.

Diagnosis
Diagnosis of primary FSGS is confirmed by kidney biopsy, with light microscopy showing scarring or sclerosis involving some (focal) glomeruli, which are affected only in a portion of the glomerular capillary bundle (segmental).

Management
Management of FSGS using ACE inhibitors or angiotensin receptor blockers (ARBs) to a target blood pressure of less than 130/80 mm Hg is indicated to forestall progression and reduce proteinuria. At disease onset, patients with nephrotic-range proteinuria should be considered for treatment with immunosuppressive regimens such as corticosteroids or calcineurin inhibitors. Of patients with primary FSGS, 39% to 45% become frequently relapsing corticosteroid-dependent or corticosteroid-resistant, and a calcineurin inhibitor can achieve remission in up to 70% of these patients; however, 60% of patients can relapse after reducing or stopping these agents. Many of these patients require chronic immunosuppressive therapy, which may also include cyclophosphamide, mycophenolate mofetil, and rituximab.

Response to treatment is the most important factor that influences prognosis. Up to 90% of patients with complete remission, 78% with partial remission, and 40% with persistent nephrotic-range proteinuria remain free of ESKD within 10 years of disease onset.

Membranous Glomerulopathy
Epidemiology and Pathophysiology
Membranous glomerulopathy is the second leading cause of primary nephrotic syndrome. Primary membranous glomerulopathy has a predilection to develop more frequently in adults older than 50 years. Untreated, approximately two thirds of patients with membranous glomerulopathy undergo spontaneous complete or partial remission, and one third of patients have a persistent or progressive disease that may result in ESKD within 10 years of onset.

Primary membranous glomerulopathy is an in situ immune complex disease in which immunoglobulins of the IgG class react with constitutive or planted antigens in the outer aspect of the glomerular basement membrane.

Membranous glomerulopathy can also be secondary to other conditions such as systemic lupus erythematosus, hepatitis B and C virus infections, malaria, malignancies, and medications such as NSAIDs.

Risk factors associated with progressive CKD in patients with membranous glomerulopathy include male gender, age greater than 50 years, elevated serum creatinine levels, low GFR, hypertension, and findings of secondary glomerulosclerosis and chronic tubulointerstitial changes on kidney biopsy. Because of the high rate of spontaneous remission of membranous glomerulopathy, persistent proteinuria of ≥4 g/24 h for more than 6 months and a decline in the slope of GFR over time are the most important risk factors associated with progression of membranous glomerulopathy to advanced CKD.

Clinical Manifestations
Membranous glomerulopathy usually presents as the nephrotic syndrome, although some patients may have asymptomatic subnephrotic proteinuria. Many patients have normal kidney function at the time of presentation. Membranous glomerulopathy has the highest prevalence of renal vein thrombosis compared with other causes of the nephrotic syndrome.

Diagnosis
Diagnosis of membranous glomerulopathy requires kidney biopsy, which shows diffuse thickening of the glomerular capillary wall on light microscopy and intramembranous electron-dense deposits initially located in the subepithelial aspect of the glomerular basement membrane on electron microscopy.

Management
Because of the potential toxicity of immunosuppressive therapies and the high rate of spontaneous remission, the clinical features and risk for disease progression should determine the most appropriate treatment in patients with primary membranous glomerulopathy (**Figure 16**). Treatment of hyperlipidemia also is recommended, with frequent (every 1-3 months) monitoring of proteinuria and GFR.

Remission is the most important factor that predicts the renal survival in patients with primary membranous glomerulopathy. Most patients with complete remission and 90% with partial remission remain free of advanced CKD or ESKD compared with 45% with persistent nephrotic syndrome within 10 years of disease onset.

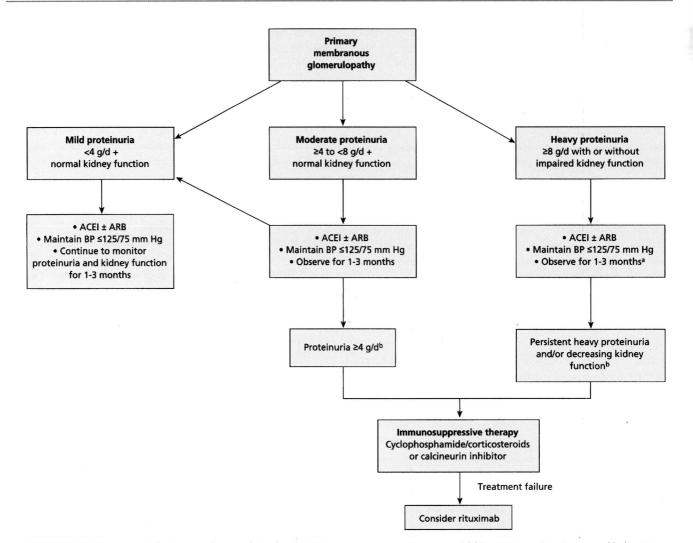

FIGURE 16. Management of primary membranous glomerulopathy. ACEI = angiotensin-converting enzyme inhibitor; ARB = angiotensin receptor blocker; BP = blood pressure.

[a]Decreasing kidney function or complication: start treatment early.

[b]Introduction of risk reduction strategies, including treatment of hyperlipidemia and consideration for prophylactic anticoagulation if patient is at low risk for bleeding and has a serum albumin level of less than 2.8 g/dL (28 g/L).

Modified with permission of the American Society of Nephrology, from J Am Soc Nephrol. Management of membranous nephropathy: when and what for treatment. Cattran D. 2005;16:1188-1194. [PMID: 15800117]; permission conveyed through Copyright Clearance Center, Inc.

Minimal Change Glomerulopathy

Epidemiology and Pathophysiology

Minimal change glomerulopathy ([MCG]; also known as minimal change disease) is associated with atopic diseases and lymphomas. It is believed to be a disorder of lymphocytes, which release immunoglobulins and cytokines that alter glomerular capillary permselectivity.

Clinical Manifestations

MCG usually presents with significant proteinuria and its consequences as the major clinical finding. Progressive CKD due to MCG is rare.

Diagnosis

Diagnosis of MCG is confirmed with kidney biopsy. Light and immunofluorescence microscopy are normal (minimal change), with electron microscopy demonstrating characteristic fusion and effacement of podocyte (visceral epithelial cell) foot processes.

Management

Most patients with MCG are responsive to daily or alternate-day prednisone, 1 mg/kg/d or 2 mg/kg every other day for 8 to 16 weeks, with complete remission achieved in approximately 70% of cases. Of those who respond to corticosteroids,

73% relapse at least one time, with most responding again to corticosteroids.

Approximately 28% of patients with MCG develop a frequently relapsing corticosteroid-dependent disease, and 25% can develop a corticosteroid-resistant disease. Immunosuppressive agents may be required in these patients.

Fibrillary and Immunotactoid Glomerulopathies
Epidemiology and Pathophysiology
Fibrillary and immunotactoid glomerulopathies are rare glomerular diseases that cause less than 1% of cases of the nephrotic syndrome in adults. Fibrillary glomerulopathy is characterized by the finding of randomly arranged fibrils with a diameter between 18 and 22 nm on electron microscopy that stain for complement and immunoglobulin, suggesting that it is an immune complex–mediated disease.

Immunotactoid glomerulopathy is characterized by the presence of organized microtubular structures with a diameter between 30 and 80 nm in the mesangium and along the subendothelial and/or subepithelial aspects of the glomerular basement membrane. In more than 60% of cases, it is associated with lymphoproliferative disorders.

Clinical Manifestations
Both fibrillary and immunotactoid glomerulopathy present in middle aged to older persons with the nephrotic syndrome, accompanied by hematuria and hypertension. Progression of kidney failure is common, with more than 50% of patients having ESKD within 10 years despite treatment.

Diagnosis
Diagnosis of both fibrillary and immunotactoid glomerulopathy is made on electron microscopy of kidney biopsy specimens showing the characteristic findings of each disorder. Assessment for the potential presence of diseases associated with these kidney findings is appropriate.

Management
No controlled trials on treatment for either disorder have been performed. Corticosteroids, cytotoxic agents, and plasmapheresis have been used, although kidney failure may progress despite therapy. Response to the treatment of an underlying lymphoproliferative disorder in immunotactoid glomerulopathy is associated with overall patient survival. **H**

KEY POINTS
- Of patients with primary focal segmental glomerulosclerosis, 39% to 45% become frequently relapsing corticosteroid-dependent or corticosteroid-resistant; many of these patients require chronic immunosuppressive therapy.

- Because of the potential toxicity of immunosuppressive therapies and the high rate of spontaneous remission, the clinical features and risk for disease progression should determine the most appropriate treatment in patients with primary membranous glomerulopathy
- Treatment with daily or alternate-day prednisone is indicated for patients with minimal change glomerulopathy.

Systemic Diseases that Cause the Nephrotic Syndrome
Diabetic Nephropathy
Epidemiology and Pathophysiology
Diabetic nephropathy is the most common glomerulopathy, developing in approximately 35% of patients with type 1 or type 2 diabetes mellitus. American Indian, Mexican-American, and black patients have a higher risk for developing diabetic nephropathy compared with white patients. Other risk factors include poor glycemic control, hypertension and/or family history of hypertension, cigarette smoking, family history of kidney involvement, and older age of onset of diabetes.

In the United States, diabetic nephropathy constitutes approximately 44% of new cases of ESKD: 6% due to type 1 diabetes and 38% due to type 2 diabetes. Hyperglycemia, hypertension, and albuminuria and/or proteinuria are modifiable risk factors associated with progressive CKD.

Hyperglycemia promotes the formation of advanced glycosylation end products in the kidney tissue and other target organs, which stimulate oxidative stress pathways conducive to damage. Glomerular hyperfiltration mediated by nitric oxide, the renin-angiotensin-aldosterone system, natriuretic peptides, and other vasoactive pathways also are important in the pathogenesis and progression of diabetic nephropathy.

Clinical Manifestations
Diabetic nephropathy results in characteristic structural changes to the kidney, including expansion of the mesangium, thickening of the basement membrane, and sclerosis of the glomeruli. Clinical manifestations typically include progressive proteinuria, a decline in kidney function, and hypertension, although the findings at presentation depend on the clinical stage at the time of diagnosis, which may be delayed, particularly in type 2 diabetes. Acute nephritic syndrome is an uncommon manifestation and should raise suspicion of concurrent glomerulonephritis.

Diagnosis
Detection of early-stage diabetic nephropathy and microalbuminuria requires annual measurement of the urine albumin–creatinine ratio for patients who have had type 1 diabetes

CONT.

for 5 years or more and for all patients with type 2 diabetes beginning at the time of diagnosis.

Longitudinal studies of high-risk patients with type 1 diabetes have delineated five clinical stages based on changes in GFR, degree of albuminuria, and development of hypertension (**Table 29**). These stages also appear to apply to type 2 diabetes except that nephropathy may occur earlier and progress more quickly, and hypertension may develop before nephropathy. However, not all patients may progress in a step-wise progression; microalbuminuria has been noted to regress in younger patients with aggressive glycemic and blood pressure control, and some patients may develop CKD without significant albuminuria. The mechanisms underlying kidney disease in these patients are not well defined.

Management

Treatment of patients with microalbuminuria or overt proteinuria in diabetic nephropathy includes tight glycemic control and careful management of hypertension with preferential use of ACE inhibitors or ARBs. In type 1 and 2 diabetic patients with microalbuminuria, randomized controlled trials indicate that achieving a hemoglobin A_{1c} of approximately 7% significantly decreased the risk of developing overt proteinuria. In type 1 or type 2 diabetic patients with nephropathy and hypertension, treatment with ACE inhibitors or ARBs significantly reduces the risk of progression compared with other antihypertensive agents. The optimal blood pressure target in type 1 and 2 diabetic patients with established nephropathy is less than 130/80 mm Hg.

Lower blood pressures may further decrease the risk of developing overt proteinuria, although more aggressive treatment is associated with potential adverse effects, including the sudden elevation of serum creatinine or reduction in the GFR, hypotension, and syncope.

Amyloidosis

Epidemiology and Pathophysiology

Amyloidosis is caused by the pathologic deposition of a protein with an altered structure that polymerizes into an insoluble form (amyloid) that is deposited into the tissues. More than 20 types of amyloidosis are classified according to the precursor protein that aggregates to form amyloid deposits. In AL amyloidosis, the most common form, the precursor protein is a monoclonal light chain, usually of the lambda isotype. AH amyloidosis results from increased production and tissue deposition of truncated monoclonal heavy chains. In AA amyloidosis, the precursor protein is amyloid AA protein, an acute phase reactant released in chronic inflammatory states such as rheumatoid arthritis, tuberculosis, and osteomyelitis. Up to 20% of patients with AL amyloidosis have a coexisting multiple myeloma or other lymphoproliferative disease.

Clinical Manifestations

AL amyloidosis is a systemic disease, and the kidney is one of the most prominently affected organs, in addition to the heart, lungs, and gastrointestinal tract. Virtually every kidney compartment can be affected by amyloidosis, but glomerular lesions predominate, resulting in the nephrotic syndrome. AL

TABLE 29. Clinical Stages of Diabetic Nephropathy in Patients with Type 1 Diabetes Mellitus		
Clinical Stage	**Manifestations**	**Occurrence**
Stage 1: Hyperfiltration	Supernormal GFR Albuminuria <30 mg/d Normal blood pressure Large kidneys on ultrasound	Within the first 5 years after onset of diabetes
Stage 2: Microalbuminuric	Normal or high GFR Albuminuria from 30-300 mg/d Prehypertension or hypertension	5-15 years after onset of diabetes
Stage 3: Overt Proteinuric	Normal or decreasing GFR Albuminuria >300 mg/d (overt proteinuria) Hypertension	10-20 years after onset of diabetes
Stage 4: Progressive	Decreasing GFR Nephrotic syndrome Hypertension	15-25 years after onset of diabetes
Stage 5: End-Stage Kidney Disease	GFR <15 mL/min/1.73 m² Difficult to control hypertension	20-30 years after onset of diabetes
GFR = glomerular filtration rate.		

amyloidosis has a poor prognosis with a short median survival ranging between 5 and 34 months after onset of the disease. AL amyloidosis survivors with kidney involvement generally have progressive CKD leading to ESKD within 5 years of onset. The prognosis in patients with AA amyloidosis is determined by its cause and in general is more favorable than AL amyloidosis.

Diagnosis

Definitive diagnosis of amyloidosis requires histologic confirmation. A fat pad aspirate is a minimally invasive and high-value diagnostic method for suspected amyloidosis; kidney biopsy should be considered when either fat pad aspirate or a rectal biopsy is nondiagnostic. On kidney biopsy, light microscopy reveals amorphous material effacing varying proportions of glomeruli, vessels, or interstitium that demonstrate green birefringence with the Congo red stain on polarized microscopy. Immunofluorescence microscopy demonstrates specific staining for monoclonal light or heavy chains or amyloid AA protein. The diagnosis of AL or AH amyloidosis warrants further evaluation for possible underlying multiple myeloma, including serum and urine protein electrophoresis and immunoelectrophoresis.

Management

For appropriate patients (younger patients with relatively well-preserved organ function), autologous hematopoietic stem cell transplantation may be considered. A regimen of low-dose melphalan and corticosteroids is often employed for patients who are not deemed candidates for autologous hematopoietic stem cell transplantation. The newer agents bortezomib and lenalidomide show promise and are being evaluated in ongoing clinical trials.

Multiple Myeloma
Epidemiology and Pathophysiology

Multiple myeloma is a plasma cell dyscrasia that results in neoplastic proliferation and production of a monoclonal immunoglobulin. Although multiple myeloma may cause kidney injury through different mechanisms (see Chronic Tubulointerstitial Disorders and Acute Kidney Injury), the glomerular manifestations of myeloma include amyloidosis, membranoproliferative glomerulonephritis, and deposition of light and heavy chains resulting in monoclonal immunoglobulin deposition disease.

Clinical Manifestations

The degree of kidney failure at presentation may range from mild to severe. Proteinuria is variable but generally mild, with less than 25% of patients presenting with nephrotic-range proteinuria.

Diagnosis

Kidney biopsy is recommended to confirm suspected myeloma-related kidney disease and to exclude other kidney disorders.

Management

Carefully administered intravenous fluids to establish euvolemia and maintain high urine output are used to treat dehydration, hypercalcemia, and hyperuricemia, if present. Use of plasmapheresis to remove the monoclonal immunoglobulin remains an area of controversy. Systemic chemotherapy to treat the underlying myeloma is indicated.

HIV-Associated Nephropathy
Epidemiology and Pathophysiology

HIV-associated nephropathy (HIVAN), a form of collapsing focal segmental glomerulosclerosis, occurs in approximately 3.5% to 12% of patients with HIV infection. HIVAN has a predilection to develop in black persons who are HIV positive and is currently the third leading cause of ESKD in black persons between the ages of 20 and 64 years. Other glomerular lesions seen less commonly in patients with HIV infection include IgA nephropathy, immune complex–mediated glomerulonephritis, membranoproliferative glomerulonephritis, lupus-like glomerulonephritis, membranous glomerulopathy, thrombotic microangiopathy, minimal change glomerulopathy, and amyloidosis.

Clinical Manifestations

HIVAN classically presents as the nephrotic syndrome accompanied by progressive kidney failure and large kidneys on ultrasound. HIVAN more commonly occurs in patients with advanced HIV infection but can also be seen early in infection. Hypertension and edema are uncommon.

Diagnosis

Diagnosis of HIVAN is often made on clinical grounds in patients with advanced HIV infection and typical clinical features. Patients with a rapid decline in kidney function, hypocomplementemia, dysmorphic hematuria or erythrocyte casts, or abnormal serologic studies such as cryoglobulins merit further evaluation with kidney biopsy. Because HIVAN is rare in white persons and those of Northwest European descent, biopsy should be more strongly considered in these persons if HIVAN is suspected. Light microscopic features on HIVAN include collapsing focal segmental glomerulosclerosis.

Management

Combination antiretroviral therapy is indicated and has reduced the incidence of progression to ESKD. ACE inhibitors and ARBs should be used to treat hypertension and proteinuria.

H CONT.

Hepatitis B Virus–Associated Kidney Disease
Epidemiology and Pathophysiology

Hepatitis B virus (HBV)–associated kidney disease is most prevalent in endemic areas, such as Asia, sub-Saharan Africa, the South Pacific, and the Middle East, and is less common in North America and Western Europe. HBV-associated kidney disease affects approximately 16% to 56% of patients with HBV infection.

The most common form of kidney disease associated with HBV infection is membranous glomerulopathy, although it may also be associated with membranoproliferative glomerulonephritis and polyarteritis nodosa (see Conditions that Cause the Nephritic Syndrome, Hepatitis B Virus–Associated Kidney Disease). Membranous glomerulopathy is particularly common in children infected with hepatitis B. It is believed that deposition of hepatitis B antigen-antibody immune complexes in the subepithelial membrane is responsible for the increased glomerular permeability and membranous glomerulopathy.

Clinical Manifestations

HBV glomerulopathy may occur in patients with serologically proven active hepatitis B, although clinically significant hepatitis may not be present. Patients with membranous glomerulopathy usually present with typical findings of the nephrotic syndrome.

Diagnosis

Diagnosis of HBV-associated kidney disease includes serologic studies for the presence of active HBV infection and kidney biopsy results consistent with membranous glomerulopathy. Complement levels may be low in HBV-associated kidney disease.

Management

Spontaneous resolution may occur, particularly in children. Remission is less common in adults, with some patients developing progressive kidney disease.

The use of an ACE inhibitor or ARB for proteinuria and/or blood pressure control is appropriate. Treatment of the underlying hepatitis infection with antiviral agents appears to be of benefit in treating the associated kidney disease. However, the use of immunosuppressive agents for treatment of severe membranous glomerulonephritis is less clear in the presence of active HBV infection. **H**

KEY POINTS

- Detection of early-stage diabetic nephropathy and microalbuminuria requires annual measurement of the urine albumin–creatinine ratio for patients who have had type 1 diabetes for 5 years or more and for all patients with type 2 diabetes beginning at the time of diagnosis.

- Treatment of patients with microalbuminuria or overt proteinuria in diabetic nephropathy includes tight glycemic control and careful management of hypertension with preferential use of ACE inhibitors or angiotensin receptor blockers.

- Up to 20% of patients with AL amyloidosis have a coexisting multiple myeloma or other lymphoproliferative disease.

Conditions that Cause the Nephritic Syndrome

Table 30 lists the causes of the nephritic syndrome.

IgA Nephropathy
Epidemiology and Pathophysiology

IgA nephropathy, the most common primary glomerulonephritis, is an immune complex disease in which IgA antigen-antibody complexes are deposited primarily in the mesangium. IgA nephropathy may primarily involve only the kidney or may be secondarily associated with other conditions such as HIV infection, chronic liver disease, inflammatory bowel disease, or celiac disease. IgA nephropathy is the renal

H

TABLE 30. Causes of the Nephritic Syndrome		
Disorder	**Frequency as a Cause of Primary Nephritic Syndrome[a]**	**Serum Complement Pattern**
IgA nephropathy	25%-30%	Normal
Lupus nephritis	20%	Low C3 and C4
Pauci-immune crescentic glomerulonephritis	15%-25%	Normal
Membranoproliferative glomerulonephritis	6%-10%	Low C3 and/or low C4
Thrombotic microangiopathy	5%-8%	Low C3 in some persons
Postinfectious glomerulonephritis	4%-8%	Low C3
Anti–glomerular basement membrane antibody disease	3%	Normal
C3 glomerulopathy	<1%	Low C3

[a]Based on biopsy series and therefore may not reflect true prevalence.

lesion of Henoch-Schönlein purpura, a systemic vasculitis most commonly seen during childhood.

Primary IgA nephropathy occurs at any age and has a predilection to develop in men who are white or Asian. Approximately 20% to 30% of patients have progressive disease that can lead to ESKD within 10 to 20 years of onset. Risk factors associated with progressive CKD include younger age at onset; hypertension; proteinuria ≥1 g/24 h; elevated serum creatinine levels; low GFR; and secondary glomerulosclerosis, chronic tubulointerstitial changes, and crescents on biopsy. Persistent proteinuria (≥1 g/24 h) and hypertension are two modifiable risk factors that increase the risk of progression to advanced CKD.

Clinical Manifestations

Most patients with IgA nephropathy are asymptomatic at presentation, with only microscopic hematuria and proteinuria discovered on evaluation of the urine. A common presentation of primary IgA nephropathy is recurrent gross hematuria occurring synchronously with an episode of respiratory ("synpharyngitic hematuria") or gastrointestinal infection. This may be associated with acute kidney injury precipitated by occlusion of tubular lumina by erythrocytes and erythrocyte casts. Less frequently, patients may present with the nephrotic syndrome or RPGN.

Diagnosis

Diagnosis is confirmed by kidney biopsy, which demonstrates mesangioproliferative glomerulonephritis with IgA-dominant mesangial immune deposits on immunofluorescence microscopy.

Management

Patients who have IgA nephropathy and a low risk for progressive disease should be treated with ACE inhibitors or ARBs, with the goal to maintain urine protein excretion to less than 1 g/24 h. Hypertension is common in patients with IgA nephropathy, and optimal treatment to a blood pressure goal of less than 130/80 mm Hg is recommended. Immunosuppressive therapy should be considered for patients with persistent proteinuria (usually >1 g/24 h), progressive kidney dysfunction, or histologic findings (such as crescents) indicative of more aggressive disease.

For patients at highest risk for progressive disease, pulse and oral corticosteroids as well as alkylating regimens such as cyclophosphamide followed by azathioprine with ACE inhibitors and/or ARBs have shown a significant reduction in the risk for ESKD. Patients with milder disease are often treated with omega-3 fatty acids.

Membranoproliferative Glomerulonephritis

Epidemiology and Pathophysiology

Membranoproliferative glomerulonephritis (MPGN) most often is secondary to immune complex formation in response to chronic antigen stimulation. Traditionally, when the source of the antigen has been identified, the glomerulonephritis has been categorized as secondary MPGN I. Causes include hepatitis C virus infection (see Hepatitis C Virus–Associated Glomerulonephritis); other chronic indolent infections such as hepatitis B, syphilis, subacute bacterial endocarditis, osteomyelitis, and mastoiditis; autoimmune diseases (lupus and Sjögren); essential cryoglobulinemia (types I and II); and malignancies (carcinomas, sarcomas, lymphomas, and leukemias).

When the source of the chronic antigen cannot be identified, the process has been historically termed *primary MPGN*, with one of three histopathologic phenotypes: MPGN I, MPGN II (dense deposit disease), and MPGN III. Some cases of primary MPGN with immune complex deposition are also likely related to chronic antigen stimulation from an as yet undefined autoimmune, infectious, or neoplastic process. However, other cases are immune complex negative, develop as a consequence of abnormalities in complement regulation, and are more properly classified as C3 glomerulopathy.

Clinical Manifestations

MPGN most commonly manifests as the nephritic syndrome but may also present with heavy proteinuria, referred to as a mixed nephritic-nephrotic picture. MPGN may follow a more indolent course but may also present as an RPGN. The most important factors associated with progression of primary MPGN to advanced CKD include decreased GFR, heavy proteinuria, hypertension, and crescents and chronic tubulointerstitial disease on biopsy.

Diagnosis

Diagnosis of MPGN requires a kidney biopsy demonstrating the characteristic pathologic findings. Immunofluorescence microscopy in addition to electron microscopy may be helpful in appropriately classifying and determining the cause of the disease.

Management

Corticosteroids with immunosuppressive agents and antiplatelet agents may be beneficial in the management of primary MPGN, but more than 50% of patients progress to advanced CKD. Treatment of secondary MPGN I is directed toward the underlying cause. **H**

KEY POINTS

- IgA nephropathy may primarily involve only the kidney or may be secondarily associated with other conditions such as HIV infection, chronic liver disease, inflammatory bowel disease, or celiac disease.

- Causes of membranoproliferative glomerulonephritis include hepatitis C virus infection, other chronic indolent infections, autoimmune diseases, essential cryoglobulinemia, and malignancies.

Hepatitis C Virus–Associated Glomerulonephritis

Epidemiology and Pathophysiology

Hepatitis C virus–associated glomerulonephritis (HCV-GN) is an immune complex disease that occurs in as many as 21% of patients who have HCV infection. It most commonly presents as MPGN and mixed cryoglobulinemia and is characterized by an indolent course in one third of patients, remission in another third, and a relapsing course in the remaining patients, with potential progression to advanced CKD.

The pathogenesis of HCV-GN involves viral infection of B lymphocytes that synthesize polyclonal or monoclonal antibodies with or without a cryoprecipitating property. Circulating immune complexes are usually IgG-IgM complexes, which are often cryoglobulins, with or without HCV viral proteins that are deposited in the glomeruli. The virus also directly infects the kidney tissue.

Clinical Manifestations

HCV-GN usually manifests as the nephritic syndrome. Other manifestations include combined nephrotic-nephritic syndrome, isolated proteinuria with hematuria, RPGN, and acute and chronic kidney failure. In patients with HCV infection, HCV-GN can also be a component of a systemic cryoglobulinemic vasculitis with involvement of the skin, peripheral nerves, and musculoskeletal system.

Diagnosis

Most patients with HCV-GN have low complement levels, particularly C4, and a positive rheumatoid factor. Diagnosis is confirmed by kidney biopsy, which demonstrates the pattern of membranoproliferative glomerulonephritis with or without capillary cryoglobulin deposition on light microscopy.

Management

Combination therapy with peginterferon and ribavirin (when GFR is >50 mL/min/1.73 m^2) is indicated for patients with HCV-GN who have relatively well-preserved kidney function. Triple therapy using the protease inhibitors telaprevir or boceprevir in combination with peginterferon and ribavirin (when GFR is >50 mL/min/1.73 m^2) is indicated for patients with hepatitis C genotype I. Rituximab may benefit patients with associated hepatitis C–related cryoglobulinemia.

Hepatitis B Virus–Associated Kidney Disease

Epidemiology and Pathophysiology

HBV infection may be associated with MPGN and polyarteritis nodosa. MPGN is believed to result from deposition of virally associated antigen-antibody complexes in the subendothelial space and mesangium. Polyarteritis nodosa (PAN), a systemic medium- to large-vessel necrotizing vasculitis that occurs in up to 5% of patients with HBV infection, may also be induced by deposition of antigen-antibody immune complexes in blood vessel walls. PAN may specifically affect the medium-sized renal arteries (lobar, lobular, arcuate, and interlobular), while sparing capillaries and venules. The acute arterial injury is characterized by fibrinoid necrosis and infiltration of inflammatory cells with thrombosis, infarction, and inflammatory aneurysms.

Clinical Manifestations

HBV-associated nephritis typically presents with subnephrotic-range proteinuria and hematuria, usually without erythrocyte casts; hypertension and decreased kidney function are common. Complement levels may be low. The clinical course may be variable, with some patients having a rapidly progressive course and others developing a more chronic glomerulonephritis with a remitting-relapsing pattern. Patients with PAN typically present with fever, abdominal pain, arthralgia, and weight loss that develop over days to months. PAN also usually involves other organ systems, including the skin, muscles, nerves, gastrointestinal tract, and arterial ischemia.

Diagnosis

Diagnosis is based on demonstration of active HBV infection and compatible kidney biopsy results, although demonstration of specific antigen deposition in the kidney is not readily available. PAN is diagnosed by biopsy of affected organs or radiographically with conventional angiography, CT angiography, or MR angiography.

Management

Treatment of patients with HBV-associated kidney disease involves antiviral therapy for HBV infection. In patients with RPGN, brief courses of corticosteroids are sometimes used. In PAN, glucocorticoids with or without plasma exchange are often used in addition to treatment of the HBV infection. The optimal duration of antiviral therapy for HBV-associated kidney disease has not been established.

KEY POINTS

- Hepatitis C virus–associated glomerulonephritis is an immune complex disease that most commonly presents as membranoproliferative glomerulonephritis and mixed cryoglobulinemia.
- Hepatitis B virus infection may be associated with membranoproliferative glomerulonephritis and polyarteritis nodosa.

Postinfectious Glomerulonephritis

Epidemiology and Pathophysiology

Acute postinfectious glomerulonephritis (PIGN) is an immunologic disease triggered by acute, usually self-limited, infections. Many bacteria, viruses, and parasites can cause PIGN; the most common microbes are nephritogenic strains of streptococci and staphylococci. PIGN has traditionally been associated with streptococcal infections of the throat and/or skin, particularly in children; however, this etiology has been declining in developed countries with more aggressive treatment of these infections. PIGN secondary to staphylococcal infections has increased, particularly in adults with diabetes, chronic liver disease, and other immunocompromised conditions.

Clinical Manifestations

PIGN presents with acute nephritis with rapid onset of edema, hypertension, oliguria, and erythrocyte casts in the urine sediment. Less commonly, PIGN manifests as RPGN or as persistent mixed nephritic-nephrotic syndrome that may progress to advanced CKD. Symptoms typically begin to remit after several weeks, with hematuria usually resolving over the course of 3 to 6 months. Proteinuria may persist 6 months or longer.

Diagnosis

Diagnosis of PIGN is usually made clinically in patients with acute onset of nephritis ≥1 week following an acute pyogenic infection. Confirmation of recent streptococcal infection by culture or an increase in anti-streptococcal antibodies such as anti-streptolysin O or anti-DNAse B lends further support to the diagnosis. C3 levels are decreased, and C4 levels are usually normal. Kidney biopsy is reserved for patients with atypical features such as progressive kidney dysfunction or when the clinical findings fail to remit at the expected rate.

Management

Early treatment of bacterial infections with appropriate antibiotics can prevent or lessen the severity of PIGN.

Management of established PIGN is supportive, aiming to control the manifestations of the disease, particularly volume overload with diuretics, antihypertensives, and, if necessary, dialysis. Corticosteroids with or without immunosuppressive agents are occasionally used but without evidence of proven benefit.

Lupus Nephritis

Epidemiology and Pathophysiology

Kidney involvement is common in patients with systemic lupus erythematosus (SLE). The cumulative incidence of lupus nephritis is higher in Asian, black, and Hispanic patients compared with white patients.

Lupus nephritis is an immune complex–mediated disease typically occurring in patients with readily identifiable extrarenal manifestations of SLE. Involvement of the renal vasculature is also common, ranging from indolent vascular immune deposits to fibrinoid necrosis and thrombotic microangiopathy. Nephritogenic anti–double-stranded DNA antibodies play a critical role in the pathogenesis of lupus nephritis.

Lupus nephritis can be divided into six distinct histologic categories (**Table 31**). Classes I and II have a similar indolent course and are common in white patients. Classes III and IV, and class V when combined with class III or IV, are severe, leading to permanent, chronic damage; these classes are more frequent in black, Hispanic, and Asian patients. Class V, alone without class III or IV, may have an indolent prolonged course but also can have a severe course, particularly when occurring with resistant nephrotic syndrome. Class VI is the result of permanent damage secondary to severe lupus nephritis. The categorization of lupus nephritis is not a continuum of the same disease, and most patients remain with

TABLE 31. International Society of Nephrology/Renal Pathology Society 2003 Classification of Glomerulonephritis in Systemic Lupus Erythematosus

Class	Histopathology	Comments
I	Minimal mesangial glomerulonephritis	Normal in light microscopy, but immune-complex deposits with immunofluorescence microscopy and/or electro-dense deposits by electron microscopy; good prognosis
II	Mesangial proliferative glomerulonephritis	Mesangial hypercellularity on light microscopy; mesangial immune-complex deposits; good prognosis
III	Focal proliferative glomerulonephritis	Involves <50% of all glomeruli with intracapillary proliferation, segmental or global active lesions; subendothelial immune-complex deposits; bad prognosis without adequate management
IV	Diffuse proliferative glomerulonephritis	Involves ≥50% of all glomeruli with intracapillary proliferation, segmental or global active lesions; subendothelial immune-complex deposits; bad prognosis without adequate management
V	Membranous glomerulonephritis	Characterized by thickening of the basement membrane, subepithelial immune-complex deposits. It can occur in combination with class III or IV; bad prognosis without adequate management
VI	Advanced sclerosing glomerulonephritis	≥90% of glomeruli globally sclerosed without residual activity; the results of progressive unresponsive severe glomerulonephritis

Modified with permission of the American Society of Nephrology, from The classification of glomerulonephritis in systemic lupus erythematosus revisited. Weening JJ, D'Agati VD, Schwartz MM, et al. J Am Soc Nephrol. 2004;15(2):241-250. [PMID: 14747370], Copyright 2004.

CONT.

the same class; however, transformation may be observed from one class to another.

Clinical Manifestations

Kidney manifestations often develop concurrently or shortly following the onset of SLE. Risk factors for progressive kidney disease are male gender; black and Hispanic ethnicity; young age; crescents in more than 50% of the glomeruli and high chronicity index on biopsy; initial high serum creatinine levels that do not normalize with treatment; the nephrotic syndrome that does not undergo remission with treatment; relapse; hypertension; noncompliance; anemia; and the presence of antiphospholipid antibodies.

Diagnosis

Diagnosis of lupus nephritis is suggested by proteinuria (>500 mg/24 h) or cellular casts (erythrocytes or leukocytes) in the urine sediment of patients fulfilling the formal criteria for the diagnosis of SLE (see MKSAP 16 Rheumatology). Most patients with active lupus nephritis have low complement levels. Kidney biopsy is indicated to define both the histologic subtype and the degree of disease activity and chronicity essential for planning appropriate therapy.

Management

Treatment with ACE inhibitors or ARBs is indicated for proteinuria in patients with class I or II lupus nephritis. Extrarenal manifestations may require treatment with corticosteroids or quinine derivatives. Patients with the proliferative classes III, IV, and V in combination with III or IV require immunosuppressive agents to induce remission, prevent relapse, and reduce the risk of progressive CKD without substantial adverse events. Several treatment regimens for induction and maintenance have been shown to be effective.

Without adequate management, classes III, IV, or class V combined with class III or IV generally are progressive, with a probability of ESKD as high as 50% to 70% after 5 to 10 years of diagnosis. However, overall survival in SLE patients with severe lupus nephritis has improved to more than 80% over the past two decades, which is likely attributable to the rational use of effective immunosuppressive therapy as well as the availability of dialysis and kidney transplantation.

KEY POINTS

- Postinfectious glomerulonephritis presents with acute nephritis with rapid onset of edema, hypertension, oliguria, and erythrocyte casts in the urine sediment.

- In patients with lupus nephritis, kidney biopsy is indicated to define both the histologic subtype and the degree of disease activity and chronicity essential for planning appropriate therapy.

Anti–Glomerular Basement Membrane Antibody Disease

Epidemiology and Pathophysiology

Anti–glomerular basement membrane (GBM) antibody disease is mediated by an autoantibody to the GBM. Antigen-antibody complexes develop along the extent of the GBM, leading to an influx of inflammatory cells and mediators and resulting in necrotizing crescentic glomerulonephritis. The disease may be renal-limited, in which case it is called anti–GBM nephritis. When both the lung and the kidney are involved, it is referred to as Goodpasture syndrome.

Anti-GBM antibody disease is found in approximately 15% of patients who manifest RPGN. Younger patients are more likely to present with Goodpasture syndrome with both diffuse pulmonary hemorrhage and glomerulonephritis, whereas older patients may have only glomerulonephritis. Anti-GBM antibody disease is generally severe, with approximately 60% to 70% of patients rapidly progressing to ESKD within a few months after onset. At presentation, serum creatinine levels of more than 5.0 mg/dL (442 micromoles/L), oliguria, crescents in more than 80% of glomeruli (particularly of the circumferential and fibrous types), and a high degree of tubular atrophy and interstitial fibrosis observed on biopsy are risk factors associated with poor kidney survival. Patient survival is approximately 75% to 90% after 1 year of presentation. Risk factors associated with high mortality include sepsis as well as severe kidney and pulmonary manifestations.

Clinical Manifestations

Anti-GBM antibody disease usually manifests as RPGN. Nephrotic-range proteinuria is rare. Pulmonary manifestations often develop concurrently or shortly before and/or after onset of the glomerulonephritis. Hemoptysis is a common pulmonary manifestation usually seen in the context of moderate to severe respiratory failure, with patchy or diffuse alveolar infiltrates.

Diagnosis

Anti-GBM antibody disease can be rapidly confirmed by kidney biopsy, which shows diffuse necrotizing crescentic glomerulonephritis with linear staining of the GBM with fluorescein-tagged anti-IgG antibodies on immunofluorescence microscopy. The presence of circulating antibodies of the IgG type specific for the GBM may be useful in the diagnosis of this disease.

Management

The combined use of plasmapheresis using albumin replacement for 1 to 2 weeks with cyclophosphamide and corticosteroids for 3 to 6 months is more effective at inducing remission when instituted early during the disease for both kidney and lung manifestations. Although relapse is rare, azathioprine maintenance for 1 to 2 years is recommended.

Small- and Medium-Vessel Vasculitis

Epidemiology and Pathophysiology

A group of vasculitis-related conditions that may affect the kidney is termed *pauci-immune crescentic glomerulonephritis* (PICG). The three major disease entities associated with PICG are granulomatosis with polyangiitis (also known as Wegener granulomatosis), microscopic polyangiitis, and Churg-Strauss syndrome. These diseases are the most common form of crescentic glomerulonephritis and are defined pathologically by the absence of glomerular immune complexes or anti–GBM antibodies on immunofluorescence microscopy. ANCA detected in most patients is pathogenic. PICG may occur as a renal-limited process or as an element of systemic small-vessel vasculitis. Patients with granulomatous inflammation (often involving the respiratory tract) and PICG are categorized as having granulomatosis with polyangiitis; those without granulomatous inflammation and systemic vasculitis are classified as having microscopic polyangiitis; and those with concurrent asthma and eosinophilia have Churg-Strauss syndrome.

PICG associated with granulomatosis with polyangiitis or microscopic polyangiitis is an aggressive disorder, with approximately 43% of patients progressing to ESKD within 12 months after onset. Risk factors associated with poor renal survival include oliguria, crescents in more than 80% of glomeruli (particularly of the circumferential and fibrous types), and a high degree of tubular atrophy and interstitial fibrosis. Patient survival is more than 75% 2 years after presentation. Risk factors associated with high mortality include older age, severe kidney and pulmonary involvement, and the development of sepsis.

Clinical Manifestations

PICG usually presents as RPGN (glomerular hematuria, proteinuria, pyuria, hypertension, signs of hypervolemia, and a rapid decline of GFR).

Diagnosis

Kidney biopsy shows necrotizing crescentic glomerulonephritis or necrotizing vasculitis of microscopic vessels such as the small arteries, arterioles, capillaries, or venules. Proteinase 3- or myeloperoxidase-ANCA, as determined by enzyme-linked immunoassay, is positive in approximately 90% of patients with granulomatosis with polyangiitis, 70% of patients with microscopic polyangiitis, and 50% of patients with Churg-Strauss syndrome, lending further support for the diagnosis.

Management

Treatment with immunosuppressive agents is indicated to induce remission, prevent relapse, and reduce the risk of ESKD and mortality. Induction with cyclophosphamide and corticosteroids followed by long-term maintenance therapy with azathioprine and corticosteroids is highly effective in inducing remission and preventing relapse in patients with moderate disease. Patients with severe kidney injury may also benefit from plasmapheresis using albumin replacement. The use of rituximab for patients with PICG and moderate small-vessel vasculitis has shown an equivalent efficacy and safety compared with regimens of immunosuppressive agents with corticosteroids in patients with relatively well-preserved kidney function. Rituximab is generally reserved for patients who cannot tolerate or refuse therapy with cyclophosphamide.

Cryoglobulinemic Vasculitis

Epidemiology and Pathophysiology

Cryoglobulinemia is characterized by the presence of temperature-sensitive monoclonal immunoglobulins, which may precipitate and deposit in vessel walls most prominently in the skin and glomerular capillaries, eliciting an inflammatory response, systemic vasculitis, and glomerulonephritis. Cryoglobulinemic vasculitis is most often associated with hepatitis C virus infection but has also been reported in patients with HIV infection, lymphoproliferative disorders, and plasma cell dyscrasias.

Clinical Manifestations

Extrarenal manifestations of cryoglobulinemia may include cutaneous vasculitis and Raynaud phenomenon. Cryoglobulinemia-associated kidney disease findings may vary based on the degree of immune complex and thrombotic disease, but most patients have progressive disease within 3 to 5 years of diagnosis.

Diagnosis

In cryoglobulinemia, kidney biopsy demonstrates a membranoproliferative pattern on light microscopy, with curved microtubular aggregates of cryoglobulins in the subendothelial zone on electron microscopy.

Management

Cryoglobulinemia is treated by addressing the underlying cause, and plasmapheresis and immunosuppressive agents may be indicated to remove and decrease the production of cryoglobulins.

Thrombotic Microangiopathy

Epidemiology and Pathophysiology

Thrombotic microangiopathy is a systemic disease that is usually characterized by thrombocytopenia and microangiopathic hemolytic anemia, which commonly involves the kidney. The causes of thrombotic microangiopathy are listed in **Table 32**.

Thrombotic thrombocytopenic purpura (TTP) is associated with decreased activity of the von Willebrand factor–cleaving protease (now termed a disintegrin and metalloprotease with a thrombospondin type 1 motif, member 13 [*ADAMTS13*]). In addition, inhibitory antibodies can be

TABLE 32.	Causes of Thrombotic Microangiopathy

Infectious agents
  Enteric pathogens
    Escherichia coli O157:H7
    Escherichia coli O104:H4
    Campylobacter jejuni
    Yersinia, Shigella, and *Salmonella* species
  HIV infection
  Mycoplasma pneumoniae
  Legionella species
  Coxsackie A and B viruses
Systemic disorders
  Systemic lupus erythematosus
  Thrombotic thrombocytopenic purpura
  Hemolytic uremic syndrome
  The antiphospholipid syndrome
  Systemic sclerosis
  Malignant hypertension
  Neoplasms
Medications
  Clopidogrel
  Ticlopidine
  Calcineurin inhibitors
  Mitomycin C
  Vinblastine
  Cisplatin
  Bleomycin
  Cytosine arabinoside
  Gemcitabine
  Daunorubicin
  Quinine
Vaccinations
  Yellow fever
  Influenza
  Measles-mumps-rubella
Organ transplantation

consumptive thrombocytopenia, neurologic findings, and kidney failure.

In other forms of thrombotic microangiopathy, clinical manifestations may occur that are related to the underlying disorder. Scleroderma renal crisis, for example, presents in patients with signs of systemic sclerosis often accompanied by severe hypertension and progressive kidney disease.

Diagnosis

Diagnosis is often made based on clinical findings of microangiopathic hemolytic anemia and acute kidney injury. Kidney biopsy is often not possible due to severe thrombocytopenia. If the diagnosis remains uncertain, patients with acceptable coagulation parameters may be candidates for kidney biopsy.

Management

Treatment of thrombotic microangiopathy varies according to its cause. Plasma exchange therapy with immunosuppressive agents is indicated for most adults with TTP, HUS, and SLE. Plasma exchange, however, is generally not indicated for patients with thrombotic microangiopathy that develops following transplantation or cancer chemotherapy. Aggressive control of blood pressure with antihypertensive agents such as ACE inhibitors or ARBs is indicated in patients with systemic sclerosis and malignant hypertension. Treatment with anticoagulation, glucocorticoids, and plasma exchange with or without intravenous immune globulin is recommended for patients with catastrophic antiphospholipid syndrome and associated thrombotic microangiopathy. Eculizumab, a monoclonal antibody directed toward complement component C5, has been approved for treatment of atypical HUS in adults. However, it is very expensive, and its role in treatment of HUS has not yet been established. **H**

KEY POINTS

- When both the lung and the kidney are involved, anti–glomerular basement membrane antibody disease is referred to as Goodpasture syndrome.
- Pauci-immune crescentic glomerulonephritis associated with granulomatosis with polyangiitis (also known as Wegener granulomatosis) or microscopic polyangiitis is treated with immunosuppressive agents to induce remission, prevent relapse, and reduce the risk of end-stage kidney disease and mortality.
- Cryoglobulinemic vasculitis is most often associated with hepatitis C virus infection but has also been reported in patients with HIV infection, lymphoproliferative disorders, and plasma cell dyscrasias.
- Thrombotic thrombocytopenic purpura and hemolytic uremic syndrome are forms of thrombotic microangiopathy that share a similar clinical presentation of fever, hemolytic anemia, consumptive thrombocytopenia, neurologic findings, and kidney failure.

H CONT. produced, resulting in ultra-large von Willebrand factor multimers that promote thrombosis.

Hemolytic uremic syndrome (HUS) is typically caused by enteric pathogens such as the *Escherichia coli* O157:H7 strain and is characterized by the binding of Shiga-like toxin to the endothelium, causing activation of inflammatory pathways and platelets and resulting in thrombosis. Atypical HUS is defined by the absence of diarrhea or Shiga toxin–producing infection and is associated with HIV infection, streptococcal pneumonia, and a number of genetic disorders resulting from abnormalities in complement regulation.

Clinical Manifestations

TTP and HUS are forms of thrombotic microangiopathy that share a similar clinical presentation of fever, hemolytic anemia,

Genetic Disorders and Kidney Disease

Kidney Cystic Disorders

End-stage kidney disease (ESKD) is caused by kidney cystic disorders in approximately 10% of patients. **Table 33** outlines the genetic and clinical findings in various inherited kidney cystic disorders.

Autosomal Dominant Polycystic Kidney Disease

Autosomal dominant polycystic kidney disease (ADPKD) is the most common inherited kidney disorder. In the United States, ADPKD is the cause of dialysis initiation in 5% to 10% of patients. Genetic mutations identified on chromosomes 16 (*PKD1*) and 4 (*PKD2*) account for approximately 85% and 15% of cases, respectively.

Screening and Diagnosis

Screening for and diagnosis of ADPKD is best performed by kidney ultrasonographic imaging. Typical findings include large kidney size and multiple cysts throughout both kidneys.

Potential transplant donors are screened for all types of kidney disease, including ADPKD. In asymptomatic adults with a positive family history, the risks and benefits of screening for ADPKD should be discussed with experienced counseling staff.

In patients at risk over the age of 30, absence of cysts nearly always excludes disease, with a false-negative rate of 2%. In those under age 30, a normal ultrasound is not conclusive. A single cyst in at-risk patients under age 30 is specific for ADPKD.

Clinical Manifestations and Management

Clinical manifestations of ADPKD include kidney enlargement up to four times the normal size. Urinary concentrating defects and decreased ammonium production are common. Chronic kidney disease (CKD) is common and usually occurs in the third or fourth decade. ESKD occurs, on average, at age 54 in patients with *PKD1* and age 74 in those with *PKD2*.

In more than 50% of patients with ADPKD, recurrent pain localized to the flank or back occurs, which can result from kidney enlargement, bleeding, infection, and stones. Hematuria usually indicates cyst rupture and is commonly self-limited, resolving within a week. If it persists, radiographic imaging is indicated. The incidence of renal cancers is the same as in the general population.

Infections are most commonly due to infected cysts and acute pyelonephritis caused by gram-negative organisms that ascend from the urinary tract. Treatment of cyst infection requires antibiotics that are capable of penetrating the cyst such as a fluoroquinolone or trimethoprim-sulfamethoxazole.

In patients with ADPKD, kidney stones are predominantly composed of uric acid, with most others comprised of calcium oxalate. Short-term therapy includes analgesics and hydration. Hypertension is common in patients with ADPKD, and treatment with an ACE inhibitor or an angiotensin receptor blocker to a blood pressure target of less than 130/80 mm Hg is indicated. Low-grade proteinuria is typically present and is tubular in origin. Nephrotic-range proteinuria should raise suspicion for an additional glomerular process.

Cardiovascular disease is the most common cause of death in patients with ADPKD; therefore, modifiable cardiovascular risk factors should be treated aggressively. Extrarenal manifestations include diverticulosis; hernias; cysts in the pancreas, spleen, thyroid, and seminal vesicles; and cysts in the liver in approximately 40% of patients. Intracranial cerebral aneurysms (ICAs) occur in approximately 8% of patients with ADPKD; experts recommend screening for ICAs using MR angiography of the cerebral arteries in patients with a positive family history of ICAs.

Therapies under investigation include rapamycin and vasopressin receptor antagonists to slow the progression of ADPKD. Increased fluid intake should be encouraged to suppress excess plasma vasopressin secretion to possibly inhibit cyst growth.

TABLE 33. Genetically Based Kidney Cystic Disorders			
Disorder	**Inheritance**	**Gene Mutation**	**Clinical Features**
ADPKD	AD	*PKD1*; *PKD2*	Cerebral aneurysm; mitral valve prolapse; extrarenal (hepatic) cysts; kidney stones; diverticulitis
ARPKD	AR	*PKHD1*	Presents in infancy; hypertension; hepatic fibrosis
Tuberous Sclerosis	AD	*TSC1*; *TSC2*	Angiofibromas; angiolipomas; hamartomas
MCKD I; MCKD II	AD	Unknown; uromodulin abnormalities	Hyperuricemia and gout in MCKD II; progress variably to ESKD between ages 20 and 70 years

AD = autosomal dominant; ADPKD = autosomal dominant polycystic kidney disease; AR = autosomal recessive; ARPKD = autosomal recessive polycystic kidney disease; ESKD = end-stage kidney disease; MCKD = medullary cystic kidney disease.

- Kidney manifestations of autosomal dominant poly-cystic kidney disease include kidney enlargement, back or flank pain, hematuria, infections, kidney stones, hypertension, and low-grade proteinuria.

- Treatment of hypertension with an ACE inhibitor or angiotensin receptor blocker to a blood pressure target of less than 130/80 mm Hg is indicated for patients with autosomal dominant polycystic kidney disease.

- Extrarenal manifestations of autosomal dominant polycystic kidney disease include diverticulosis; hernias; cysts in the liver, pancreas, spleen, thyroid, and seminal vesicles; and intracranial cerebral aneurysms.

Autosomal Recessive Polycystic Kidney Disease

Autosomal recessive polycystic kidney disease (ARPKD) is a rare inherited disorder caused by mutations in the *PKHD1* gene, which encodes for fibrocystin on chromosome 6. More severe disease presents earlier in life; massive kidney enlargement due to cystic dilation of the renal tubules may be seen at birth. Progressive kidney failure is common, with hepatic fibrosis and portal hypertension being more pronounced in patients presenting after infancy. Most patients present with hypertension and growth retardation.

There are no specific treatments to delay the progression of ARPKD. Dialysis and kidney or kidney-liver transplantation are appropriate therapies. Parents of children with ARPKD should be counseled about the 1 in 4 chance of disease in future children.

Tuberous Sclerosis Complex

Clinical Manifestations

Tuberous sclerosis complex (TSC) is an autosomal dominant disorder resulting from mutations in the *TSC1* or *TSC2* gene. This neurocutaneous disorder involves many organ systems and is characterized by benign hamartomas of the kidney, brain, skin, or other organs.

The most common kidney manifestations are kidney cysts and angiomyolipomas. Angiomyolipomas occur in 75% of patients and are detected by CT or MRI. Complications include pain and hemorrhage, which can be benign or, rarely, can result in kidney failure or death. Renal cell carcinoma is much less common, occurring in 1% to 2% of adults with the disorder. Ultrasonographic surveillance is recommended to monitor lesion growth and malignant transformation.

Diagnosis

Diagnostic criteria require either the presence of at least two major features or one major feature and two minor features. Major criteria include facial angiofibromas, three or more hypomelanotic macules, kidney angiomyolipomas, and retinal hamartomas. Minor criteria include nonrenal hamartomas, multiple kidney cysts, and various dental abnormalities such as pits on dental enamel and gingival fibromas.

Management

Everolimus has shown promise in reducing kidney angiomyolipomas but is not yet an established therapy. Other interventions include arterial embolization of angiomyolipomas, which can decrease the risk of bleeding, pain, and concern for malignancy.

Medullary Cystic Kidney Disease

The medullary cystic kidney diseases (MCKD I and MCKD II) are rare autosomal dominant disorders that often appear during the teenage years. The causative mutation is unknown, but most cases result from mutations in the gene for uromodulin, also called Tamm-Horsfall mucoprotein.

Types I and II have similar clinical manifestations, including impaired kidney function, mild urinary concentrating defects, minimal proteinuria, and a benign urine sediment. On ultrasonographic imaging, medullary cysts can be seen but are not present in most cases. Diagnosis is often suspected based on clinical findings and family history and can be confirmed by genetic testing.

Optimal treatment strategies are not clear, aside from the general management of CKD. Allopurinol should be considered for patients with hyperuricemia and gout.

- Hepatic fibrosis and portal hypertension are more pronounced in patients who present with autosomal recessive polycystic kidney disease after infancy.

- The most common kidney manifestations of tuberous sclerosis complex are angiomyolipomas and kidney cysts.

Noncystic Disorders

Alport Syndrome

Alport syndrome, also termed hereditary nephritis, is an inherited glomerular disease arising from mutations in genes that code for $\alpha 3$, $\alpha 4$, or $\alpha 5$ chain of type IV collagen. This disease is X-linked in 80% of patients, autosomal recessive in 15%, and autosomal dominant in 5%. Alport syndrome most commonly occurs in men, and women usually have a milder form of disease.

Alport syndrome is characterized by sensorineural hearing loss, ocular abnormalities, microscopic hematuria, and a family history of kidney disease and deafness. These signs and symptoms are due to disruption of the basement membrane in the affected organ. Proteinuria, hypertension, and CKD usually develop over time. ESKD commonly occurs between the late teenage years and the fourth decade of life. The autosomal dominant form may manifest somewhat later.

Diagnosis is confirmed by either skin or kidney biopsy, which reveals the absence of type IV collagen. Expression of type IV collagen can be variable in women owing to lyonization of the X chromosome.

There are no specific therapies for Alport syndrome. Kidney transplantation is the optimal treatment for ESKD, and patients have no risk for disease recurrence. However, approximately 5% of patients develop anti–glomerular basement membrane antibody disease after transplantation.

Thin Glomerular Basement Membrane Disease

Thin glomerular basement membrane disease, also known as benign familial hematuria, is a set of heterogeneous conditions that result in hematuria. Some are heterozygous mutations that encode for α3 and α4 chains of type IV collagen. Up to 5% of the population may be affected. This disease is characterized by microscopic or macroscopic hematuria, which often initially occurs in childhood, as well as a family history suggestive of the condition. Long-term prognosis is excellent, with rare progression to CKD. Blood pressure control and drugs to decrease proteinuria are reasonable goals in this population.

Fabry Disease

Fabry disease is a rare X-linked disorder of α-galactosidase A deficiency, an error of the glycosphingolipid pathway. Clinical manifestations arise from the progressive deposit of globotriaosylceramide (Gb3) in lysosomes.

This disease should be considered in young men with urinary concentrating defects, proteinuria, or CKD. Other manifestations include premature coronary artery disease, severe neuropathic pain, telangiectasias, and angiokeratomas.

Screening for Fabry disease is recommended for family members of affected patients. Enzyme replacement therapy with recombinant human α-galactosidase A is effective.

KEY POINTS

- Alport syndrome is characterized by sensorineural hearing loss, ocular abnormalities, microscopic hematuria, and a family history of kidney disease and deafness.

- Thin glomerular basement membrane disease is characterized by microscopic or macroscopic hematuria, which often initially occurs in childhood, as well as a family history suggestive of the condition.

- Clinical manifestations of Fabry disease include urinary concentrating defects, proteinuria, chronic kidney disease, premature coronary artery disease, severe neuropathic pain, telangiectasias, and angiokeratomas.

Acute Kidney Injury

Pathophysiology and Epidemiology

Acute kidney injury (AKI) indicates recent-onset damage to the kidneys. As opposed to chronic kidney disease (CKD), which by definition is present for 3 months, AKI occurs within hours to weeks. Kidney injury refers to the impaired ability of the kidneys to perform their normal physiologic functions: maintaining electrolyte and volume balance and homeostasis. Patients with AKI may recover some or all of the lost kidney function.

Multiple pathophysiologic mechanisms can lead to AKI, which can be grouped into three categories: prerenal, intrinsic, or postrenal. The likelihood of the cause of injury depends on the clinical setting. Prerenal causes occur more commonly in outpatient settings, and intrinsic causes are more common in the hospital. Prerenal kidney injury and intrinsic kidney injury due to ischemia are part of a spectrum, with ischemic intrinsic kidney injury a possible outcome in severe prerenal kidney injury. The incidence of AKI is estimated at 1% of patients who present to the hospital. Among hospitalized patients, the incidence can range from 7% to up to 50% of patients in the intensive care unit. **H**

KEY POINTS

- Acute kidney injury indicates recent-onset damage to the kidneys and occurs within hours to weeks.

- The three categories of acute kidney injury are prerenal, intrinsic, and postrenal; the likelihood of the cause of injury depends on the clinical setting.

Definition and Classification

The Acute Dialysis Quality Initiative initially developed the RIFLE criteria to help clarify the definition of AKI. Subsequently, the Acute Kidney Injury Network (AKIN) modified and simplified these criteria (**Table 34**). AKI can be defined by either an increase in serum creatinine or a decline in urine output, with different stages defined by the amount of elevation in serum creatinine or decrease in urine output.

Clinical Manifestations and Diagnosis

The underlying cause of AKI (such as hypovolemia or vasculitis) often determines the symptoms. Excluding the symptoms attributable to the underlying diagnosis, the symptoms from AKI are variable and dependent on the severity of the kidney insult. Many patients have AKI without any symptoms; in these cases, the episode of AKI is recognized only by laboratory test results. If the AKI is severe, symptoms of uremia (malaise, anorexia, nausea, vomiting) can occur. There may be decreased urine output, which may go unnoticed by

TABLE 34. Acute Kidney Injury Network Criteria for the Classification of Acute Kidney Injury

Stage	Serum Creatinine Criteria	Urine Output Criteria
1	Cr ↑ by 1.5-2× or Cr ↑ by 0.3 mg/dL (26.5 µmol/L) or more	<0.5 mL/kg/h for 6 h
2	Cr ↑ by 2-3×	<0.5 mL/kg/h for 12 h
3	Cr ↑ by more than 3× or Cr increase of 0.5 mg/dL, with baseline Cr ≥4 mg/dL (354 µmol/L)	<0.3 mL/kg/h for 24 h (or anuria for 12 h)

Cr = serum creatinine.

Data from Bellomo R, Ronco C, Kellum JA, Mehta RL, Palevsky P; Acute Dialysis Quality Initiative Workgroup: Acute renal failure-definition, outcome measures, animal models, fluid therapy and information technology needs: the Second International Consensus Conference of the Acute Dialysis Quality Initiative (ADQI) Group. Crit Care. 2004;8(4):R204-R212. [PMID:15312219]

the patient. Symptoms from volume overload (edema, dyspnea) and electrolyte abnormalities (muscle weakness, palpitations/arrhythmias) may also occur.

Diagnosis of AKI relies on an accurate history and physical examination as well as laboratory tests, including urine studies and imaging. A complete history includes both a full review of systems to evaluate for systemic diseases that can cause AKI and a detailed review of recent historical events that could cause kidney damage or compromise blood flow to the kidneys. The presence of diseases that damage the kidneys over time (diabetes mellitus, hypertension, vascular disease) helps identify patients at higher risk for kidney damage. A history of AKI is associated with future development of CKD as well as a predisposition to future AKI.

The diagnostic evaluation for AKI includes a review of recent serum creatinine levels, repeat kidney function studies, urine electrolytes and osmolality, and a urinalysis. **Figure 17** shows the typical urine microscopy and urine chemistry findings for the classes of AKI.

When testing for measures of kidney function, special mention should be made concerning certain medications. Trimethoprim-sulfamethoxazole or histamine H_2 receptor blockers can cause a rise in serum creatinine that may be interpreted as AKI. This rise is due to decreased tubular secretion of creatinine and is reversible when the medications are discontinued.

The urine sodium, fractional excretion of sodium (FE_{Na}), and urine osmolality help differentiate between prerenal and intrinsic causes of AKI (see Figure 17), particularly oliguric AKI, with oliguria defined as urine output less than 500 mL/d. Prerenal causes of AKI are associated with kidney retention of sodium, a low FE_{Na}, and elevated urine osmolality. Recent diuretic use can alter the urine sodium, making urine sodium and FE_{Na} less reliable in assessing for a prerenal cause; the fractional excretion of other substances (urea, uric acid) may be more accurate in this setting. **Table 35** shows how to calculate a fractional excretion and lists which tests are useful in the presence of diuretics. Multiple calculators for fractional excretion are available online.

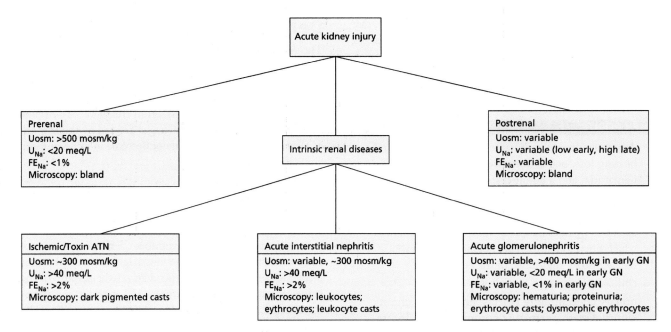

FIGURE 17. Urine findings associated with acute kidney injury. ATN = acute tubular necrosis; FE_{Na} = fractional excretion of sodium; GN = glomerulonephritis; U_{Na} = urine sodium; Uosm = urine osmolality.

TABLE 35. Fractional Excretion of Various Solutes in Oliguric Acute Kidney Injury[a]

Fractional Excretion of	Level Suggesting Prerenal Acute Kidney Injury	Altered by Diuretics
Sodium	<1%	Yes
Urea	<35%	No
Uric acid	<10%	No

[a]Calculation of fractional excretion of substance X:

(Urine Concentration of X/Plasma Concentration of X) ÷ (Urine Concentration of Creatinine/Plasma Concentration of Creatinine)

Preexisting kidney disease may also alter urine sodium handling and decrease the effectiveness of fractional excretion calculations at differentiating prerenal azotemia from other intrinsic AKI causes.

Although glomerulonephritis can cause a low urine sodium and a low FE_{Na}, glomerulonephritis is better differentiated from prerenal causes of kidney injury by blood, protein, and/or casts found in the urine. Urinalysis findings of blood, protein, dysmorphic erythrocytes, or erythrocyte casts suggest a glomerular insult. The urine sediment in prerenal kidney injury and obstructive kidney injury is often bland. Pigmented granular casts suggest acute tubular necrosis or rhabdomyolysis.

In patients with AKI, it is important to use imaging to look for obstructive causes. Ultrasonography is the preferred test because it does not involve radiation or contrast. A noncontrast CT can also evaluate for obstruction but exposes the patient to radiation. The use of contrast agents in patients with AKI is discussed in the Contrast-Induced Nephropathy section. **H**

KEY POINTS

- Patients with suspected acute kidney injury (AKI) should undergo a complete history to evaluate for systemic diseases as well as a detailed review of recent historical events that could cause AKI.

- Urine studies and urinalysis findings can help differentiate between prerenal and intrinsic causes of acute kidney injury.

- In patients with acute kidney injury, ultrasonography is the preferred test to look for obstructive causes because it does not involve radiation or contrast.

Causes

Prerenal Azotemia

Prerenal azotemia results from hypovolemia and low blood flow to the kidney. In the classic setting of hypovolemia, the kidneys sense both the lower blood pressure in the afferent arteriole and the lower solute and urine flow rate through the juxtaglomerular apparatus; as a result, activation of the renin-angiotensin-aldosterone system leads to increased tubular

reabsorption of sodium. In prerenal azotemia, the tubules are still functional; therefore, the urine sodium is low, which reflects the reabsorption of sodium from the tubular urine. Increased water reabsorption under the influence of increased antidiuretic hormone results in concentrated urine and decreased urine output. The typical urine studies for prerenal azotemia are listed in Figure 17.

Prerenal azotemia is often associated with a high blood urea nitrogen (BUN)–creatinine ratio. In the tubules, urea is reabsorbed via urea transporters, whereas creatinine is secreted. In patients with prerenal azotemia, both BUN and creatinine can increase, but BUN often increases disproportionately more than creatinine, as the slow flow through the tubules allows more time for BUN to be reabsorbed (decreasing BUN clearance and increasing the BUN) and creatinine to be secreted (increasing creatinine clearance, particularly when compared with BUN clearance). Antidiuretic hormone also increases the expression of urea transporters, thereby further enhancing urea reabsorption in states of hypovolemia.

Prerenal azotemia is the most common cause of AKI in the outpatient setting. The kidney functions properly in patients with prerenal azotemia, and appropriate treatment with hydration should result in a quick recovery. The cause is usually evident from the history, which may reveal poor oral intake, increased volume losses (such as from diarrhea, vomiting, or diuretics), or both poor intake and increased losses. Symptoms such as dizziness and lightheadedness may accompany the hypovolemia. The physical examination may be notable for signs of volume depletion with decreased skin turgor, a low blood pressure, tachycardia, and orthostasis; however, these findings are not sensitive, and laboratory tests are indicated to confirm the diagnosis.

Treatment with 0.9% saline should reverse the prerenal state in patients with true volume depletion. Patients can also have prerenal physiology (a sodium avid kidney) in the setting of a decreased effective arterial blood volume from decompensated heart failure, cirrhosis, or the nephrotic syndrome. In these conditions, the kidney retains salt and water even though the patient has an increased total body volume and edema. For this type of prerenal azotemia, correction of the underlying disease is indicated (see Hepatorenal Syndrome and Cardiorenal Syndrome). **H**

KEY POINTS

- Prerenal azotemia is the most common cause of acute kidney injury in the outpatient setting.

- The kidney functions properly in patients with prerenal azotemia, and appropriate treatment with hydration should result in a quick recovery.

Intrinsic Kidney Diseases
Acute Tubular Necrosis

Acute tubular necrosis (ATN) is the most common cause of intrinsic kidney disease causing AKI. ATN usually occurs after an ischemic event or exposure to nephrotoxic agents. Prerenal azotemia, if severe and prolonged, can cause ischemic ATN. Urine studies typically reveal high urine sodium, high FE_{Na}, and isosthenuria (defined as a urine osmolality near 300 mosm/kg H_2O, which is similar to the plasma osmolality) (see Figure 17). Urinalysis classically shows dark, pigmented, granular (muddy brown) casts (**Figure 18**), renal tubular epithelial cells, or epithelial cell casts that result from tubular damage. Otherwise, the urine is often bland, with minimal or no blood or protein.

The diagnostic approach to ATN begins with identifying when the serum creatinine level began to increase or when the urine output began to decrease. Then, the clinical course during the days preceding the kidney injury is evaluated for kidney insults. Events that might compromise kidney perfusion, such as a decrease in blood pressure, an arrhythmia, or hypoxia, should be sought. If the patient underwent surgery or a procedure, the operative note and anesthesia record may reveal a hemodynamic kidney insult not evident in other parts of the chart. A history or chart review for administration of nephrotoxic agents is also necessary (**Table 36**). Even if an ischemic or toxic insult is not found, some kidney insults may be multifactorial in nature and the cause not readily apparent.

Certain patients are at risk for ATN due to impaired autoregulation of kidney blood flow that makes the kidney more susceptible to injury. **Table 37** lists clinical features associated with impaired autoregulation. In these patients, even modest decrements in blood pressure may result in ischemic kidney injury because of impaired autoregulation. A patient accustomed to higher blood pressures may have an autoregulatory range higher than normal. Such a patient may develop ischemic ATN with a drop in blood pressure even though the blood pressure is considered to be within a normal range. Low kidney blood flow may also increase susceptibility to nephrotoxic agents.

Standard treatment of ATN involves maintaining an adequate perfusion pressure, discontinuing potential nephrotoxic agents, and adjusting the dose of renally excreted medications

TABLE 36. Common Agents that Cause Direct Tubular Toxicity
Antibiotics
Aminoglycosides
Amikacin
Gentamicin
Kanamycin
Streptomycin
Tobramycin
Amphotericin B
Pentamidine
Foscarnet
Tenofovir
Intravenous dye
NSAIDs
Chemotherapy
Cisplatin
Carboplatin
Ifosfamide
Herbal medications/exposures (toxicity may be tubular damage from chronic interstitial disease)
Aristolochia/aristolochic acid
Germanium
Heavy metals/lead

for the current level of kidney function. Data on the use of ACE inhibitors (and angiotensin receptor blockers) in patients with ATN are limited; these agents generally are discontinued because they may compromise perfusion through their effects on renal blood flow.

Recovery from ATN is variable and depends on the severity of the initial insult. Mild ATN usually resolves quickly if the inciting insult is corrected. Severe ATN can lead to dialysis-dependent kidney failure; patients with this condition may regain kidney function after weeks to months, although the longer the time on dialysis the less likely recovery becomes. If a patient is oliguric, one of the first signs of kidney recovery is a spontaneous increase in urine output. In general, nonoliguric kidney injury has a better prognosis than oliguric kidney injury. Although diuretics may be useful to manage volume status in patients with oliguric kidney failure, a response to diuretics does not mean patients have a greater likelihood of kidney recovery than oliguric patients who do not respond to diuresis; thus, diuretics should not be used in AKI except to treat volume overload. Low-dose dopamine has not been shown to be beneficial in expediting renal recovery from ATN.

Contrast-Induced Nephropathy

Iodinated contrast can induce vasospasm and cause ischemic injury or direct damage to the kidneys. Contrast-induced nephropathy (CIN) is defined as either an increase in serum

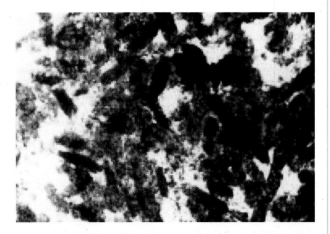

FIGURE 18. Muddy brown casts seen on urine microscopy in a patient with acute tubular necrosis.

TABLE 37. Clinical Features Associated with Impaired Renal Autoregulation and Increasing Susceptibility to Ischemic Acute Tubular Necrosis

Clinical History
Older age (>70 years old)
History of vascular disease/atherosclerosis/renal artery stenosis
Long-standing hypertension
Chronic kidney disease/nephrosis
Diabetes mellitus
Liver disease/hepatorenal syndrome
Heart failure
Medications
Agents that affect the renin-angiotensin system
ACE inhibitors
Angiotensin receptor blockers
Renin inhibitors
Agents that affect prostaglandin synthesis
NSAIDs
Cyclooxygenase-2 inhibitors

Data from Abuelo JG. Normotensive ischemic acute renal failure. N Engl J Med. 2007;357(8):797-805. [PMID: 17715412]

creatinine of 0.5 mg/dL (44.2 micromoles/L) or an increase in serum creatinine of 25% from baseline at 48 hours after contrast administration.

Risk factors for severe kidney damage from contrast are summarized in **Table 38**. Physicians should assess the need for the contrast study in terms of the patient's risk. Although CIN may occur in persons with normal baseline kidney function, the risk of contrast-associated injury is substantially higher in patients with preexisting acute or chronic kidney disease, and contrast studies in these patients should be approached with caution. A calculator that estimates a patient's risk for developing CIN is available at www.zunis.org/Contrast-Induced %20Nephropathy%20Calculator2.htm. This calculator was

TABLE 38. Predictors of Severe Contrast-Induced Nephropathy[a]

Initial serum creatinine
Chronic heart failure
Diabetes mellitus
Urgent/emergent procedure
Intra-aortic balloon pump (preprocedure)
Age ≥80 years

[a]The predictors are in order of relative weight. Severe contrast nephropathy in this study was defined as ≥50% increase in serum creatinine, ≥2 mg/dL (177 μmol/L) rise in serum creatinine, or the requirement of dialysis postprocedure.

Reprinted from American Heart Journal. 155(2). Brown JR, DeVries JT, Piper WD, et al; Northern New England Cardiovascular Disease Study Group. Serious renal dysfunction after percutaneous coronary interventions can be predicted. 260-266. 2008, [PMID: 18215595] with permission from Elsevier.

validated in patients undergoing cardiac catheterization and may overestimate risk in other circumstances. Although it provides a limited range of risk categories, it can provide a starting point to discuss risk of CIN with patients. If the contrast study is not necessary or if useful information can be obtained without contrast exposure (for example, with non-contrast studies or ultrasonography), avoiding contrast is the safest option in all patients.

If contrast administration is unavoidable, minimizing the risk of contrast is the priority. Several guidelines have been published, and the main points are listed in **Table 39**. Optimizing hemodynamics is recommended, and the intravenous fluids of choice are normal saline or isotonic sodium bicarbonate. There is no clear evidence supporting one of these fluid choices over the other. Finally, the use of a low or iso-osmolar iodinated contrast is recommended. High osmolar contrast has an osmolality of 2000 mosm/kg H_2O, and there is evidence that it is the most nephrotoxic. Low osmolar (osmolality of 600-800 mosm/kg H_2O) and iso-osmolar (osmolality of approximately 300 mosm/kg H_2O) contrast are thought to be safer than high osmolar contrast. There is no clear difference in CIN risk between low and iso-osmolar agents, and a lack of consensus suggests a small real difference between the two options. *N*-acetylcysteine has been shown in some studies to prevent a rise in serum creatinine after contrast administration. Because it has minimal toxicity, *N*-acetylcysteine is used as prophylaxis to prevent CIN, although efficacy of *N*-acetylcysteine for CIN prevention is not proved.

TABLE 39. Approach to the Prevention of Contrast-Induced Nephropathy

Use a noncontrast study if possible:
  Noncontrast CT or MRI
  Ultrasonography

If contrast needed, minimize the dye volume:
  Biplanar imaging if angiography
  Avoid left ventriculography with cardiac catheterization
  Use a low or iso-osmolar iodinated contrast agent

Hydration with normal saline or isotonic fluid with sodium bicarbonate in patients without volume overload (particularly if GFR <60 mL/min/1.73 m²):
  Hold NSAIDs and metformin
  Hold diuretics in patients without volume overload

Oral *N*-acetylcysteine may be beneficial and is not harmful

GFR = glomerular filtration rate.

CONT.

Forty-eight hours after contrast administration, the serum creatinine level should be measured to determine if any kidney damage has occurred. An increase in serum creatinine should be followed with repeat measurements to determine the severity of the damage. Fortunately, the increase in serum creatinine may only be a transient phenomenon. A persistently increasing creatinine should prompt evaluation for other possible contributors to the kidney damage as well as close follow-up for any complications of impaired kidney function or the possible need for kidney replacement therapy.

In patients with preexisting kidney failure, MRI is frequently used instead of contrast imaging. However, the MRI contrast agent gadolinium has been associated with nephrogenic systemic fibrosis, an irreversible condition seen primarily in patients with an estimated glomerular filtration rate (GFR) of less than 30 mL/min/1.73 m². Therefore, except under very specific clinical situations, MRI with gadolinium contrast should be avoided in patients with abnormal kidney function (see Chronic Kidney Disease, Management, Special Considerations, Imaging).

Pigment Nephropathy

Pigment nephropathy refers to kidney damage from either hemoglobin or myoglobin present in excessive concentrations in the renal tubules. Both are thought to damage the kidney through multiple mechanisms: they may induce ischemia, block tubules, and cause direct toxic damage to the tubules. The patient history is usually remarkable for a precipitating cause for the hemolysis in hemoglobin-induced pigment nephropathy or muscle damage in rhabdomyolysis.

Hemolysis, the destruction of erythrocytes, causes release of excessive amounts of hemoglobin along with other erythrocyte contents into the circulation. When the level of erythrocyte destruction overwhelms normal clearance mechanisms, adequate hemoglobin may be delivered to the renal tubule to cause damage. Rhabdomyolysis is muscle damage leading to release of intracellular muscle contents into the circulation, including the heme pigment myoglobin, which when present in adequate amounts can cause kidney damage.

Laboratory values in hemolysis-induced kidney disease are consistent with massive hemolysis (anemia, increased lactate dehydrogenase, decreased haptoglobin) and kidney failure (increased creatinine). In rhabdomyolysis, laboratory test results are notable for an increased creatine kinase and serum and/or urine markers of increased myoglobin consistent with muscle damage, as well as increased creatinine due to kidney damage. Because of increased release of creatine kinase from damaged muscle, the creatine kinase increase can be dramatic in rhabdomyolysis.

Evaluation of the urine can be particularly helpful in identifying pigment nephropathy. The urine dipstick tests positive for blood in the urine in the presence of either hemoglobin or myoglobin but does not differentiate between hemoglobin and myoglobin. The urine sediment, however, may not reveal blood cells. The discrepancy between the urine dipstick identifying blood and the urine microscopy showing no erythrocytes suggests hemoglobin- or myoglobin-induced kidney injury. The classic urine sediment in pigment nephropathy shows dark (pigmented) granular casts (see Figure 18). Complications of rhabdomyolysis include hypocalcemia, hyperphosphatemia, hyperuricemia, metabolic acidosis, acute muscle compartment syndrome, and limb ischemia.

Treatment of pigment nephropathy consists of reversing the underlying cause (hemolysis or rhabdomyolysis) and intravenous fluids to dilute and possibly promote excretion of the pigment through the kidneys. The goal urine output is 200 to 300 mL/h. Whether bicarbonate-containing fluid is better than other fluid options (normal saline) is not established. Administration of intravenous fluid as soon after the injury as possible is important. Electrolytes must be monitored because alkalosis and hypocalcemia or acidosis can develop, depending on the type of fluid given and the degree of tubular injury. Treatment is then supportive, monitoring for compartment syndrome, further kidney damage, and hyperkalemia while avoiding nephrotoxins and assessing for complications of kidney failure and potential dialysis needs. Patients with suspected compartment syndrome require urgent surgical consultation to evaluate for possible fasciotomy. There is no evidence to support using dialysis to help remove hemoglobin or myoglobin; the decision to initiate dialysis is based on clinical and metabolic needs only.

Acute Interstitial Nephritis

Although some systemic diseases such as multiple myeloma or autoimmune diseases may cause acute interstitial nephritis (AIN), AIN typically is caused by a hypersensitivity reaction to a medication (**Table 40**). The clinical presentation of AIN is variable and in part dependent on the underlying medication. The classic presentation of AIN is fever, rash, and

TABLE 40. Causes of Acute Interstitial Nephritis
Medications
Antibiotics
β-Lactams
Fluoroquinolones
Sulfonamides
Antivirals
Indinavir
Abacavir
Analgesics
NSAIDs
Cyclooxygenase-2 inhibitors
Gastrointestinal
Proton pump inhibitors
5-Aminosalicylates
Herbal medications
Chinese herb nephropathy
Heavy metals (germanium; lead)
Miscellaneous
Allopurinol
Phenytoin
Autoimmune Disorders
Systemic lupus erythematosus
Sarcoidosis
Tubulointerstitial nephritis and uveitis (TINU syndrome)
Systemic Diseases
Sarcoidosis
HIV infection
Multiple myeloma
Leukemia
Lymphoma

eosinophilia in a patient with an elevated serum creatinine level, but this presentation is found in only 10% of patients.

Diagnosis is most often made by a history of exposure to a drug with a high likelihood of causing AIN. AIN usually occurs after 7 to 10 days of drug exposure; however, prior exposure to a drug may result in a more sudden onset. The urine may show leukocytes and leukocyte casts with negative urine cultures (sterile pyuria) and erythrocytes.

The mainstay of AIN treatment is discontinuation of the offending agent. The symptoms usually resolve, and the serum creatinine level decreases soon after stopping the medication. Recovery may sometimes be prolonged. Evidence for using corticosteroids in patients with AIN is limited. Corticosteroids are often considered in patients with severe or prolonged AIN, particularly when kidney biopsy results confirm a significant component of acute inflammation. If used, corticosteroids seem to be more effective the earlier they are initiated.

Thrombotic Microangiopathy

Thrombotic thrombocytopenic purpura (TTP) and hemolytic uremic syndrome (HUS) are two forms of thrombotic microangiopathy that can cause AKI. In TTP and HUS, obstruction of small blood vessels due to endothelial activation, intimal expansion, and thrombi causes kidney injury, which can range from chronic and smoldering to acute and oliguric. The urine sediment may be bland or show blood and protein and therefore mimic glomerulonephritis. Treatment is dictated by the underlying etiology and may range from supportive care for most cases of Shiga-like toxin–associated (typical) HUS to plasma exchange for idiopathic TTP. For further discussion of thrombotic microangiopathy, see the Glomerular Diseases chapter.

Other Syndromes of Acute Kidney Injury

Vancomycin may be associated with nephrotoxicity, possibly mediated through extra osmoles introduced during the manufacturing process, causing osmotic nephropathy. A similar mechanism of kidney injury has been reported with certain IgG preparations. The evidence for vancomycin-induced AKI is limited, but care should be taken to dose this medication appropriately for a patient's body weight and GFR.

Phosphate nephropathy has been described in patients using oral phosphorus bowel preparations. Phosphate deposition in the renal tubules can occur, particularly in patients with CKD or who are dehydrated, resulting in kidney injury that can be permanent and lead to a need for dialysis. Oral phosphorus bowel preparations should not be given to patients with CKD and probably are best avoided. High-dose vitamin C, orlistat, carambola juice (star fruit), and gastric bypass surgery can cause acute oxalate nephropathy.

KEY POINTS

- Acute tubular necrosis usually occurs after an ischemic event or exposure to nephrotoxic agents and is commonly associated with muddy brown casts on urinalysis and a fractional excretion of sodium greater than 2%.

- Contrast-induced nephropathy is defined as either an increase in serum creatinine of 0.5 mg/dL (44.2 micromoles/L) or an increase in serum creatinine of 25% from baseline at 48 hours after contrast administration.

- Interventions to decrease the incidence and severity of contrast-induced nephropathy include minimizing the amount of iodinated contrast used, optimizing hemodynamics, and using a low or iso-osmolar iodinated contrast.

- Acute interstitial nephritis typically is caused by a hypersensitivity reaction to a medication; the clinical presentation is variable and in part dependent on the underlying medication.

Postrenal Disease

Urinary obstruction is an important reversible cause of AKI. AKI results from obstruction that affects both kidneys (or obstruction of a single kidney or a unilaterally functioning kidney). Because relief of obstruction can reverse kidney injury and prevent chronic damage, timely diagnosis of urinary obstruction is essential. Urinary obstruction can be asymptomatic and can be associated with no noted change in urine output. Bladder outlet obstruction should be excluded by bladder ultrasonography or catheterization. Without evidence of outlet obstruction, kidney imaging, typically ultrasonography, should be performed in all patients with AKI. Findings in the medical history, such as pelvic tumors or irradiation, congenital urinary abnormalities, kidney stones, genitourinary infections, procedures or surgeries, or prostatic enlargement, should increase suspicion for obstruction. In obstruction, the urinalysis is bland. Urine electrolytes are variable; in early obstruction, the urine sodium and FE_{Na} may be low, but in late obstruction, the urine sodium and FE_{Na} may be high, indicative of tubular damage. Because of impaired kidney potassium, acid, and water excretion, hyperkalemic metabolic acidosis and hyponatremia can be present. Kidney ultrasonography or noncontrast CT can be used to identify obstruction, although early obstruction and obstruction with concomitant dehydration or retroperitoneal fibrosis may be missed. Diuretic radionuclide kidney clearance scanning is often used to more definitively evaluate for obstruction if other imaging is equivocal. Treatment by removing or bypassing the obstruction is most effective if implemented early. **H**

> **KEY POINT**
>
> - Without evidence of outlet obstruction, kidney imaging, typically ultrasonography, should be performed in all patients with acute kidney injury.

Acute Kidney Injury in Specific Clinical Settings

Critical Care

Increased intra-abdominal pressure (IAP) may cause AKI. Although the pathophysiology is not completely elucidated, contributing deleterious processes likely include a depressed cardiac output, decreased renal blood flow (both arterial and venous), and increased pressure on the ureter.

Intra-abdominal hypertension is defined as an IAP ≥12 mm Hg. IAP can be estimated by measuring the bladder pressure through a bladder catheter. Abdominal compartment syndrome (ACS) is new organ dysfunction with an IAP greater than 20 mm Hg. ACS should be suspected in patients with oliguria or increasing serum creatinine level who have had abdominal surgery, who have received massive fluid resuscitation, who have a tense abdomen, or who have liver disease with ascites. Diagnosis of ACS is made by measuring bladder pressures to confirm the high IAP in the setting of

organ dysfunction. Although medical treatment (diuresis, dialysis, management of ascites) can be tried, surgical decompression of the abdomen is often necessary to definitively treat ACS. **H**

> **KEY POINTS**
>
> - Abdominal compartment syndrome is defined by new organ dysfunction in the setting of an intra-abdominal pressure greater than 20 mm Hg.
> - Surgical decompression of the abdomen is often necessary to definitively treat abdominal compartment syndrome.

Cardiovascular Disease

Cardiorenal Syndrome

There is an intricate physiologic interaction between the heart and the kidneys. Cardiorenal syndrome occurs when one organ system dysfunction affects another. Cardiorenal syndrome is divided into five types: acute heart failure compromising kidney function (AKI), chronic heart failure causing CKD, AKI compromising heart function acutely, CKD contributing to chronic heart disease, and concomitant cardiac and kidney dysfunction caused by another process (such as sepsis).

Treatment of any type of cardiorenal syndrome focuses on reversing (if possible) any specific underlying cause or improving the compromised organ function, usually through improving hemodynamic parameters. The difficulty in treating cardiorenal syndrome is the delicate balance between fluid removal and hemodynamics, specifically kidney perfusion. Diuretics may be used, and if not successful, ultrafiltration or dialysis may be indicated. Diuretic boluses seem to be as effective as diuretic drips for diuresis as long as adequate doses are used. Isolated ultrafiltration has shown greater fluid removal compared with diuretics in some studies. However, the benefit of this therapy over adequately dosed diuretics is unproved, especially when the risk of the procedure (central line placement) and increased hypotension are considered.

Atheroembolic Disease

Atherosclerotic plaque dislodgement from arterial walls during invasive procedures or spontaneously can cause cholesterol embolization and result in systemic findings, including kidney injury. Atheroembolic disease usually occurs in patients with vascular disease risk factors (hypertension, hyperlipidemia, smoking, older age, diabetes) or known atherosclerotic disease (bruits on examination, history of coronary artery disease, arterial stents, or bypass procedures) who undergo intra-arterial intervention. Soon after the procedure, a livedo reticularis rash may appear. Evidence of emboli (blue digits or ischemic tips of digits) may be noted, particularly downstream from the instrumented vessels. A Hollenhorst plaque (a cholesterol plaque in the retinal artery or its branches) may be noted on funduscopic examination. An increase in the serum creatinine level indicates AKI, and eosinophilia is found in two thirds of patients. Hypocomplementemia may also be seen. Although intravenous contrast can also cause an increase in serum creatinine, contrast should not cause the other clinical findings associated with atheroembolic disease.

In high-risk patients, avoiding invasive vascular procedures is the best prevention. Devices that are deployed downstream to catch plaque are sometimes used but are not always effective. There is no proven treatment once the disease has occurred; however, therapy, including statins, treatment of hypertension, and aspirin, should be initiated for secondary prevention of cardiovascular disease.

KEY POINTS

- Cardiorenal syndrome is divided into five categories based on the interactions of abnormal renal and cardiac physiology.
- Treatment of cardiorenal syndrome focuses on reversing any specific underlying cause or improving the compromised organ function.
- Atheroembolic disease usually occurs in patients with vascular disease risk factors or known atherosclerotic disease who undergo intra-arterial intervention.
- There is no proven treatment for atheroembolic disease; however, therapy should be initiated for secondary prevention of cardiovascular disease.

Liver Disease

Hepatorenal syndrome (HRS), kidney dysfunction occurring in the setting of liver disease without another identifiable etiology, is believed to be due to altered vasoregulation arising from changes in the splanchnic circulation. HRS is essentially a diagnosis of exclusion; hypotension/shock, hypovolemia, and renal parenchymal damage should be ruled out before making the diagnosis. The urine sodium is often low in HRS because the kidney senses decreased blood volume and avidly retains sodium and water. Diagnostic criteria are listed in Table 41.

TABLE 41. Diagnostic Criteria for Hepatorenal Syndrome in Cirrhosis

Liver disease: cirrhosis with ascites
Kidney disease: serum creatinine level >1.5 mg/dL (133 µmol/L)
Kidney function not improved by fluid challenge: diuretics held and albumin 1 g/kg given for 2 days (maximum 100 g/d)
No other etiology for kidney dysfunction: shock not present; no precipitating/current nephrotoxins
No evidence of parenchymal kidney disease (proteinuria, hematuria, or abnormal kidney ultrasound)

Modified from Gut. Diagnosis, prevention and treatment of hepatorenal syndrome in cirrhosis. Salerno F, Gerbes A, Ginès P, Wong F, Arroyo V. 56(9):1310-1318, [PMID: 17389705] Copyright 2008 with permission from BMJ Publishing Group.

There are two types of HRS. Type I HRS, in which acute liver failure leads to AKI, is severe, progresses rapidly, and requires intensive care monitoring. Type II HRS is found in chronic liver disease, usually with refractory ascites. The hemodynamic derangements from the liver disease result in splanchnic vasodilation and reduced renal blood flow, causing a slow progressive decline in kidney function.

Management of both types of HRS consists of reversing any precipitating causes (gastrointestinal bleeding, peritonitis, other infections) and optimizing hemodynamics. The use of albumin in patients with cirrhosis and spontaneous bacterial peritonitis has been shown to reduce mortality and the incidence of HRS. A liver transplant is definitive therapy and can be curative for both types. Midodrine and octreotide have shown some promise in treating type II HRS, although evidence is limited. Vasopressin analogs, such as terlipressin, are being investigated as potential therapies for HRS.

KEY POINTS

- Hepatorenal syndrome is kidney dysfunction occurring in the setting of liver disease without another identifiable etiology.
- The use of albumin in patients with cirrhosis and spontaneous bacterial peritonitis has been shown to reduce mortality and the incidence of hepatorenal syndrome.

Malignancy
Tumor Lysis Syndrome

Tumor lysis syndrome refers to the release of intracellular contents from breakdown of tumor cells and release of their contents into the circulation. Manifestations include AKI and arrhythmias resulting from the release of potassium, phosphorus, and uric acid. The cell death can be spontaneous with highly proliferative malignancies but more commonly is induced by chemotherapy. Patients with tumor lysis syndrome present with hyperkalemia, hyperuricemia, and hyperphosphatemia and may require urgent medical intervention. Precipitation of uric acid and calcium phosphate crystals in the renal tubules may result in AKI, often with oliguria.

Treatment of tumor lysis syndrome begins with recognizing the at-risk patient. Those with fast-growing tumors, a high tumor burden, or a tumor highly responsive to treatment are at increased risk. Once the patient with increased risk is identified, treatment with intravenous fluid is recommended. Intravenous hydration with saline is preferred given the risk of metabolic alkalosis and possible precipitation of phosphorus at higher urine pH associated with sodium bicarbonate therapy. Allopurinol, a xanthine oxidase inhibitor, can be given prophylactically to reduce uric acid formation, and rasburicase, a urate oxidase that catalyzes the degradation of uric acid, can be used to actively lower uric acid levels. Rasburicase is considerably more expensive than allopurinol and is therefore used primarily in patients with high risk for

CONT.

tumor lysis syndrome or if excessively high uric acid levels occur in the context of chemotherapy. If kidney function is compromised, the patient must be assessed closely for the need for dialysis. Early initiation of continuous dialysis may be beneficial in tumor lysis syndrome with decreased kidney function and oliguria to prevent accumulation of potassium, phosphorus, uric acid, and the extra volume given to prevent and treat tumor lysis syndrome.

Chemotherapy-Induced Disease

Chemotherapy, besides precipitating tumor lysis syndrome, can also cause direct kidney injury. Platinum-based therapies can cause nonoliguric AKI with magnesium and potassium wasting, similar to aminoglycosides. Ifosfamide can also cause acute tubular injury. Prolonged use of nitrosoureas can cause chronic interstitial disease. Vascular endothelial growth factor inhibitors are known to induce proteinuria usually secondary to thrombotic microangiopathy. To minimize toxicity, the doses of renally excreted agents should be adjusted for GFR.

Myeloma Cast Nephropathy

Kidney involvement is common in multiple myeloma, with up to 25% of patients having kidney insufficiency at the time of diagnosis. Kidney failure may be the presenting finding. There is a correlation of the presence of kidney disease, its severity, and its response to therapy with overall survival in multiple myeloma.

Myeloma-related kidney disease occurs through several mechanisms. Myeloma-related hypercalcemia may cause a decreased GFR and an increased serum creatinine level. Certain glomerular diseases (membranoproliferative glomerulonephritis, cryoglobulinemia, and amyloidosis) may also result from monoclonal light chain deposition in the glomeruli (see Glomerular Diseases). Light chains may also accumulate in the tubules and form complexes with Tamm-Horsfall mucoprotein, leading to development of tubular casts (myeloma cast nephropathy) with obstruction, direct tubular injury, and AKI (see Chronic Tubulointerstitial Disorders).

In patients with myeloma cast nephropathy, urine examination is generally bland, and the urine dipstick typically does not reveal albuminuria. However, the addition of sulfosalicylic acid to the urine will precipitate all nonalbumin proteins, including light chains. Serum and urine protein electrophoresis with immunofixation can identify and quantify the monoclonal immunoglobulin.

Treatment of myeloma cast nephropathy requires reducing the burden of the paraproteins. Chemotherapy for multiple myeloma reduces paraprotein production; plasmapheresis to remove excess paraproteins is controversial. Autologous stem cell transplantation may be a treatment option for appropriate patients. Kidney transplantation has been successful in patients with multiple myeloma who have achieved full remission, but recurrence of light chain nephropathy and kidney failure has been reported.

HIV Infection

Patients with HIV infection have a high incidence of prerenal AKI thought to be due to volume depletion, concomitant liver disease, and hypoperfusion with infections. HIV infection is associated with some parenchymal diseases (HIV nephropathy, interstitial/infiltrative diseases, immune complex–mediated nephritis), which can present as AKI (see Glomerular Diseases). Medications used to treat HIV infection can cause AKI. Indinavir and atazanavir can cause AKI from obstruction, although using lower doses should cause less crystalluria. Tenofovir is absorbed by the proximal tubule and can also cause AKI and proximal renal tubular acidosis. Kidney biopsy should be considered in patients with HIV infection who have unexplained AKI. **H**

KEY POINTS

- Tumor lysis syndrome refers to the release of intracellular contents from breakdown of tumor cells and release of their contents into the circulation.

- Management of tumor lysis syndrome consists of early recognition, intravenous hydration with saline, medication to lower uric acid levels, and dialysis if needed to control the metabolic abnormalities.

- Myeloma cast nephropathy is associated with tubular obstruction, tubular injury, and acute kidney injury.

- Kidney biopsy should be considered in patients with HIV infection who have unexplained acute kidney injury.

Kidney Stones

Kidney stones are common, and the lifetime incidence has increased to nearly 10% in the United States. An initial kidney stone was most commonly seen in patients in their 30s and 40s; however, epidemiologic data now suggest that there has been an increase in nephrolithiasis in younger patients, which may coincide with the increase in metabolic syndrome and obesity in younger Americans.

The constituents of urine are typically insoluble at concentrations excreted each day, but several urine proteins and inhibitors limit stone formation. However, this balance is easily disrupted by low urine volume, anatomic abnormalities that cause urine stasis, medications, supplements, and dietary and metabolic factors.

Types of Kidney Stones

Calcium Stones

Calcium-containing stones account for nearly 80% of all kidney stones. Most calcium-containing stones are composed of calcium oxalate, which is relatively insoluble in acid urine; 10% are composed of calcium phosphate, which is insoluble in alkaline urine.

Risk Factors

Hypercalciuria

Hypercalciuria is the most common metabolic factor associated with calcium oxalate kidney stones. Hypercalciuria may occur in the setting of hypercalcemia, in which the filtered load of calcium is increased, as seen in primary hyperparathyroidism, sarcoidosis, and vitamin D excess. More frequently, the cause of hypercalciuria is not identified and is called idiopathic hypercalciuria, a disorder that is commonly familial.

Management of idiopathic hypercalciuria includes thiazide diuretics, which promote reabsorption of calcium by inducing mild hypovolemia and increased proximal tubular calcium reabsorption. A diet low in sodium increases the effectiveness of thiazide diuretics. Patients should not limit calcium intake, which paradoxically appears to increase urine calcium. Instead, patients should aim for age-appropriate calcium intake.

Hyperoxaluria

Excess oxalate excretion can also contribute to calcium oxalate stones. Excessive intake of dietary oxalate (chocolate, spinach, green and black tea) can lead to hyperoxaluria.

Enteric hyperoxaluria occurs in the setting of gastrointestinal malabsorption when free fatty acids bind to calcium, allowing free oxalate to be absorbed in the colon. This is particularly common in patients who undergo Roux-en-Y gastric bypass procedures for obesity; these patients have an increased risk of nephrolithiasis. Oral calcium carbonate in doses up to 4 g/d is used for patients with enteric hyperoxaluria to bind oxalate within the gastrointestinal tract.

Primary hyperoxaluria is an autosomal recessive disorder in which excess oxalate is produced, leading to deposition of calcium oxalate in the kidneys and other organs. The increased urine excretion of oxalate can lead to calcium oxalate kidney stones. Calcium oxalate can also deposit in the kidney parenchyma, blood vessels, and other major organs. Treatment includes increased fluid intake, avoidance of food with high oxalate content, and the use of pyridoxine (vitamin B_6) to limit the formation of oxalate.

Hypocitraturia

Reduced urine citrate can occur in settings of metabolic acidosis (such as distal renal tubular acidosis) when there is increased proximal absorption of urine citrate. A high protein diet also promotes proximal reabsorption of citrate. Citrate normally chelates calcium and limits the formation of calcium oxalate in the urine. If urine citrate is reduced, patients may take potassium citrate supplements.

Struvite Stones

Less than 10% of patients with kidney stones have struvite stones, which are composed of magnesium ammonium phosphate (struvite) and calcium carbonate apatite. Infections caused by urease-splitting organisms such as *Proteus* and *Klebsiella* species hydrolyze urea to ammonium, which alkalinizes the urine and leads to precipitation of phosphate ion complexes.

Without adequate treatment, the process tends to promulgate, and the stones may form "staghorn" shapes that fill the kidney pelvis. Antibiotic therapy and stone removal are the mainstays of therapy for struvite stones.

Uric Acid Stones

Uric acid stones cause approximately 10% of kidney stones. Uric acid is insoluble in an acid pH, but remarkably few patients develop uric acid stones. Patients who develop uric acid stones typically have low urine volume or hyperuricosuria. The latter may result from a high protein diet or rapid purine metabolism as in tumor lysis syndrome. Other risk factors include gout, conditions associated with uric acid overproduction, diabetes mellitus, the metabolic syndrome, and chronic diarrhea. Alkalinization of the urine and increased fluid intake are essential for management of uric acid stones. In addition, allopurinol can be used if the patient has gout or when urine uric acid excretion exceeds 1 g/24 h (5.9 mmol/d).

Cystine Stones

Cystine stones are an exceedingly rare cause of nephrolithiasis seen in patients with cystinuria. In this autosomal recessive disorder, patients lack the proximal tubular transporter for dibasic amino acids, including cystine. Cystine stones occur because cystine is insoluble in an acid pH. Crystals have a telltale hexagon shape. Without treatment, stones can be large.

Treatment is directed at alkalinization of the urine and use of agents that can chelate cystine with a sulfhydryl group such as penicillamine or the better-tolerated tiopronin.

KEY POINTS

- Hypercalciuria is the most common metabolic factor associated with calcium oxalate kidney stones.

- Management of idiopathic hypercalciuria includes thiazide diuretics, and calcium intake should not be limited, which paradoxically appears to increase urine calcium.

- Struvite stones may develop in patients with infections caused by urease-splitting organisms such as *Proteus* and *Klebsiella* species.

- Patients who develop uric acid stones typically have low urine volume or hyperuricosuria.

Clinical Manifestations

Patients with kidney stones usually present with colicky flank pain; however, pain may be localized along the path of the urinary tract to the groin, penis, or testicle, or it may be abdominal. On occasion, it may mimic an acute abdomen. When stones reach the bladder, irritative symptoms such as urinary urgency and frequency may occur. Patients may experience severe paroxysmal pain, nausea, and vomiting.

Diagnosis

CONT. Physical examination is important to identify other conditions. Urinalysis usually demonstrates hematuria. If crystals are present in the urine, this may be helpful in determining the composition of the kidney stones but is not diagnostic. Laboratory studies are indicated to evaluate kidney function, electrolyte levels, and the possible presence of coincident infection.

Imaging studies aid in the diagnosis of nephrolithiasis and help guide management based on the size and location of the stone. Noncontrast abdominal helical CT is the gold standard for diagnosing nephrolithiasis. This study can identify every type of kidney stone throughout its path in the urinary tract and may be able to suggest the type of stone present. Plain abdominal radiography has no role in acute diagnosis but may be used to assess the stone burden in patients with known radiopaque stones. Ultrasonography may identify stones in the kidneys but does not detect ureteral stones and may not detect early hydronephrosis. **H**

KEY POINTS

- Patients with kidney stones usually present with colicky flank pain; however, pain may be localized along the path of the urinary tract to the groin, penis, or testicle, or it may be abdominal.
- Noncontrast helical CT is the gold standard for diagnosing nephrolithiasis and can identify every type of kidney stone throughout its path in the urinary tract and may be able to suggest the type of stone present.

Acute Management

Patients with kidney stones whose pain can be controlled with oral analgesia and who can achieve oral hydration with a goal of at least 2 L of urine output daily can be managed conservatively with close follow-up. Because knowledge of stone type is helpful in management, patients should be instructed to strain their urine, and recovered stones should be sent for chemical analysis if the stone type and risk factors have not yet been established. Medical expulsive therapy with the α-blocker tamsulosin or a calcium channel blocker such as nifedipine has been shown to accelerate the passage of small stones. Utilization of these agents to facilitate stone passage is off label but common practice. Head-to-head comparisons show similar efficacy, but most clinicians prefer to use tamsulosin to avoid hypotension. With these strategies, more than 90% of small stones (<5 mm) pass spontaneously. In contrast, stones that are more than 7 mm are unlikely to pass without intervention (**Figure 19**). If urgent decompression of the collecting system is needed because of concerns of infection, bilateral obstruction, or obstruction of a solitary kidney, then percutaneous nephrostomy or ureteral stenting should be performed; the appropriate procedure is determined by the location of the stone and the clinical condition of the patient.

Patients who do not have an urgent indication for urologic intervention may still require intervention if the stone does not pass after a period of observation. The American Urological Association recommends careful counseling regarding all technical options. Extracorporeal shock wave lithotripsy is a widely used, noninvasive strategy used to treat symptomatic calculi located in the proximal ureter or within the kidney. Although generally well tolerated, tissue injury

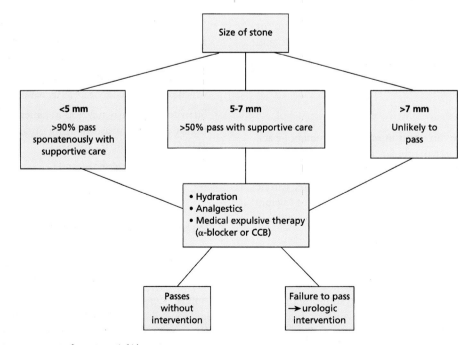

FIGURE 19. Acute management of symptomatic kidney stones.

can occur, and several studies have found new-onset hypertension following treatment. This association, however, is controversial. On occasion, very large complex stones require intervention with percutaneous nephrolithotomy.

In contrast, stones located in the distal ureter are usually accessible by directed therapy guided by ureteroscopy. During ureteroscopy, "intracorporeal" lithotripsy can be performed using lasers, ultrasonography, or other techniques. Stone fragments can be snared in baskets, or ureteral stents may be placed to facilitate stone fragment passage. 🅷

Risk Factor Evaluation and Subsequent Treatment

Historically, clinicians have been taught to look for the cause after the second kidney stone; however, in 1988, the NIH consensus conference on this topic suggested that an evaluation be pursued after the first stone. This assessment includes urinalysis and measurement of serum electrolytes, blood urea nitrogen, creatinine, calcium, phosphorus, and uric acid.

Analysis of passed stones and evaluation of the cause of kidney stones using a 24-hour urine collection are also recommended to guide management of kidney stones. Because the evaluation of the constituents of urine requires different preservatives, more than one collection may be required unless a special collection kit is utilized. Each 24-hour urine collection must include urine creatinine to assure a complete collection and facilitate comparison of future collections. Collections should also measure urea (to assess dietary protein intake), calcium, phosphate, citrate, oxalate, uric acid, and sodium. A radiologic assessment of "stone burden" should be performed at the onset of treatment, at 1 year, and, if negative, every 2 to 4 years thereafter. This can be done with kidney ultrasonography or plain radiography of the abdomen if stones are radiopaque.

After evaluation, patients should be counseled with general advice on how to prevent new stone formation as well as specific measures directed at identified metabolic abnormalities (**Table 42**). Without intervention, recurrence is common. Approximately 40% of patients have another stone within 5 years and nearly double that at 20 years.

KEY POINTS

- Medical expulsive therapy with the α-blocker tamsulosin or a calcium channel blocker such as nifedipine has been shown to accelerate the passage of small kidney stones.

- Extracorporeal shock wave lithotripsy is a widely used, noninvasive strategy used to treat symptomatic calculi located in the proximal ureter or within the kidney.

- Stones located in the distal ureter are usually accessible by directed therapy guided by ureteroscopy.

- Analysis of passed stones and evaluation of the cause of kidney stones using a 24-hour urine collection are recommended to guide management of kidney stones.

The Kidney in Pregnancy

Normal Physiologic Changes in Pregnancy

Hemodynamic Changes

During normal pregnancy, blood pressure lowers as a result of peripheral vasodilation and relative loss in response to vasoconstrictive hormones such as angiotensin II and vasopressin. These changes begin shortly after the first missed menstrual period and plateau in the middle of the second trimester. Concurrently, the plasma volume increases steadily because of increasing renal sodium and water retention. The increase in plasma volume leads to an increase in renal plasma flow and glomerular filtration rate (GFR). The increase in GFR results in a decrease in the serum creatinine level from the normal prepregnancy value of 0.8 mg/dL (70.7 micromoles/L) to 0.5 mg/dL (44.2 micromoles/L). The increased GFR may result in a small increase in proteinuria in healthy women and more substantial increases in women with preexisting proteinuria.

Changes in the Urinary Tract

Coincident with the increase in plasma volume, maternal hormones cause dilatation of the renal pelvis, calices, and ureters that may be mistaken for kidney obstruction. The dilated urinary system may be more prone to ascending pyelonephritis; therefore, standard practice includes a urine culture on the first prenatal visit and treatment of asymptomatic bacteriuria (>100,000 colony-forming units/mL). Finally, the incidence of kidney stones is slightly greater during the third trimester.

Changes in Acid-Base Regulation

Maternal hormones affect the configuration of the thoracic cage and stimulate ventilation, causing an increase in tidal volume and relative hyperventilation. The resulting hypocapnia, with an average arterial PCO_2 of 30 mm Hg (4.0 kPa), favors carbon dioxide transfer from the fetus to the maternal circulation. The kidney responds secondarily with increased bicarbonate excretion, resulting in a serum bicarbonate level of 18 to 20 meq/L (18-20 mmol/L) and a serum pH of 7.4 to 7.45 throughout pregnancy.

Changes in Water Homeostasis

Although both sodium and water retention occur, which increase plasma volume during pregnancy, water retention exceeds sodium retention. The decrease in the osmotic threshold for suppression of arginine vasopressin and thirst leads to a decline in the serum sodium level of approximately 4 meq/L (4 mmol/L), matched by a decrease in the plasma osmolality of 8 to 10 mosm/kg H_2O.

TABLE 42. Prevention of New Kidney Stone Formation

Stone Type	Risk Factor	Treatment	Therapeutic Targets/Comments
General stone advice		Increase fluid intake	>2 L/d
		Low sodium diet	<100 meq/d (100 mmol/d)
		Low protein diet	0.8-1 g/kg/d
		Dietary calcium intake	Age-appropriate calcium intake
Calcium (primarily calcium oxalate except with high urine pH, which predisposes to calcium phosphate)	Idiopathic hypercalciuria	Thiazide diuretics	Chlorthalidone, 12.5-25 mg daily or hydrochlorothiazide, 25 mg twice daily
	Hypocitraturia	Potassium citrate	20-30 meq twice daily
	Enteric hyperoxaluria	Calcium carbonate or citrate	1-2 g with meals
		Avoid high oxalate foods	e.g., chocolate, spinach
		Cholestyramine	4 g with meals
	Primary hyperoxaluria (urine oxalate >80 g/d)	Increase fluid intake	>3 L/d
		Avoid high oxalate foods	e.g., chocolate, spinach
		High-dose pyridoxine	5-20 mg/kg/d
	High urine pH	Correct metabolic acidosis	Serum bicarbonate 22-24 meq/L (22-24 mmol/L); keep urine pH <6.6
Uric acid	Urine pH <6.0	Potassium citrate or bicarbonate	40-80 meq/d (40-80 mmol/d): titrate to urine pH of 6.1-7.0
	Hyperuricosuria (>1000 mg/d [59 mmol/d])	Allopurinol	100-300 mg/d
Struvite	Urinary tract infection	Urologic interventions: percutaneous nephrolithotomy; surgery	Complete removal of all stone material
		Aggressive treatment of infection when present	Antibiotics as indicated
		Urease inhibitor (acetohydroxamic acid)	Rarely used due to toxicity
Cystine	Cystinuria	Potassium citrate or bicarbonate	Urine pH >7.0; 3-4 meq/kg/d (3-4 mmol/kg/d)
		Chelating agents	Tiopronin; penicillamine (captopril if hypertension)

KEY POINTS

- Pregnancy is normally associated with a lowering in blood pressure, a small increase in proteinuria, and a decrease in the serum creatinine level.
- Maternal hormones cause dilatation of the renal pelvis, calices, and ureters that may be mistaken for kidney obstruction.

Hypertensive Disorders Associated with Pregnancy

Chronic Hypertension

The normal systemic vasodilation seen early in pregnancy typically results in blood pressure values that are lower than those of nongravid women; therefore, women with chronic hypertension may have normal or low blood pressure during pregnancy.

When hypertension is noted before the 20th week of gestation, it is most consistent with a new diagnosis of chronic hypertension. There is no evidence that tight control of hypertension during pregnancy will prevent preeclampsia; instead, antihypertensive therapy is warranted only to limit maternal end-organ damage in those with severe hypertension. Therefore, most experts recommend that blood pressure should be maintained below 150/100 mm Hg and possibly lower in the setting of chronic kidney disease (CKD). If treatment is necessary, it is important to note that all antihypertensive agents cross the placenta. Methyldopa and labetalol appear to be the safest choices, whereas ACE inhibitors, angiotensin receptor blockers (ARBs), and likely renin inhibitors are not safe (**Table 43**). Women of child-bearing age who require blockade of the renin-angiotensin system for control of blood pressure and proteinuria should be counseled regarding the risk of birth defects should they become pregnant; these agents should be discontinued if conception is possible or anticipated.

Because many healthy women receive regular medical care for the first time during pregnancy, this may also be the first time that chronic hypertension is diagnosed. Such hypertension may be essential or secondary. CKD is the most common cause of secondary hypertension. Renovascular hypertension is another important cause of hypertension in young women, but diagnosis is particularly difficult during pregnancy when renin, angiotensin, and aldosterone are all normally elevated to achieve the sodium retention required to increase the plasma volume. Similarly, the diagnosis of primary hyperaldosteronism is challenging.

KEY POINTS

- Antihypertensive therapy is warranted only to limit maternal end-organ damage in pregnant patients with severe hypertension.

- In pregnant patients, blood pressure should be maintained below 150/100 mm Hg and possibly lower in the setting of chronic kidney disease.

- Blockade of the renin-angiotensin system should be discontinued before conception because of the risk of birth defects.

Gestational Hypertension

Gestational hypertension refers to hypertension that develops after 20 weeks of pregnancy in the absence of proteinuria or other maternal end-organ damage. Blood pressure should return to normal within 6 weeks of delivery; if the blood pressure remains high, it is more consistent with chronic hypertension. Some women with gestational hypertension may have undiagnosed chronic hypertension masked by the early decline in blood pressure seen in the first trimester that returned to prepregnancy values after 20 weeks. Up to 45% of women initially diagnosed with gestational hypertension develop preeclampsia, and the risk is greatest if the hypertension develops remote from term.

Preeclampsia

Preeclampsia is characterized by new-onset hypertension accompanied by the development of proteinuria. This condition can develop any time after 20 weeks of pregnancy. New generalized edema also may occur but is not part of the diagnostic criteria, because edema is common during uncomplicated pregnancy. Severe disease is characterized by thrombocytopenia, heavy proteinuria, rising serum creatinine levels, and elevated liver chemistry test results. Risk factors for preeclampsia include a family history of preeclampsia, nulliparity, multiple gestations, obesity, CKD, chronic hypertension, diabetes mellitus, and thrombophilia (such as antiphospholipid antibodies).

Pathophysiology

The broad spectrum of clinical manifestations and predisposing factors associated with preeclampsia suggest that it is a heterogeneous disorder. Nevertheless, increasing evidence suggests a cascade of events following insufficient maternal uterine vascular response to the placenta and placental ischemia. In addition, anti-angiogenic factors made by the placenta circulate in high levels shortly before the development of preeclampsia. Measurement of these factors may soon aid in the early diagnosis of preeclampsia.

TABLE 43.	Management of Hypertension During Pregnancy	
Medication	**Role in Management**	**Comments**
Methyldopa	First line for gestational/chronic hypertension	May cause thirst, nausea, drowsiness
Labetalol	First line for acute/severe hypertension; first line for gestational/chronic hypertension	Increasingly preferred over methyldopa because of side-effect profile; may cause headache
Sustained-release nifedipine	Second line for chronic hypertension (less long-term experience than labetalol)	Avoid short-acting agents; avoid with magnesium
Hydralazine	Second line for acute/severe hypertension; third line for chronic management	Frequent dosing impractical for chronic treatment; lupus-like syndrome may occur in chronic setting
β-Blockers	Third line for chronic management	Conflicting data on atenolol safety; metoprolol appears to be safe
Thiazide diuretics	Third line for chronic management; may continue if patient taking prior to pregnancy	Theoretical concern for decrease in maternal plasma volume but no deleterious effects reported; hypokalemia may occur
ACE inhibitors; angiotensin receptor blockers; renin inhibitors	Contraindicated in pregnancy	Early exposure associated with cardiac anomalies; late exposure associated with kidney agenesis

Clinical Manifestations

CONT.

Preeclampsia may be complicated by fetal injury (including fetal growth restriction) and maternal end-organ damage. Patients with preeclampsia may develop headache, visual disturbances, nausea, and vomiting. Variants include HELLP (hemolysis, elevated liver enzymes, low platelet count) and eclampsia (the development of seizures).

Prevention and Treatment

Many agents have been advocated to decrease the risk of preeclampsia; however, at present, only low-dose aspirin appears to modestly reduce risk. The definitive treatment of preeclampsia is delivery; in women at or near term, induction of labor is appropriate. Women who have mild disease and are remote from term can be managed with close monitoring of the mother and fetus, bed rest, and antihypertensive therapy for systolic blood pressures greater than 150 to 160 mm Hg. Antenatal corticosteroids can be given to promote fetal lung maturity if delivery is anticipated before the 34th week of gestation. Magnesium sulfate is the antiepileptic drug of choice and can be administered intrapartum or immediately postpartum in severe preeclampsia to prevent seizures. The clinical manifestations of preeclampsia typically resolve in the postpartum period, although resolution of hypertension may take longer with higher blood pressures. Similarly, higher proteinuria levels take longer to resolve.

KEY POINTS

- Gestational hypertension refers to hypertension that develops after 20 weeks of pregnancy in the absence of proteinuria or other maternal end-organ damage.
- Preeclampsia is characterized by new-onset hypertension accompanied by proteinuria and can develop any time after 20 weeks of pregnancy.
- Low-dose aspirin appears to modestly reduce the risk of preeclampsia.
- The definitive treatment of preeclampsia is delivery; in women at or near term, induction of labor is appropriate.
- Women with mild preeclampsia who are remote from term can be managed with close monitoring of the mother and fetus, bed rest, and antihypertensive therapy.
- In patients with severe preeclampsia, magnesium sulfate can be administered intrapartum or immediately postpartum to prevent seizures.

Kidney Disease in the Pregnant Patient

Women with CKD need significant counseling before considering pregnancy. Data suggest that women whose serum creatinine level is greater than 1.4 mg/dL (124 micromoles/L, stage 3 CKD or higher) have a significantly greater risk of complications from pregnancy, including preeclampsia and a significant decline in kidney function. In addition, there is a far greater risk of preterm delivery and intrauterine growth restriction.

Diabetes Mellitus

Patients with diabetes mellitus or gestational diabetes typically have excellent outcomes if they are able to maintain tight glycemic control. Women with diabetes and albuminuria who are treated with ACE inhibitors or ARBs must discontinue these agents before conception because of their teratogenic effects. In pregnant patients with albuminuria and hypertension who require treatment, specific calcium channel blockers have been shown to have a renoprotective effect and are considered safe for use in pregnancy (see MKSAP 16 Endocrinology and Metabolism).

Systemic Lupus Erythematosus

Patients with active systemic lupus erythematosus (SLE) have a high risk of maternal and fetal complications. Some of these complications relate to the autoimmune profile of the mother. In the setting of antiphospholipid antibodies, miscarriages and hypertensive disorders are common. In contrast, other autoantibodies increase the risk of neonatal lupus erythematosus. In addition, pregnancy may result in an exacerbation of SLE. Patients who receive cyclophosphamide or mycophenolate mofetil for nephritis should be counseled to avoid pregnancy. Therapy during pregnancy is ideally limited to corticosteroids and azathioprine.

Management of End-Stage Kidney Disease During Pregnancy

Pregnancy is very uncommon in women who are undergoing dialysis. Most of these patients have anovulatory cycles and decreased libido related to kidney failure and comorbid conditions. When pregnancy does occur, care should focus on adequacy of dialysis with goals greater than those for nonpregnant persons. Goals include maintaining normal electrolytes, lowering blood urea nitrogen levels (<40-45 mg/dL [14.3-16.1 mmol/L]), and maintaining adequate nutrition, with little fluctuation in weight or blood pressure. To achieve this end, hemodialysis is increased from an average of 12 hours per week to more than 20 hours per week. Peritoneal dialysis confers additional challenges, as the uterus grows and assumes an increasing amount of space in the abdomen; near term, it is difficult to achieve sufficient clearance without nearly continuous exchanges.

In contrast, successful pregnancy is increasingly common after kidney transplantation. Women should be counseled to wait 1 to 2 years after transplantation when they are on a stable medication regimen. In addition, women who take mycophenolate mofetil must shift to alternative agents, because this medication is not safe in pregnancy. There is experience with calcineurin inhibitors, azathioprine, and corticosteroids, but there are limited data for sirolimus. During pregnancy, transplant recipients may be more prone to anemia, glucose intolerance, hypertension, infection, and preeclampsia. There also is an increased risk of fetal complications, including intrauterine growth restriction, congenital anomalies, hypoadrenalism (if the mother is taking corticosteroids), and infections.

KEY POINTS

- Women with diabetes mellitus and albuminuria who are treated with ACE inhibitors or angiotensin receptor blockers must discontinue these agents before conception because of their teratogenic effects.
- Hemodialysis is increased from an average of 12 hours per week to more than 20 hours per week in pregnant patients with end-stage kidney disease.
- Kidney transplant recipients should wait 1 to 2 years after transplantation before conceiving.

Chronic Kidney Disease
Pathophysiology and Epidemiology

Chronic kidney disease (CKD) is abnormal kidney function persisting for more than 3 months. Abnormal kidney function can be defined by either a decreased glomerular filtration rate (GFR) or by anatomic or structural abnormalities. CKD is functionally classified according to the degree of impairment in the GFR (**Table 44**). This classification system may overestimate the prevalence of CKD (particularly stages 1 and 2) but allows patients with CKD to be appropriately identified and evaluated.

Approximately 13% of the U.S. population has CKD. It generally has been thought that once the kidney is damaged, kidney disease will progress over time and require dialysis because of the increased work of the remaining nephron mass; however, patients with stages 1 through 4 CKD are more likely to die than to progress to kidney replacement therapy.

Screening

Recognizing patients at risk for CKD is imperative in a disease that can be asymptomatic. **Table 45** lists relevant medical history and predisposing risk factors that should prompt screening for CKD. In particular, evaluation for diseases that can damage the kidneys directly or can cause damage through their treatment is indicated. A family history of CKD is a risk factor, as more evidence points to an inherited predisposition to CKD. A history of acute kidney injury (AKI) is recognized as a risk for future AKI and CKD. Various genitourinary abnormalities also can cause CKD.

Screening for CKD includes measurement of the serum creatinine level, estimation of GFR, and urinalysis to evaluate for blood, protein, and casts. Kidney imaging (usually ultrasonography) should be considered, particularly if the serum

TABLE 44. Expanded Classification System for Chronic Kidney Disease

Stage[a]	GFR, mL/min/1.73 m²	Description	U.S. Population, %
1	≥90	Normal or increased GFR with other evidence of kidney damage	2
2	60-89	Slight decrease in GFR, with other evidence of kidney damage	3
3[b]	30-59	Moderate decrease in GFR, with or without other evidence of kidney damage	8
3A	45-59		
3B	30-44		
4	15-29	Severe decrease in GFR, with or without other evidence of kidney damage	0.4
5	<15	Established end-stage kidney disease	0.2

GFR = glomerular filtration rate.

[a]Suffixes are used to further describe the stages (for example, stage 2P, stage 3T):

"P" denotes the presence of proteinuria defined as a urine albumin–creatinine ratio greater than 30 mg/g or a urine protein–creatinine ratio greater than 0.5 mg/mg.

"T" denotes a patient with a functioning transplant.

"D" denotes a patient on dialysis (usually stage 5D).

[b]Stage 3 is sometimes divided in stages 3A and 3B to recognize the increased rate of cardiovascular complications in stage 3B compared with stage 3A. In persons older than 70 years of age, an estimated GFR between 45 to 59 mL/min/1.73 m², if stable over time and without any other evidence of kidney damage, is unlikely to be associated with complications related to chronic kidney disease.

National Institute for Health and Clinical Excellence (2008). Adapted from CG 73 Chronic kidney disease: early identification and management of chronic kidney disease in adults in primary and secondary care. London: NICE. Available from: www.nice.org.uk/cg73. Reproduced with permission.

TABLE 45. Medical History and Historical Features Associated with Chronic Kidney Disease

Medical History/Possible Causes of CKD

Causing Direct Kidney Damage	Important Historical Features
Diabetes mellitus	Duration
Hypertension	Duration
Glomerulonephritis	Autoimmune disease history
Multiple myeloma	History of treatment
AKI episodes	Episodes of kidney failure; dialysis
Chronic viral infections	History of hepatitis B, hepatitis C, or HIV

Kidney Damage from Treatment	Important Historical Features
Cancer	History of chemotherapy use
Chronic pain	Pain medications and duration used
Infections	Antibiotics used

Genitourinary Abnormalities	Important Historical Features
Kidney stones	Flank pain; hematuria
Kidney cancer	Kidney surgery/resection
Obstruction	Voiding issues; prostate issues; endometrial/pelvic cancers
Ureteral reflux	Urine infections; kidney infections

Exposures	Important Historical Features
Contrast	Repeat imaging studies/angiography
Heavy metals	Exposure history
Herbal supplements	Nonprescription/OTC use

Increased Risk

Increased Predisposition	Important Historical Features
Patient demographics	Older age (>70 years); obesity (BMI >30)
Family history	Family history of dialysis, proteinuria, kidney failure, or genetic kidney diseases (such as polycystic kidney disease)
Prior AKI even if baseline serum creatinine level is normal	Episodes of kidney failure; dialysis; prolonged hospitalizations; sepsis
Kidney transplant	Immunosuppressive drug use; episodes of rejection
Liver disease	Hepatitis; alcohol use

AKI = acute kidney injury; CKD = chronic kidney disease; OTC = over the counter.

creatinine level or urinalysis is abnormal or if there is suspicion of a structural abnormality.

Clinical Manifestations

The ability of the kidney to compensate for lost function can result in delayed presentation of clinical kidney disease; minimal or no symptoms may be present. The symptoms of CKD can be vague and include dysgeusia, pruritus, anorexia, fluid retention, fatigue, and impaired cognitive function. Pericarditis, serositis, gastrointestinal bleeding, encephalopathy, and uremic neuropathy typically do not develop until the GFR falls below 10 to 15 mL/min/1.73 m².

KEY POINTS

- Chronic kidney disease is characterized by a decreased glomerular filtration rate or by anatomic or structural abnormalities that have persisted for more than 3 months.

- Many conditions, including diabetes mellitus, hypertension, cancer, genitourinary abnormalities, and autoimmune diseases, are associated with chronic kidney disease.

- In patients with risk factors for chronic kidney disease, screening includes measurement of the serum creatinine level, estimation of glomerular filtration rate, and urinalysis to evaluate for the presence of blood, protein, and casts.

- The symptoms of chronic kidney disease include dysgeusia, pruritus, anorexia, fluid retention, fatigue, and impaired cognitive function.
- Pericarditis, serositis, gastrointestinal bleeding, encephalopathy, and uremic neuropathy typically do not develop until the glomerular filtration rate falls below 10 to 15 mL/min/1.73 m^2.

Management

Prevention of Progression

The approach to delaying or halting kidney disease progression involves an accurate diagnosis of the cause of CKD. If the diagnosis is not evident from the history, physical examination, laboratory studies, and imaging, a kidney biopsy may be appropriate.

Specific therapy to treat the underlying cause should then be instituted, such as treatment of an autoimmune disease, glomerulonephropathy, or interstitial nephritis. If treatment specific to the underlying cause of CKD is not indicated, management to delay kidney disease progression focuses on blood pressure control, cardiovascular risk reduction, use of sodium bicarbonate therapy, avoidance of further insults to the kidney, and proteinuria reduction.

Hypertension

Blood pressure control has been shown to delay CKD progression. The Seventh Report of the Joint National Committee on Prevention, Detection, Evaluation, and Treatment of High Blood Pressure (JNC 7) recommends a target blood pressure of less than 130/80 mm Hg for patients with kidney disease (as of publication, the eighth report reflecting current research data is in progress). **Figure 20** gives an algorithmic approach to the management of hypertension in patients with CKD.

Certain agents may help preserve kidney function beyond their blood pressure–lowering effect. ACE inhibitors have been shown to delay progression in patients with moderate to severe kidney disease and are particularly beneficial in patients with proteinuric (>1000 mg/24 h) CKD. Angiotensin receptor blockers (ARBs) may have effects on CKD progression similar to ACE inhibitors; the evidence is more limited, but growing.

Serum potassium levels should be monitored in patients taking ACE inhibitors or ARBs. If hyperkalemia develops, dietary potassium restriction, discontinuation of NSAIDs or other contributing medications, and the addition of loop or thiazide diuretics can be implemented to facilitate continuation of angiotensin blockade whenever possible.

The serum creatinine level should also be followed for progressive increases. A small increase in the serum creatinine level (<30% increase from baseline) can occur and may be a marker of effective renoprotection: decreased glomerular pressure causes an increase in the serum creatinine level, but the lower glomerular pressure results in less kidney damage over time. If the serum creatinine level increases by more than 30% after initiating an ACE inhibitor or ARB, evaluation for other sources of the decline in kidney function, such as bilateral renal artery stenosis, may be appropriate. If no other cause of AKI is apparent, the ACE inhibitor or ARB should be discontinued. If the serum creatinine level has increased to less than 30% from baseline but stabilizes, the benefits of renoprotection from the ACE inhibitor or ARB generally favor continuation of angiotensin blockade for most patients.

In patients in whom the GFR is marginal (such as <20 mL/min/1.73 m^2), discontinuation of the ACE inhibitor or ARB has been shown in one observational study to delay progression to end-stage kidney disease (ESKD) in patients with advanced diabetic nephropathy on average by 1 year. ACE inhibitors or ARBs can be resumed in patients who do not show improvement in kidney function after discontinuation in the absence of other contraindications such as hyperkalemia. After initiating ACE inhibitor or ARB therapy, the GFR should be monitored closely in the following months. If a patient has a progressive decline in GFR in the months after starting ACE inhibitor or ARB therapy, and this rate of decline is faster than prior to initiation of the medication, the patient may have underlying vascular disease. The risk of accelerated CKD progression on angiotensin blockade in such patients likely outweighs the potential benefits.

Diuretics are effective agents for blood pressure control in patients with CKD and should be used in patients with edema. These agents generally require higher doses in patients with CKD to be effective. If a patient has CKD and uncontrolled blood pressure on hydrochlorothiazide, switching to a loop diuretic should be a first consideration. The addition of a thiazide to a loop diuretic such as furosemide can result in enhanced diuresis. Adequate dosing of loop and thiazide diuretics should increase potassium excretion, which lowers serum potassium levels and allows for more liberal use of other agents that block the renin-angiotensin-aldosterone system (such as ACE inhibitors, ARBs, or spironolactone).

The ACCOMPLISH trial demonstrated that combination therapy with a dihydropyridine calcium channel blocker and an ACE inhibitor was superior in preserving kidney function in patients with CKD compared to an ACE inhibitor with a thiazide diuretic. In the absence of edema, this combination is appropriate for patients requiring two agents to achieve target blood pressures. Spironolactone can also be a particularly effective antihypertensive agent in patients with resistant hypertension, but the serum potassium level must be monitored closely, particularly in patients with CKD who take ACE inhibitors or ARBs. Spironolactone is generally well tolerated in patients with an estimated GFR greater than 45 mL/min/17.3 m^2 and a baseline serum potassium level less than 4.5 meq/L (4.5 mmol/L).

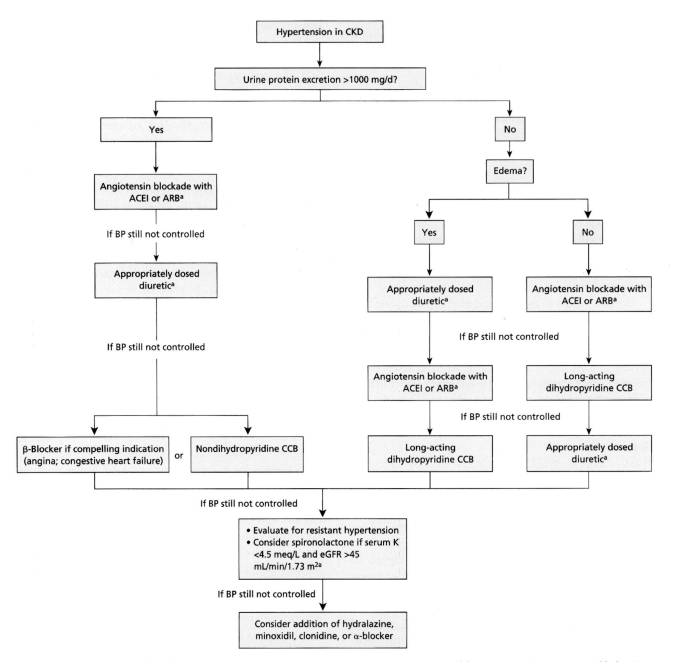

FIGURE 20. Management of hypertension in chronic kidney disease. ACEI = angiotensin-converting enzyme inhibitor; ARB = angiotensin receptor blocker; BP = blood pressure; CCB = calcium channel blocker; CKD = chronic kidney disease; eGFR = estimated glomerular filtration rate; K = potassium.

[a]Monitor serum potassium and creatinine levels. If serum potassium is greater than 5 meq/L (5 mmol/L), implement dietary potassium restriction, discontinue contributing agents such as NSAIDs, and consider increasing diuretic dose.

The peripheral vasodilators hydralazine and minoxidil are usually reserved for more refractory hypertension, which is more likely to occur in patients with CKD. Hydralazine or minoxidil should only be used as part of a multidrug regimen. Before initiating a peripheral vasodilator, the antihypertensive regimen should consist of an appropriate diuretic regimen and β-blockade to prevent edema and reflex tachycardia.

Metabolic Acidosis

Metabolic acidosis commonly develops in patients with CKD due to the loss of the ability of the kidney to regenerate bicarbonate. A delay in CKD progression with alkali therapy has been shown in several studies. The largest study involved more than 100 patients with stage 4 CKD who had baseline serum bicarbonate levels of 16 to 20 meq/L (16-20 mmol/L); those who received oral sodium bicarbonate

(600 mg, three times a day, with dose adjusted to achieve a serum bicarbonate level of at least 23 meq/L [23 mmol/L]) had a slower decline in GFR. Despite increased sodium intake, there was no difference in blood pressure or evidence of volume overload. Alkali treatment was given in addition to standard care, which included blood pressure control and ACE inhibitors. Alkali-treated patients also have been shown to have improved nutritional parameters. The low cost and low side-effect profile of this therapy make it an attractive treatment.

Nephrotoxins

An important part of preserving kidney function is avoiding the potentially harmful administration of medications that can damage kidney function. In patients with kidney disease, avoidance of certain over-the-counter medications, herbal supplements, nephrotoxic medications, or medications that can raise blood pressure is indicated (**Table 46**). Prescribed medications need to be dosed appropriately for the patient's GFR.

Iodinated contrast should be avoided if possible in patients with kidney disease, especially when the estimated GFR is less than 60 mL/min/1.73 m^2 (see Special Considerations, Imaging).

Proteinuria

Greater degrees of proteinuria have been associated with a more rapid decline of kidney function in diabetic and nondiabetic kidney disease. Proteinuria reduction is generally thought to be beneficial for the preservation of GFR in kidney disease. Blood pressure should first be lowered to a target of 130/80 mm Hg, preferentially using agents that block angiotensin (ACE inhibitors or ARBs). Spironolactone also has been shown to reduce proteinuria in patients with diabetes. The ONTARGET study showed that adding an ARB (telmisartan) to an ACE inhibitor (ramipril) reduced proteinuria but actually worsened renal outcomes in patients over the age of 55 years who have diabetes and end-organ damage or atherosclerotic vascular disease. This study, however, did not include many patients with high degrees of proteinuria. In general, using an ACE inhibitor and ARB in combination is not recommended, but in high-risk (heavy proteinuria) patients, this combination is under investigation.

Protein Restriction

Protein restriction has been shown to delay kidney disease progression in animals. Evidence in humans remains unclear; studies indicate a small but insignificant improvement in the rate of decrease of GFR in protein-restricted patients who have CKD. A protein restriction of 0.6 to 0.8 g/kg/d to delay CKD progression can be instituted in very adherent patients. Body weight and serum albumin levels should be followed to ensure adequate nutrition. When used, protein restriction should be used in combination with measures proved to forestall progression, such as hypertension control or angiotensin blockade.

TABLE 46. Over-the-Counter Medications to Avoid in Patients with Chronic Kidney Disease

Agent	Potential Adverse Effects
NSAIDs	Hemodynamic changes due to prostaglandin inhibition; interstitial nephritis
Decongestants	Increased blood pressure
Herbal supplements	
Aristolochia/aristolochic acid	Tubular atrophy and interstitial fibrosis
Chromium	Chronic interstitial nephritis
Creatine	Chronic interstitial nephritis; rhabdomyolysis; AKI
Germanium	Tubular injury and degeneration
Ma Huang/Ephedra	Increased blood pressure; rhabdomyolysis; AKI
Salt substitutes	High in potassium
Gastrointestinal medications	
Laxatives/enemas	
Sodium phosphate	Elevated serum phosphate levels
Magnesium hydroxide	Elevated serum magnesium levels
Magnesium citrate	Elevated serum magnesium levels
Antacids/antidyspepsia agents	
Aluminum and magnesium hydroxide	Elevated serum magnesium and aluminum levels
Sodium bicarbonate, potassium bicarbonate, and citric acid	Elevated serum sodium and potassium levels

AKI = acute kidney injury.

- Prevention of kidney disease progression focuses on management of hypertension, cardiovascular risk reduction, use of sodium bicarbonate therapy, avoidance of further insults to the kidney, and proteinuria reduction.

- ACE inhibitors and angiotensin receptor blockers have been shown to delay progression in patients with moderate to severe kidney disease and are particularly beneficial in patients with proteinuric (>1000 mg/24 h) chronic kidney disease.

- In patients with kidney disease, avoidance of nephrotoxic medications, iodinated contrast, certain over-the-counter medications, medications that can raise the blood pressure, and herbal supplements is indicated.

Complications

In addition to measures to prevent kidney disease progression, efforts should be undertaken to recognize and manage complications specific to CKD.

Cardiovascular Disease

CKD is associated with an increased risk of cardiovascular disease, specifically, myocardial infarction, stroke, peripheral vascular disease, and cardiovascular death. This risk is greater in patients with CKD than in the general population, even after adjusting for traditional risk factors such as hypertension and diabetes. The risk of cardiovascular events (and death and hospitalizations) has been shown to increase steadily with increased CKD stage (or decreased GFR) when GFR was stratified into stages 3A, 3B, 4, and 5 (see Table 44). Addressing cardiovascular risk is a management priority in patients with CKD. Patients with CKD are more likely to experience cardiovascular complications and death than to progress to ESKD and the need for kidney replacement therapy.

Lifestyle modification, including smoking cessation, exercise, and weight loss in overweight patients, may have benefit in delaying kidney disease progression and should be implemented to help reduce cardiovascular risk. Other treatment targets (hypertension, dyslipidemia, and coronary artery disease) are discussed in the next sections.

Hypertension

The prevalence of hypertension is higher in patients with CKD than in the general population. The prevalence of hypertension in the general adult population is almost 25%. The prevalence increases with increasing stage of kidney disease—from approximately 35% in stage 1 to more than 80% in stages 4 and 5. Although patients with CKD often have been excluded from hypertension trials, the cardiovascular benefit of lowering blood pressure found in the general population is also likely true for patients with CKD.

The treatment of hypertension in patients with CKD is discussed in the Prevention of Progression section. A preference for agents that inhibit angiotensin (ACE inhibitors and ARBs) is reasonable, as these agents can also delay CKD progression (particularly when proteinuria is present) and have been shown in some studies to reduce cardiovascular mortality.

Dyslipidemia

No consistent pattern of lipid abnormalities has been identified in patients with CKD. Alterations in apolipoproteins have been noted before the serum cholesterol levels change, and a decrease in HDL cholesterol and increase in triglycerides has been reported as CKD progresses. The variability of lipid levels in CKD may reflect the underlying cause of the CKD. Although treatment of dyslipidemia with statins has not been shown to delay CKD progression, lowering cholesterol levels with statins reduces cardiovascular risk. Statins may also reduce proteinuria and have beneficial anti-inflammatory and vascular effects.

A 2009 Cochrane review of statins in patients with CKD showed reduced cardiovascular mortality in those with stages 3 and 4 CKD, and the incidence of side effects was similar in the CKD population to the general population. Although effective in patients with stages 1 through 4 CKD, large studies have not shown a mortality benefit to statin use in the dialysis CKD population.

Coronary Artery Disease

The prevalence of coronary artery disease in patients with CKD is estimated at 40% to 65%. The event rate for myocardial infarction is higher in CKD patients without diabetes than in non-CKD patients with diabetes. A portion of the increased cardiovascular risk in patients with CKD may be attributable to decreased use of appropriate medications, perhaps because of concern about a higher rate of side effects. ACE inhibitors, aspirin, and statins are less likely to be used in patients with CKD. These agents should not be withheld on the basis of a diagnosis of CKD; in fact, treatment with these medications may benefit the CKD population more than the general population. CKD may also cause some confusion with diagnostic blood tests. The levels of cardiac enzymes in the blood, specifically creatine kinase, B-type natriuretic peptide, and troponin, may be elevated in those with CKD relative to patients with normal kidney function, particularly in patients on dialysis. These elevated levels should not be attributed to CKD alone without an appropriate evaluation.

Coronary artery bypass grafting can be beneficial in selected patients with CKD and should be considered for appropriate patients, although these patients have a higher risk of postoperative AKI. The risk of kidney disease requiring dialysis in a patient with CKD undergoing heart surgery can be estimated by a calculator available online at www.zunis.org/Need%20For%20Dialysis%20After%20Heart%20Surgery%20Calculator.htm.

Chronic Kidney Disease-Mineral Bone Disorder

The kidney plays a critical role in calcium and phosphorus homeostasis; as kidney function deteriorates, adaptations occur that maintain normal serum calcium levels. Yet these accommodations may lead to a spectrum of adverse consequences, including serious bone disease and extraskeletal vascular calcification. The term *chronic kidney disease-mineral bone disorder* (CKD-MBD) has been adopted to reflect these abnormalities. The 2009 Kidney Disease Improving Global Outcomes (KDIGO) guidelines on the evaluation and treatment of CKD-MBD are available at www.kdigo.org/guidelines/mbd/index.html.

Calcium and Phosphorus Homeostasis

Cholecalciferol (vitamin D_3) is synthesized in the skin with exposure to ultraviolet light and can also be obtained from fortified dietary sources. Vitamin D deficiency is common, particularly in the setting of CKD. Vitamin D is hydroxylated in the liver and then in the kidney into calcitriol (1,25-dihydroxy vitamin D). Calcitriol promotes absorption of dietary calcium and phosphorus in the gastrointestinal tract. As the kidney loses the ability to hydroxylate vitamin D, the plasma level of calcitriol often decreases as the GFR declines, which prompts an increase in the parathyroid hormone (PTH) level via both direct and indirect mechanisms, termed *secondary hyperparathyroidism*. Low calcitriol levels can result in hypocalcemia, leading to a compensatory increase in serum PTH levels.

Vitamin D deficiency removes the inhibitory effect of calcitriol on the vitamin D receptor of parathyroid cells.

PTH liberates calcium and phosphorus from bone and limits urine calcium excretion; routine serum calcium levels may be normal as the PTH levels increase due to increased mobilization of calcium from bone (**Figure 21**).

Reduced kidney function leads to a decrease in phosphate filtration and increases in serum phosphorus levels. This also results in an increased release of PTH, which inhibits proximal tubular reabsorption of phosphorus and results in increased phosphorus excretion. Yet when the GFR is reduced, this effect is limited; the concurrent PTH-driven liberation of phosphorus from bone increases the filtered load of phosphate and exacerbates the hyperphosphatemia. A vicious cycle may ensue in which hyperparathyroidism worsens steadily in response to hypocalcemia and hyperphosphatemia.

Laboratory Abnormalities

A large multicenter observational study noted that an elevation in PTH level is often the first detectable change associated with CKD-MBD, which may occur very early in the course of CKD; therefore, KDIGO guidelines recommend testing for MBD beginning with stage 3 CKD.

Assessment includes measurement of serum calcium and phosphorus levels and measurement of PTH levels using the "intact" assay that measures active PTH hormone in two sites (fragments of the PTH molecule are cleared by the kidney

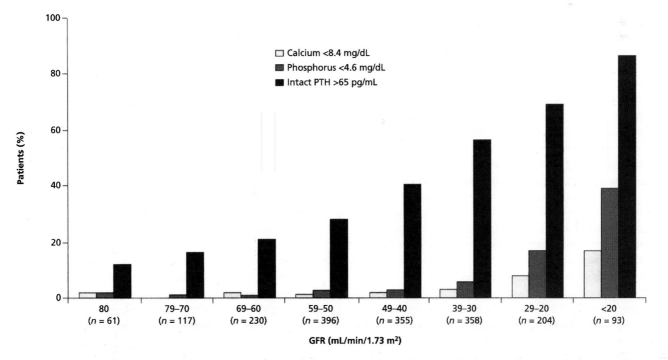

FIGURE 21. Prevalence of abnormal serum calcium, phosphorus, and intact parathyroid hormone by glomerular filtration rate in patients with chronic kidney disease. GFR = glomerular filtration rate; PTH = parathyroid hormone.

and may be elevated in CKD). Calcidiol (25-hydroxy vitamin D) should be measured because it has a long half-life and reflects both nutritional intake and skin synthesis. Alkaline phosphatase also may be used as an adjunct to interpret testing; however, if levels are elevated, a liver source should be excluded. If the PTH is in normal range and kidney function is stable, annual measurements of calcium, phosphorus, and PTH should suffice; however, if the patient's kidney function declines or if the patient requires treatment, then calcium, phosphate, and PTH should be monitored every 3 months.

Vascular Calcification
Severe vascular calcification appears to play a significant role in the risk of cardiovascular disease in patients with CKD. Whereas patients with atherosclerosis develop calcification in the intima of arteries, even young patients with CKD can develop medial vascular calcifications. This pathology leads to a decrease in vascular compliance, which is associated with hypertension, left ventricular hypertrophy, and reduced end-organ perfusion. Although calcification was thought to be the result of a simple physicochemical relationship of the high calcium and phosphorus product, it now appears that the mineral imbalance initiates a complex response with damage to the vascular smooth muscle cells and perhaps phenotypic transformation of these cells into osteoblast-like cells. As the bone is demineralized, the vasculature becomes more calcified. Calcific uremic arteriolopathy (calciphylaxis) is the most severe form of this process and involves the small cutaneous arteries. This disorder is characterized by ischemic and painful skin ulceration and is associated with a high mortality rate. It is not yet clear whether improved calcium and phosphorus control will translate to a reduction in vascular calcification and an improvement in clinical outcomes in patients with CKD.

Renal Osteodystrophy
Renal osteodystrophy refers to the skeletal complications associated with CKD. Bone disease may result in bone pain or fractures. Although there are several patterns of pathology, all patterns confer a markedly increased risk of fracture. The most common forms of renal osteodystrophy are osteitis fibrosa cystica, osteomalacia, and adynamic bone disease; patients may also have a mixed disorder or additional conditions such as osteoporosis or amyloidosis. Distinction between these types of bone disease can only be made by bone biopsy, which is generally reserved for patients with unexplained findings when pathology may help guide therapy. Instead, treatment decisions are generally based on biochemical profiles.

Osteitis fibrosis cystica describes the high-turnover bone disease associated with chronic secondary hyperparathyroidism. Patients typically are asymptomatic but may develop bone pain and have an increased risk of fractures. Classic radiograph findings include subperiosteal bone reabsorption, especially in the distal clavicles and the phalanges. Treatment includes maintaining serum calcium and phosphorus levels in the normal range through use of phosphate binders as well as use of calcitriol or other 1,25-dihydroxy vitamin D analogs or cinacalcet to maintain serum PTH levels at target levels.

Osteomalacia is characterized by decreased bone mineralization at the newly formed osteoid in sites of bone turnover. This disorder can occur in children with vitamin D deficiency and is called rickets when the unfused growth plates are also involved. Although vitamin D deficiency is common in CKD, this form of bone pathology is unusual and is typically associated with an additional abnormality. In the past, the most common etiology was aluminum toxicity, which is taken up by bone and leads to abnormal bone mineralization. Avoidance of aluminum in over-the-counter and prescribed medications as well as limitation of aluminum in water supplies and in phosphate-binding agents has greatly decreased the incidence of this disorder. Treatment of aluminum toxicity requires prolonged chelation therapy.

Adynamic bone disease is characterized by low turnover of bone with both reduced bone formation and resorption. Although the pathophysiology is poorly understood, it appears to be associated with oversuppression of PTH. This may be seen in the setting of excessive treatment with vitamin D and calcium or following parathyroidectomy. Patients typically have PTH levels below 100 pg/mL (100 ng/L), bone pain, and fractures. Alkaline phosphatase levels are usually not elevated. A decrease or discontinuation of vitamin D analogs and calcium-based binders is indicated.

Patients with CKD can also develop osteoporosis; however, the diagnosis may be more difficult in the setting of CKD because bone mineral density studies in patients with either osteoporosis or CKD-MBD may demonstrate reduction in bone density and cannot reliably determine risk for fracture nor differentiate osteoporosis from other pathology. For this reason, it is currently recommended that patients with mild kidney impairment (stages 1 or 2 CKD) be treated for suspected osteoporosis like the general population. Patients with stage 3 CKD should be evaluated for evidence of secondary hyperparathyroidism. If these biochemical markers are normal, they can also be treated like the general population for osteoporosis.

In contrast, when the estimated GFR is less than 30 mL/min/1.73 m^2, the focus of therapy should be on correcting secondary hyperparathyroidism. Bisphosphonates are cleared by the kidney and have not been adequately tested in patients with reduced kidney function. In this setting, the dose must be reduced or stopped altogether. Furthermore, because the mechanism of action is to inhibit osteoclast reabsorption, bisphosphonates may subsequently limit new bone formation and result in adynamic bone disease. Other antiresorptive agents used in the treatment of osteoporosis such as raloxifene have not been extensively studied in patients with reduced kidney function.

Treatment
The initial goal in the treatment of CKD-MBD is correction of hyperphosphatemia and hypocalcemia. Hyperphosphatemia can be treated by dietary phosphate restriction

and oral medications that bind dietary phosphate in the gastrointestinal tract. The goal of therapy is to maintain the serum phosphorus level in the normal range. Aluminum salts work well to bind phosphate, but long-term use results in neurologic, skeletal, and hematologic toxicity. Calcium salts (carbonate and acetate) also can serve to bind phosphate; however, large doses are needed, and recent concerns regarding their role in vascular calcification have prompted clinicians to select newer and more costly noncalcium-, nonaluminum-based agents such as sevelamer and lanthanum. However, this shift has not yet produced any clear clinical improvements.

Patients with vitamin D deficiency should receive supplemental vitamin D. If vitamin D levels are robust and the phosphate level is normal, but the PTH level is elevated above target levels, active vitamin D analogs should be initiated. The National Kidney Foundation guidelines suggest graded PTH goals based on the level of kidney function; in stage 3 CKD, the goal should be at the upper limit of normal, whereas in stage 5 CKD, the goal could be much higher. In contrast, the KDIGO guidelines suggest aiming for normal values at all stages of CKD with more permissive rises once a patient begins dialysis. Both sets of guidelines are opinion-based, and both agree that vitamin D analogs should be discontinued in the setting of hypercalcemia or hyperphosphatemia.

In contrast to vitamin D analogs, calcimimetic agents modulate the calcium-sensing receptor on the parathyroid cells and increase the signal of extracellular ionized calcium. As a result, these agents "mimic" calcium at the receptor and decrease PTH release. There is currently one calcimimetic available, cinacalcet, which is FDA approved only for use in patients who are on dialysis. This agent is very expensive, and its role in patients with CKD has not yet been defined.

Anemia

Anemia is common in patients with CKD and usually occurs when the estimated GFR falls below 30 mL/min/1.73 m². Erythropoietin is made by interstitial peritubular fibroblasts of the kidney. Patients with reduced kidney function may have low erythropoietin levels, but erythropoietin resistance also occurs. When patients with reduced kidney function develop anemia, evaluation for other causes is appropriate; in particular, relative iron deficiency is common. If iron stores are adequate and other causes have also been eliminated, the anemia can be attributed to CKD. There is no role for the routine measurement of erythropoietin levels in this setting because this expensive test does not aid in the diagnosis or guide treatment decisions.

The erythropoiesis-stimulating agents (ESAs) epoetin and darbepoetin have been found to limit the development of left ventricular hypertrophy and the need for blood transfusions as well as to improve quality-of-life markers in patients on dialysis. Although target hemoglobin levels were never established, standard practice was to treat patients to a target hemoglobin level of 11 to 12 g/dL (110-120 g/L). In recent years, a number of trials have investigated outcomes when

ESAs have been dosed to achieve normal hemoglobin levels. A large randomized trial of men with cardiovascular disease on hemodialysis was terminated early due to a trend toward increased mortality in the normal hemoglobin group. Investigators suspected that this was related to hemoconcentration and hyperviscosity in patients undergoing hemodialysis. Targeting a normal hematocrit was also studied in patients with CKD in three large randomized trials. These trials did not demonstrate benefit in cardiovascular morbidity or mortality from the higher target hemoglobin level. In addition, one study suggested that patients with higher hemoglobin targets were more likely to have adverse outcomes, and another found nearly a doubling in the risk of strokes. Subsequent analyses have shown that decreased responsiveness to ESAs, and therefore, higher pharmacologic doses, also conferred a worse prognosis.

Multiple recent trials on the use of ESAs in the treatment of anemia associated with cancer suggest that ESAs may increase the risk of tumor growth and shorten survival in patients with cancer. For this reason, the FDA has issued a warning, and patients with cancer can only use ESAs with appropriate counseling and enrollment in a monitoring program.

ESAs should be considered for patients with symptomatic anemia attributable to erythropoietin deficiency when the hemoglobin level is less than 10 g/dL (100 g/L). Patients with CKD must be carefully counseled about the risks of ESAs, which include increased risk of thrombotic and cardiovascular events as well as increased blood pressure. In addition, clinicians should explain that the targets for hemoglobin are lower than those used in the past, and that patients must be monitored regularly to titrate the dose to a target hemoglobin level of 10 to 11 g/dL (100-110 g/L).

KEY POINTS

- Complications associated with chronic kidney disease include cardiovascular disease, chronic kidney disease-mineral bone disorder, and anemia.

- Patients with chronic kidney disease may develop renal osteodystrophy that manifests as osteitis fibrosa cystica, osteomalacia, and adynamic bone disease.

- The initial goal in the treatment of chronic kidney disease-mineral bone disorder is correction of hyperphosphatemia and hypocalcemia.

- Anemia of chronic kidney disease is a diagnosis of exclusion; erythropoietin levels are not diagnostic and should not be pursued.

- Erythropoiesis-stimulating agents should be considered for patients with symptomatic anemia attributable to erythropoietin deficiency when the hemoglobin level is less than 10 g/dL (100 g/L).

- Erythropoiesis-stimulating agent therapy requires careful monitoring to titrate the dose to target hemoglobin levels of 10 to 11 g/dL (100-110 g/L).

Special Considerations

Special considerations for patients with CKD include medication dosing, medication selection, imaging, and vascular access. Medications that are renally excreted should be dosed based on the GFR of the patient. When intravenous or new medications are started, levels should be monitored if possible to avoid toxic levels and to ensure appropriate therapeutic levels. Non-nephrotoxic medications should be used when possible, and intravenous contrast should be avoided unless necessary. Fluid and electrolyte replacement should be administered carefully because patients with CKD can have impaired renal excretion of sodium, potassium, phosphorus, and magnesium.

Imaging

Iodinated contrast used in imaging studies can cause AKI in patients who have CKD and should be avoided. Alternatives include ultrasonography, noncontrast studies, plain radiography, and MRI (see Clinical Evaluation of Kidney Function, Imaging Studies). If a radiocontrast study is necessary, minimizing the amount of contrast and optimizing patient hemodynamics are cornerstones of treatment. Optimizing kidney perfusion entails avoiding hypovolemia, optimizing cardiac function (particularly in patients with heart failure), and discontinuing agents that can compromise kidney perfusion such as ACE inhibitors, ARBs, renin inhibitors, or NSAIDs. N-acetylcysteine is frequently given to prevent contrast-induced nephropathy; although the benefit may not be robust, N-acetylcysteine is associated with minimal risk. Once a patient with minimal urine output is on dialysis, iodinated contrast administration is thought to be safe.

The MRI contrast agent gadolinium is associated with nephrogenic systemic fibrosis (NSF) and should be avoided in patients with CKD, particularly those with a GFR less than 30 mL/min/1.73 m². NSF manifests as cutaneous plaques, papules, and nodules with a brawny wooden texture that start symmetrically in legs and may then involve the arms and trunk with sparing of the face. NSF usually occurs within a few months of gadolinium exposure but may take years to appear (or be recognized). In addition to skin and periarticular fibrosis, the heart, lungs, skeletal muscle, and diaphragm can also be affected. Patients with NSF often have a progressive course, resulting in worsening morbidity (from limited mobility and pain) and ultimately death. Although reversal with kidney transplantation has been reported, the best treatment is prevention. **H**

Vaccination

Patients with CKD are considered to have impaired immune systems. Vaccination should be addressed aggressively in patients with CKD because potential outcomes include dialysis and kidney transplantation. Providing vaccination before transplantation or dialysis may result in a superior immune response.

Annual influenza vaccination, as well as vaccination against *Streptococcus pneumoniae* at the time of CKD diagnosis and at 5-year intervals, is indicated. Hepatitis B vaccine series is recommended for patients with progressive CKD. Live virus vaccines are contraindicated in transplant recipients and should be avoided 3 months before planned transplantation. The role of the live varicella zoster vaccine in progressive CKD is not yet clear.

Hospitalization

Patients with CKD may ultimately need dialysis, and maintaining vein patency will make future arteriovenous hemodialysis access creation (fistula or graft) possible. Veins can be protected by avoiding intravenous lines and blood draws as much as possible. Use of the hands for veins for blood draws and peripheral intravenous lines is preferred. Peripherally inserted central catheter lines and subclavian central access should be avoided, and internal jugular central venous access is preferred if central access is needed to limit the risk of subsequent subclavian vein stenosis. Avoiding central veins, if possible, is preferred. Minimizing phlebotomy protects veins and reduces the potential for anemia. For patients on hemodialysis, phlebotomy can be done with their dialysis, which can spare these patients unnecessary venipuncture. **H**

KEY POINTS

- The MRI contrast agent gadolinium is associated with nephrogenic systemic fibrosis and should be avoided in patients with chronic kidney disease, particularly those with a glomerular filtration rate less than 30 mL/min/1.73 m².

- Vaccination should be addressed aggressively in patients with chronic kidney disease because the response to vaccination is superior before dialysis or transplantation.

- In patients with chronic kidney disease, avoiding intravenous lines and venipuncture in the arms is helpful to preserve veins for future dialysis access; use of the hands for venipuncture and peripheral intravenous lines is preferred.

Treatment of End-Stage Kidney Disease

Despite efforts to slow CKD progression, sometimes the residual renal mass is insufficient, and kidney function continues to decline. Discussions regarding the decline in kidney function and modalities of kidney replacement therapy should begin at least 1 year before the patient is likely to need kidney replacement therapy. When the estimated GFR approaches 20 mL/min/1.73 m², referral to a transplant center is appropriate, and more comprehensive "options teaching" should occur.

Transplantation is the treatment of choice for ESKD because the mortality and morbidity are far lower than with other modalities of kidney replacement therapy. Patients can undergo preemptive transplantation before initiating dialysis, which has a better prognosis than transplantation after dialysis. Preemptive transplantation is usually performed using a living donor but sometimes a patient may receive a kidney from a deceased donor. Nevertheless, many patients may not be appropriate candidates for transplantation or may not have an appropriate donor. Instead, they will need to pursue dialysis and, if appropriate, wait for a kidney while undergoing dialysis (**Table 47**).

Recent studies have shown that there is no benefit from early initiation of dialysis when kidney function is above an estimated GFR ≥12 mL/min/1.73 m². Patients should wait until they have uremic symptoms, electrolyte abnormalities that cannot be managed easily with medications, or evidence of malnutrition. Dialysis is typically initiated when the estimated GFR is between 8 and 11 mL/min/1.73 m²; most patients will be symptomatic at this level. Management of volume overload often necessitates earlier initiation compared with patients who can tolerate extra volume. **H**

KEY POINTS

- Discussions regarding the decline in kidney function and modalities of kidney replacement therapy should begin at least 1 year before the patient is likely to need kidney replacement therapy.

- Kidney transplantation is the treatment of choice for patients with end-stage kidney disease.

- Patients can undergo preemptive kidney transplantation before initiating dialysis, which has a better prognosis than transplantation after dialysis.

- Dialysis should be initiated in patients with uremic symptoms, electrolyte abnormalities that cannot be easily managed with medications, uncontrollable volume overload, or evidence of malnutrition.

Dialysis

Hemodialysis

The most common modality for dialysis in the United States is hemodialysis. Hemodialysis is typically done three times a week for 4 hours. Longer nocturnal strategies, which are employed six times a week, are gaining popularity. In anticipation of hemodialysis, patients should be referred for vascular access. Ideally, an autologous arteriovenous fistula is created by anastomosing a vein to an artery. The vein becomes thickened or "arterialized" and is then able to sustain repeated cannulation when dialysis is needed. If there are no appropriate veins, a synthetic conduit can be used, but these are more likely to develop thrombosis or infection. Finally, if initiation of dialysis is more urgent and the patient does not have access, a catheter can be placed. Large-gauge tunneled catheters are typically placed in the internal jugular vein rather than the subclavian vein because the latter may lead to subclavian venous stenosis and limit venous return of future arteriovenous access on the ipsilateral side. Catheters are easy to use but have a high rate of infection.

Because treatments are usually only three times a week, patients must adhere to a strict diet and limit sodium, potassium, and fluids between treatments. During dialysis, volume, electrolytes, anemia, and bone disease are carefully managed.

Peritoneal Dialysis

Peritoneal dialysis, in which the peritoneum is used as a dialysis membrane, is an alternative to hemodialysis for most patients with ESKD. Patients with heart failure tolerate peritoneal dialysis well because there are smaller fluid shifts than during hemodialysis, but patients who have had prior extensive abdominal surgeries may have too much scarring to utilize this modality. A catheter is placed in the peritoneum and tunneled through the abdominal wall. The incision requires 1 month to heal, and the patient receives training to perform exchanges. Peritoneal dialysis can be done by manually instilling and removing the dialysis fluid (an exchange), or a cycling

TABLE 47. Kidney Transplantation and Graft Survival[a]					
Transplantation	**Comment**	**1-Year Graft Survival**	**1-Year Patient Survival**	**5-Year Graft Survival**	**5-Year Patient Survival**
Living donor (related or unrelated)	Elective surgery may allow avoidance of dialysis	97%	99%	81%	91%
Deceased donor	Waiting time varies by blood type but typically >4 years for type O	93%	96%	72%	84%
Extended criteria Deceased donor	Shorter wait time; may include donors >60 years or those with hypertension; history of cerebrovascular accident or serum creatinine level >1.5 mg/dL (133 µmol/L)	86%	92%	57%	72%

[a]1-year data is from 2007 and 5-year data is from 2002 to 2007.

Data from Axelrod DA, McCullough KP, Brewer ED, Becker BN, Segev DL, Rao PS. Kidney and pancreas transplantation in the United States, 1999-2008: the changing face of living donation. Am J Transplant. 2010;10(4 Pt 2):987-1002. [PMID: 20420648]

machine can be utilized during the night that is programmed to perform exchanges automatically. In both techniques, fluid with a high concentration of dextrose is instilled into the peritoneum. Diffusion and convection aid in the movement of water, urea, and electrolytes into the dialysate, which is then drained and discarded. This modality offers independence for patients able to participate in their own care and more gradual shifts in electrolytes and fluid, but it may worsen control of diabetes from absorption of the dextrose in the peritoneal fluid. **H**

Management without Dialysis

Patients may decide not to participate in dialysis or may decide to stop dialysis after initiation ("withdrawal"). In these cases, the decision should be explored with the assistance of the patient's nephrologist. Patients who have been established on dialysis and then choose to stop typically survive less than 2 weeks; the progression to death is painless, and patients typically drift into a coma before death. If patients with a very low estimated GFR decide to continue on a protein-restricted diet without dialysis, the course can be much slower but similarly painless. Hospice services are infrequently utilized for patients with ESKD who choose to avoid or withdraw from dialysis but would be a potential benefit.

Complications of Dialysis

Cardiovascular Disease

Cardiovascular disease is the leading cause of death in patients on dialysis. The increased risk is multifactorial, but conventional cardiovascular risk factors do not fully explain the excess risk. Additional factors may be present in the uremic milieu, including mediators of inflammation, sympathetic nerve activity, disturbed mineral balance, and endothelial dysfunction. In addition, electrolyte abnormalities associated with intermittent hemodialysis make patients more susceptible to arrhythmias and sudden death. **H**

Acquired Renal Cystic Disease

Patients with CKD commonly develop multiple small bilateral cysts in the kidneys that may be noted incidentally on imaging. Although cysts may be seen before dialysis, the incidence increases as the number of months or years on dialysis increases. Most cysts are asymptomatic, but on occasion, patients may develop hematuria or flank pain. The most serious complication of acquired renal cystic disease is the development of renal cell carcinoma. The incidence of renal cell carcinoma is not clear, but some experts recommend screening after 3 to 5 years of dialysis.

KEY POINT

- Patients on dialysis have an increased risk for cardio-vascular disease and acquired renal cystic disease.

Kidney Transplantation

Kidney transplants can be from living or deceased donors. A living donor may be a relative, unrelated but emotionally related, or altruistic. Donor evaluation includes age-appropriate screening tests, kidney imaging, and assessment of kidney function and proteinuria. Donors are typically excluded if they have diabetes or hypertension. Recent studies show that carefully screened donors have no greater risk of ESKD than the general population.

Careful screening of the potential recipient is also essential. There are multiple potential barriers to transplantation, including ischemic heart disease, substance abuse, malignancy, and infection. In addition, cognitive, behavioral, and financial issues must be addressed.

Immunosuppressive Therapy

Kidney graft and patient survival have steadily improved; however, immunosuppressive therapy is needed to prevent the host immune system from rejecting the transplanted organ. Immunosuppressive regimens are complex and must balance the risk of rejection with that of excessive immunosuppression and adverse effects. Clinical practice guidelines from the American Transplantation Society are available at www.kdigo.org/clinical_practice_guidelines/pdf/TxpGL_publVersion.pdf.

Initial treatment includes induction immunosuppressive therapy because this is the period when the risk of acute rejection is greatest. Induction therapy may include T-cell–depleting antibodies or antibodies that block the IL-2 receptor. Maintenance therapy typically includes a calcineurin inhibitor and an antiproliferative agent with or without corticosteroids. Combination therapy with low doses of several agents that have different mechanisms of action may allow improved efficacy with less toxicity (**Table 48**).

Risks of Transplantation

Infection

Polyoma BK virus is an increasingly recognized cause of graft nephropathy. Screening with polymerase chain reaction testing and urine cytology is recommended in the first year and when there is a decline in kidney function. Definitive diagnosis requires kidney biopsy. When BK nephropathy occurs, reduction of immunosuppression to the minimum level possible to avoid rejection is required.

Cytomegalovirus (CMV) remains an important pathogen in the posttransplant period. Risk of infection depends on the serology of the donor and the recipient and is greatest when the donor is positive for CMV but the recipient is negative. Chemoprophylaxis with valganciclovir decreases the risk of infection. Patients with acute CMV infection may have a nonspecific febrile syndrome or more serious illness with enteritis, pneumonitis, or hepatitis. CMV infection is also associated with both acute and chronic rejection.

TABLE 48. Maintenance Immunosuppressive Therapy for Kidney Transplantation

Class	Medication	Mechanism	Adverse Effects
Anti-inflammatory	Prednisone	Inhibits T-cell activation by blocking IL-1, IL-6, IL-2, and IFN synthesis	Glucose intolerance; avascular necrosis; cataracts; hypertension; central obesity; bone loss
Calcineurin inhibitor	Tacrolimus and cyclosporine	Inhibits calcineurin activity necessary for transcription of genes that activate T cells	Both agents are nephrotoxic; tacrolimus: causes more glucose intolerance and neurologic toxicity (tremors, headaches); cyclosporine: causes more hypertension, hirsutism, and gingival hyperplasia
Antimetabolite	Mycophenolate mofetil and azathioprine	Blocks T- and B-cell proliferation by interrupting purine synthesis	Mycophenolate mofetil: nausea, diarrhea, leucopenia, anemia, viral infections; azathioprine: leukopenia, thrombocytopenia, hepatitis, susceptibility to infection and cancer (particularly squamous cell)
Inhibits rapamycin	Sirolimus	Blocks IL-2 dependent T-cell proliferation	Leukopenia; hyperlipidemia; proteinuria; glucose intolerance; decreased wound healing; pneumonitis; infertility

IFN = interferon; IL = interleukin.

Transplant recipients also are at increased risk of urinary tract infection in the first 6 months following transplantation. Prophylaxis with trimethoprim-sulfamethoxazole is usually recommended. This strategy also provides prophylaxis for *Pneumocystis jirovecii* pneumonia, and many centers will continue prophylaxis for the latter indefinitely. In addition, prophylaxis to prevent oral and esophageal candidiasis is recommended in the immediate posttransplant period.

Cancer
Kidney transplant recipients are at an increased risk for posttransplant lymphoproliferative disease (PTLD), which is often related to the Epstein-Barr virus. Reduction or withdrawal of immunosuppressive therapy may be sufficient to address PTLD, but some patients may require additional strategies to control the disease.

The incidence of squamous cell carcinoma of the skin is increased, particularly in those with long exposure to azathioprine, and all patients with CKD should be counseled to limit exposure to ultraviolet light.

Special Considerations in Transplant Recipients
Disease Recurrence
Several primary kidney diseases may recur in the transplanted kidney; the most concerning is primary focal segmental glomerulosclerosis. In this situation, the nephrotic syndrome may recur early in the posttransplant period but may respond to plasmapheresis. Thrombotic microangiopathy may also recur, particularly in the setting of calcineurin inhibitors, and may respond to withdrawal of these agents and use of plasma exchange. Diabetic nephropathy and IgA nephropathy may also recur as a late complication.

Cardiovascular Disease
The predilection for cardiovascular disease in patients with CKD continues after transplantation. Lipid abnormalities are common; however, they can be difficult to manage because use of calcineurin inhibitors together with statins increases the risk for rhabdomyolysis. Pravastatin and fluvastatin appear to have the lowest risk of myopathy and are not metabolized by CYP3A4; however, many transplant teams still prefer atorvastatin because it is the only statin that also lowers triglycerides and in low doses still has a low risk of myopathy.

Bone Disease
Although kidney transplantation may improve CKD-MBD, it may not completely resolve. Persistent posttransplant hyperparathyroidism is common and can manifest with hypophosphatemia and progressive decline in bone density. In addition, exposure to corticosteroids may lead to rapid bone loss or avascular necrosis.

Vaccinations
Ideally, patients should receive appropriate vaccinations before transplantation. At 6 months posttransplantation, a routine vaccination schedule can be resumed with the annual influenza vaccine, pneumococcal pneumonia vaccine every 5 years, and the tetanus vaccine every 10 years. Live vaccines such as varicella zoster, bacillus Calmette-Guerin, and oral polio are contraindicated after transplantation.

Nonadherence
Nonadherence is common and is associated with a high risk of rejection and graft loss. The most common reasons for nonadherence include side effects and costs of medications. Inadequate social support, substance use, and poor follow-up with transplant specialists are also important risk factors. This is best addressed by a team approach, which includes education, monitoring, detection, and intervention.

KEY POINTS

- Immunosuppression with both induction and maintenance therapy is needed in kidney transplant recipients to prevent the host immune system from rejecting the transplanted organ.

- Kidney transplant recipients have an increased risk for infection, cardiovascular disease, and malignancy as well as recurrence of their original kidney disease.

- Nonadherence by kidney transplant recipients is associated with a high risk of rejection and graft loss; the most common reasons include side effects and costs of medications.

Bibliography

Clinical Evaluation of Kidney Function

Brown RS. Has the time come to include urine dipstick testing in screening asymptomatic young adults? JAMA. 2011;306(7):764-765. [PMID: 21846861]

Chou R, Dana T. Screening adults for bladder cancer: a review of the evidence for the U.S. preventive services task force. Ann Intern Med. 2010;153(7):461-468. [PMID: 20921545]

Glassock RJ, Winearls C. Screening for CKD with eGFR: doubts and dangers. Clin J Am Soc Nephrol. 2008;3(5):1563-1568. [PMID: 18667744]

Guy M, Newall R, Borzomato J, Kalra PA, Price C. Use of a first-line urine protein-to-creatinine ratio strip test on random urines to rule out proteinuria in patients with chronic kidney disease. Nephrol Dial Transplant. 2009;24(4):1189-1193. [PMID: 18987264]

Levey AS, Stevens LA, Schmid CH, et al; CKD-EPI (Chronic Kidney Disease Epidemiology Collaboration). A new equation to estimate glomerular filtration rate. Ann Intern Med. 2009;150(9): 604-612. [PMID: 19414839]

Melamed ML, Bauer C, Hostetter TH. eGFR: is it ready for early identification of CKD? Clin J Am Soc Nephrol. 2008;3(5):1569-1572. [PMID: 18667739]

National Kidney Foundation. K/DOQI clinical practice guidelines for chronic kidney disease: evaluation, classification, and stratification. Am J Kidney Dis. 2002;39(2 Suppl 1):S1-S266. [PMID: 11904577]

Stevens LA, Schmid CH, Greene T, et al. Comparative performance of the CKD Epidemiology Collaboration (CKD-EPI) and the Modification of Diet in Renal Disease (MDRD) Study equations for estimating GFR levels above 60 mL/min/1.73 m2. Am J Kidney Dis. 2010;56(3):486-495. [PMID: 20557989]

Vivante A, Afek A, Frenkel-Nir Y, et al. Persistent asymptomatic isolated microscopic hematuria in Israeli adolescents and young adults and risk for end-stage renal disease. JAMA. 2011;306(7):729-736. [PMID: 21846854]

Fluids and Electrolytes

Alshayeb HM, Showkat A, Babar F, Mangold, Wall BM. Severe hypernatremia correction rate and mortality in hospitalized patients. Am J Med Sci. 2011;341(5):356-360. [PMID: 21358313]

Fenske W, Maier SKG, Blechschmidt A, Allolio B, Störk S. Utility and limitations of the traditional diagnostic approach to hyponatremia: a diagnostic study. Am J Med. 2010;123(7):652-657. [PMID: 20609688]

Liamis G, Milionis HJ, Elisaf M. Medication-induced hypophosphatemia: a review. QJM. 2010;103(7):449-459. [PMID: 20356849]

Sterns RH, Hix JK, Silver S. Treatment of hyponatremia. Curr Opin Nephrol Hypertens. 2010;19(5): 493-498. [PMID: 20539224]

Unwin RJ, Luft FC, Shirley DG. Pathophysiology and management of hypokalemia: a clinical perspective. Nat Rev Nephrol. 2011;7(2):75-84. [PMID: 21278718]

Weir MR, Rolfe M. Potassium homeostasis and renin-angiotensin-aldosterone system inhibitors. Clin J Am Soc Nephrol. 2010;5(3):531-548. [PMID: 20150448]

Acid-Base Disorders

Adrogué HJ, Madias NE. Secondary responses to altered acid-base status: the rules of engagement. J Am Soc Nephrol. 2010;21(6):920-923. [PMID: 20431042]

Gennari FJ, Weise WJ. Acid-base disturbances in gastrointestinal disease. Clin J Am Soc Nephrol. 2008;3(6):1861-1868. [PMID: 18922984]

Kraut JA, Kurtz I. Toxic alcohol ingestions: clinical features, diagnosis, and management. Clin J Am Soc Nephrol. 2008;3(1):208-225. [PMID: 18045860]

Kraut JA, Madias NE. Metabolic acidosis: pathophysiology, diagnosis and management. Nat Rev Nephrol. 2010;6(5):274-285. [PMID: 20308999]

Hypertension

American Diabetes Association. Standards of medical care in diabetes—2011. Diabetes Care. 2011;34(Suppl 1):S11-S61. [PMID: 21193625]

Bangalore S, Messerli FH, Wun CC, et al; Treating to New Targets Steering Committee and Investigators. J-curve revisited: an analysis of blood pressure and cardiovascular events in the Treating to New Targets (TNT) Trial. Eur Heart J. 2010;31(23):2897-2908. [PMID: 20846991]

Beckett NS, Peters R, Fletcher AE, et al; HYVET Study Group. Treatment of hypertension in patients 80 years of age or older. N Engl J Med. 2008;358(18):1887-1898. [PMID: 18378519]

Calhoun DA, Jones D, Textor S, et al; American Heart Association Professional Education Committee. Resistant hypertension: diagnosis, evaluation, and treatment: a scientific statement from the American Heart Association Professional Education Committee of the Council for High Blood Pressure Research. Circulation. 2008;117(25):e510-e526. [PMID: 18574054]

Chobanian AV, Bakris GL, Black HR, et al; Joint National Committee on Prevention, Detection, Evaluation, and Treatment of High Blood Pressure. National Heart, Lung, and Blood Institute; National High Blood Pressure Education Program Coordinating Committee. Seventh report of the Joint National Committee on Prevention, Detection, Evaluation, and Treatment of High Blood Pressure. Hypertension. 2003;42(6):1206-1252. [PMID: 14656957]

ACCORD Study Group, Cushman WC, Evans GW, Byington RP, et al. Effects of intensive blood-pressure control in type 2 diabetes mellitus. N Engl J Med. 2010;362(17):1575-1585. [PMID: 20228401]

Egan BM, Zhao Y, Axon RN. US trends in prevalence, awareness, treatment, and control of hypertension, 1988-2008. JAMA. 2010;303(20):2043-2050. [PMID: 20501926]

Flack JM, Sica DA, Bakris G, et al; International Society on Hypertension in Blacks. Management of high blood pressure in blacks: an update of the International Society on Hypertension in Blacks consensus statement. Hypertension. 2010;56(5):780-800. [PMID: 20921433]

Green BB, Cook AJ, Ralston JD, et al. Effectiveness of home blood pressure monitoring, Web communication, and pharmacist care on hypertension control: a randomized controlled trial. JAMA. 2008;299(24):2857-2867. [PMID: 18577730]

Jamerson K, Weber MA, Bakris GL, et al; ACCOMPLISH Trial Investigators. Benazepril plus amlodipine or hydrochlorothiazide for hypertension in high-risk patients. N Engl J Med. 2008;359(23):2417-2428. [PMID: 19052124]

Law MR, Morris JK, Wald NJ. Use of blood pressure lowering drugs in the prevention of cardiovascular disease: meta-analysis of 147 randomised trials in the context of expectations from prospective epidemiological studies. BMJ. 2009;338:b1665. [PMID: 19454737]

Pickering TG, Miller NH, Ogedegbe G, Krakoff LR, Artinian NT, Goff D; American Heart Association; American Society of Hypertension; Preventive Cardiovascular Nurses Association. Call to action on use and reimbursement for home blood pressure monitoring: executive summary: a joint scientific statement from the American Heart Association, American Society of Hypertension, and Preventive Cardiovascular Nurses Association. Hypertension. 2008;52(1):1-9. [PMID: 18497371]

Rossi GP, Bernini G, Caliumi C, et al; PAPY Study Investigators. A prospective study of the prevalence of primary aldosteronism in 1,125 hypertensive patients. J Am Coll Cardiol. 2006;48(11):2293-2300. [PMID: 17161262]

Chronic Tubulointerstitial Disorders

Appel GB. The treatment of acute interstitial nephritis: more data at last. Kidney Int. 2008;73(8):905-907. [PMID: 18379525]

Bendz H, Schön S, Attman PO, Aurell M. Renal failure occurs in chronic lithium treatment but is uncommon. Kidney Int. 2010;77(3):219-224. [PMID: 19940841]

Menè P, Punzo G. Uric acid: bystander or culprit in hypertension and progressive renal disease? J Hypertens. 2008;26(11):2085-2092. [PMID: 18854744]

Glomerular Diseases

ACCORD Study Group, Cushman WC, Evans GW, Byington RP, et al. Effects of intensive blood-pressure control in type 2 diabetes mellitus. N Engl J Med. 2010;362(17):1575-1585. [PMID: 20228401]

de Boer IH, Rue TC, Hall YN, Heagerty PJ, Weiss NS, Himmelfarb J. Temporal trends in the prevalence of diabetic kidney disease in the United States. JAMA. 2011;305(24):2532-2539. [PMID: 21693741]

Dooley MA, Jayne D, Ginzler EM, et al; ALMS Group. Mycophenolate versus azathioprine as maintenance therapy for lupus nephritis. N Engl J Med. 2011;365(20):1886-1895. [PMID: 22087680]

Duckworth W, Abraira C, Moritz T, et al; VADT Investigators. Glucose control and vascular complications in veterans with type 2 diabetes [errata in N Engl J Med. 2009;361(10):1024-1025 and N Engl J Med. 2009;361(10):1028]. N Engl J Med. 2009;360(2):129-139. [PMID: 19092145]

Jayne DR, Gaskin G, Rasmussen N, et al; European Vasculitis Study Group. Randomized trial of plasma exchange or high-dosage methylprednisolone as adjunctive therapy for severe renal vasculitis. J Am Soc Nephrol. 2007;18(7):2180-2188. [PMID: 17582159]

Sethi S, Nester CM, Smith RJ. Membranoproliferative glomerulonephritis and C3 glomerulopathy: resolving the confusion. Kidney Int. 2012;81(5):434-441. [PMID: 22157657]

Waldman M, Crew RJ, Valeri A, et al. Adult minimal-change disease: clinical characteristics, treatment, and outcomes. Clin J Am Soc Nephrol. 2007;2(3):445-453. [PMID: 17699450]

Working Group of the International IgA Nephropathy Network and the Renal Pathology Society, Cattran DC, Coppo R, Cook HT, et al. The Oxford classification of IgA nephropathy: rationale, clinicopathological correlations, and classification. Kidney Int. 2009;76(5):534-545. [PMID: 19571791]

Genetic Disorders and Kidney Disease

Curatolo P, Bombardieri R, Jozwiak S. Tuberous sclerosis. Lancet. 2008;372(9639):657-668. [PMID: 18722871]

Gubler MC. Inherited diseases of the glomerular basement membrane. Nat Clin Pract Nephrol. 2008;4(1):24-37. [PMID: 18094725]

Haas M. Alport syndrome and thin glomerular basement membrane nephropathy: a practical approach to diagnosis. Arch Pathol Lab Med. 2009;133(2):224-232. [PMID: 19195966]

Kashtan CE, Segal Y. Genetic disorders of glomerular basement membranes. Nephron Clin Pract. 2011;118(1):c9-c18. [PMID: 21071975]

Pei Y, Obaji J, Dupuis A, et al. Unified criteria for ultrasonographic diagnosis of ADPKD. J Am Soc Nephrol. 2009;20(1):205-212. [PMID: 18945943]

Torres VE, Harris PC. Autosomal dominant polycystic kidney disease: the last 3 years. Kidney Int. 2009;76(2):149-168. [PMID: 19455193]

Walz G, Budde K, Mannaa M, et al. Everolimus in patients with autosomal dominant polycystic kidney disease. N Engl J Med. 2010;363(9):830-840. [PMID: 20581392]

Acute Kidney Injury

Abu-Alfa AK, Younes A. Tumor lysis syndrome and acute kidney injury: evaluation, prevention, and management. Am J Kidney Dis. 2010;55(5 Suppl 3):S1-S13. [PMID: 20420966]

Bosch X, Poch E, Grau JM. Rhabdomyolysis and acute kidney injury. N Engl J Med. 2009;361(1):62-72. [PMID: 19571284]

Coiffier B, Altman A, Pui CH, Younes A, Cairo MS. Guidelines for the management of pediatric and adult tumor lysis syndrome: an evidence-based review [erratum in J Clin Oncol. 2010;28(4):708]. J Clin Oncol. 2008;26(16):2767-2778. [PMID: 18509186]

European Association for the Study of the Liver. EASL clinical practice guidelines on the management of ascites, spontaneous bacterial peritonitis, and hepatorenal syndrome in cirrhosis. J Hepatol. 2010;53(3):397-417. [PMID: 20633946]

Felker GM, Lee KL, Bull DA, et al; NHLBI Heart Failure Clinical Research Network. Diuretic strategies in patients with acute decompensated heart failure. N Engl J Med. 2011;364(9):797-805. [PMID: 21366472]

Hutchison CA, Bradwell AR, Cook M, et al. Treatment of acute renal failure secondary to multiple myeloma with chemotherapy and extended high cut-off hemodialysis. Clin J Am Soc Nephrol. 2009;4(4):745-754. [PMID: 19339414]

Perazella MA, Markowitz GS. Drug-induced acute interstitial nephritis. Nat Rev Nephrol. 2010;6(8):461-470. [PMID: 20517290]

Ronco C, Haapio M, House AA, Anavekar N, Bellomo R. Cardiorenal syndrome. J Am Coll Cardiol. 2008;52(19):1527-1539. [PMID: 19007588]

Scolari F, Ravani P. Atheroembolic renal disease. Lancet. 2010;375(9726):1650-1660. [PMID: 20381857]

Shah-Khan F, Scheetz MH, Ghossein C. Biopsy-proven acute tubular necrosis due to vancomycin toxicity. Int J Nephrol. 2011;2011:436856. [PMID: 21716699]

Kidney Stones

American Urological Association. Management of ureteral calculi: EAU/AUA nephrolithiasis panel (2007). Available at www.auanet.org/content/guidelines-and-quality-care/clinical-guidelines.cfm. Accessed July 3, 2012.

Eisner BH, Eisenberg ML, Stoller ML. Relationship between body mass index and quantitative 24-hour urine chemistries in patients with nephrolithiasis. Urology. 2010;75(6):1289-1293. [PMID: 20018350]

Goldfarb DS. In the clinic. Nephrolithiasis. Ann Intern Med. 2009;151(3):ITC2. [PMID: 19652185]

Krambeck AE, Rule AD, Li X, Bergstralh EJ, Gettman MT, Lieske JC. Shock wave lithotripsy is not predictive of hypertension among community stone formers at long-term followup [erratum in J Urol. 2011;185(3):1161]. J Urol. 2011;185(1):164-169. [PMID: 21074794]

Maalouf NM, Tondapu P, Guth ES, Livingston EH, Sakhaee K. Hypocitraturia and hyperoxaluria after Roux-en-Y gastric bypass surgery. J Urol. 2010;183(3):1026-1030. [PMID: 20096421]

Taylor EN, Fung TT, Curhan GC. DASH-style diet associates with reduced risk for kidney stones. J Am Soc Nephrol. 2009;20(10):2253-2259. [PMID: 19679672]

Worcester EM, Coe FL. Clinical practice. Calcium kidney stones. N Engl J Med. 2010;363(10):954-963. [PMID: 20818905]

The Kidney in Pregnancy

Berks D, Steegers EA, Molas M, Visser W. Resolution of hypertension and proteinuria after preeclampsia. Obstet Gynecol. 2009;114(6):1307-1314. [PMID: 19935034]

Lykke JA, Langhoff-Roos J, Sibai BM, Funai EF, Triche EW, Paidas MJ. Hypertensive pregnancy disorders and subsequent cardiovascular morbidity and type 2 diabetes mellitus in the mother. Hypertension. 2009;53(6):944-951. [PMID: 19433776]

Noori M, Donald AE, Angelakopoulou A, Hingorani AD, Williams DJ. Prospective study of placental angiogenic factors and maternal vascular function before and after preeclampsia and gestational hypertension. Circulation. 2010;122(5):478-487. [PMID: 20644016]

Podymow T, August P. Update on the use of antihypertensive drugs in pregnancy. Hypertension. 2008;51(4):960-969. [PMID: 18259046]

Seely EW, Ecker J. Clinical practice. Chronic hypertension in pregnancy. N Engl J Med. 2011;365(5):439-446. [PMID: 21812673]

Steegers EA, von Dadelszen P, Duvekot JJ, Pijnenborg R. Pre-eclampsia. Lancet. 2010;376(9741):631-644. [PMID: 20598363]

Chronic Kidney Disease

Axelrod DA, McCullough KP, Brewer ED, Becker BN, Segev DL, Rao PS. Kidney and pancreas transplantation in the United States, 1999-2008: the changing face of living donation. Am J Transplant. 2010;10(4 Pt 2):987-1002. [PMID: 20420648]

Bakris GL, Sarafidis PA, Weir MR, et al; ACCOMPLISH Trial investigators. Renal outcomes with different fixed-dose combination therapies in patients with hypertension at high risk for cardiovascular events (ACCOMPLISH): a prespecified secondary analysis of a randomised controlled trial. Lancet. 2010;3;375(9721):1173-1181. [PMID: 20170948]

Bomback AS, Kshirsagar AV, Amamoo MA, Klemmer PJ. Change in proteinuria after adding aldosterone blockers to ACE inhibitors or angiotensin receptor blockers in CKD: a systematic review. Am J Kidney Dis. 2008;51(2):199-211. [PMID: 18215698]

Cooper BA, Branley P, Bulfone L, et al; IDEAL Study. A randomized controlled trial of early versus late initiation of dialysis. N Engl J Med. 2010;363(7):609-619. [PMID: 20581422]

de Brito-Ashurst I, Varagunam M, Raftery MJ, Yaqoob MM. Bicarbonate supplementation slows progression of CKD and improves nutritional status. J Am Soc Nephrol. 2009;20(9):2075-2084. [PMID: 19608703]

Drawz P, Rahman M. In the clinic. Chronic kidney disease. Ann Intern Med. 2009;150(3):ITC2-1-ITC2-15. [PMID: 19189903]

Fellström BC, Jardine AG, Schmieder RE, et al; AURORA Study Group. Rosuvastatin and cardiovascular events in patients undergoing hemodialysis [erratum in N Engl J Med. 2010;362(15):1450]. N Engl J Med. 2009;360(14):1395-1407. [PMID: 19332456]

Go AS, Chertow GM, Fan D, McCulloch CE, Hsu CY. Chronic kidney disease and the risks of death, cardiovascular events, and hospitalization. N Engl J Med. 2004;351(13):1296-1305. [PMID: 15385656]

Gordon PL, Frassetto LA. Management of osteoporosis in CKD Stages 3 to 5. Am J Kidney Dis. 2010;55(5):941-956. [PMID: 20438987]

Ibrahim HN, Foley R, Tan L, et al. Long-term consequences of kidney donation. N Engl J Med. 2009;360:459-469 [PMID: 19179315]

Kidney Disease: Improving Global Outcomes (KDIGO) CKD-MBD Work Group. KDIGO clinical practice guideline for the diagnosis, evaluation, and treatment of chronic kidney disease-mineral and bone disorder (CKD-MBD). Kidney Int Suppl. 2009;(113):S1-S130. [PMID: 19644521]

Kidney Disease: Improving Global Outcomes (KDIGO) Transplant Work Group. KDIGO clinical practice guideline for the care of kidney transplant recipients. Am J Transplant. 2009;9(Suppl 3):S1-S155. [PMID: 19845597]

Mann JF, Schmieder RE, McQueen M, et al; ONTARGET Investigators. Renal outcomes with telmisartan, ramipril, or both, in people at high vascular risk (the ONTARGET study): a multicentre, randomised, double-blind, controlled trial. Lancet. 2008;372(9638):547-553. [PMID: 18707986]

Navaneethan SD, Nigwekar SU, Perkovic V, Johnson DW, Craig JC, Strippoli GF. HMG CoA reductase inhibitors (statins) for dialysis patients. Cochrane Database Syst Rev. 2009;(3):CD004289. [PMID: 19588351]

Navaneethan SD, Pansini F, Perkovic V, et al. HMG CoA reductase inhibitors (statins) for people with chronic kidney disease not requiring dialysis. Cochrane Database Syst Rev. 2009;(2):CD007784. [PMID: 19370693]

Palmer SC, Hayen A, Macaskill P, et al. Serum levels of phosphorus, parathyroid hormone, and calcium and risks of death and cardiovascular disease in individuals with chronic kidney disease: a systematic review and meta-analysis. JAMA. 2011;305(11):1119-1127. [PMID: 21406649]

Pfeffer MA, Burdmann EA, Chen CY, et al; TREAT Investigators. A trial of darbepoetin alfa in type 2 diabetes and chronic kidney disease. N Engl J Med. 2009;361(21):2019-2032. [PMID: 19880844]

Solomon SD, Uno H, Lewis EF, et al; Trial to Reduce Cardiovascular Events with Aranesp Therapy (TREAT) Investigators. Erythropoietic response and outcomes in kidney disease and type 2 diabetes. N Engl J Med. 2010;363(12):1146-1155. [PMID: 20843249]

U.S. Food and Drug Administration. FDA Drug Safety Communication: erythropoiesis-stimulating agents (ESAs): procrit, epogen and aranesp. www.fda.gov/Drugs/DrugSafety/Postmarket DrugSafetyInformationforPatientsandProviders/ucm200297.htm. Accessed July 3, 2012.

Wright JT Jr, Bakris G, Greene T, et al; African American Study of Kidney Disease and Hypertension Study Group. Effect of blood pressure lowering and antihypertensive drug class on progression of hypertensive kidney disease: results from the AASK trial. JAMA. 2002;288(19):2421-2431. [PMID: 12435255]

Nephrology Self-Assessment Test

This self-assessment test contains one-best-answer multiple-choice questions. Please read these directions carefully before answering the questions. Answers, critiques, and bibliographies immediately follow these multiple-choice questions. The American College of Physicians is accredited by the Accreditation Council for Continuing Medical Education (ACCME) to provide continuing medical education for physicians.

The American College of Physicians designates MKSAP 16 Nephrology for a maximum of 16 *AMA PRA Category 1 Credits*™. Physicians should claim only the credit commensurate with the extent of their participation in the activity.

Earn "Same-Day" CME Credits Online

For the first time, print subscribers can enter their answers online to earn CME credits in 24 hours or less. You can submit your answers using online answer sheets that are provided at mksap.acponline.org, where a record of your MKSAP 16 credits will be available. To earn CME credits, you need to answer all of the questions in a test and earn a score of at least 50% correct (number of correct answers divided by the total number of questions). Take any of the following approaches:

> ➤ Use the printed answer sheet at the back of this book to record your answers. Go to mksap.acponline.org, access the appropriate online answer sheet, transcribe your answers, and submit your test for same-day CME credits. There is no additional fee for this service.

> ➤ Go to mksap.acponline.org, access the appropriate online answer sheet, directly enter your answers, and submit your test for same-day CME credits. There is no additional fee for this service.

> ➤ Pay a $10 processing fee per answer sheet and submit the printed answer sheet at the back of this book by mail or fax, as instructed on the answer sheet. Make sure you calculate your score and fax the answer sheet to 215-351-2799 or mail the answer sheet to Member and Customer Service, American College of Physicians, 190 N. Independence Mall West, Philadelphia, PA 19106-1572, using the courtesy envelope provided in your MKSAP 16 slipcase. You will need your 10-digit order number and 8-digit ACP ID number, which are printed on your packing slip. Please allow 4 to 6 weeks for your score report to be emailed back to you. Be sure to include your email address for a response.

If you do not have a 10-digit order number and 8-digit ACP ID number or if you need help creating a username and password to access the MKSAP 16 online answer sheets, go to mksap.acponline.org or email custserv@acponline.org.

CME credit is available from the publication date of December 31, 2012, until December 31, 2015. You may submit your answer sheets at any time during this period.

Each of the numbered items is followed by lettered answers. Select the ONE lettered answer that is BEST in each case.

Item 1

A 41-year-old woman is evaluated during a follow-up visit for high blood pressure. She is a vegetarian and does not smoke cigarettes. She feels well except for an occasional tension headache. She takes no medications.

On physical examination, blood pressure is 162/100 mm Hg, which is similar to the values measured at her initial visit. Other vital signs are normal. BMI is 21. The remainder of the examination is unremarkable.

Laboratory studies reveal normal electrolytes, complete blood count, fasting glucose, and fasting lipid profile as well as normal kidney function.

Electrocardiogram is unremarkable.

Which of the following is the most appropriate next step in the management of this patient's hypertension?

(A) Combination drug therapy
(B) Lifestyle modifications
(C) Single-drug therapy
(D) Reevaluate patient in 2 weeks

Item 2

A 52-year-old woman is evaluated for a 2-day history of right flank pain, mild nausea, and fever. She has autosomal dominant polycystic kidney disease.

On physical examination, the patient appears ill. Temperature is 38.6 °C (101.4 °F), blood pressure is 149/94 mm Hg, pulse rate is 92/min, and respiration rate is 20/min. BMI is 26. Abdominal examination reveals right costovertebral angle tenderness on palpation; the abdomen is nondistended, and bowel sounds are normal.

Laboratory studies reveal a leukocyte count of 13,000/µL (13×10^9/L), a serum creatinine level of 1.9 mg/dL (168 µmol/L), and negative urine culture results.

On kidney ultrasound, the left kidney is 16.2 cm, and the right kidney is 16.9 cm; multiple bilateral intraparenchymal cysts are noted.

Which of the following is the most appropriate treatment for this patient?

(A) Amoxicillin
(B) Cephalexin
(C) Ciprofloxacin
(D) Nitrofurantoin

Item 3

A 51-year-old man is being followed in the hospital after receiving chemotherapy for acute myeloid leukemia 1 day ago. Kidney function was normal at the start of his treatment, which consisted of normal saline at a rate of 200 mL/h and rasburicase on the day of chemotherapy. He reports no symptoms except for some fatigue and nausea. He has no shortness of breath or fever.

On physical examination, the patient is afebrile. Blood pressure is 122/70 mm Hg, pulse rate is 72/min, and respiration rate is 12/min. BMI is 25. Some bruising is noted on the skin. There is no jugular venous distention. Heart rate is regular. Lungs are clear to auscultation. There is no edema.

Urine output has been around 50 mL/h.

Laboratory studies:

Albumin	3.2 g/dL (32 g/L)
Blood urea nitrogen	14 mg/dL (5.0 mmol/L)
Calcium	9 mg/dL (2.3 mmol/L)
Serum creatinine	1.0 mg/dL (88.4 µmol/L) (baseline: 0.9 mg/dL [79.6 µmol/L])
Electrolytes	
Sodium	139 meq/L (139 mmol/L)
Potassium	5.2 meq/L (5.2 mmol/L)
Chloride	100 meq/L (100 mmol/L)
Bicarbonate	25 meq/L (25 mmol/L)
Phosphorus	5.7 mg/dL (1.84 mmol/L)
Uric acid	7.1 mg/dL (0.42 mmol/L)

Which of the following is the most appropriate next step in management?

(A) Add sodium bicarbonate to intravenous fluid at current rate
(B) Add sodium polystyrene sulfonate
(C) Increase intravenous saline rate
(D) Substitute allopurinol for rasburicase

Item 4

A 31-year-old woman is seen to discuss treatment of her progressive chronic kidney disease resulting from membranoproliferative glomerulonephritis. She has had a steady decline in kidney function and is approaching the need for kidney replacement therapy. Her identical twin sister has agreed to donate a kidney but is currently pregnant, and donation will likely not be possible for at least a year. She is otherwise doing well and is actively involved in her medical care. In discussing future treatment options, she has expressed a desire to pursue peritoneal dialysis should kidney replacement therapy be needed before the availability of the transplant from her sister. Medications are epoetin alfa, sevelamer, amlodipine, and sodium bicarbonate.

On physical examination, blood pressure is 126/78 mm Hg. BMI is 24. Cardiac examination is normal without a rub. Lungs are clear. Abdominal examination is normal, with no evidence of prior surgery. There is no asterixis. Trace edema is present.

Laboratory studies reveal a blood urea nitrogen level of 88 mg/dL (31.4 mmol/L), a serum creatinine level of 4.7 mg/dL (415 µmol/L), and a urine protein–creatinine ratio of 3.3 mg/mg.

In counseling this patient, which of the following is the most appropriate recommendation for management?

(A) Plan for hemodialysis when needed
(B) Plan for peritoneal dialysis when needed

(C) Pursue a deceased donor kidney transplant

(D) Start either form of dialysis now

Item 5

A 20-year-old woman is evaluated for a 4-week history of fatigue, polyarthritis, oral ulcers, and edema. Her medical history is unremarkable, and she takes no medications.

On physical examination, blood pressure is 165/100 mm Hg; other vital signs are normal. There are ulcers on the hard palate and buccal mucosa. Symmetric swelling, erythema, and tenderness of the metacarpophalangeal and proximal interphalangeal joints are noted. There is 2+ pitting edema of the lower extremities.

Laboratory studies:

Hemoglobin	10.8 g/dL (108 g/L)
Leukocyte count	2000/µL (2.0×10^9/L)
Platelet count	110,000/µL (110×10^9/L)
Albumin	3.4 g/dL (34 g/L)
Serum creatinine	1.4 mg/dL (124 µmol/L)
Urinalysis	15-20 erythrocytes/hpf; 10-15 leukocytes/hpf; erythrocyte casts
Urine protein–creatinine ratio	2.8 mg/mg

Which of the following is the most likely diagnosis?

(A) Focal segmental glomerulosclerosis

(B) IgA nephropathy

(C) Postinfectious glomerulonephritis

(D) Proliferative lupus nephritis

Item 6

A 50-year-old man returns for a follow-up visit to discuss his blood pressure results. At his new patient office visit 6 weeks ago, his blood pressure was 138/82 mm Hg, and the evaluation was otherwise unremarkable. At his follow-up visit 2 weeks later, his blood pressure was 136/85 mm Hg. He does not smoke cigarettes or use alcohol or drugs. Family history is significant for his mother who has hypertension. He takes no medications.

On physical examination today, blood pressure is 135/84 mm Hg; other vital signs are normal. BMI is 26. The remainder of the examination, including cardiac and pulmonary examinations, is normal.

Laboratory studies:

Complete blood count	Normal
Serum creatinine	Normal
Electrolytes	Normal
Glucose	Normal
Total cholesterol	192 mg/dL (4.97 mmol/L)
LDL cholesterol	145 mg/dL (3.76 mmol/L)
HDL cholesterol	38 mg/dL (0.98 mmol/L)
Triglycerides	Normal

Electrocardiogram is normal.

In addition to lifestyle modifications, which of the following is the most appropriate next step in the management of this patient's blood pressure?

(A) Ambulatory blood pressure monitoring

(B) High-sensitivity C-reactive protein measurement

(C) Hydrochlorothiazide

(D) Recheck blood pressure in 1 year

Item 7

A 56-year-old man is evaluated in the emergency department after his wife found him unconscious. She reports that he has a history of alcohol abuse. Upon arrival, he has a generalized seizure that resolves spontaneously. He is treated with lorazepam, thiamine, and a 1-L bolus of 5% dextrose-0.9% saline.

On physical examination, the patient is thin, disheveled, and somnolent. Temperature is 35.8 °C (96.4 °F), blood pressure is 100/50 mm Hg, pulse rate is 110/min, and respiration rate is 18/min. Repeat examination 30 minutes later reveals an increased level of consciousness and normal strength. The remainder of the examination is normal.

Laboratory studies:

	Initial	30 Minutes Later
Blood urea nitrogen	56 mg/dL (20 mmol/L)	42 mg/dL (15 mmol/L)
Serum creatinine	1.6 mg/dL (141 µmol/L)	1.5 mg/dL (133 µmol/L)
Electrolytes		
Sodium	133 meq/L (133 mmol/L)	135 meq/L (135 mmol/L)
Potassium	3.5 meq/L (3.5 mmol/L)	3.4 meq/L (3.4 mmol/L)
Chloride	92 meq/L (92 mmol/L)	97 meq/L (97 mmol/L)
Bicarbonate	16 meq/L (16 mmol/L)	20 meq/L (20 mmol/L)
Ethanol	88 mg/dL (19 mmol/L)	–
Glucose	90 mg/dL (5.0 mmol/L)	102 mg/dL (5.7 mmol/L)
Osmolality	320 mosm/kg H_2O	–
Arterial blood gas studies (ambient air):		
pH	7.15	7.30
$P\text{CO}_2$	40 mm Hg (5.3 kPa)	37 mm Hg (4.9 kPa)
$P\text{O}_2$	86 mm Hg (11.4 kPa)	92 mm Hg (12.2 kPa)
Urinalysis	pH 5.4; trace protein; 1+ ketones; few hyaline casts	–

CONT. Which of the following is the most appropriate next step in management?

(A) Fomepizole
(B) Hemodialysis
(C) Sodium bicarbonate
(D) Supportive care

Item 8

A 55-year-old woman is evaluated during a routine visit. She was diagnosed with chronic kidney disease 3 years ago. For the past year, she has had increasing fatigue. She reports no shortness of breath or chest pain. Medications are lisinopril, furosemide, calcium acetate, ferrous sulfate, and a multivitamin.

On physical examination, temperature is normal, blood pressure is 100/70 mm Hg, pulse rate is 76/min, and respiration rate is 14/min. BMI is 30. Abdominal examination is normal. A stool specimen is negative for occult blood.

Laboratory studies:

Hemoglobin	8.9 g/dL (89 g/L) (1 year ago: 11 g/dL [110 g/L])
Mean corpuscular hemoglobin	30 pg
Mean corpuscular hemoglobin concentration	33 g/dL (330 g/L)
Mean corpuscular volume	91 fL
Reticulocyte count	1% of erythrocytes
Serum creatinine	2 mg/dL (177 µmol/L)
Ferritin	250 ng/mL (250 µg/L)
Transferrin saturation	33%
Folate	Normal
Vitamin B_{12}	Normal

Which of the following is the most appropriate intervention for this patient's management?

(A) Add ascorbic acid
(B) Add an erythropoiesis-stimulating agent
(C) Perform a blood transfusion
(D) Switch from oral to intravenous iron therapy

Item 9

A 42-year-old man hospitalized for recurrent variceal bleeding is evaluated 48 hours after admission for severe metabolic alkalosis. He has a 4-year history of alcoholic cirrhosis. He received endoscopic therapy for the varices. In the first 24 hours following admission, he required six units of packed red blood cells and four units of fresh frozen platelets to maintain hemodynamic stability. Today he feels confused but otherwise reports no symptoms. Medications are nadolol, octreotide, and intravenous ciprofloxacin.

On physical examination, temperature is normal, blood pressure is 100/70 mm Hg, and pulse rate is 96/min. BMI is 20. Cardiopulmonary examination is normal. Ascites is noted. There is 2+ presacral edema and 2+ leg edema.

Laboratory studies:

	On Admission	Hospital Day 2
Serum creatinine	1.2 mg/dL (106 µmol/L)	–
Electrolytes		
Sodium	138 meq/L (138 mmol/L)	136 meq/L (136 mmol/L)
Potassium	3.8 meq/L (3.8 mmol/L)	5.0 meq/L (5.0 mmol/L)
Chloride	105 meq/L (105 mmol/L)	85 meq/L (85 mmol/L)
Bicarbonate	21 meq/L (21 mmol/L)	38 meq/L (38 mmol/L)
Urine chloride	–	<5 meq/L (5 mmol/L) (normal range for men, 25-371 meq/L [25-371 mmol/L])
Arterial blood gas studies (ambient air):		
pH	–	7.52
Pco_2	–	48 mm Hg (6.4 kPa)

Which of the following is the most appropriate management?

(A) Add acetazolamide
(B) Add furosemide
(C) Add isotonic saline
(D) Discontinue octreotide

Item 10

A 26-year-old man is evaluated for a 3-day history of fever, lower abdominal pain, tenesmus, hematochezia, and watery diarrhea. Seven months ago, he underwent a cadaveric kidney transplantation. At the time of transplantation, the transplant donor was seropositive for cytomegalovirus, and the patient was seronegative for this virus. Current medications are tacrolimus, mycophenolate mofetil, prednisone, and trimethoprim-sulfamethoxazole. Valganciclovir was discontinued 1 month ago after 6 months of prophylaxis as per standard protocol.

On physical examination, temperature is 38.8 °C (101.8 °F), blood pressure is 100/70 mm Hg, pulse rate is 104/min, and respiration rate is 18/min. BMI is 24. Cardiopulmonary examination is normal. Abdominal examination reveals increased bowel sounds but no tenderness to palpation. There is no organomegaly.

Laboratory studies:

Leukocyte count	2100/µL (2.1×10^9/L)
Alanine aminotransferase	72 units/L
Aspartate aminotransferase	60 units/L
Serum creatinine	1.4 mg/dL (124 µmol/L)

Chest radiograph is normal.

Which of the following is the most likely diagnosis?

(A) *Clostridium difficile* infection
(B) Cytomegalovirus infection

(C) Mycophenolate mofetil toxicity

(D) Tacrolimus toxicity

Item 11

A 62-year-old man is evaluated for a 1-month history of low-grade back pain, generalized weakness, and progressive fatigue. He also notes dyspnea with exertion. He has had no joint aches, fevers, or cough.

On physical examination, temperature is 36.9 °C (98.5 °F), blood pressure is 124/70 mm Hg, pulse rate is 69/min, and respiration rate is 14/min. There are no rashes or bruises on the skin. There are no enlarged lymph nodes. Cardiac examination is unremarkable. Lungs are clear. Abdominal examination is benign with no masses. Some tenderness is noted on the back along the spine. There is no edema. Neurologic examination is intact.

Laboratory studies:

Hemoglobin	8.1 g/dL (81 g/L)
Leukocyte count	6800/µL (6.8 × 10⁹/L) with normal differential
Platelet count	124,000/µL (124 × 10⁹/L)
Albumin	3.5 g/dL (35 g/L)
Blood urea nitrogen	59 mg/dL (21.1 mmol/L)
Calcium	11.1 mg/dL (2.8 mmol/L)
Serum creatinine	7.5 mg/dL (663 µmol/L) (5 years ago: 1.0 mg/dL [88.4 µmol/L])
Electrolytes	
Sodium	138 meq/L (138 mmol/L)
Potassium	4.5 meq/L (4.5 mmol/L)
Chloride	110 meq/L (110 mmol/L)
Bicarbonate	23 meq/L (23 mmol/L)
Glucose	102 mg/dL (5.7 mmol/L)
Phosphorus	6.4 mg/dL (2.07 mmol/L)
Total protein	8.1 g/dL (81 g/L)
Urinalysis	Specific gravity 1.018; pH 6.5; trace protein; 0-3 erythrocytes/hpf; 6-10 leukocytes/hpf; no casts
Urine protein–creatinine ratio	3.3 mg/mg

Chest radiograph is unremarkable. Kidney ultrasound shows no evidence of urinary obstruction.

Which of the following is the most appropriate diagnostic study to evaluate this patient's kidney injury?

(A) ANCA testing

(B) Kidney biopsy

(C) Parathyroid hormone measurement

(D) Serum and urine electrophoresis

Item 12

An 81-year-old woman is evaluated during a follow-up visit for a 3-year history of hypertension. She feels relatively well. She does not smoke cigarettes. She appears to be adherent to her medication regimen, which consists of maximum doses of chlorthalidone, enalapril, amlodipine, and carvedilol.

On physical examination, seated blood pressure is 158/68 mm Hg, and pulse rate is 68/min; other vital signs are normal. BMI is 26. A systolic crescendo-decrescendo murmur is noted at the right upper sternal border. The carotid upstrokes are normal, and no bruits are heard. Trace pedal edema is noted.

Laboratory studies reveal normal electrolytes, complete blood count, fasting glucose, and fasting lipid profile as well as normal kidney function.

Which of the following is the most appropriate next step in management?

(A) Ambulatory blood pressure monitoring

(B) Echocardiography

(C) Hydralazine

(D) Urine metanephrine measurement

Item 13

A 75-year-old man is evaluated for a 3-week history of increasing abdominal girth. He has alcoholic liver disease with cirrhosis. He is not a candidate for liver transplantation at this time because of recent alcohol use and medical non-adherence. His only medication is propranolol.

On physical examination, the patient is alert and oriented. Temperature is 36.2 °C (97.2 °F), blood pressure is 106/58 mm Hg, pulse rate is 58/min, and respiration rate is 16/min. BMI is 20. There are no focal neurologic deficits. There is no asterixis. Abdominal examination reveals shifting abdominal dullness. There is 1+ lower extremity edema.

Laboratory studies:

Albumin	2.0 g/dL (20 g/L)
Blood urea nitrogen	8 mg/dL (2.9 mmol/L)
Serum creatinine	1.6 mg/dL (141 µmol/L)
Electrolytes	
Sodium	119 meq/L (119 mmol/L)
Potassium	3.6 meq/L (3.6 mmol/L)
Chloride	87 meq/L (87 mmol/L)
Bicarbonate	21 meq/L (21 mmol/L)
Glucose	95 mg/dL (5.3 mmol/L)
Osmolality	250 mosm/kg H₂O
Urine studies:	
Osmolality	156 mosm/kg H₂O (normal range, 300-900 mosm/kg H₂O)
Potassium	5 meq/L (5 mmol/L) (normal range for men, 11-99 meq/L [11-99 mmol/L])
Sodium	<5 meq/L (5 mmol/L) (normal range for men, 18-301 meq/L [18-301 mmol/L])

A diagnostic paracentesis reveals findings consistent with transudative ascites; the ascitic fluid absolute neutrophil count is 50/µL.

Which of the following is the most appropriate management for this patient's hyponatremia?

(A) 3% Saline

(B) Conivaptan

(C) Demeclocycline

(D) Fluid restriction

Item 14

A 27-year-old woman seeks preconception counseling. She has IgA nephropathy established by kidney biopsy. She feels well, has no other medical problems, and takes no medications.

On physical examination, temperature is normal, blood pressure is 138/88 mm Hg, pulse rate is 68/min, and respiration rate is 16/min. Cardiovascular and pulmonary examinations are normal.

Serum creatinine level 1 year ago was 1.2 mg/dL (106 µmol/L). Urinalysis today shows 10-20 erythrocytes/hpf and 1+ protein.

Which of the following should be done next to further assess the maternal and fetal risk of pregnancy outcome?

(A) Measure IgA levels

(B) Measure serum creatinine level

(C) Obtain 24-hour ambulatory blood pressure measurement

(D) Repeat kidney biopsy

Item 15

An 81-year-old man is evaluated for progressive fatigue. Nine months ago, he was diagnosed with giant cell arteritis; at that time, prednisone, omeprazole, risedronate, and vitamin D were initiated. His symptoms improved, and the prednisone was tapered. Five months ago he began to feel more fatigued. Evaluation was unremarkable other than the urinalysis, which was positive for leukocytes and leukocyte esterase. He was treated with ciprofloxacin without improvement of his symptoms. A subsequent urine culture was negative.

On physical examination, temperature is 37.3 °C (99.1 °F), blood pressure is 151/65 mm Hg, pulse rate 98/min, and respiration rate is 14/min. The remainder of the examination is unremarkable.

Laboratory studies:

Hemoglobin	10.7 g/dL (107 g/L)
Leukocyte count	8700/µL (8.7×10^9/L) (65% neutrophils, 23% lymphocytes, 11% monocytes, and 1% eosinophils)
Platelet count	198,000/µL (198×10^9/L)
Blood urea nitrogen	51 mg/dL (18.2 mmol/L)
Serum creatinine	3.1 mg/dL (274 µmol/L) (baseline: 1.1 mg/dL [97.2 µmol/L])
Lactate dehydrogenase	80 units/L
Urinalysis	Specific gravity 1.014; pH 6.0; trace protein; + leukocyte esterase; occasional leukocytes; rare erythrocytes; occasional hyaline casts

Which of the following is the most likely diagnosis?

(A) Acute interstitial nephritis

(B) Acute tubular necrosis

(C) Glomerulonephritis

(D) Thrombotic thrombocytopenic purpura

Item 16

A 58-year-old man is evaluated for a 6-month history of lower extremity edema and a weight gain of 12 kg (26 lb). He has frothy urine but reports no burning while urinating or blood in the urine. The patient is black. Medical history is otherwise unremarkable, and he takes no medications.

On physical examination, blood pressure is 155/105 mm Hg; other vital signs are normal. BMI is 30. There is 3+ pitting edema of the lower extremities. The remainder of the examination is unremarkable.

Laboratory studies:

Albumin	2.4 g/dL (24 g/L)
Complement (C3 and C4)	Normal
Serum creatinine	1.6 mg/dL (141 µmol/L)
Total cholesterol	280 mg/dL (7.25 mmol/L)
LDL cholesterol	170 mg/dL (4.40 mmol/L)
HDL cholesterol	35 mg/dL (0.91 mmol/L)
Triglycerides	250 mg/dL (2.83 mmol/L)
Serum protein electrophoresis	Normal
Rheumatoid factor	Negative
Antinuclear antibodies	Negative
Hepatitis B surface antigen	Negative
Hepatitis C virus antibodies	Negative
HIV antibodies	Negative
Rapid plasma reagin	Negative
Urinalysis	1-3 erythrocytes/hpf; 1-3 leukocytes/hpf
Urine protein–creatinine ratio	7.4 mg/mg

A kidney biopsy is performed.

Which of the following is the most likely diagnosis?

(A) Focal segmental glomerulosclerosis

(B) IgA nephropathy

(C) Lupus nephritis

(D) Postinfectious glomerulonephritis

Item 17

A 23-year-old woman is evaluated in the emergency department for a 2-month history of progressive leg weakness. She has been unable to ambulate for 1 day. She reports no diarrhea or weight loss. Medical history is remarkable for Sjögren syndrome. She takes no medications.

On physical examination, vital signs are normal. BMI is 22. Diffuse weakness is noted most prominently in the legs, graded at 3/5. There is no muscle atrophy or tenderness.

Laboratory studies:

Albumin	4.5 g/dL (45 g/L)
Blood urea nitrogen	13 mg/dL (4.6 mmol/L)
Calcium	9.1 mg/dL (2.3 mmol/L)
Serum creatinine	1.1 mg/dL (97.2 μmol/L)
Electrolytes	
Sodium	141 meq/L (141 mmol/L)
Potassium	1.9 meq/L (1.9 mmol/L)
Chloride	117 meq/L (117 mmol/L)
Bicarbonate	14 meq/L (14 mmol/L)
Magnesium	2.2 mg/dL (0.91 mmol/L)
Phosphorus	3.5 mg/dL (1.13 mmol/L)
Total protein	8.9 g/dL (89 g/L)
Urine anion gap	Positive
Urinalysis	Specific gravity 1.014; pH 7.0; no blood; trace protein; no glucose; no leukocyte esterase; no nitrites

Kidney ultrasound shows nephrocalcinosis bilaterally.

Which of the following is the most likely diagnosis?

(A) Gitelman syndrome
(B) Hypokalemic distal (type 1) renal tubular acidosis
(C) Laxative abuse
(D) Proximal (type 2) renal tubular acidosis

Item 18

A 28-year-old man is found to have blood in the urine on testing related to an insurance physical examination. Family history is significant for his father who died of metastatic bladder cancer at the age of 55 years. The patient takes no medications.

On physical examination, temperature is 36.9 °C (98.4 °F), blood pressure is 138/85 mm Hg, pulse rate is 72/min, and respiration rate is 12/min. BMI is 28. The remainder of the examination is normal.

Urinalysis reveals no protein, 5-10 erythrocytes/hpf (all of which are isomorphic), and 0-2 leukocytes/hpf.

Which of the following is the most appropriate diagnostic test to perform next?

(A) CT urography
(B) Cystoscopy
(C) Repeat urinalysis
(D) Urine culture
(E) Urine cytology

Item 19

A 55-year-old woman is evaluated for a possible kidney transplant. She has end-stage kidney disease secondary to systemic lupus erythematosus (SLE). Her SLE has been quiescent since initiating hemodialysis 11 months ago. She feels well and has a stable weight and appetite. She has no arthritis, rashes, or other symptoms attributable to SLE. She reports voiding a minimal amount of urine once or twice a day.

On physical examination, vital signs are normal. Cardiopulmonary examination is normal. Abdominal examination is unremarkable.

Laboratory studies reveal a hemoglobin level of 10.8 g/dL (108 g/L), a leukocyte count of 8700/μL (8.7 × 10^9/L) with a normal differential, and a normal platelet count.

Kidney ultrasound reveals a complex-appearing mass suspicious for a renal neoplasm in the right kidney.

Which of the following is the most appropriate imaging study to perform next?

(A) CT with contrast
(B) Intravenous pyelography
(C) MRI with gadolinium
(D) Positron emission tomography

Item 20

A 59-year-old man is evaluated in the emergency department for a 3-month history of arthralgia, edema of the lower extremities, rash, and weakness. Medical history is remarkable for injection drug use.

On physical examination, blood pressure is 148/100 mm Hg. There is a diffuse, palpable erythematous rash. The lower extremities are notable for numbness, weakness, and 2+ pitting edema.

Laboratory studies on admission:

Hemoglobin	9.3 g/dL (93 g/L)
Leukocyte count	10,500/μL (10.5 × 10^9/L)
Platelet count	230,000/μL (230 × 10^9/L)
C3	Normal
C4	Decreased
Serum creatinine	1.8 mg/dL (159 μmol/L)
Lactate dehydrogenase	250 units/L
Cryoglobulin	Positive
Rheumatoid factor	Positive
Antinuclear antibodies	1:80
ANCA	Negative
Anti–glomerular basement membrane antibodies	Negative
Hepatitis B surface antibodies	Positive
Hepatitis B surface antigen	Negative
Hepatitis C virus antibodies	Positive
HIV antibodies	Negative
Peripheral blood smear	Erythrocytes of normal size and shape without schistocytosis
Urinalysis	Erythrocyte casts; leukocyte casts

Kidney biopsy results show a membranoproliferative glomerulonephritis with capillary microthrombi and diffuse IgM immune deposition in the capillary loops.

Which of the following is the most likely cause of this patient's kidney findings?

(A) Hepatitis B virus infection
(B) Hepatitis C virus infection

(C) Polyarteritis nodosa

(D) Thrombotic microangiopathy

Item 21

A 51-year-old man is evaluated for unilateral flank pain and a low-grade fever of several days' duration. He reports no nausea or vomiting. He has not experienced urinary changes such as hesitancy or frequency. He has a 10-year history of hyperlipidemia managed with simvastatin.

On physical examination, temperature is 37.8 °C (100.0 °F), blood pressure is 159/93 mm Hg, pulse rate is 92/min, and respiration rate is 12/min. BMI is 26. Abdominal examination reveals a soft and nondistended abdomen, normal bowel sounds, no masses, and mild diffuse tenderness, which is slightly worse in the right flank and right upper quadrant.

Laboratory studies:

Hemoglobin	14.1 g/dL (141 g/L)
Leukocyte count	11,500/µL (11.5 × 10^9/L)
Urinalysis	pH 5.5; 2+ blood; trace protein; 1+ leukocyte esterase; 5-10 erythrocytes/hpf; 2-5 leukocytes/hpf; no nitrites

Which of the following is the most appropriate test to perform next?

(A) Abdominal MRI

(B) Abdominal radiography of the kidneys, ureters, and bladder

(C) Intravenous pyelography

(D) Kidney ultrasonography

(E) Noncontrast abdominal helical CT

Item 22

A 47-year-old woman is evaluated during a follow-up visit for diabetic nephropathy. She also has chronic kidney disease, hypertension, retinopathy, and mild neuropathy. She has been well and is maintaining a healthy lifestyle. Medications are glyburide, amlodipine, and gabapentin.

On physical examination, blood pressure is 124/80 mm Hg. Cardiac examination is normal without a rub. Lungs are clear. Abdominal examination is unremarkable. Trace edema is present.

Laboratory studies:

Bicarbonate	17 meq/L (17 mmol/L)
Blood urea nitrogen	88 mg/dL (31.4 mmol/L)
Calcium	8.4 mg/dL (2.1 mmol/L)
Serum creatinine	3.1 mg/dL (274 µmol/L)
Phosphorus	4.5 mg/dL (1.45 mmol/L)
Potassium	4.8 meq/L (4.8 mmol/L)
Sodium	134 meq/L (134 mmol/L)
Uric acid	8 mg/dL (0.47 mmol/L)
Estimated glomerular filtration rate	16 mL/min/1.73 m^2

Based on the laboratory studies, which of the following is the most appropriate addition to this patient's chronic kidney disease therapeutic regimen?

(A) Allopurinol

(B) Noncalcium-containing phosphate binder

(C) Sodium bicarbonate therapy

(D) Sodium polystyrene

Item 23

A 51-year-old woman is evaluated during a follow-up visit for hypertension. Her office blood pressure measurements are high; however, her home readings range from 118 to 140 mm Hg systolic and 82 to 88 mm Hg diastolic, averaging 126/84 mm Hg. She has no known cardiovascular disease. She consumes a heart-healthy diet, exercises regularly, and does not smoke cigarettes.

Using the patient's home device, blood pressure measurements are 150/86 mm Hg and 147/83 mm Hg. BMI is 25. Other vital signs are normal. The remainder of the examination is unremarkable.

Within the past 10 months, she has had normal chemistry laboratory test results and a normal electrocardiogram.

Ambulatory blood pressure monitoring is ordered, and results show an average 24-hour systolic blood pressure of 127 mm Hg and an average 24-hour diastolic blood pressure of 82 mm Hg; the average daytime pressure is less than 130/80 mm Hg, and the average nighttime pressure is less than 120/70 mm Hg (all values normal).

Which of the following is the most appropriate next step in management?

(A) Continue home blood pressure measurements

(B) Initiate chlorthalidone

(C) Order echocardiography

(D) Order a plasma aldosterone-plasma renin activity ratio

(E) Order a spot urine albumin–creatinine ratio

Item 24

A 41-year-old woman is evaluated for urinary frequency and some urgency. She reports no dysuria. Medical history is notable for chronic hepatitis C virus infection unresponsive to treatment and nephrolithiasis. She also has HIV infection that is well controlled with atazanavir, tenofovir, emtricitabine, and ritonavir.

On physical examination, the patient is comfortable and in no distress. Temperature is normal, blood pressure is 132/78 mm Hg, and pulse rate is 80/min. There are no rashes. Cardiac and pulmonary examinations are normal. Abdominal examination reveals no tenderness or flank pain.

Laboratory studies:

Blood urea nitrogen	27 mg/dL (9.6 mmol/L)
Calcium	9.2 mg/dL (2.3 mmol/L)
Serum creatinine	1.6 mg/dL (141 µmol/L) (6 months ago: 0.9 mg/dL [79.6 µmol/L])

Electrolytes
Sodium	138 meq/L (138 mmol/L)
Potassium	3.4 meq/L (3.4 mmol/L)
Chloride	108 meq/L (108 mmol/L)
Bicarbonate	18 meq/L (18 mmol/L)
Glucose	104 mg/dL (5.8 mmol/L)
Phosphorus	2.3 mg/dL (0.74 mmol/L)
CD4	625/μL
HIV RNA viral load	Undetectable
Hepatitis C viral load	250,000 units/L

Urine studies:
Creatinine	85 mg/dL (normal range for women, 15-327 mg/dL)
Sodium	70 meq/L (70 mmol/L) (normal range for women, 15-267 meq/L [15-267 mmol/L])
Fractional excretion of sodium	1%
Urinalysis	Specific gravity 1.008; pH 6.5; 1+ blood; 1+ protein; 1+ glucose; 1-3 erythrocytes/hpf; 1-2 leukocytes/hpf; no casts

Kidney ultrasound shows no hydronephrosis.

Which of the following is the most likely cause of this patient's acute kidney injury?

(A) Hepatitis C virus–associated glomerulonephritis
(B) HIV-associated focal segmental glomerulosclerosis
(C) Nephrolithiasis
(D) Tenofovir-induced toxicity

Item 25

A 26-year-old man is evaluated in the emergency department after being found on the floor in his apartment by friends who had not seen him in several days.

On physical examination, the patient is somnolent and minimally responsive. Temperature is 37.2 °C (98.9 °F), blood pressure is 92/54 mm Hg, pulse rate is 118/min, and respiration rate is 14/min with 97% oxygen saturation on ambient air. BMI is 25. Skin is mottled and edematous on the posterior surface of the legs, buttocks, and back. He withdraws from painful stimuli. Pupils are reactive. Neurologic examination reveals no focal or lateralizing findings. The remainder of the examination is normal.

Laboratory studies:
Blood urea nitrogen	174 mg/dL (62.1 mmol/L)
Calcium	7.8 mg/dL (2.0 mmol/L)
Creatine kinase	125,000 units/L
Serum creatinine	8.3 mg/dL (734 μmol/L)

Electrolytes
Sodium	151 meq/L (151 mmol/L)
Potassium	5.8 meq/L (5.8 mmol/L)
Chloride	121 meq/L (121 mmol/L)
Bicarbonate	19 meq/L (19 mmol/L)
Glucose	94 mg/dL (5.2 mmol/L)
Phosphorus	8.5 mg/dL (2.75 mmol/L)

Urinalysis	Specific gravity 1.012; pH 6.5; 3+ blood; 1+ protein; 0-5 erythrocytes/hpf; 1-3 leukocytes/hpf; dark granular casts
Toxicology screening	Pending

During the 3 hours he has been in the hospital, total urine output has been 60 mL.

Electrocardiogram reveals sinus tachycardia with normal intervals and no ST- or T-wave changes.

Which of the following is the most appropriate treatment for this patient?

(A) Hemodialysis
(B) Intravenous mannitol
(C) Rapid infusion of intravenous 0.9% saline
(D) Rapid infusion of intravenous 5% glucose

Item 26

A 52-year-old man is hospitalized for ganciclovir-resistant cytomegalovirus encephalitis. Therapy with foscarnet is initiated. He has advanced AIDS and does not currently take antiretroviral medications.

On physical examination, the patient is lethargic and oriented only to person. Temperature is 37.8 °C (100.0 °F), blood pressure is 136/56 mm Hg, pulse rate is 102/min, and respiration rate is 14/min. BMI is 17. During the first week of hospitalization, the serum sodium level increases from 143 meq/L (143 mmol/L) on admission to 156 meq/L (156 mmol/L); during this time, he has been receiving intravenous hydration with 0.9% saline.

Laboratory studies:
	On Admission	Day 7
Blood urea nitrogen	10 mg/dL (3.6 mmol/L)	15 mg/dL (5.4 mmol/L)
Serum creatinine	0.6 mg/dL (53 μmol/L)	1.2 mg/dL (106 μmol/L)
Glucose	88 mg/dL (4.9 mmol/L)	75 mg/dL (4.2 mmol/L)
Sodium	143 meq/L (143 mmol/L)	156 meq/L (156 mmol/L)
Plasma osmolality	300 mosm/kg H$_2$O	326 mosm/kg H$_2$O
Urine osmolality	186 mosm/kg H$_2$O (normal, 300-900 mosm/kg H$_2$O)	190 mosm/kg H$_2$O (normal, 300-900 mosm/kg H$_2$O)
Urine output	–	3020 mL/d

Following administration of desmopressin, the urine osmolality increases to 614 mosm/kg H$_2$O.

Which of the following is the most likely diagnosis?

(A) Central diabetes insipidus
(B) Cerebral salt wasting
(C) Nephrogenic diabetes insipidus
(D) Osmotic diuresis

Item 27

A 74-year-old woman is evaluated for a 2-month history of fatigue, anorexia, and a 6-kg (13.2-lb) weight loss. She was treated with chemotherapy for ovarian cancer 6 months ago. She also has hypertension managed with hydrochlorothiazide.

On physical examination, temperature is 36.2 °C (97.2 °F), blood pressure is 132/75 mm Hg without postural changes, pulse rate is 86/min without postural changes, and respiration rate is 14/min. BMI is 23. There are no neurologic findings. Estimated central venous pressure is less than 5 cm H_2O. Cardiac and pulmonary examinations are normal. There is no peripheral edema.

Laboratory studies:

Blood urea nitrogen	5 mg/dL (1.8 mmol/L)
Serum creatinine	0.4 mg/dL (35.4 µmol/L)
Electrolytes	
Sodium	128 meq/L (128 mmol/L)
Potassium	3.8 meq/L (3.8 mmol/L)
Chloride	90 meq/L (90 mmol/L)
Bicarbonate	25 meq/L (25 mmol/L)
Glucose	60 mg/dL (3.3 mmol/L)
Osmolality	266 mosm/kg H_2O
Cortisol (8 AM)	20 µg/dL (552 nmol/L) (normal range, 5-25 µg/dL [138-690 nmol/L])
Thyroid-stimulating hormone	1.3 µU/mL (1.3 mU/L)
Urine studies:	
Osmolality	50 mosm/kg H_2O (normal range, 300-900 mosm/kg H_2O)
Potassium	15 meq/L (15 mmol/L) (normal range for women, 17-164 meq/L [17-164 mmol/L])
Sodium	12 meq/L (12 mmol/L) (normal range for women, 15-267 meq/L [15-267 mmol/L])

Which of the following is the most likely cause of this patient's hyponatremia?

(A) Hypovolemia
(B) Low solute intake
(C) Measurement error (pseudohyponatremia)
(D) Primary adrenal insufficiency

Item 28

A 61-year-old woman is evaluated for the recent finding of a low estimated glomerular filtration rate (GFR). Laboratory studies performed by her previous physician revealed a serum creatinine level of 1.0 mg/dL (88.4 µmol/L), and the estimated GFR using the Modification of Diet in Renal Disease study equation was 56 mL/min/1.73 m².

She feels well and is active, exercising 5 days a week. She has no pertinent personal or family history. Medications are calcium carbonate and a daily multivitamin.

On physical examination, the patient appears younger than her age and is muscular. Vital signs and the remainder of the examination are normal.

Dipstick urinalysis results show no significant findings.

Which of the following is the most appropriate diagnostic test to perform next?

(A) 24-Hour urine collection for creatinine clearance
(B) Estimate GFR using the Chronic Kidney Disease Epidemiology Collaboration equation
(C) Estimate GFR using the Cockcroft-Gault equation
(D) Radionuclide kidney clearance scanning

Item 29

A 54-year-old woman is evaluated during a follow-up visit for a 15-year history of type 2 diabetes mellitus and a 10-year history of hypertension and hyperlipidemia. She is overweight and has been unsuccessful with weight loss. Medications are metformin, glipizide, irbesartan, hydrochlorothiazide, and simvastatin.

On physical examination, blood pressure is 154/82 mm Hg, and pulse rate is 88/min. BMI is 28. Cardiovascular examination is normal. The remainder of the examination is noncontributory.

Laboratory studies reveal a serum potassium level of 4.9 meq/L (4.9 mmol/L) and an estimated glomerular filtration rate of >60 mL/min/1.73 m². A urine albumin–creatinine ratio performed 3 months ago was 15 mg/g.

In addition to reinforcing lifestyle modifications, which of the following is the most appropriate next step in management?

(A) Add diltiazem
(B) Add furosemide
(C) Add lisinopril
(D) Add spironolactone

Item 30

A 36-year-old woman is evaluated during a follow-up visit for three episodes of nephrolithiasis that occurred during the past year. Each episode was treated with analgesics in an acute care setting. She had uncomplicated passage of the stones, although none was recovered for analysis. Her father and brother have a history of kidney stones. Her only medication is a multivitamin.

On physical examination, blood pressure is 126/78 mm Hg, and pulse rate is 96/min. BMI is 27. There is no costovertebral angle tenderness. The remainder of the examination is unremarkable.

Laboratory studies:

Blood urea nitrogen	15 mg/dL (5.4 mmol/L)
Calcium	8.9 mg/dL (2.2 mmol/L)
Serum creatinine	0.8 mg/dL (70.7 µmol/L)
Parathyroid hormone	Normal
Urine studies:	
Calcium excretion	379 mg/24 h (9.5 mmol/24 h)
Citrate excretion	521 mg/24 h (normal range, 320-1240 mg/24 h)
Oxalate excretion	26 mg/24 h (296 µmol/24 h) (normal range, 9.7-40.5 mg/24 h [111-462 µmol/24 h])
Uric acid excretion	359 mg/24 h (2.12 mmol/24 h)
Urine volume	1500 mL/24 h

Radiographs of the kidneys, ureters, and bladder show a 6-mm calcification in the lower pole of the right kidney.

In addition to recommending adequate fluid intake, which of the following is the most appropriate next step in management?

(A) Calcium-restricted diet
(B) Chlorthalidone
(C) Potassium chloride supplements
(D) Sodium citrate

Item 31

A 66-year-old man is evaluated for a 3-year history of chronic kidney disease (CKD). Medical history is significant for gout and hypertension, both of which were diagnosed at the same time as his CKD. He is retired as an industrial worker in a battery factory. His weight is stable, and his appetite is good. He has no history of drug abuse and does not smoke cigarettes. Medications are hydrochlorothiazide, amlodipine, and allopurinol. He does not take over-the-counter medications or remedies.

On physical examination, temperature is 36.9 °C (98.4 °F), blood pressure is 128/72 mm Hg, pulse rate is 82/min, and respiration rate is 13/min. BMI is 30. There are no rashes. There is no joint swelling or pitting edema of the extremities.

Laboratory studies:

Bicarbonate	21 meq/L (21 mmol/L)
Blood urea nitrogen	18 mg/dL (6.4 mmol/L)
Calcium	8.9 mg/dL (2.2 mmol/L)
Serum creatinine	1.9 mg/dL (168 µmol/L)
Glucose	95 mg/dL (5.3 mmol/L)
Lead	16 µg/dL (0.77 µmol/L) (normal range, <25 µg/dL [1.2 µmol/L])
Phosphorus	3.4 mg/dL (1.10 mmol/L)
Uric acid	5.8 mg/dL (0.34 mmol/L)
Urinalysis	pH 5.5; trace protein; + glucose; 0 erythrocytes/hpf; 1-3 leukocytes/hpf; no ketones
Urine protein–creatinine ratio	0.4 mg/mg

Which of the following is the most appropriate diagnostic study to perform next?

(A) Chelation mobilization testing
(B) Erythrocyte protoporphyrin measurement
(C) Long bone radiography
(D) Peripheral blood smear

 ## Item 32

A 53-year-old man is hospitalized for treatment of osteomyelitis of the foot resulting from a chronic diabetic ulcer. Medical history is significant for type 1 diabetes mellitus, hypertension, and chronic kidney disease with a baseline serum creatinine level of 3.2 mg/dL (283 µmol/L) and an estimated glomerular filtration rate of 19 mL/min/1.73 m². The ulcer was surgically debrided, and

a deep culture of the bone grew an *Escherichia coli* species sensitive only to piperacillin-tazobactam.

Although maintaining peripheral intravenous access was difficult, he responded well to antibiotic therapy, and his current examination shows a clean and dry healing surgical site. The remainder of the physical examination is unremarkable except for a baseline dense lower extremity sensory neuropathy. Kidney function is unchanged from admission. Continued intravenous antibiotics to complete a 4-week course are planned following discharge.

Which of the following is the most appropriate route of access for ongoing antibiotic administration for this patient?

(A) Left internal jugular temporary dialysis catheter
(B) Left subclavian catheter
(C) Peripheral intravenous access
(D) Right peripherally inserted central catheter

Item 33

A 40-year-old man is evaluated during a follow-up visit for high blood pressure. Three weeks ago, his blood pressure was 150/94 mm Hg. He has no knowledge of prior blood pressure measurements. He has no history of cardiovascular disease. He takes no medications.

On physical examination, temperature is 37.1 °C (98.8 °F), blood pressure is 148/96 mm Hg seated and 156/100 mm Hg standing, pulse rate is 82/min, and respiration rate is 18/min. BMI is 27. Funduscopic examination shows arteriolar narrowing with two arteriovenous crossing defects ("nicking"). The remainder of the examination is unremarkable.

Initial laboratory studies, including serum electrolyte levels, complete blood count, lipid profile, and urinalysis, are normal. Normal kidney function is noted.

Which of the following is the most appropriate next step in management?

(A) Atenolol
(B) Electrocardiography
(C) Home blood pressure monitoring
(D) Plasma aldosterone-plasma renin activity ratio

Item 34

A 54-year-old man is evaluated during a follow-up visit for five previous episodes of nephrolithiasis. Two of these stones were composed primarily of uric acid. After his third episode, potassium citrate was initiated. Medical history is notable for type 2 diabetes mellitus, hypertension, and hyperlipidemia. He does not have a known history of gout. He eats a fairly high protein diet, and his fluid intake is inconsistent. Other medications are metformin, metoprolol, amlodipine, atorvastatin, and aspirin.

On physical examination, blood pressure is 136/82 mm Hg, and pulse rate is 68/min. BMI is 32. There is no costovertebral angle tenderness. The remainder of the examination is unremarkable.

Laboratory studies:

Blood urea nitrogen	15 mg/dL (5.4 mmol/L)
Calcium	8.5 mg/dL (2.1 mmol/L)
Serum creatinine	1.1 mg/dL (97.2 μmol/L)
Uric acid	7.8 mg/dL (0.46 mmol/L)
Urine studies:	
Calcium excretion	220 mg/24 h (5.5 mmol/24 h)
Citrate excretion	400 mg/24 h (normal range, 320-1240 mg/24 h)
Oxalate excretion	26 mg/24 h (296 μmol/24 h) (normal range, 9.7-40.5 mg/24 h [111-462 μmol/24 h])
Uric acid excretion	710 mg/24 h (4.19 mmol/24 h)
Urinalysis	Specific gravity 1.025; pH 6.2; no blood, protein, or leukocyte esterase
Urine volume	1600 mL/24 h

In addition to increased fluid intake and dietary changes, which of the following is the most appropriate treatment for this patient?

(A) Acetazolamide

(B) Allopurinol

(C) Calcium carbonate

(D) Chlorthalidone

Item 35

A 64-year-old man is evaluated for an 8-week history of fatigue, dyspnea, a sore tongue, leg edema, and painful burning feet. He has never smoked cigarettes and does not drink alcohol or use illicit drugs. He takes no medications.

On physical examination, the patient is afebrile; blood pressure is 156/84 mm Hg, pulse rate is 100/min, and respiration rate is 20/min. BMI is 22. Macroglossia and multiple ecchymoses are present. Jugular venous distention is noted. There is an S_3 at the cardiac apex. Crackles are heard at the posterior lung bases. Hepatomegaly is noted. There is 3+ pitting edema of the lower extremities. There is diminished sensation in the feet bilaterally.

Laboratory studies:

Hemoglobin	11.2 g/dL (112 g/L)
Hemoglobin A_{1c}	5.8%
Albumin	2.0 g/dL (20 g/L)
Calcium	9.2 mg/dL (2.3 mmol/L)
Serum creatinine	1.5 mg/dL (133 μmol/L)
Total protein	8.0 g/dL (80 g/L)
Urinalysis	0-3 erythrocytes/hpf; 3-5 leukocytes/hpf
Urine protein–creatinine ratio	8.9 mg/mg

Electrocardiogram reveals sinus tachycardia and low voltage. Chest radiograph reveals cardiomegaly and vascular congestion.

Which of the following is the most likely diagnosis?

(A) AL amyloidosis

(B) Diabetic nephropathy

(C) Polyarteritis nodosa

(D) Primary membranous glomerulopathy

Item 36

A 22-year-old man is evaluated for hypertension and hypokalemic metabolic alkalosis. He is asymptomatic. He does not have a history of licorice ingestion. He does not use NSAIDs, illicit drugs, alcohol, or tobacco products. Medications are amlodipine and benazepril.

On physical examination, temperature is 37.1 °C (98.8 °F), blood pressure is 164/98 mm Hg, pulse rate is 70/min, and respiration rate is 14/min. BMI is 29. The remainder of the examination is normal.

Laboratory studies:

Blood urea nitrogen	10 mg/dL (3.6 mmol/L)
Serum creatinine	0.7 mg/dL (61.9 μmol/L)
Electrolytes	
Sodium	142 meq/L (142 mmol/L)
Potassium	3.0 meq/L (3.0 mmol/L)
Chloride	102 meq/L (102 mmol/L)
Bicarbonate	34 meq/L (34 mmol/L)
Aldosterone	<4 ng/dL (110 pmol/L)
Plasma renin activity	<0.6 ng/mL/h (0.6 μg/L/h) (normal range, 0.6-4.3 ng/mL/h [0.6-4.3 μg/L/h])
24-Hour urine free cortisol	Normal
Urinalysis	Specific gravity 1.012; pH 6.0; no blood, protein, casts, or cells

Kidney ultrasound reveals normal-sized kidneys without hydronephrosis.

Which of the following is the most likely diagnosis?

(A) Liddle syndrome

(B) Pheochromocytoma

(C) Primary hyperaldosteronism

(D) Renovascular hypertension

Item 37

An 80-year-old woman is hospitalized for a 1-week history of progressive weakness, nausea, and anorexia. She lives independently but has become bedridden and confused during the past 3 days. She has hypertension managed with enalapril as well as chlorthalidone, which was initiated 2 weeks ago.

On physical examination, the patient is lethargic and unable to recognize family members. Temperature is 37.3 °C (99.2 °F), blood pressure is 160/86 mm Hg, pulse rate is 68/min, and respiration rate is 14/min. BMI is 20. Cardiac and pulmonary examinations are normal. Neurologic examination shows no focal deficits. There is no edema, ascites, or evidence of hypovolemia.

Laboratory studies are consistent with hypotonic hyponatremia; her serum sodium level is 110 meq/L (110 mmol/L). Therapy with 3% saline is initiated, and her mentation rapidly improves to baseline.

H CONT. Laboratory studies 10 hours after admission:

Serum sodium	121 meq/L (121 mmol/L)
Urine sodium	48 meq/L (48 mmol/L); 82 meq/L (82 mmol/L) on admission (normal range for women, 15-267 meq/L [15-267 mmol/L])
Urine osmolality	206 mosm/kg H₂O; 486 mosm/kg H₂O on admission (normal range, 300-900 mosm/kg H₂O)
Urine output	Approximately 400 mL/h since admission

Which of the following is the most appropriate treatment for this patient?

(A) 0.9% Saline
(B) 5% Dextrose in water
(C) Fluid restriction
(D) Tolvaptan

H ## Item 38

A 75-year-old man is hospitalized for community-acquired pneumonia and is treated with antibiotics and intravenous normal saline. His fever resolves and his breathing improves after 2 days. On day 3, he is preparing for discharge but reports his breathing has not returned to baseline. His dyspnea, although improved since admission, is particularly noticeable on exertion. Medical history is remarkable for hypertension, hyperlipidemia, and ischemic cardiomyopathy with an ejection fraction of 25%. Current medications are moxifloxacin, hydrochlorothiazide, metoprolol, lisinopril, simvastatin, and aspirin.

On physical examination, temperature is 36.4 °C (97.5 °F), blood pressure is 115/64 mm Hg, pulse rate is 102/min, and respiration rate is 18/min. Jugular venous pulsation is elevated. Cardiac examination reveals an S₃; there are no murmurs. Pulmonary examination reveals mild basilar crackles. There is trace lower extremity edema.

Laboratory studies:

Blood urea nitrogen	45 mg/dL (16.1 mmol/L)
Serum creatinine	1.9 mg/dL (168 μmol/L) (2 days ago: 1.3 mg/dL [115 μmol/L])
Electrolytes	
Sodium	133 meq/L (133 mmol/L)
Potassium	3.6 meq/L (3.6 mmol/L)
Chloride	102 meq/L (102 mmol/L)
Bicarbonate	23 meq/L (23 mmol/L)
Urinalysis	Specific gravity 1.019; pH 6.0; 0-1 erythrocytes/hpf; 0-1 leukocytes/hpf; occasional hyaline casts; no other casts

Which of the following is the most appropriate treatment?

(A) Administer a 500-mL bolus of normal saline
(B) Begin intravenous furosemide
(C) Increase lisinopril
(D) Increase metoprolol

Item 39

A 72-year-old man is evaluated during a follow-up visit for difficult-to-control hypertension. He has diabetes mellitus and stage 4 chronic kidney disease (CKD). A review of his laboratory studies shows his serum creatinine level has gradually increased over the past 3 years, consistent with progression of his CKD. He has been on the same antihypertensive regimen for years and takes hydrochlorothiazide, 25 mg/d; lisinopril, 40 mg/d; amlodipine, 10 mg/d; and metoprolol, 100 mg/d (long acting). He adheres to his medication regimen and reports no side effects. He is not taking any over-the-counter medications. He eats a low salt diet and exercises 20 to 30 minutes daily.

On physical examination, the patient is afebrile. Blood pressure is 162/74 mm Hg, and pulse rate is 62/min, without orthostatic changes. There is no elevation in jugular venous pressure. Cardiac examination is normal with no murmurs. Lungs are clear. There is trace edema of the lower extremities.

Laboratory studies:

Serum creatinine	3.2 mg/dL (283 μmol/L)
Potassium	4.7 meq/L (4.7 mmol/L)
Estimated glomerular filtration rate	24 mL/min/1.73 m²
Urine albumin–creatinine ratio	650 mg/g

Which of the following is the most appropriate adjustment to this patient's hypertensive medication regimen?

(A) Add clonidine
(B) Add hydralazine
(C) Add valsartan
(D) Change hydrochlorothiazide to furosemide

Item 40

A 34-year-old woman is evaluated for urinary frequency. She has no dysuria, fever, chills, or sweats. She is otherwise healthy, and her only medication is a daily multivitamin.

On physical examination, temperature is 37.1 °C (98.7 °F), blood pressure is 149/95 mm Hg, pulse rate is 72/min, and respiration rate is 18/min. BMI is 23. The remainder of the examination is normal.

Dipstick urinalysis shows a pH of 5.5, 1+ blood, 1+ protein, and negative leukocyte esterase. The urine microscopy is shown (see next page).

Which of the following diagnostic tests is most appropriate to perform next?

(A) Kidney biopsy
(B) Kidney ultrasonography and cystoscopy
(C) Urine culture
(D) Urine protein–creatinine ratio and serum creatinine measurement

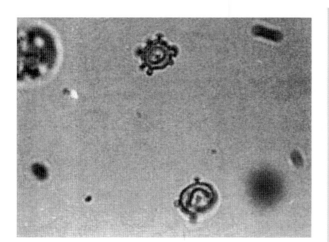

ITEM 40

Item 41

A 32-year-old woman is evaluated during a new patient visit. She is healthy, exercises regularly without symptoms, and takes no medications. Medical history is unremarkable. Family history is notable for her father and paternal aunt who both have hypertension and chronic kidney disease. There is no family history of polycystic kidney disease. Her father began dialysis when he was 50 years old and now has a kidney transplant.

Physical examination and vital signs are normal.

Which of the following should be done to screen for chronic kidney disease?

(A) 24-Hour urine collection for creatinine clearance
(B) Kidney ultrasonography
(C) Radionuclide kidney clearance scanning
(D) Serum creatinine, estimated glomerular filtration rate, and urinalysis

Item 42

A 68-year-old woman is evaluated following the results of a dual-energy x-ray absorptiometry measurement obtained at a hospital system–sponsored health fair, which revealed a T score of −3.0 in the lumbosacral spine and −3.2 in the left hip. She has chronic kidney disease. Her only medication is a calcium supplement, 1000 mg/d.

On physical examination, blood pressure is 124/80 mm Hg. BMI is 24. The remainder of the examination is unremarkable.

Laboratory studies:

Calcium	9.1 mg/dL (2.3 mmol/L)
Serum creatinine	2.4 mg/dL (212 µmol/L)
Phosphorus	4.5 mg/dL (1.45 mmol/L)
Intact parathyroid hormone	65 pg/mL (65 ng/L)
25-hydroxyvitamin D	38 ng/mL (95 nmol/L)
Estimated glomerular filtration rate	26 mL/min/1.73 m²

In addition to recommending physical activity, which of the following is the most appropriate next step in management?

(A) Add cinacalcet
(B) Add risedronate
(C) Add sevelamer
(D) Discontinue the calcium supplement
(E) Maintain current therapeutic regimen

Item 43

A 75-year-old woman is evaluated during a follow-up visit for escalating hypertension. She has a 54-pack-year history of smoking; she quit 5 years ago after she had a transient ischemic attack. She is adherent to her medication regimen, which consists of a β-blocker, a calcium channel blocker, and a diuretic. Six months ago her blood pressure was 148/82 mm Hg, and three months ago it was 158/90 mm Hg.

On physical examination, temperature is normal, blood pressure is 174/96 mm Hg, and pulse rate is 60/min. BMI is 20. Cardiopulmonary examination reveals bilateral carotid bruits as well as midline and bilateral epigastric bruits. An S_4 gallop is noted. There is trace pedal edema.

Laboratory studies reveal a serum creatinine level of 1.7 mg/dL (150 µmol/L), an estimated glomerular filtration rate of 29 mL/min/1.73 m², and a negative urine dipstick.

Which of the following is the most appropriate next step in management?

(A) Add an ACE inhibitor
(B) Increase the β-blocker dose
(C) Obtain Doppler ultrasonography of the renal arteries
(D) Obtain kidney angiography

Item 44

An 83-year-old woman is hospitalized for a total knee replacement to manage her osteoarthritis. She also has hypertension and stage 3 chronic kidney disease. Current medications are amlodipine, fondaparinux, and celecoxib for postoperative pain. She is allergic to opioids, which cause delirium.

On physical examination, temperature is 36.0 °C (96.8 °F), blood pressure is 142/65 mm Hg, pulse rate is 80/min, and respiration rate is 15/min. BMI is 28. On postoperative day 3, her serum potassium level has increased from 4.2 meq/L (4.2 mmol/L) to 6.2 meq/L (6.2 mmol/L). A stool specimen is negative for occult blood.

Laboratory studies (postoperative day 3):

Hemoglobin	12.2 g/dL (122 g/L)
Leukocyte count	6700/µL (6.7 × 10⁹/L)
Platelet count	396,000/µL (396 × 10⁹/L)
Blood urea nitrogen	22 mg/dL (7.9 mmol/L)
Serum creatinine	1.2 mg/dL (106 µmol/L)
Electrolytes	
Sodium	136 meq/L (136 mmol/L)
Potassium	6.2 meq/L (6.2 mmol/L)
Chloride	106 meq/L (106 mmol/L)
Bicarbonate	20 meq/L (20 mmol/L)

Glucose	90 mg/dL (5 mmol/L)
Osmolality	288 mosm/kg H_2O
Estimated glomerular filtration rate	52 mL/min/1.73 m²
Urine studies:	
Creatinine	100 mg/dL (normal range for women, 15-327 mg/dL)
Osmolality	576 mosm/kg H_2O (normal range, 300-900 mosm/kg H_2O)
Potassium	30 meq/L (30 mmol/L) (normal range for women, 17-164 meq/L [17-164 mmol/L])

Electrocardiogram reveals tall, symmetric, peaked T waves.

Which of the following is the most likely cause of this patient's hyperkalemia?

(A) Adrenal hemorrhage
(B) Celecoxib toxicity
(C) High potassium diet
(D) Pseudohyperkalemia

Item 45

An 18-year-old woman is evaluated for a 6-month history of progressive weakness and a 5-kg (11-lb) weight loss. She reports increased fatigue and myalgia following exercise during the past 2 months.

On physical examination, the patient is thin. Temperature is 36.4 °C (97.6 °F), blood pressure is 110/60 mm Hg, pulse rate is 96/min, and respiration rate is 18/min. BMI is 18. The remainder of the examination is unremarkable.

Laboratory studies:

Blood urea nitrogen	4 mg/dL (1.4 mmol/L)
Serum creatinine	0.5 mg/dL (44.2 µmol/L)
Electrolytes	
Sodium	135 meq/L (135 mmol/L)
Potassium	3.1 meq/L (3.1 mmol/L)
Chloride	108 meq/L (108 mmol/L)
Bicarbonate	18 meq/L (18 mmol/L)
Urine studies:	
Creatinine	120 mg/dL (normal range for women, 15-327 mg/dL)
Sodium	22 meq/L (22 mmol/L) (normal range for women, 15-267 meq/L [15-267 mmol/L])
Potassium	15 meq/L (15 mmol/L) (normal range for women, 17-164 meq/L [17-164 mmol/L])
Chloride	45 meq/L (45 mmol/L) (normal range for women, 20-295 meq/L [20-295 mmol/L])
Urea	112 mg/dL (normal range for women, 132-1629 mg/dL)
Osmolality	290 mosm/kg H_2O (normal range, 300-900 mosm/kg H_2O)
Urinalysis	Specific gravity 1.012; pH 5.8; no blood, protein, glucose, leukocyte esterase, ketones, or nitrites

Which of the following is the most likely cause of this patient's acid-base disorder?

(A) Diuretic abuse
(B) Hypokalemic distal (type 1) renal tubular acidosis
(C) Laxative abuse
(D) Surreptitious vomiting

Item 46

A 54-year-old woman is evaluated for an abnormal electrocardiogram obtained at a local health screening fair. She has no cardiovascular symptoms or risk factors and takes no medications.

On physical examination, blood pressure is 136/80 mm Hg; other vital signs are normal. The remainder of the examination is unremarkable.

Laboratory studies, including complete blood count, serum creatinine, electrolytes, and lipids, are normal.

The electrocardiogram demonstrates voltage criteria for left ventricular hypertrophy. A follow-up echocardiogram confirms the presence of symmetric left ventricular hypertrophy without evidence of aortic valve disease or resting outflow gradient.

Which of the following is the most appropriate next step in management?

(A) 24-Hour ambulatory blood pressure monitoring
(B) Cardiac MRI
(C) Chlorthalidone
(D) Coronary artery calcium score

Item 47

H

A 19-year-old woman is hospitalized for acute kidney injury (AKI) associated with bloody diarrhea that developed after she returned from a trip to South America. She also has nausea, vomiting, abdominal pain, fever, chills, and decreased urine output. Medical history is otherwise unremarkable, and she takes no medications.

On physical examination, temperature is 37.8 °C (100.0 °F), blood pressure is 135/90 mm Hg, and pulse rate is 110/min. The oral mucosa is dry. There is diffuse abdominal pain with guarding. The remainder of the physical examination is normal.

Laboratory studies:

Haptoglobin	8 mg/dL (80 mg/L)
Hemoglobin	5.2 g/dL (52 g/L)
Leukocyte count	20,000/µL (20 × 10⁹/L)
Platelet count	36,000/µL (36 × 10⁹/L)
Reticulocyte count	7.8%
Serum creatinine	5.7 mg/dL (504 µmol/L)
Lactate dehydrogenase	2396 units/L
Peripheral blood smear	Many schistocytes
Urinalysis	Many erythrocytes and erythrocyte casts
Urine protein–creatinine ratio	0.5 mg/mg

Which of the following is the most likely cause of this patient's acute kidney injury?

(A) Acute tubular necrosis
(B) Hemolytic uremic syndrome
(C) Postinfectious glomerulonephritis
(D) Scleroderma renal crisis

Item 48

A 28-year-old woman is evaluated during a follow-up visit. A life insurance examination revealed proteinuria. She is otherwise healthy and has no pertinent personal or family history.

On physical examination, temperature is 36.1 °C (97.0 °F), blood pressure is 110/64 mm Hg, pulse rate is 72/min, and respiration rate is 12/min. BMI is 23. The remainder of the examination is normal.

Laboratory studies today:

Serum creatinine	0.8 mg/dL (70.7 µmol/L)
Estimated glomerular filtration rate	>60 mL/min/1.73 m²
24-Hour urine collection for protein	200 mg/24 h
Urinalysis	1+ protein; 0-2 erythrocytes/hpf; 0 leukocytes/hpf

Which of the following is the most appropriate next step in management?

(A) Kidney biopsy
(B) Repeat 24-hour urine collection for protein
(C) Split urine collection
(D) Spot urine protein–creatinine ratio
(E) Reassurance

Item 49

A 47-year-old man is evaluated during a follow-up visit for stage 3 chronic kidney disease attributed to type 2 diabetes mellitus and hypertension. He feels well and has no complaints. Medications are fosinopril, amlodipine, and glipizide.

On physical examination, blood pressure is 148/82 mm Hg, and pulse rate is 80/min. BMI is 25. There is no jugular venous distention. Cardiac and pulmonary examinations are unremarkable. There is no edema.

Laboratory studies:

Blood urea nitrogen	45 mg/dL (16.1 mmol/L)
Calcium	9.0 mg/dL (2.3 mmol/L)
Serum creatinine	1.7 mg/dL (150 µmol/L)
Electrolytes	
Sodium	139 meq/L (139 mmol/L)
Potassium	4.3 meq/L (4.3 mmol/L)
Chloride	101 meq/L (101 mmol/L)
Bicarbonate	22 meq/L (22 mmol/L)
Phosphorus	4.3 mg/dL (1.39 mmol/L)
Parathyroid hormone	69 pg/mL (69 ng/L)
Estimated glomerular filtration rate	41 mL/min/1.73 m²
Urine protein–creatinine ratio	0.17 mg/mg

Which of the following changes to this patient's therapeutic regimen should be made next?

(A) Add sodium bicarbonate
(B) Begin activated vitamin D therapy
(C) Increase antihypertensive therapy
(D) No change

Item 50

A 33-year-old man is evaluated for nausea, anorexia, diarrhea, and weight loss. He has recurrent testicular germ cell cancer and is undergoing chemotherapy with vinblastine, ifosfamide, and cisplatin. He reports no tinnitus, dyspnea, or confusion. Other medications are ondansetron and aspirin as needed.

On physical examination, the patient appears thin, with bitemporal wasting. Temperature is 36.4 °C (97.6 °F), blood pressure is 128/84 mm Hg, pulse rate is 82/min, and respiration rate is 16/min. BMI is 22. There is no edema. The remainder of the examination is unremarkable.

Laboratory studies:

Albumin	3.9 g/dL (39 g/L)
Alkaline phosphatase	126 units/L
Blood urea nitrogen	22 mg/dL (7.9 mmol/L)
Calcium	8.5 mg/dL (2.1 mmol/L)
Serum creatinine	1.3 mg/dL (115 µmol/L)
Electrolytes	
Sodium	141 meq/L (141 mmol/L)
Potassium	3.4 meq/L (3.4 mmol/L)
Chloride	112 meq/L (112 mmol/L)
Bicarbonate	19 meq/L (19 mmol/L)
Glucose	82 mg/dL (4.6 mmol/L)
Magnesium	2.1 mg/dL (0.87 mmol/L)
Phosphorus	2 mg/dL (0.65 mmol/L)
Urinalysis	Specific gravity 1.012; pH 5.0; no blood; trace protein; 1+ glucose
Fractional excretion of phosphate	20% (Normal, <5%)

Which of the following is the most likely cause of this patient's hypophosphatemia?

(A) Malnutrition
(B) Oncogenic osteomalacia
(C) Primary hyperparathyroidism
(D) Proximal (type 2) renal tubular acidosis

Item 51

A 25-year-old man is evaluated for dark urine and decreased urine output. He reports a 5-day history of an upper respiratory infection with a dry cough, runny nose, sore throat, and low-grade fever that he has treated with over-the-counter NSAIDs. He also notes mild diffuse myalgia and bilateral flank pain but reports no vomiting, diarrhea, or burning while urinating.

On physical examination, blood pressure is 135/88 mm Hg. The pharynx is erythematous but without exudate. Shotty neck lymphadenopathy is noted. There is 1+ pitting edema.

Laboratory studies:

Hemoglobin	9.8 g/dL (98 g/L)
Leukocyte count	9800/μL (9.8 × 10⁹/L) with normal differential
Platelet count	258,000/μL (258 × 10⁹/L)
C3	100 mg/dL (1000 mg/L)
C4	Normal
Creatine kinase	95 units/L
Serum creatinine	2.3 mg/dL (203 μmol/L)
Antistreptolysin O antibodies	Negative
Urine myoglobin	Negative
Urinalysis	Dark red–appearing urine with >100 erythrocytes/hpf; 2-3 leukocytes/hpf; no bacteria

Kidney ultrasound shows normal-sized kidneys and no evidence of obstruction.

Which of the following is the most likely cause of this patient's acute kidney injury?

(A) Analgesic toxicity
(B) IgA nephropathy
(C) Postinfectious glomerulonephritis
(D) Rhabdomyolysis

Item 52

An 86-year-old man is hospitalized for heart failure. He has coronary artery disease that is managed with pravastatin, metoprolol, nitroglycerin, and aspirin.

On physical examination, temperature is 37.1 °C (98.8 °F), blood pressure is 105/60 mm Hg, pulse rate is 98/min, and respiration rate is 18/min. BMI is 31. Jugular venous distention, an S₃, pulmonary crackles, and pedal edema are noted.

After initial clinical improvement following the first day of treatment with furosemide and enalapril, he develops increased abdominal distention, vomiting, and watery diarrhea.

Laboratory studies:

	On Admission	Hospital Day 3
Blood urea nitrogen	26 mg/dL (9.3 mmol/L)	12 mg/dL (4.3 mmol/L)
Serum creatinine	1.3 mg/dL (115 μmol/L)	1.2 mg/dL (106 μmol/L)
Electrolytes		
Sodium	136 meq/L (136 mmol/L)	134 meq/L (134 mmol/L)
Potassium	3.8 meq/L (3.8 mmol/L)	2.8 meq/L (2.8 mmol/L)
Chloride	98 meq/L (98 mmol/L)	94 meq/L (94 mmol/L)
Bicarbonate	30 meq/L (30 mmol/L)	28 meq/L (28 mmol/L)
Urine studies:		
Creatinine	–	120 mg/dL (normal range for men, 22-392 mg/dL)
Potassium	–	16 meq/L (16 mmol/L) (normal range for men, 11-99 meq/L [11-99 mmol/L])

Abdominal radiographs reveal colonic dilatation from the cecum to the splenic flexure with preservation of haustral markings. CT scan of the abdomen shows no evidence of mechanical obstruction.

A nasogastric tube is placed to gravity drain, with drainage of 300 mL.

Which of the following is the most likely cause of this patient's hypokalemia?

(A) Colonic pseudo-obstruction
(B) Furosemide
(C) Nasogastric fluid loss
(D) Redistribution

Item 53

A 19-year-old man is evaluated for a 3-day history of lower extremity and periorbital edema that developed 3 weeks after an upper respiratory tract infection. He is otherwise in good health and takes no medications.

On physical examination, blood pressure is 150/94 mm Hg; other vital signs are normal. There is 2+ pitting leg edema.

Laboratory studies:

Blood urea nitrogen	35 mg/dL (12.5 mmol/L)
C3	Decreased
Serum creatinine	2 mg/dL (177 μmol/L)
Antistreptolysin O antibodies	Elevated
Anti-DNase B antibodies	Elevated
Throat culture	Negative for group A β-hemolytic streptococcus
Urinalysis	30-35 erythrocytes/hpf; 1-2 erythrocyte casts/hpf
Urine protein–creatinine ratio	2.2 mg/mg

Which of the following is the most appropriate treatment for this patient?

(A) Cyclosporine
(B) Intravenous pulse methylprednisolone followed by prednisone
(C) Plasmapheresis followed by cyclophosphamide with prednisone
(D) Prednisone and cyclophosphamide for 6 months
(E) Supportive care

Item 54

A 63-year-old woman is evaluated for a 4-week history of lower extremity edema and a weight gain of 3 kg (6.6 lb). She reports no burning while urinating or blood in the urine but has noticed frothy urine. She also has a 20-year history of hypertension and a 14-year history of type 2 diabetes mellitus and hyperlipidemia, all of which have been well controlled. Medications are lisinopril, metformin, and simvastatin.

On physical examination, blood pressure is 135/85 mm Hg. Retinal examination is normal. Bilateral edema of the legs is noted. Six months ago, blood pressure was 125/70 mm Hg, hemoglobin A_{1c} level was 6.2%, total cholesterol level was 155 mg/dL (4.01 mmol/L), and urine albumin–creatinine ratio was less than 30 mg/g.

Laboratory studies today:

Albumin	3.3 g/dL (33 g/L)
Blood urea nitrogen	21 mg/dL (7.5 mmol/L)
Complement (C3 and C4)	Normal
Total cholesterol	282 mg/dL (7.30 mmol/L)
Serum creatinine	0.7 mg/dL (61.9 µmol/L)
Glucose	96 mg/dL (5.3 mmol/L)
Cryoglobulin	Negative
Serum protein electrophoresis	Normal
Rheumatoid factor	Negative
Antinuclear antibodies	Negative
Hepatitis B surface antigen	Negative
Hepatitis C virus antibodies	Negative
HIV antibodies	Negative
Urinalysis	4+ protein; 0-5 leukocytes/hpf
Urine protein–creatinine ratio	7 mg/mg

Percutaneous kidney biopsy results show diffuse thickening of the glomerular basement membrane. There is no increase in cellularity or evidence of active inflammation. Immune staining reveals diffuse granular deposits of IgG and C3 along the basement membrane, and electron microscopy confirms numerous subepithelial electron-dense deposits with moderate podocyte foot process effacement.

Which of the following is the most likely diagnosis?

(A) Diabetic nephropathy
(B) Membranous lupus nephritis
(C) Minimal change glomerulopathy
(D) Primary membranous glomerulopathy

Item 55

A 48-year-old man is evaluated during a follow-up visit for urinary frequency. He reports no hesitancy, urgency, dysuria, or change in urine color. He has not experienced fevers, chills, sweats, nausea, vomiting, diarrhea, or other gastrointestinal symptoms. He feels thirsty very often; drinking water and using lemon drops seem to help. He has a 33-pack-year history of smoking. He has hypertension, chronic kidney disease, and bipolar disorder. Medications are amlodipine, lisinopril, and lithium. He has tried other agents in place of lithium for his bipolar disorder, but none has controlled his symptoms as well as lithium.

On physical examination, temperature is 37.3 °C (99.2 °F), blood pressure is 142/75 mm Hg, pulse rate is 82/min, and respiration rate is 14/min. BMI is 29. There are no rashes. There is no pitting edema of the extremities.

Laboratory studies:

Serum creatinine	1.9 mg/dL (168 µmol/L)
Serum sodium	143 meq/L (143 mmol/L)

Urine osmolality	206 mosm/kg H_2O (normal range, 300-900 mosm/kg H_2O)
Urinalysis	Specific gravity 1.009; pH 5.5; trace protein; 0 erythrocytes/hpf; 0-2 leukocytes/hpf
Urine cultures	Negative

Which of the following is the most appropriate treatment intervention for this patient?

(A) Amiloride
(B) Fluid restriction
(C) Prednisone
(D) Tolvaptan

Item 56

A 65-year-old man is hospitalized following emergent surgery for peritonitis consequent to a perforated diverticulum. A sigmoid colectomy and diverting colostomy are performed. He has stage 4 chronic kidney disease due to autosomal dominant polycystic kidney disease. He also has hypertension treated with amlodipine.

On physical examination, temperature is 38.1 °C (100.5 °F), blood pressure is 150/95 mm Hg, pulse rate is 102/min, and respiration rate is 18/min. BMI is 31. On abdominal examination, the colostomy site is well perfused; bowel sounds are present.

Postoperatively, the serum potassium level increases from 4.8 meq/L (4.8 mmol/L) on admission to 6.9 meq/L (6.9 mmol/L); the serum creatinine level increases from 5.4 mg/dL (477 µmol/L) on admission to 6.4 mg/dL (566 µmol/L); and the urine output decreases to 50 mL over the initial 8 hours postoperatively and does not improve following a fluid challenge.

Laboratory studies:

Hemoglobin	8.6 g/dL (86 g/L)
Leukocyte count	15,900/µL (15.9 × 10⁹/L)
Platelet count	206,000/µL (206 × 10⁹/L)
Blood urea nitrogen	86 mg/dL (30.7 mmol/L)
Serum creatinine	6.4 mg/dL (566 µmol/L)
Electrolytes	
Sodium	135 meq/L (135 mmol/L)
Potassium	6.9 meq/L (6.9 mmol/L)
Chloride	101 meq/L (101 mmol/L)
Bicarbonate	17 meq/L (17 mmol/L)

Electrocardiogram reveals tall, symmetric, peaked T waves and a shortened QT interval.

In addition to intravenous calcium and insulin-dextrose, which of the following is the most appropriate treatment?

(A) Furosemide
(B) Hemodialysis
(C) Sodium bicarbonate
(D) Sodium polystyrene sulfonate

Item 57

A 42-year-old man is evaluated in the emergency department for increased confusion. Earlier in the day, he visited a homeopathic practitioner for his psoriasis; he was treated with cream and a body wrap for 1 hour. He subsequently developed nausea and vomiting. He reports feeling "out of his body" and hearing water in his ears. He also has hypertension and type 2 diabetes mellitus complicated by proteinuria. Medications are enalapril and metformin.

On physical examination, the patient is irritable, anxious, and intermittently somnolent but easily aroused. Temperature is 37.6 °C (99.7 °F), blood pressure is 160/100 mm Hg, pulse rate is 106/min standing, and respiration rate is 20/min. BMI is 40. Erythematous plaques are noted on the scalp, back, and extensor surfaces of the elbows and knees. There are no focal neurologic findings.

Laboratory studies:

Hemoglobin	14.4 g/dL (144 g/L)
Leukocyte count	6300/µL (6.3 × 10⁹/L)
Blood urea nitrogen	15 mg/dL (5.4 mmol/L)
Serum creatinine	1.3 mg/dL (115 µmol/L)
Electrolytes	
Sodium	145 meq/L (145 mmol/L)
Potassium	3.6 meq/L (3.6 mmol/L)
Chloride	109 meq/L (109 mmol/L)
Bicarbonate	22 meq/L (22 mmol/L)
Glucose	158 mg/dL (8.8 mmol/L)
Lactic acid	7.2 mg/dL (0.8 mmol/L)
Osmolality	308 mosm/kg H₂O
Arterial blood gas studies (ambient air):	
pH	7.51
P_{CO_2}	35 mm Hg (4.7 kPa)
P_{O_2}	96 mm Hg (12.8 kPa)
Urinalysis	Specific gravity 1.024; pH 6.0; trace blood; 2+ protein; 1+ glucose; trace leukocyte esterase; no ketones, nitrites, cells, or formed elements

Which of the following is the most likely cause of this patient's clinical presentation?

(A) Metformin toxicity
(B) Methanol toxicity
(C) Salicylate toxicity
(D) Sepsis

Item 58

A 27-year-old woman is evaluated during a follow-up visit for high blood pressure that manifested 4 months after she began taking an oral contraceptive pill. Despite stopping the oral contraceptive pill, her blood pressure has remained high. She states that she feels well. Medical history is otherwise unremarkable, and she takes no medications.

On physical examination, blood pressure measurements are 150 to 166 mm Hg systolic and 100 to 108 mm Hg diastolic without orthostasis; other vital signs are normal. There is a bruit in the right epigastric region. The remainder of the examination is unremarkable.

Kidney function is normal, and urinalysis is unremarkable.

A kidney angiogram is shown.

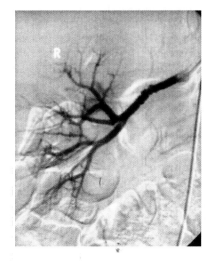

Which of the following is the most appropriate next step in management?

(A) ACE inhibitor
(B) Calcium channel blocker/ACE inhibitor combination
(C) Percutaneous transluminal kidney angioplasty
(D) Surgical revascularization

Item 59

A 28-year-old man is evaluated during a follow-up visit for Alport syndrome. He feels well and reports no fever, chills, or gastrointestinal symptoms. He has good exercise tolerance with normal fatigue levels with usual activity. He also has hypertension, and his kidney function has been declining steadily. Family history is notable for a brother who has chronic kidney disease and an uncle who has undergone kidney transplantation; his sister is healthy. Medications are furosemide, amlodipine, erythropoietin, and losartan.

On physical examination, the patient appears mildly fatigued. He wears hearing aids and eyeglasses. Temperature is 36.8 °C (98.1 °F), blood pressure is 138/88 mm Hg, pulse rate is 72/min, and respiration rate is 14/min. BMI is 23. His lungs are clear to auscultation. There is no edema. The remainder of the examination is unremarkable.

Laboratory studies:

Hemoglobin	10.1 g/dL (101 g/L)
Serum creatinine	5.4 mg/dL (477 µmol/L)
Estimated glomerular filtration rate	13 mL/min/1.73 m²
Spot urine protein–creatinine ratio	1.7 mg/mg

Kidney ultrasound performed last year revealed hyperechoic kidneys; the right kidney is 8.9 cm, and the left kidney is 9.1 cm.

Which of the following is the best management option?

(A) Add everolimus
(B) Begin hemodialysis
(C) Evaluate for kidney transplantation
(D) Switch losartan to lisinopril

Item 60

A 59-year-old man is evaluated for worsening kidney function. He was hospitalized 24 hours ago with a diabetic foot ulcer and associated cellulitis of 4 weeks' duration. He also has chronic diabetic kidney disease, hypertension, and type 2 diabetes mellitus. Medications are metformin, insulin glargine, lisinopril, and piperacillin-tazobactam.

On physical examination, blood pressure is 160/100 mm Hg (3 months ago: 130/78 mm Hg); other vital signs are normal. BMI is 30. An area of erythema extends about 3 cm around a 3- × 3-mm ulcer on the right heel. The involved area is tender and warm. There is 2+ pedal edema.

Laboratory studies:

Albumin	2.4 g/dL (24 g/L)
Complement (C3 and C4)	Decreased
Serum creatinine	4.1 mg/dL (362 µmol/L) (2 weeks ago: 1.4 mg/dL [124 µmol/L])
Urine studies:	
Urine sodium	15 meq/L (15 mmol/L) (normal range for men, 18-301 meq/L [18-301 mmol/L])
Urinalysis	25 erythrocytes/hpf; 1-2 erythrocyte casts/hpf
Urine albumin–creatinine ratio	1500 mg/g

Which of the following is the most likely cause of this patient's acute kidney injury?

(A) Diabetic nephropathy
(B) IgA nephropathy
(C) Postinfectious glomerulonephritis
(D) Primary membranous glomerulopathy

Item 61

A 34-year-old woman is scheduled to have a kidney biopsy. She has a 5-year history of systemic lupus erythematosus and a 3-year history of hypertension. Medications are prednisone, hydrochlorothiazide, atenolol, lisinopril, calcium carbonate, and a daily multivitamin.

On physical examination, blood pressure is 172/96 mm Hg, and pulse rate is 92/min. BMI is 26. A malar rash is present. There is no jugular venous distention. Cardiac examination reveals no murmurs, rubs, or gallops. Lungs are clear to auscultation. There is trace lower extremity edema.

Laboratory studies:

Hemoglobin	10.4 g/dL (104 g/L)
Platelet count	110,000/µL (110 × 10⁹/L)
Serum creatinine	1.1 mg/dL (97.2 µmol/L) (1 year ago: 0.9 mg/dL [79.6 µmol/L])

Urinalysis	1+ blood; 2+ protein; 2-5 erythrocytes/hpf; 0-2 leukocytes/hpf

Kidney ultrasound from 1 week ago reveals normal-sized kidneys without hydronephrosis or other anatomic abnormalities.

Which of the following is a contraindication to kidney biopsy in this patient?

(A) BMI greater than 25
(B) Daily prednisone treatment
(C) Hemoglobin level less than 11 g/dL (110 g/L)
(D) Uncontrolled hypertension

Item 62

A 51-year-old man is evaluated for a 1-year history of uncontrolled hypertension. He has not responded to treatment with metoprolol and clonidine. He has no family history of hypertension. He has never smoked cigarettes and has no other medical problems. Current medications are maximum doses of chlorthalidone, lisinopril, and amlodipine.

On physical examination, seated blood pressure is 160/94 mm Hg, and pulse rate is 76/min. The remainder of the examination is unremarkable.

Laboratory studies reveal a serum creatinine level of 1.1 mg/dL (97.2 µmol/L), a potassium level of 4.1 meq/L (4.1 mmol/L), and an estimated glomerular filtration rate of >60 mL/min/1.73 m².

Which of the following is the most appropriate next step in management?

(A) Discontinue chlorthalidone; begin furosemide
(B) Discontinue lisinopril; begin aliskiren
(C) Obtain kidney Doppler ultrasonography
(D) Obtain a plasma aldosterone-plasma renin activity ratio

Item 63

A 62-year-old man is hospitalized after being found on the floor of his apartment by a neighbor. The patient is confused and can provide only minimal history and says that he was involved in a fight several days ago. He states that he has high blood pressure and high cholesterol but does not know the names of his medications. The neighbor notes that the patient has a history of alcohol abuse.

On physical examination, the patient is thin, disheveled, and malodorous. He is sleepy but arousable, and he is able to move all extremities but has pain when doing so. Numerous bruises and mild lacerations are seen on his body. He is oriented only to his name. Temperature is 37.3 °C (99.2 °F), blood pressure is 165/85 mm Hg, pulse rate is 102/min, and respiration rate is 18/min. There is no icterus; mucous membranes are dry. Cardiac examination is normal. Lungs are clear to auscultation. The abdomen is soft with diffuse, mild tenderness and no distention. There is no peripheral edema. The cranial nerves appear intact.

Laboratory studies:

Hemoglobin	9.3 g/dL (93 g/L)
Leukocyte count	6500/µL (6.5 × 10⁹/L)
Platelet count	113,000/µL (113 × 10⁹/L)
Blood urea nitrogen	85 mg/dL (30.3 mmol/L)
Calcium	8.3 mg/dL (2.1 mmol/L)
Creatine kinase	15,832 units/L
Serum creatinine	4.5 mg/dL (398 µmol/L)
Electrolytes	
Sodium	145 meq/L (145 mmol/L)
Potassium	5.1 meq/L (5.1 mmol/L)
Chloride	103 meq/L (103 mmol/L)
Bicarbonate	21 meq/L (21 mmol/L)
Phosphorous	5.8 mg/dL (1.87 mmol/L)
Liver chemistry tests	Normal
Serum ethanol	0 mg/dL
Urine studies:	
Creatinine	115 mg/dL (normal range for men, 22-392 mg/dL)
Sodium	85 meq/L (85 mmol/L) (normal range for men, 18-301 meq/L [18-301 mmol/L])
Fractional excretion of sodium	5.7%
Urinalysis	Specific gravity 1.015; pH 6.5; 3+ blood; no ketones; trace leukocyte esterase; 5-10 erythrocytes/hpf; 0-3 leukocytes/hpf; rare hyaline casts; several granular casts

Which of the following is the most likely diagnosis?

(A) Acute interstitial nephritis
(B) Hepatorenal syndrome
(C) Intra-abdominal compartment syndrome
(D) Pigment nephropathy

Item 64

A 30-year-old woman is evaluated for a 2-month history of lower extremity edema and a weight gain of 3 kg (7 lb). Medical history is unremarkable, and she takes no medications.

On physical examination, blood pressure is 132/82 mm Hg; other vital signs are normal. There is 3+ pitting leg edema. The remainder of the examination is unremarkable.

Laboratory studies:

Albumin	3.1 g/dL (31 g/L)
Blood urea nitrogen	19 mg/dL (6.8 mmol/L)
Serum creatinine	0.7 mg/dL (61.9 µmol/L)
Total cholesterol	237 mg/dL (6.14 mmol/L)
LDL cholesterol	147 mg/dL (3.81 mmol/L)
Hepatitis B surface antigen	Negative
Hepatitis C virus antibodies	Negative
HIV antibodies	Negative
Rheumatoid factor	Negative
Antinuclear antibodies	Negative
Antistreptolysin O antibodies	Negative
Urinalysis	3+ protein; 0-3 erythrocytes/hpf; 0-5 leukocytes/hpf
Urine protein–creatinine ratio	3.7 mg/mg

Kidney biopsy results reveal changes consistent with membranous glomerulopathy and no evidence of mesangium involvement, secondary glomerulosclerosis, or chronic tubulointerstitial changes.

Which of the following is the most appropriate treatment for this patient?

(A) ACE inhibitor and statin
(B) Calcineurin inhibitor
(C) Corticosteroids
(D) Cyclophosphamide
(E) Mycophenolate mofetil

Item 65

A 46-year-old man is hospitalized for a subarachnoid hemorrhage after collapsing shortly after developing a severe headache. He has stage 2 chronic kidney disease due to autosomal dominant polycystic kidney disease. He also has hypertension managed with enalapril.

Mechanical ventilation is initiated, and a ventriculostomy drain is placed. Sedation is maintained with propofol and morphine, and he is treated with fosphenytoin for seizure prophylaxis.

On physical examination, temperature is 35.8 °C (96.4 °F), blood pressure is 126/70 mm Hg, and pulse rate is 96/min. Cardiac and pulmonary examinations are normal.

Laboratory studies:

	Initial	Day 3
Blood urea nitrogen	42 mg/dL (15.0 mmol/L)	52 mg/dL (18.6 mmol/L)
Creatine kinase	45 units/L	1885 units/L
Serum creatinine	1.4 mg/dL (124 µmol/L)	2.3 mg/dL (203 µmol/L)
Electrolytes		
Sodium	140 meq/L (140 mmol/L)	135 meq/L (135 mmol/L)
Potassium	4.8 meq/L (4.8 mmol/L)	6.2 meq/L (6.2 mmol/L)
Chloride	104 meq/L (104 mmol/L)	99 meq/L (99 mmol/L)
Bicarbonate	25 meq/L (25 mmol/L)	14 meq/L (14 mmol/L)
Glucose	125 mg/dL (6.9 mmol/L)	146 mg/dL (8.1 mmol/L)
Lactic acid	14 mg/dL (1.5 mmol/L)	50 mg/dL (5.5 mmol/L)
Urinalysis	–	pH 5.4; 1+ blood; 1+ protein; no ketones; few granular casts; no cells

The patient's serum is noted to be lipemic in appearance.

Which of the following is the most likely cause of this patient's laboratory findings?

(A) Fosphenytoin
(B) Propofol
(C) Propylene glycol
(D) Pyroglutamate

Item 66

An 82-year-old woman is evaluated in the emergency department for a 1-week history of progressive fatigue and shortness of breath. She lives independently, but her family reports that during the past month she has had increased difficulty walking because of low back pain, for which she self-medicates with aspirin. She also has COPD managed with ipratropium.

On physical examination, temperature is 37.6 °C (99.7 °F), blood pressure is 146/82 mm Hg, pulse rate is 86/min, and respiration rate is 24/min. BMI is 23. Tachypnea and increased respiratory effort are noted. Gag reflex is intact. The remainder of the examination is unremarkable.

Laboratory studies:

Blood urea nitrogen	42 mg/dL (15.0 mmol/L)
Serum creatinine	1.3 mg/dL (115 µmol/L)
Electrolytes	
Sodium	138 meq/L (138 mmol/L)
Potassium	3.4 meq/L (3.4 mmol/L)
Chloride	106 meq/L (106 mmol/L)
Bicarbonate	18 meq/L (18 mmol/L)
Glucose	86 mg/dL (4.8 mmol/L)
Salicylate	62 mg/dL (4.5 mmol/L) (therapeutic range, 10-25 mg/dL [0.72-1.8 mmol/L])
Arterial blood gas studies (ambient air):	
pH	7.42
P_{CO_2}	29 mm Hg (3.9 kPa)
P_{O_2}	68 mm Hg (9.0 kPa)
Urinalysis	Specific gravity 1.024; pH 5.2; no blood, protein, leukocyte esterase, ketones, or nitrites

Chest radiograph shows no infiltrates or edema.

Which of the following is the most appropriate treatment?

(A) Acetazolamide
(B) Hemodialysis
(C) Mechanical ventilation
(D) Sodium bicarbonate infusion

Item 67

A 48-year-old woman is evaluated in the emergency department for fatigue, diffuse weakness, and lightheadedness. Her symptoms developed after attending an outdoor music festival, where she was exposed to the sun most of the day.

She has a 2-year history of systemic lupus erythematosus; her last flare occurred 6 months ago. She also has hypertension, which is well controlled with hydrochlorothiazide. Other medications are hydroxychloroquine and as-needed ibuprofen. She took ibuprofen before arriving at the emergency department.

On physical examination, temperature is 37.1 °C (98.7 °F), blood pressure is 97/52 mm Hg, pulse rate is 98/min, and respiration rate is 12/min. When standing, blood pressure is 90/45 mm Hg, and pulse rate is 108/min. No rashes or edema are present. Cardiac and pulmonary examinations are normal.

Laboratory studies:

Blood urea nitrogen	21 mg/dL (7.5 mmol/L)
Serum creatinine	1.1 mg/dL (97.2 µmol/L) (baseline: 0.7 mg/dL [61.9 µmol/L])
Electrolytes	
Sodium	143 meq/L (143 mmol/L)
Potassium	4 meq/L (4 mmol/L)
Chloride	108 meq/L (108 mmol/L)
Bicarbonate	26 meq/L (26 mmol/L)
Urine studies:	
Sodium	34 meq/L (34 mmol/L) (normal range for women, 15-267 meq/L [15-267 mmol/L])
Creatinine	23 mg/dL (normal range for women, 15-327 mg/dL)
Urea	118 mg/dL (normal range for women, 132-1629 mg/dL)
Fractional excretion of sodium	1.2%
Fractional excretion of urea	27.4%
Urinalysis	Specific gravity 1.025; pH 6.5; trace blood; trace protein; occasional nondysmorphic erythrocytes; 3-5 hyaline casts; no renal tubular epithelial cells

Which of the following is the most likely diagnosis?

(A) Acute interstitial nephritis
(B) Acute tubular necrosis
(C) Lupus nephritis
(D) Prerenal azotemia

Item 68

A 45-year-old woman is evaluated as a new patient. She recently emigrated from Romania. She has chronic kidney disease (CKD). She also has hypertension, which was diagnosed at the same time as her CKD. Family history includes a cousin with CKD. She reports no urinary symptoms. Her only medication is captopril.

On physical examination, temperature is 37.7 °C (99.8 °F), blood pressure is 138/67 mm Hg, pulse rate is 72/min, and respiration rate is 12/min. BMI is 22. There are no rashes. Cardiac examination reveals normal heart sounds and no murmurs. The abdomen is nontender and without masses. There is trace pitting edema to the ankles.

Laboratory studies:

Serum creatinine	2.8 mg/dL (248 μmol/L)
Electrolytes	
Sodium	138 meq/L (138 mmol/L)
Potassium	4.9 meq/L (4.9 mmol/L)
Chloride	109 meq/L (109 mmol/L)
Bicarbonate	21 meq/L (21 mmol/L)
Urinalysis	pH 5.5; no blood; trace protein; no glucose; + leukocyte esterase; no nitrites; 0-1 erythrocytes/hpf; 2-5 leukocytes/hpf; rare granular and waxy casts
Urine cultures	Negative

Kidney ultrasound reveals small kidneys bilaterally without hydronephrosis or hydroureter.

Which of the following is the most likely diagnosis?

(A) Analgesic nephropathy
(B) Balkan nephropathy
(C) Hypertensive nephropathy
(D) IgA nephropathy

Item 69

A 76-year-old woman is evaluated in the emergency department for a 1-day history of nausea, vomiting, weakness, and confusion. Today, she has difficulty walking and has fallen several times.

On physical examination, the patient appears chronically ill; she is unable to stand without assistance because of generalized weakness. Temperature is 36.2 °C (97.2 °F), blood pressure is 130/78 mm Hg, pulse rate is 68/min without postural changes, and respiration rate is 18/min. BMI is 19. Neurologic, cardiac, and pulmonary examinations are normal. There is no peripheral edema.

Laboratory studies:

Albumin	3.6 g/dL (36 g/L)
Blood urea nitrogen	10 mg/dL (3.6 mmol/L)
Serum creatinine	0.9 mg/dL (79.6 μmol/L)
Electrolytes	
Sodium	120 meq/L (120 mmol/L)
Potassium	3.6 meq/L (3.6 mmol/L)
Chloride	83 meq/L (83 mmol/L)
Bicarbonate	27 meq/L (27 mmol/L)
Glucose	105 mg/dL (5.8 mmol/L)
Osmolality	255 mosm/kg H$_2$O
Total protein	9.1 g/dL (91 g/L)
Urine studies:	
Osmolality	408 mosm/kg H$_2$O (normal, 300-900 mosm/kg H$_2$O)
Potassium	32 meq/L (32 mmol/L) (normal range for women, 17-164 meq/L [17-164 mmol/L])
Sodium	90 meq/L (90 mmol/L) (normal range for women, 15-267 meq/L [15-267 mmol/L])

Which of the following is the most appropriate treatment?

(A) 0.9% Saline infusion
(B) 3% Saline infusion
(C) Furosemide
(D) Tolvaptan

Item 70

A 25-year-old woman comes for a preconception evaluation. She has a history of hypertension that is well controlled with lisinopril. Medical history is otherwise unremarkable.

On physical examination, blood pressure is 134/86 mm Hg in both upper extremities; other vital signs are normal. Results of the cardiovascular examination are unremarkable. There is no edema, cyanosis, digital clubbing, or radial artery–femoral artery pulse delay.

Laboratory studies reveal normal electrolytes, complete blood count, thyroid-stimulating hormone level, kidney function, and urinalysis.

An electrocardiogram is normal.

In addition to starting a prenatal vitamin, which of the following medication adjustments should be made before this patient proceeds with pregnancy?

(A) Discontinue lisinopril
(B) Substitute labetalol for lisinopril
(C) Substitute losartan for lisinopril
(D) Substitute spironolactone for lisinopril

Item 71

A 60-year-old man is evaluated as a new patient. He was diagnosed with type 2 diabetes mellitus during a health insurance evaluation 6 months ago. At that time, metformin was initiated. Medical history is otherwise unremarkable.

On physical examination, blood pressure is 145/94 mm Hg; other vital signs are normal. BMI is 29. The remainder of the examination is unremarkable.

Laboratory studies:

Hemoglobin A$_{1c}$	6.8%
Blood urea nitrogen	10 mg/dL (3.6 mmol/L)
Serum creatinine	0.9 mg/dL (79.6 μmol/L)
Glucose	126 mg/dL (7 mmol/L)
Urinalysis	Normal
Urine albumin–creatinine ratio	20 mg/g

Electrocardiogram reveals left ventricular hypertrophy.

Which of the following is the most appropriate next step in management?

(A) Add an ACE inhibitor
(B) Add a β-blocker
(C) Add a calcium channel blocker
(D) Add a diuretic
(E) Continue current regimen

Item 72

A 71-year-old man is evaluated during a follow-up visit 6 months after undergoing a kidney transplant because of ANCA-associated vasculitis. His postoperative course was uncomplicated, and his serum creatinine level was 1.3 mg/dL (115 µmol/L) at discharge. Over the past 3 months, his serum creatinine level has steadily increased. Current medications are tacrolimus, mycophenolate mofetil, metoprolol, and trimethoprim-sulfamethoxazole.

On physical examination, blood pressure is 110/64 mm Hg. BMI is 19. Cardiac examination is normal without rubs. Lungs are clear. There is a left brachiocephalic arteriovenous fistula with a palpable thrill and audible bruit. Abdominal examination is notable for a well-healed incision at the right lower quadrant; the kidney graft is nontender, and there is no bruit. There is no lower extremity edema.

Laboratory studies:

Blood urea nitrogen	42 mg/dL (15 mmol/L)
Serum creatinine	1.9 mg/dL (168 µmol/L)
Tacrolimus level (trough)	9 ng/mL (9 µg/L) (target, 8-10 ng/mL [8-10 µg/L])
Polymerase chain reaction	Positive for polyoma BK virus in the blood and urine
Urinalysis	1+ blood; 1+ protein; 1+ leukocyte esterase; 8-10 nondysmorphic erythrocytes/hpf; 4-8 leukocytes/hpf; rare leukocyte casts; no bacteria

Kidney biopsy results demonstrate an inflammatory interstitial infiltrate with evidence of tubulitis and scattered intranuclear viral inclusions in the tubular epithelial cells.

Which of the following is the most appropriate next step in management?

(A) Add acyclovir
(B) Add ganciclovir
(C) Add muromonab-CD3
(D) Decrease immunosuppression

Item 73

A 59-year-old woman is evaluated during a routine follow-up visit. She was recently diagnosed with type 2 diabetes mellitus and hyperlipidemia. She feels well. Medications are metformin, atorvastatin, and aspirin.

Physical examination findings and vital signs are normal. BMI is 27.

Laboratory studies reveal a serum creatinine level of 0.9 mg/dL (79.6 µmol/L), an estimated glomerular filtration rate of >60 mL/min/1.73 m², and normal urinalysis results.

Which of the following is the most appropriate diagnostic test to perform next?

(A) 24-Hour urine collection for protein
(B) Kidney ultrasonography
(C) Spot urine albumin–creatinine ratio
(D) No additional testing

Item 74

A 59-year-old man is evaluated during a follow-up visit for hypertension. He also has diabetes mellitus and stage 3 chronic kidney disease. One month ago, his dose of lisinopril was increased. Other medications are metoprolol, felodipine, and furosemide.

On physical examination, blood pressure is 158/75 mm Hg, and pulse rate is 70/min. There is dependent edema. The remainder of the examination is unremarkable.

Laboratory studies:

Serum creatinine	2.2 mg/dL (194 µmol/L)
Electrolytes	
Sodium	139 meq/L (139 mmol/L)
Potassium	5.3 meq/L (5.3 mmol/L)
Chloride	103 meq/L (103 mmol/L)
Bicarbonate	24 meq/L (24 mmol/L)

In addition to a low potassium diet, which of the following is the most appropriate treatment for this patient?

(A) Add sodium polystyrene sulfonate
(B) Add spironolactone
(C) Discontinue lisinopril
(D) Increase furosemide

Item 75

A 45-year-old man is evaluated for abdominal pain that began the previous night. The pain was intermittent and crampy. Over the course of the day, the pain has worsened and now radiates to the scrotum on the right side. He vomited once and reports anorexia. Medical history is notable for prostatitis 2 years ago and an appendectomy. He takes no medications.

On physical examination, the patient appears ill and is curled up on the examination table. Temperature is 37.9 °C (100.3 °F), blood pressure is 140/92 mm Hg, and pulse rate is 98/min. Cardiac and pulmonary examinations are normal. There is abdominal guarding. Genital examination is notable for the absence of penile discharge; there are normal-sized testes without tenderness. Rectal examination reveals normal tone and a smooth, nontender prostate. There is no edema.

Laboratory studies:

Leukocyte count	11,500/µL (11.5 × 10⁹/L)
Blood urea nitrogen	15 mg/dL (5.4 mmol/L)
Serum creatinine	1.2 mg/dL (106 µmol/L)
Urinalysis	pH 5.0; + blood; no protein, glucose, bilirubin, or leukocyte esterase; 10-15 erythrocytes/hpf; 1-3 leukocytes/hpf

Which of the following is the most appropriate imaging study to determine the cause of this patient's pain?

(A) Abdominal radiography of the kidneys, ureters, and bladder
(B) Intravenous pyelography
(C) Noncontrast abdominal helical CT
(D) Testicular ultrasonography

Item 76

A 55-year-old woman is evaluated for a 6-month history of increased fatigue and decreased exercise tolerance. History is notable for HIV infection. Medications are trimethoprim-sulfamethoxazole, atazanavir, emtricitabine, and tenofovir.

On physical examination, temperature is 36.0 °C (96.8 °F), blood pressure is 146/80 mm Hg, pulse rate is 86/min, and respiration rate is 18/min. BMI is 28. Mild diffuse weakness is noted.

Laboratory studies:

Albumin	3.8 g/dL (38 g/L)
Blood urea nitrogen	12 mg/dL (4.3 mmol/L)
Calcium	8.1 mg/dL (2.0 mmol/L)
Serum creatinine	1.3 mg/dL (115 µmol/L)
Electrolytes	
Sodium	140 meq/L (140 mmol/L)
Potassium	2.9 meq/L (2.9 mmol/L)
Chloride	114 meq/L (114 mmol/L)
Bicarbonate	16 meq/L (16 mmol/L)
Glucose	105 mg/dL (5.8 mmol/L)
Phosphorus	1.8 mg/dL (0.58 mmol/L)
Venous blood gas studies:	
pH	7.32
P_{CO_2}	36 mm Hg (4.8 kPa)
Urine studies:	
Urinalysis	Specific gravity 1.012; pH 5.1; no blood; trace protein; 1+ glucose; no ketones, nitrites, or leukocyte esterase
Urine protein–creatinine ratio	0.525 mg/mg

Kidney ultrasound shows no nephrocalcinosis.

Which of the following is the most appropriate management?

(A) Discontinue tenofovir
(B) Discontinue trimethoprim-sulfamethoxazole
(C) Measure serum lactate level
(D) Order a stool laxative screen

Item 77

A 66-year-old woman is evaluated in the hospital for acute kidney injury 4 days following a partial colectomy for perforated diverticulitis. She had no intraoperative hypotension but has required a total of 15 L of intravenous fluids to maintain her blood pressure. Urine output has gradually diminished, and she is now oliguric with an indwelling bladder catheter in place. She received one dose of tobramycin postoperatively; additional medications are vancomycin and imipenem.

On physical examination, the patient is intubated and sedated. Temperature is 37.2 °C (98.9 °F), blood pressure is 91/52 mm Hg, pulse rate is 108/min, and respiration rate on ventilation is 14/min. BMI is 35. Cardiac examination is notable for tachycardia, with a regular rate and no murmur. Pulmonary examination is normal. Abdominal examination reveals a tense and distended abdomen, with hypoactive bowel sounds. The abdominal wall is edematous. There is pitting edema of the legs.

Laboratory studies:

Blood urea nitrogen	45 mg/dL (16.1 mmol/L)
Serum creatinine	Preoperative: 0.9 mg/dL (79.6 µmol/L); postoperative day 4: 2.9 mg/dL (256 µmol/L)
Fractional excretion of sodium	1.5%
Urinalysis	Specific gravity 1.011; pH 6.0; trace erythrocytes/hpf; 1-2 leukocytes/hpf; occasional granular casts

Kidney ultrasound reveals normal-sized kidneys and no hydronephrosis.

Which of the following is the most likely cause of this patient's kidney failure?

(A) Abdominal compartment syndrome
(B) Aminoglycoside nephrotoxicity
(C) Prerenal acute kidney injury
(D) Urinary obstruction

Item 78

A 53-year-old woman is evaluated for a 3-month history of swelling of the face, hands, and feet. She has untreated hepatitis C virus infection. She takes lithium for bipolar disorder. She has no additional symptoms.

On physical examination, temperature is normal, blood pressure is 134/93 mm Hg, pulse rate is 71/min, and respiration rate is 18/min. Bilateral periorbital edema and swelling of the hands and legs are noted. The remainder of the examination is unremarkable.

Laboratory studies:

Complete blood count	Normal
Albumin	1.6 g/dL (16 g/L)
Blood urea nitrogen	28 mg/dL (10 mmol/L)
Complement (C3 and C4)	Normal
Serum creatinine	1.5 mg/dL (133 µmol/L)
Cryoglobulin	Negative
Serum protein electrophoresis	Normal
Rheumatoid factor	Negative
Hepatitis B surface antigen	Negative
Hepatitis C virus antibodies	Positive with low RNA titer
HIV antibodies	Negative
Antinuclear antibodies	Negative
Urinalysis	4+ protein; 4-7 erythrocytes/hpf; 4-7 leukocytes/hpf
24-Hour urine collection of protein	14 g/24 h

Ultrasound shows normal-sized kidneys.

Percutaneous kidney biopsy results show glomeruli of normal size and cellularity, with patent capillary lumina. Diffuse fusion of podocyte foot processes is noted on electron microscopy. Immunofluorescence studies show no immune deposits.

Which of the following is the most likely cause of this patient's nephrotic syndrome?

(A) Hepatitis C virus–associated glomerulonephritis
(B) Lupus nephritis

(C) Membranous glomerulopathy

(D) Minimal change glomerulopathy

Item 79

A 50-year-old man is seen during a follow-up visit 2 days after he was evaluated in the emergency department for renal colic. Records from the emergency department show a normal metabolic profile, and a noncontrast CT scan revealed a 4-mm stone in the distal left ureter. He continues to have pain controlled with oxycodone.

On physical examination, vital signs are normal. Mild left costovertebral angle tenderness is noted. The remainder of the examination is unremarkable.

Which of the following is the most appropriate next step in management?

(A) 24-Hour urine collection for calcium, oxalate, and uric acid

(B) Extracorporeal shock wave lithotripsy

(C) Repeat noncontrast CT

(D) Tamsulosin

(E) Ureteroscopy and intracorporeal lithotripsy

Item 80

A 74-year-old man was hospitalized 3 days ago for extensive, nonpurulent cellulitis of the right lower extremity and is now being evaluated for acute kidney injury. He has hypertension, hyperlipidemia, and peripheral vascular disease. His hypertension has been poorly controlled; his last office blood pressure measurement was 165/92 mm Hg. Medications are lisinopril, metoprolol, hydrochlorothiazide, amlodipine, pravastatin, and aspirin. On admission, cefazolin was initiated.

The patient is now afebrile, and his blood pressure has not exceeded 118/60 mm Hg since admission. There is no evidence of orthostasis. The cellulitis has improved since admission.

Since admission, his serum creatinine level has progressively increased from 1.5 mg/dL (133 μmol/L) to 2.7 mg/dL (239 μmol/L).

Other laboratory studies are as follows:

Urine sodium	45 meq/L (45 mmol/L) (normal range for men, 18-301 meq/L [18-301 mmol/L])
Fractional excretion of sodium	2.3%
Fractional excretion of urea	51%
Urinalysis	Specific gravity 1.015; trace protein; no erythrocytes or leukocytes; occasional granular casts

Kidney ultrasound is normal.

Which of the following is the most likely cause of this patient's acute kidney injury?

(A) Acute interstitial nephritis

(B) Cholesterol emboli

(C) Normotensive ischemic acute kidney injury

(D) Prerenal azotemia

Item 81

A 54-year-old woman is evaluated during a follow-up visit for recurrent kidney stones. She underwent successful gastric bypass surgery for obesity approximately 1 year ago. Steady weight loss has occurred, and her BMI has decreased from 38 to 33. However, she has had two episodes of nephrolithiasis since the time of her surgery and most recently passed another kidney stone. None of the stones has been available for analysis. Medical history is notable for type 2 diabetes mellitus and hypertension. Medications are metoprolol and glyburide.

On physical examination, blood pressure is 125/78 mm Hg. The remainder of the examination is unremarkable.

Urine studies:

Calcium excretion	Normal
Citrate excretion	Normal
Oxalate excretion	High
Uric acid excretion	Normal
Urinalysis	Specific gravity 1.025; pH 5.0; no blood; 2-4 erythrocytes/hpf; many envelope-shaped crystals
Urine volume	1300 mL/24 h

In addition to increased fluid intake, which of the following is the most appropriate next step in management?

(A) Calcium carbonate supplements

(B) Chlorthalidone

(C) Potassium citrate

(D) Tamsulosin

Item 82

A 47-year-old man is evaluated during a routine follow-up visit. He has chronic kidney disease from IgA nephropathy and hypertension and has been treated with lisinopril, resulting in stable proteinuria and blood pressures in the 125/75 mm Hg range. He reports doing well except for a 1-week flu-like syndrome for which he has treated himself with an over-the-counter cold preparation and analgesic medication. His symptoms have improved, and he reports no apparent blood in his urine, arthritis, or fever.

On physical examination, blood pressure is 152/85 mm Hg, and pulse rate is 82/min. BMI is 25. There are no rashes. The ears are clear, and the nasal and oropharyngeal mucosa are slightly edematous and erythematous with a minimal amount of discharge. Cardiac and pulmonary examinations are normal. There is no arthritis or edema.

Urine protein is less than 1 g/24 h and unchanged from baseline.

Laboratory studies:

Electrolytes	Normal
Serum creatinine	1.7 mg/dL (150 μmol/L) (unchanged from baseline)
Urinalysis	pH 5.5; no leukocytes; 5-10 erythrocytes/hpf; no casts or epithelial tubular cells

Which of the following is the most appropriate next step in managing this patient's blood pressure?

(A) Add losartan
(B) Begin prednisone
(C) Discontinue over-the-counter medications
(D) Increase lisinopril

Item 83

A 68-year-old man is hospitalized for a 3-month history of dark brown–colored urine, malaise, and an unintentional 6.8-kg (15-lb) weight loss. He has felt febrile during this time period. He reports no urinary hesitancy, frequency, dysuria, nausea, vomiting, or diarrhea. He has not had any abdominal pain, fullness, or gastrointestinal symptoms. He has type 2 diabetes mellitus and hypertension. Medications are glipizide and lisinopril. He has a 40-pack-year history of smoking.

On physical examination, the patient appears fatigued and has periorbital edema. Temperature is 37.6 °C (99.6 °F), blood pressure is 162/93 mm Hg, pulse rate is 88/min, and respiration rate is 16/min. BMI is 29. Cardiac examination reveals no murmurs, rubs, or gallops. Lungs are clear to auscultation. The abdomen is nontender and nondistended, and bowel sounds are normal. There is 1+ pitting edema of the extremities.

Laboratory studies:

Hemoglobin	11.8 g/dL (118 g/L)
Albumin	3.4 g/dL (34 g/L)
Serum creatinine	3.2 mg/dL (283 µmol/L) (6 months ago: 1.6 mg/dL [141 µmol/L])
Urinalysis	1+ blood; 1+ protein; 5-10 erythrocytes/hpf; 50% acanthocytes; erythrocyte casts

Which of the following is the most likely diagnosis?

(A) Acute interstitial nephritis
(B) Acute tubular necrosis
(C) Polyarteritis nodosa
(D) Rapidly progressive glomerulonephritis

Item 84

A 63-year-old woman is evaluated during a follow-up visit for a 3-year history of type 2 diabetes mellitus and hypertension. Her diabetes has been well controlled on a twice daily dose of metformin. She takes lisinopril, 20 mg/d, for her hypertension; her blood pressure measurements are typically around 125/75 mm Hg.

On physical examination, vital signs recorded by a medical assistant show a temperature of 37.3° C (99.2 °F), blood pressure of 154/78 mm Hg, and pulse rate of 82/min. BMI is 32. The remainder of the examination is normal.

Laboratory studies reveal normal electrolytes, complete blood count, fasting lipid profile, and urine albumin–creatinine ratio as well as normal kidney function; hemoglobin A_{1c} level is 7.1%.

Which of the following is the most appropriate next step in management?

(A) Add hydrochlorothiazide
(B) Ambulatory blood pressure monitoring
(C) Increase lisinopril
(D) Repeat blood pressure measurement

Item 85

A 30-year-old woman is evaluated during a prenatal visit. She is 18 weeks pregnant, and this is her first pregnancy. She has a history of borderline hypertension, and her blood pressure measurements since conception have been in the range of 120 to 130/80 to 90 mm Hg without antihypertensive therapy. She adheres to a low sodium diet; a dietary assessment shows adequate amounts of dietary calcium. Family history is notable for her mother who had preeclampsia at 37 weeks' gestation. She takes prenatal vitamins.

Urinalysis is negative for protein.

Which of the following interventions may reduce this patient's risk of preeclampsia?

(A) Low-dose aspirin
(B) Methyldopa
(C) Oral calcium supplement
(D) Oral magnesium supplement
(E) Reduce blood pressure to less than 120/80 mm Hg

Item 86

A 57-year-old man is evaluated for a 20-year history of hypertension. He reports a 4.5-kg (10-lb) weight gain during the past 6 months. The patient is black. He does not smoke cigarettes. His only medication is low-dose chlorthalidone.

On physical examination, seated blood pressure is 146 to 150/88 mm Hg, and pulse rate is 78/min. BMI is 29. The remainder of the examination is unremarkable.

Laboratory studies reveal a serum creatinine level of 1.7 mg/dL (150 µmol/L), an estimated glomerular filtration rate of 51 mL/min/1.73 m², and a urine protein–creatinine ratio of 0.45 mg/mg.

Which of the following is the most appropriate next step in managing this patient's hypertension?

(A) Add amlodipine
(B) Add metoprolol
(C) Add ramipril
(D) Increase the chlorthalidone dose

Item 87

A 65-year-old man is evaluated in the emergency department for a 4-month history of fatigue and sinus symptoms and a 1-week history of low-grade fever, worsening fatigue, and hemoptysis. His medical history is otherwise unremarkable.

On physical examination, temperature is 37.9 °C (100.3 °F), blood pressure is 153/89 mm Hg, pulse rate is 95/min, and respiration rate is 22/min. Periorbital edema is noted. There is dried blood in the nares. Pulmonary examination reveals crackles and moderate respiratory distress. There is 1+ pitting edema of the lower extremities.

Laboratory studies on admission:

Hemoglobin	9.8 g/dL (98 g/L)
Leukocyte count	12,000/µL (12×10^9/L)
Bicarbonate	14 meq/L (14 mmol/L)
Blood urea nitrogen	70 mg/dL (25 mmol/L)
Serum creatinine	6.7 mg/dL (592 µmol/L) (3 months ago: 1.3 mg/dL [115 µmol/L]; 1 year ago: 0.7 mg/dL [61.9 µmol/L])
Potassium	6.1 meq/L (6.1 mmol/L)
p-ANCA	1:1240
Anti–glomerular basement membrane antibodies	Negative
Blood cultures	Negative
Sputum cultures	Negative
Arterial blood gas studies (ambient air):	
pH	7.32
P_{CO_2}	30 mm Hg (4.0 kPa)
P_{O_2}	75 mm Hg (10.0 kPa)
Urinalysis	2 erythrocytes/hpf; many erythrocyte casts

Chest radiograph reveals infiltrates in the lung fields.

Kidney biopsy results reveal diffuse necrotizing crescentic glomerulonephritis with a pauci-immune pattern.

Broad-spectrum antibiotics and intermittent hemodialysis support are initiated. He is transferred to the intensive care unit and placed on noninvasive positive-pressure ventilation for worsened respiratory failure.

Which of the following is the most appropriate induction therapy?

(A) Cyclophosphamide and corticosteroids
(B) Mycophenolate mofetil and corticosteroids
(C) Plasmapheresis
(D) Plasmapheresis, cyclophosphamide, and corticosteroids

Item 88

A 17-year-old teenager is evaluated during a follow-up visit. His mother states that he struggles in school and was held back a grade. Family history includes a first-degree cousin with cognitive impairment and a grandmother who died of "kidney failure." He takes no medications.

On physical examination, the patient appears generally well. Temperature is 37.1 °C (98.7 °F), blood pressure is 149/94 mm Hg, pulse rate is 72/min, and respiration rate is 16/min. BMI is 23. The patient wears eyeglasses but has no obvious ophthalmic lesions. There is poor dentition, including pitted tooth enamel and gum lesions. Several hypomelanotic lesions are present on the back and shoulders.

Laboratory studies reveal a serum creatinine level of 1.9 mg/dL (168 µmol/L), and urinalysis results are normal.

On kidney ultrasound, the left kidney is 9.8 cm, and the right kidney is 10.2 cm; there are two cystic lesions in each kidney.

Which of the following is the most likely diagnosis?

(A) Autosomal dominant polycystic kidney disease
(B) Autosomal recessive polycystic kidney disease
(C) Fabry disease
(D) Tuberous sclerosis complex

Item 89

A 67-year-old man is evaluated following a recent diagnosis of type 2 diabetes mellitus.

On physical examination, blood pressure is 134/84 mm Hg; other vital signs are normal. BMI is 30. The remainder of the examination is unremarkable.

Laboratory studies:

Hemoglobin A_{1c}	7.8%
Blood urea nitrogen	15 mg/dL (5.4 mmol/L)
Serum creatinine	1.0 mg/dL (88.4 µmol/L)
Urinalysis	No protein; 3+ glucose; 0-2 erythrocytes/hpf; 0-3 leukocytes/hpf

In addition to therapeutic lifestyle changes, which of the following is the most appropriate next step in management?

(A) Estimated glomerular filtration rate using the Modification of Diet in Renal Disease study equation
(B) Urine albumin–creatinine ratio in 5 years
(C) Urine albumin–creatinine ratio now
(D) Urine protein–creatinine ratio in 5 years
(E) Urine protein–creatinine ratio now

Item 90

A 69-year-old man is evaluated during a new patient visit. Medical history includes a 23-year history of hypertension as well as several kidney stones 15 years ago. Family history includes his mother who began dialysis at age 72 years for unknown reasons and died of "kidney disease" 5 years later. Medications are lisinopril, furosemide, and aspirin.

On physical examination, temperature is 36.9 °C (98.4 °F), blood pressure is 134/72 mm Hg, pulse rate is 72/min, and respiration rate is 14/min. BMI is 29. The remainder of the physical examination is normal.

Laboratory studies:

Hemoglobin	12 g/dL (120 g/L)
Serum creatinine	1.9 mg/dL (168 µmol/L) (1 year ago: 1.8 mg/dL [159 µmol/L]; 6 years ago: 1.4 mg/dL [124 µmol/L])
Estimated glomerular filtration rate	37 mL/min/1.73 m²
Urinalysis	2+ protein; 0-2 erythrocytes/hpf; 2-4 leukocytes/hpf
Urine cultures	No growth

Which of the following is the most appropriate diagnostic test to perform next?

(A) Abdominal CT with contrast
(B) Kidney biopsy
(C) Kidney ultrasonography
(D) Radionuclide kidney clearance scanning

Item 91

A 61-year-old man is evaluated for a 3-year history of hypertension. He also has pedal edema that is undetectable when he wakes up in the morning and worsens throughout the day. He feels tired and has slowly gained approximately 4.5 kg (10 lb) during the past 3 years. He does not smoke cigarettes. Medications are hydrochlorothiazide, losartan, and amlodipine.

On physical examination, the average blood pressure is between 128 and 134/70 mm Hg, which is similar to readings obtained during the past 3 years. Other vital signs are normal. BMI is 28. There are no abdominal bruits, and the distal pulses are normal. There is trace pedal edema bilaterally.

Laboratory studies:

Serum creatinine	1.6 mg/dL (141 µmol/L) (1 year ago: 1.5 mg/dL [133 µmol/L]; 3 years ago, before treatment: 1.2 mg/dL [106 µmol/L])
Estimated glomerular filtration rate	53 mL/min/1.73 m²
Urinalysis	1+ protein; no blood; no cells; otherwise unremarkable

Which of the following is the most likely cause of this patient's elevation in serum creatinine level?

(A) Angiotensin receptor blocker therapy
(B) Glomerulonephritis
(C) Inadequate blood pressure control
(D) Renovascular disease

Item 92

A 50-year-old man is hospitalized for progressively worsening right and left flank pain of 3 weeks' duration. Associated symptoms include anorexia, malaise, fever, and joint pain. He has no other medical problems and takes no medications.

On physical examination, the patient appears chronically ill. Temperature is 38.6 °C (101.5 °F), blood pressure is 168/94 mm Hg, and pulse rate is 66/min. There are no abnormal skin findings. Cardiopulmonary examination is normal. There is tenderness to deep abdominal palpation and percussion of the flanks, which is not concordant with the perceived abdominal pain level of 10 of 10.

Laboratory studies:

Erythrocyte sedimentation rate	101 mm/h
Serum creatinine	1.8 mg/dL (159 µmol/L) (1 year ago: 0.9 mg/dL [79.6 µmol/L])

ANCA	Negative
Hepatitis A total antibodies	Negative
Hepatitis B surface antigen	Positive
Hepatitis B surface antigen IgM antibody	Positive
Hepatitis B surface antigen IgG antibody	Negative
Hepatitis C virus antibodies	Negative
Urinalysis	3+ blood; 1+ protein; many erythrocytes; no dysmorphic erythrocytes; no casts

Kidney angiogram reveals multiple aneurysms and stenotic lesions of renal artery branches bilaterally.

Which of the following is the most likely diagnosis?

(A) Giant cell arteritis
(B) Granulomatosis with polyangiitis
(C) Polyarteritis nodosa
(D) Takayasu arteritis

Item 93

A 78-year-old woman is evaluated for increased fatigue. Two weeks ago, she was hospitalized for fever, chills, and weakness occurring 10 days following aortic valve replacement. At that time, blood cultures grew vancomycin-resistant *Enterococcus faecalis*, and intravenous linezolid was initiated. She has type 2 diabetes mellitus and hypertension. Medications are linezolid, amlodipine, enalapril, warfarin, and acetaminophen.

On physical examination, temperature is 37.3 °C (99.2 °F), blood pressure is 146/50 mm Hg, pulse rate is 96/min, and respiration rate is 24/min. BMI is 38. Cardiac examination is consistent with findings associated with a normal functioning prosthetic aortic valve. The lung fields are clear. The remainder of the examination is normal.

Laboratory studies:

Hemoglobin	10.4 g/dL (104 g/L)
Leukocyte count	7000/µL (7.0 × 10⁹/L)
Blood urea nitrogen	10 mg/dL (3.6 mmol/L)
Serum creatinine	0.7 mg/dL (61.9 µmol/L)
Electrolytes	
Sodium	143 meq/L (143 mmol/L)
Potassium	4.8 meq/L (4.8 mmol/L)
Chloride	106 meq/L (106 mmol/L)
Bicarbonate	9 meq/L (9 mmol/L)
Glucose	196 mg/dL (14.2 mmol/L)
Lactic acid	126 mg/dL (14 mmol/L)
Ketones	Negative
Arterial blood gas studies (ambient air):	
pH	7.23
Pco₂	22 mm Hg (2.9 kPa)
Po₂	98 mm Hg (13.0 kPa)

Which of the following is the most likely diagnosis?

(A) Diabetic ketoacidosis
(B) Pyroglutamic acidosis

(C) Sepsis

(D) Type B lactic acidosis

Item 94

A 26-year-old man is evaluated for a 6-month history of fatigue. He is subsequently diagnosed with hypokalemic metabolic alkalosis. He takes no medications.

On physical examination, temperature is 36.6 °C (97.9 °F), blood pressure is 110/64 mm Hg, pulse rate is 78/min, and respiration rate is 14/min. BMI is 20. Cardiac and pulmonary examinations are normal. There is no edema. The remainder of the examination is unremarkable.

Laboratory studies:

Blood urea nitrogen	12 mg/dL (4.3 mmol/L)
Serum creatinine	0.8 mg/dL (70.7 µmol/L)
Electrolytes	
Sodium	142 meq/L (142 mmol/L)
Potassium	2.9 meq/L (2.9 mmol/L)
Chloride	100 meq/L (100 mmol/L)
Bicarbonate	32 meq/L (32 mmol/L)

Which of the following is the most appropriate diagnostic test to perform next?

(A) Plasma aldosterone and renin levels

(B) Serum magnesium level

(C) Urine chloride level

(D) Urine osmolal gap

Item 95

A 71-year-old woman is hospitalized for chest pain. She has diabetes mellitus, hypertension, hyperlipidemia, and chronic kidney disease. Medications are lisinopril, rosuvastatin, as-needed furosemide, carvedilol, insulin, and aspirin.

On physical examination, the patient is afebrile; blood pressure is 118/50 mm Hg, and pulse rate is 70/min. There is no jugular venous distention. Cardiac examination is normal, with no murmurs or S_3. The lungs are clear. Abdominal examination is unremarkable. There is trace edema of the lower extremities, which is her baseline.

Laboratory studies:

Hematocrit	33%
Serum creatinine	3.1 mg/dL (274 µmol/L)
Electrolytes	Normal
Estimated glomerular filtration rate	19 mL/min/1.73 m²

Adenosine thallium scan reveals an area of reversible ischemia in the left anterior descending artery distribution. Cardiac catheterization is scheduled. Her lisinopril is held prior to the procedure.

Which of the following interventions will decrease this patient's risk for contrast-induced nephropathy?

(A) Hydration with isotonic saline

(B) Hydration with isotonic saline with mannitol diuresis

(C) Oral hydration

(D) Prophylactic hemodialysis

Item 96

A 68-year-old man is evaluated during a follow-up visit for chronic kidney disease. He also has hypertension, dyslipidemia, and COPD. His kidney function has remained stable, with an estimated glomerular filtration rate ranging from 30 to 40 mL/min/1.73 m². Medications are metoprolol, lisinopril, aspirin, atorvastatin, and albuterol and ipratropium inhalers.

On physical examination, blood pressure is 120/75 mm Hg, pulse rate is 80/min, and respiration rate is 14/min. There is no jugular venous distention. Cardiac examination reveals regular heart sounds and no murmur. The lungs are tympanitic with good air movement but mild diffuse expiratory wheezes. There is no lower extremity edema.

Laboratory studies:

Hemoglobin	10.5 g/dL (105 g/L)
Blood urea nitrogen	52 mg/dL (18.6 mmol/L)
Calcium	8.2 mg/dL (2.1 mmol/L)
Total cholesterol	179 mg/dL (4.64 mmol/L)
LDL cholesterol	115 mg/dL (2.98 mmol/L)
HDL cholesterol	42 mg/dL (1.09 mmol/L)
Triglycerides	110 mg/dL (1.24 mmol/L)
Serum creatinine	2.2 mg/dL (194 µmol/L)
Electrolytes	
Sodium	141 meq/L (141 mmol/L)
Potassium	4.9 meq/L (4.9 mmol/L)
Chloride	105 meq/L (105 mmol/L)
Bicarbonate	23 meq/L (23 mmol/L)
Phosphorus	4.5 mg/dL (1.45 mmol/L)
Parathyroid hormone	135 pg/mL (135 ng/L)
Estimated glomerular filtration rate	31 mL/min/1.73 m²
Urine albumin–creatinine ratio	235 mg/g

Which of the following interventions is most likely to prevent premature mortality?

(A) Begin 1,25-dihydroxy vitamin D

(B) Begin sodium bicarbonate replacement therapy

(C) Increase atorvastatin

(D) Increase lisinopril

Item 97

A 38-year-old woman is evaluated during a follow-up visit. She has a history of well-controlled hypertension and type 1 diabetes mellitus. She is at 16 weeks' gestation with her first pregnancy. Prior to conception she was taking lisinopril, which was discontinued in anticipation of the pregnancy, and labetalol was initiated. Other medications are insulin glargine, insulin lispro, and a prenatal vitamin.

On physical examination, she appears in good health. Blood pressure is 135/80 mm Hg. There is no edema. The remainder of the physical examination is normal.

Laboratory studies reveal a serum creatinine level of 0.7 mg/dL (61.9 µmol/L) and a urine protein–creatinine ratio of 0.8 mg/mg.

Which of the following is the most appropriate step in the management of this patient's hypertension?

(A) Add methyldopa
(B) Change labetalol to losartan
(C) Increase labetalol dose
(D) Continue current medication regimen

Item 98

An 82-year-old woman is evaluated during a follow-up visit for a 25-year history of hypertension. She feels well and has had no end-organ damage due to her blood pressure. Medications are maximal therapeutic daily doses of indapamide and lisinopril, which she tolerates well.

On physical examination, seated blood pressure is 146/68 mm Hg with a regular pulse rate of 72/min; after standing for 1 minute, blood pressure is 140/72 mm Hg with no change in pulse rate. The remainder of the examination is unremarkable.

Laboratory studies reveal normal electrolytes and kidney function.

Which of the following is the most appropriate next step in managing this patient's blood pressure?

(A) Add amlodipine
(B) Add metoprolol
(C) Discontinue indapamide; begin hydrochlorothiazide
(D) No change in management

Item 99

A 48-year-old man is evaluated during a follow-up visit for chronic kidney disease attributed to hypertensive nephrosclerosis. One week ago, he began to have dyspnea with exertion with increasing frequency. Episodes typically begin when he is walking, and he needs to sit for the symptoms to resolve. Occasionally the dyspnea is accompanied by nausea. He has no chest pain. He has never smoked and does not drink alcoholic beverages. Medications are lisinopril and lovastatin.

On physical examination, blood pressure is 142/86 mm Hg. BMI is 29. There is no jugular venous distention. Cardiac examination is normal. Lungs are clear. There is 1+ edema.

Laboratory studies (obtained 1 week ago):

Blood urea nitrogen	36 mg/dL (12.9 mmol/L)
Serum creatinine	2.1 mg/dL (186 µmol/L)
Total cholesterol	168 mg/dL (4.35 mmol/L)
LDL cholesterol	100 mg/dL (2.59 mmol/L)
HDL cholesterol	38 mg/dL (0.98 mmol/L)
Estimated glomerular filtration rate	41 mL/min/1.73 m²
Urine protein–creatinine ratio	0.9 mg/mg

Electrocardiogram shows changes compatible with left ventricular hypertrophy.

Which of the following is the most appropriate next step in management?

(A) Begin an albuterol inhaler
(B) Begin furosemide
(C) Obtain spirometry
(D) Refer to the emergency department

Item 100

A 32-year-old man is evaluated for a recent diagnosis of autosomal dominant polycystic kidney disease (ADPKD) by kidney ultrasound. His mother had polycystic kidney disease, hypertension, and kidney failure requiring hemodialysis, and she died of a stroke. The patient also has hypertension that is managed with metoprolol and losartan.

On physical examination, blood pressure is 132/82 mm Hg, and pulse rate is 64/min. There is no flank pain or lower extremity edema. The remainder of the examination is unremarkable.

Laboratory studies reveal a serum creatinine level of 1.2 mg/dL (106 µmol/L) and a urine protein–creatinine ratio of 0.15 mg/mg; microscopic urinalysis reveals 5-10 erythrocytes/hpf.

Which of the following is the most appropriate next step in management?

(A) 24-Hour urine collection for protein
(B) Cerebral artery MR angiography
(C) Genotype testing for ADPKD subtype
(D) Noncontrast abdominal CT

Item 101

A 38-year-old woman is evaluated during a follow-up visit for stage 3 chronic kidney disease and hypertension secondary to polycystic kidney disease. Her only medication is lisinopril. Her daily dietary calcium intake is restricted to 1000 mg.

On physical examination, blood pressure is 124/80 mm Hg. Cardiopulmonary examination is normal. Abdominal examination is notable for bilateral palpable kidneys. The remainder of the examination is normal.

Laboratory studies:

Calcium	8.2 mg/dL (2.1 mmol/L)
Serum creatinine	1.7 mg/dL (150 µmol/L)
Phosphorus	4.3 mg/dL (1.39 mmol/L)
Intact parathyroid hormone	163 pg/mL (163 ng/L)
25-hydroxyvitamin D	12 ng/mL (30 nmol/L)
Estimated glomerular filtration rate	34 mL/min/1.73 m²

Which of the following is the most appropriate next step in management?

(A) Begin calcitriol (1,25-dihydroxy vitamin D)
(B) Begin calcium carbonate
(C) Begin cholecalciferol (vitamin D₃)
(D) Begin sevelamer
(E) Continue current regimen

Item 102

A 21-year-old man is evaluated during a follow-up visit. He was initially evaluated at a student health center for flu-like symptoms and was found to have a blood pressure of 144/90 mm Hg. At his first office visit 3 weeks ago, his blood pressure was 136/83 mm Hg seated (average of three readings). Medical history is unremarkable. He takes no medications.

On physical examination today, blood pressure is 133/79 mm Hg seated (average of three readings); other vital signs are normal. The remainder of the examination is normal.

Which of the following is the most likely diagnosis?

(A) Masked hypertension
(B) Normotension
(C) Prehypertension
(D) White coat hypertension

Item 103

A 33-year-old woman is evaluated for hypertension. She is at 17 weeks' gestation with her second pregnancy. Her first pregnancy was complicated by hypertension at term. She has not followed up in the 4 years since the delivery of her first child. She has no allergies. Family history is notable for her father who has diabetes mellitus and hypertension. Her only medication is prenatal vitamins.

On physical examination, she appears well. Blood pressure is 140/90 mm Hg, and pulse rate is 90/min. Lungs are clear. The abdomen has a gravid uterus. Reflexes are normal. There is trace edema. The remainder of the examination is unremarkable.

Laboratory studies reveal a serum creatinine level of 1.7 mg/dL (150 µmol/L), 1+ protein on urinalysis, and a urine protein–creatinine ratio of 0.5 mg/mg.

Which of the following is the most likely diagnosis?

(A) Chronic kidney disease and hypertension
(B) Gestational hypertension
(C) The nephrotic syndrome
(D) Preeclampsia

Item 104

A 72-year-old woman is hospitalized for a 3-day history of fever, chills, and malaise. Three months ago, she had a complete heart block necessitating placement of a dual-chamber pacemaker.

On physical examination, temperature is 37.4 °C (99.3 °F), blood pressure is 128/56 mm Hg, pulse rate is 96/min, and respiration rate is 16/min. BMI is 26. A grade 3/6 holosystolic murmur is heard best along the left sternal border and is louder during inspiration.

Echocardiogram reveals a 1-cm vegetation on the tricuspid valve.

Blood cultures grow vancomycin-resistant *Enterococcus*. Intravenous vancomycin and gentamicin are initiated. On day 3, the patient develops increased agitation and paranoid delusions; quetiapine is initiated.

Laboratory studies:

	On Admission	10 Days Later
Blood urea nitrogen	26 mg/dL (9.3 mmol/L)	24 mg/dL (8.6 mmol/L)
Serum creatinine	0.8 mg/dL (70.7 µmol/L)	1.3 mg/dL (115 µmol/L)
Electrolytes		
Sodium	142 meq/L (142 mmol/L)	138 meq/L (138 mmol/L)
Potassium	5 meq/L (5 mmol/L)	2.9 meq/L (2.9 mmol/L)
Chloride	105 meq/L (105 mmol/L)	93 meq/L (93 mmol/L)
Bicarbonate	25 meq/L (25 mmol/L)	32 meq/L (32 mmol/L)
Urine studies:		
Chloride	–	96 meq/L (96 mmol/L) (normal range for women, 20-295 meq/L [20-295 mmol/L])
Creatinine	–	80 mg/dL (normal range for women, 15-327 mg/dL)
Potassium	–	40 meq/L (40 mmol/L) (normal range for women, 17-164 meq/L [17-164 mmol/L])
Sodium	–	103 meq/L (103 mmol/L) (normal range for women, 15-267 meq/L [15-267 mmol/L])
Urine potassium–creatinine ratio	–	50 meq/g

Which of the following is the most likely cause of this patient's electrolyte disorder?

(A) Gentamicin toxicity
(B) Primary hyperaldosteronism
(C) Quetiapine toxicity
(D) Vancomycin toxicity

Item 105

A 65-year-old woman is evaluated during a follow-up visit for long-standing diabetic nephropathy and hypertension. She feels well but reports mild dyspnea with exertion. Medications are lisinopril, metoprolol, hydrochlorothiazide, neutral protamine Hagedorn (NPH) insulin, and regular insulin.

On physical examination, blood pressure is 138/78 mm Hg, and pulse rate is 65/min. Cardiac examination is normal. Lungs are clear. The remainder of the examination is unremarkable.

Laboratory studies:

Hematocrit	29%
Leukocyte count and differential	Normal

Mean corpuscular volume	88 fL
Platelet count	Normal
Reticulocyte count	0.5% of erythrocytes
Serum creatinine	2.3 mg/dL (203 μmol/L)
Estimated glomerular filtration rate	21 mL/min/1.73 m^2
Peripheral blood smear	Consistent with normocytic anemia

Which of the following is the most appropriate next step in the management of this patient's anemia?

(A) Discontinue lisinopril
(B) Initiate erythropoiesis-stimulating agents
(C) Measure serum erythropoietin level
(D) Measure serum iron stores

Item 106

A 67-year-old man is evaluated in the hospital for an increasing serum creatinine level. He was hospitalized for pneumonia 2 days ago and is improving on levofloxacin therapy. He has experienced no episodes of hypotension during the hospitalization. His only other medication is prazosin for benign prostatic hyperplasia.

On physical examination, blood pressure is 144/75 mm Hg, and pulse rate is 64/min. BMI is 34. Cardiac and pulmonary examinations are normal. The abdomen is nontender, with normal bowel sounds and some suprapubic fullness. Urine output was 1200 mL in the past 24 hours.

Laboratory studies:

Serum creatinine	1.9 mg/dL (168 μmol/L) (1.2 mg/dL [106 μmol/L] on admission)
Potassium	5.7 meq/L (5.7 mmol/L) (4.5 meq/L [4.5 mmol/L] on admission)
Urinalysis	Specific gravity 1.011; pH 6.0; trace leukocyte esterase; 0-3 erythrocytes/hpf; 0-5 leukocytes/hpf

Which of the following is the most appropriate diagnostic test to perform next?

(A) Fractional excretion of sodium
(B) Kidney biopsy
(C) Kidney ultrasonography
(D) Serum creatine kinase level measurement

Item 107

A 20-year-old woman is evaluated in the hospital after a tonsillectomy because her blood pressure increased from 122/72 mm Hg before anesthesia induction to 210/126 mm Hg during induction. Her heart rate increased from 70/min to 106/min when her blood pressure increased. Intravenous nitroglycerin was initiated to lower her blood pressure. Other than occasional palpitations, her medical history, family history, and review of systems were unremarkable.

On physical examination 2 hours later, the patient is awake and alert. The nitroglycerin was discontinued 30 minutes ago. Current blood pressure is 118/76 mm Hg, and heart rate is 80/min. Other than a fresh tonsillectomy scar, the remainder of the examination is normal.

Which of the following is the most appropriate next step in management?

(A) CT of the adrenal glands
(B) Catheter-based kidney angiography
(C) Plasma metanephrine measurement
(D) Transthoracic echocardiography

Item 108

A 68-year-old man is hospitalized for acute kidney injury secondary to a bladder outlet obstruction. He also has benign prostatic hyperplasia, hypertension, chronic kidney disease, and bipolar disorder previously treated with lithium. Medications are doxazosin, valproate, and enalapril (held on admission).

On admission, serum creatinine level is 6.2 mg/dL (548 μmol/L); 6 months ago, it was 1.5 mg/dL (133 μmol/L). After placement of a bladder (Foley) catheter, 800 mL of urine drained immediately. Urine volume increased to 130 mL/h over the initial 48 hours of hospitalization.

On physical examination, temperature is 37.3 °C (99.2 °F), blood pressure is 160/60 mm Hg, pulse rate is 68/min, and respiration rate is 14/min. BMI is 30. Cardiopulmonary examination is normal. There is 1+ lower extremity edema.

Laboratory studies on day 3 of admission:

Blood urea nitrogen	86 mg/dL (30.7 mmol/L)
Serum creatinine	3.4 mg/dL (301 μmol/L)
Electrolytes	
Sodium	148 meq/L (148 mmol/L)
Potassium	5.2 meq/L (5.2 mmol/L)
Chloride	117 meq/L (117 mmol/L)
Bicarbonate	18 meq/L (18 mmol/L)
Glucose	106 mg/dL (5.9 mmol/L)
Urine studies:	
Osmolality	326 mosm/kg H$_2$O (normal, 300-900 mosm/kg H$_2$O)
Potassium	35 meq/L (35 mmol/L) (normal range for men, 11-99 meq/L [11-99 mmol/L])
Sodium	40 meq/L (40 mmol/L) (normal range for men, 18-301 meq/L [18-301 mmol/L])
Urinalysis	Specific gravity 1.012; pH 5.0; no blood; trace protein; no glucose

Kidney ultrasound reveals hydronephrosis bilaterally and cortical thinning bilaterally.

Which of the following is the most appropriate management?

(A) 0.45% Sodium chloride
(B) 5% Dextrose in water
(C) Desmopressin
(D) Water deprivation test

Answers and Critiques

Item 1   Answer: A

Educational Objective: Manage newly diagnosed stage 2 hypertension.

Combination drug therapy is indicated for this patient with newly diagnosed stage 2 hypertension. The Seventh Report of the Joint National Committee on Prevention, Detection, Evaluation, and Treatment of High Blood Pressure (JNC 7) guidelines classify stage 2 hypertension as a systolic blood pressure of ≥160 mm Hg or a diastolic blood pressure of ≥100 mm Hg. According to the JNC 7, in the absence of comorbidities or compelling indications, the blood pressure goal in patients younger than 80 years is 140/90 mm Hg. In patients whose blood pressure goal requires reductions of systolic pressure more than 20 mm Hg and of diastolic pressure more than 10 mm Hg, the JNC 7 indicates that combination therapy can shorten the time needed for medication adjustment and increase the likelihood of achieving the blood pressure goal, while reducing the number of visits needed for drug titrations. Initial treatment with two antihypertensive agents is therefore warranted in this patient who has blood pressure measurements at least 22/10 mm Hg above goal.

Several nondrug approaches are useful in lowering blood pressure, including weight loss if the patient is overweight, salt reduction, physical activity of at least 30 minutes per day at least 3 days per week, and a reduction in alcohol consumption. However, lifestyle modifications alone in this patient with a normal BMI who has good health habits will likely not adequately lower her blood pressure to the targeted goal.

Monotherapy is unlikely to be effective in patients whose blood pressure is more than 20 mm Hg above the blood pressure goal. This patient has newly diagnosed stage 2 hypertension, with blood pressure measurements that are unlikely to be controlled with a single agent.

A follow-up visit in 2 to 4 weeks to reevaluate this patient is also indicated; however, this is in addition to initiating treatment for her stage 2 hypertension.

KEY POINT

- **Initial treatment with two antihypertensive agents may be warranted in patients whose blood pressure is more than 20 mm Hg above the blood pressure goal.**

Bibliography

Rosendorff C, Black HR, Cannon CP, et al; American Heart Association Council for High Blood Pressure Research; American Heart Association Council on Clinical Cardiology; American Heart Association Council on Epidemiology and Prevention. Treatment of hypertension in the prevention and management of ischemic heart disease: a scientific statement from the American Heart Association Council for High Blood Pressure Research and the Councils on Clinical Cardiology and Epidemiology and Prevention [erratum in Circulation. 2007;116(5):e121]. Circulation. 2007;115(21):2761-2788. [PMID: 17502569]

Item 2   Answer: C

Educational Objective: Treat infected cysts in a patient with autosomal dominant polycystic kidney disease.

Ciprofloxacin is appropriate treatment for this patient with probable infected kidney cysts. She has autosomal dominant polycystic kidney disease (ADPKD) and now has flank pain and fever. Patients with ADPKD can have infected cysts without any abnormal findings on urinalysis or culture because the infected cyst(s) may not communicate with the rest of the urinary tract. With high suspicion of an infected cyst (flank pain and fever), treatment should consist of an antibiotic with an appropriate antimicrobial coverage spectrum for urinary tract pathogens and with good cystic penetration, such as ciprofloxacin. In this case, treatment should be continued for 2 to 4 weeks.

In patients with ADPKD, nitrofurantoin, cephalosporins, or penicillins are not considered appropriate antibiotic choices given their poor cystic penetration. Patients with ADPKD who have cystic hemorrhage can have flank pain and low-grade fever that may mimic infection; however, this patient's degree of fever with an elevated leukocyte count is out of proportion for what would be expected for a ruptured hemorrhagic cyst, suggesting infection.

KEY POINT

- **Patients with autosomal dominant polycystic kidney disease can have infected kidney cysts without abnormal findings on urinalysis or culture.**

Bibliography

Sallée M, Rafat C, Zahar JR, et al. Cyst infections in patients with autosomal dominant polycystic kidney disease. Clin J Am Soc Nephrol. 2009;4(7):1183-1189. [PMID: 19470662]

Item 3   Answer: C

Educational Objective: Prevent tumor lysis syndrome.

An increase in the intravenous saline rate is appropriate. This patient with acute myeloid leukemia received chemotherapy 1 day ago and is at risk for tumor lysis syndrome. Manifestations include acute kidney injury and arrhythmias resulting from the release of potassium, phosphorus, and uric acid from cells. The cell death can be spontaneous with highly proliferative malignancies but more commonly is induced by chemotherapy. Patients with untreated tumor lysis syndrome present with hyperkalemia, hyperuricemia, and hyperphosphatemia. Optimal treatment to prevent tumor lysis syndrome is intravenous fluids to promote a faster urine flow rate. The goal intravenous fluid rate is up to 3000 mL/m^2/d, around 6 L/d in this patient. Although his initial intravenous fluid rate was reasonable, his high phosphorus and potassium levels suggest that cell breakdown is occurring, and an increased rate of saline infusion will help promote potassium excretion and decrease the solubility of phosphorus and uric acid by increasing urine volume. In this patient, an increased intravenous fluid with normal saline at a rate of 250 mL/h would be appropriate. The use of a loop diuretic to maintain urine flow is also reasonable in selected patients.

Although intravenous fluid with sodium bicarbonate has the benefit of alkalinizing the urine and therefore increasing uric acid clearance, it also increases the risk of calcium phosphorus precipitation, which can increase damage to the kidneys, and is not appropriate for this patient with a high serum phosphorus level.

Sodium polystyrene sulfonate can be used to treat this patient's hyperkalemia but will not improve his urine flow.

Rasburicase is generally preferred to allopurinol for prophylaxis of tumor lysis syndrome because of differences in mechanism. Rasburicase directly breaks down uric acid and minimizes xanthine accumulation, whereas allopurinol does not. Because this patient's serum uric acid levels appear to be adequately controlled with rasburicase, there would be no benefit of treatment with allopurinol.

KEY POINT

- **Optimal treatment to prevent tumor lysis syndrome is intravenous fluids to promote a faster urine flow rate.**

Bibliography
Howard SC, Jones DP, Pui CH. The tumor lysis syndrome. N Engl J Med. 2011;364(19):1844-1854. [PMID: 21561350]

Item 4   Answer: B

Educational Objective: Evaluate options for kidney replacement therapy in a patient with chronic kidney disease.

Planning for pretransplant peritoneal dialysis is indicated. This patient has advanced chronic kidney disease, with an estimated glomerular filtration rate of 11 mL/min/1.73 m^2. She has a genetically identical kidney donor in the future, but it is unlikely that she will be able to wait a year without kidney replacement therapy. Thus, an interim plan is needed. She is otherwise healthy, independent, and appears able to participate in peritoneal dialysis. She has never had abdominal surgery, and her BMI is normal. She

is an ideal candidate for peritoneal dialysis, and this modality will also allow her to preserve her independence and more easily transition to a life with end-stage kidney disease. Recent studies have shown that peritoneal dialysis offers similar outcomes to hemodialysis, and that there is no particular advantage to utilizing hemodialysis versus peritoneal dialysis in eligible patients who require pretransplant dialysis.

Compared with live donors, organs from deceased donors from the extended donor criteria pool have a far inferior renal allograft survival rate. These donors are of older age or have died of stroke or had a history of hypertension or reduced kidney function at the time of death. Utilization of an extended donor criteria kidney would be ill-advised for a young healthy recipient and a poor utilization of organs from the extended donor pool.

Preemptive dialysis has not been shown to be beneficial, and posttransplant outcomes appear to be worse with a longer duration of dialysis before transplant occurs. Therefore, the preferred method of kidney replacement therapy should be started when indicated by clinical circumstances, if needed, before transplant.

KEY POINT

- **Peritoneal dialysis can preserve independence and allow a better transition to life with end-stage kidney disease.**

Bibliography
Mehrotra R, Chiu YW, Kalantar-Zadeh K, Bargman J, Vonesh E. Similar outcomes with hemodialysis and peritoneal dialysis in patients with end-stage renal disease. Arch Intern Med. 2011;171(2):110-118. [PMID: 20876398]

Item 5   Answer: D

Educational Objective: Diagnose proliferative lupus nephritis.

The most likely diagnosis is proliferative lupus nephritis. This patient likely has systemic lupus erythematosus (SLE) based on her small-joint symmetric polyarthritis, oral ulcers, cytopenias, and kidney disease. Kidney disease is very common in patients with SLE. Patients satisfy this SLE criterion by having a 24-hour urine protein excretion greater than 500 mg/24 h, urinalysis showing more than 10 erythrocytes/hpf, erythrocyte or leukocyte casts in a sterile urine sample (proven by culture), or by kidney biopsy. Findings of proliferative lupus nephritis may include new-onset hypertension or edema typically associated with high titers of anti–double-stranded DNA antibodies and hypocomplementemia, proteinuria, hematuria, and erythrocyte and granular casts in the urine. Kidney biopsy is usually needed to make the diagnosis of lupus nephritis and to classify the pattern of glomerular disease. Kidney manifestations of lupus nephritis often develop concurrently or shortly following the onset of SLE in black, Hispanic, and Asian persons. Black patients who have SLE are commonly affected with severe lupus nephritis.

Focal segmental glomerulosclerosis (FSGS) is the leading cause of primary nephrotic syndrome, with a predilection for black patients. Patients with primary FSGS usually present with microscopic hematuria, hypertension, and kidney insufficiency. This patient has the nephritic syndrome, with erythrocyte casts in the urine sediment, which is very uncommon in patients with FSGS.

IgA nephropathy may only involve the kidney or can be secondarily associated with conditions such as HIV infection, chronic liver disease, inflammatory bowel disease, or celiac disease. It is not associated with SLE. IgA nephropathy has a predilection to develop in white or Asian men.

Postinfectious glomerulonephritis (PIGN) is an immunologic disease triggered by an infection, which is followed by the release of immunoglobulins and activation of complement proteins that are deposited in the glomeruli, activating cytokine inflammatory pathways. PIGN accounts for approximately 6% of the nephritic syndrome cases. PIGN cannot explain this patient's polyarthritis, oral ulcers, or cytopenias.

KEY POINT

- Findings of proliferative lupus nephritis may include new-onset hypertension or edema typically associated with high titers of anti–double-stranded DNA antibodies and hypocomplementemia, proteinuria, hematuria, and erythrocyte and granular casts in the urine.

Bibliography

Contreras G, Lenz O, Pardo V, et al. Outcomes in African Americans and Hispanics with lupus nephritis. Kidney Int. 2006;69(10):1846-1851. [PMID: 16598205]

Item 6   Answer: D

Educational Objective: Manage prehypertension.

This patient has prehypertension, and rechecking his blood pressure in 1 year is indicated. The prehypertension category established by the Seventh Report of the Joint National Committee on Prevention, Detection, Evaluation, and Treatment of High Blood Pressure (JNC 7) designates a group at high risk for progression to hypertension, in whom lifestyle modifications may be preemptive. Although this is not considered a mild form of hypertension, it is a category used to define persons considered at increased risk for the development of true hypertension. Increasing age and family history are also associated with an increased risk of eventually developing hypertension requiring treatment. Given his mild overweight and borderline lipid profile, this patient should be aggressively counseled on lifestyle intervention to improve his diet, increase his aerobic exercise capacity, and lose weight. His blood pressure should then be rechecked in 1 year.

Ambulatory blood pressure monitoring is indicated for patients with suspected white coat hypertension, to monitor patients with difficult-to-control blood pressure or those with significant symptoms such as hypotension on therapy, or if autonomic dysfunction is suspected. None of these situations is present in this patient.

C-reactive protein is a marker of inflammation that is increasingly associated with cardiovascular events and may eventually be useful in stratifying persons with cardiovascular risk. However, its use in prehypertension risk assessment has not been established.

This patient has not met the diagnostic criteria for sustained hypertension; therefore, initiation of long-term medical treatment is not appropriate.

KEY POINT

- Lifestyle modifications and a repeat blood pressure measurement in 1 year are indicated for patients with prehypertension.

Bibliography

Chobanian AV, Bakris GL, Black HR, et al; National Heart, Lung, and Blood Institute; Joint National Committee on Prevention, Detection, Evaluation, and Treatment of High Blood Pressure; National High Blood Pressure Education Program Coordinating Committee. The Seventh Report of the Joint National Committee on Prevention, Detection, Evaluation, and Treatment of High Blood Pressure: the JNC 7 report [erratum in JAMA. 2003;290(2):197]. JAMA. 2003;289(19):2560-2572. [PMID: 12748199]

Item 7   Answer: D

Educational Objective: Treat a patient who has lactic acidosis.

Supportive care is appropriate for this patient who presents with a mixed acid-base disorder after having a probable alcohol withdrawal seizure. He has an anion gap metabolic acidosis and his arterial P_{CO_2} is greater than the level expected, which is consistent with a concurrent respiratory acidosis. The increased anion gap acidosis is most likely due to a seizure-related lactic acidosis with concurrent alcoholic ketoacidosis; the improvement in acid-base status with volume repletion and supplemental glucose supports this diagnosis. His respiratory acidosis is consistent with a postictal state and alcohol use. Treatment of seizure-related lactic acidosis is directed toward controlling and preventing further seizures along with supportive measures such as adequate volume repletion.

Fomepizole, a competitive inhibitor of alcohol dehydrogenase, is indicated for patients with methanol or ethylene glycol ingestion to minimize their conversion to toxic metabolites. Both ingestions are associated with an elevated osmolal gap, calculated by the following equation:

$$\text{Osmolal Gap} = \text{Measured Plasma Osmolality} - \text{Calculated Plasma Osmolality, where,}$$

$$\text{Plasma Osmolality (mosm/kg } H_2O) = 2 \times \text{Serum Sodium (meq/L)} + \text{Plasma Glucose (mg/dL)}/18 + \text{Blood Urea Nitrogen (mg/dL)}/2.8 \ (+ \text{Ethanol [mg/dL]}/3.7, \text{if present})$$

CONT.

The osmolal gap in this patient, when accounting for the contribution of ethanol, is less than 10; therefore, the use of fomepizole is not indicated.

Hemodialysis should be considered in patients with suspected ethylene glycol or methanol poisoning, severe propylene glycol toxicity, or severe isopropyl alcohol poisoning. This patient's improvement with supportive measures alone argues against toxic alcohol ingestion. The absence of calcium oxalate crystals also decreases the likelihood of ethylene glycol toxicity.

Supplemental sodium bicarbonate can be administered in persistent severe acidemia (pH <7.15), with the goal of maintaining the pH above 7.15, but is not indicated in this patient with evidence of improving acidosis.

KEY POINT

- Management of lactic acidosis is directed toward controlling the underlying cause along with supportive measures.

Bibliography

Rachoin JS, Weisberg LS, McFadden CB. Treatment of lactic acidosis: appropriate confusion. J Hosp Med. 2010;5(4):E1-E7. [PMID: 20394011]

Item 8   Answer: B

Educational Objective: Manage anemia associated with chronic kidney disease.

This patient has anemia associated with chronic kidney disease (CKD), and the most appropriate intervention is initiation of an erythropoiesis-stimulating agent (ESA). Anemia may develop in patients with stages 3 and 4 CKD and is primarily caused by reduced production of erythropoietin. Anemia is associated with decreased quality of life, left ventricular hypertrophy, and cardiovascular complications in patients with CKD. ESAs are indicated for patients with CKD who have hemoglobin levels less than 10 g/dL (100 g/L), but other causes of anemia, including iron deficiency, hemoglobinopathies, vitamin B_{12} deficiency, and gastrointestinal blood loss, should be considered before beginning this therapy. Because use of ESAs to correct hemoglobin levels to the normal range may be associated with an increased risk for cardiovascular events, ESAs should not be initiated in patients with hemoglobin levels greater than 12 g/dL (120 g/L). The FDA therefore recommends that patients with CKD who have not yet started dialysis have a hemoglobin level less than 10 g/dL (100 g/L) before initiating an ESA and supports a target hemoglobin level of 10 to 11 g/dL (100-110 g/L) during maintenance therapy.

Although ascorbic acid has been shown to augment oral iron absorption, there are no convincing data suggesting that the addition of this agent is worth the cost or increase in gastrointestinal side effects.

Blood transfusion is generally avoided in patients with chronic anemia in the absence of critical tissue ischemia, for example, chest pain and neurologic symptoms. This intervention can sensitize persons to HLA antigens, which may complicate the potential for kidney transplantation.

Because this patient's iron levels are adequate, switching from oral to intravenous iron therapy would not help to improve her anemia and is associated with an increased risk of anaphylaxis.

KEY POINT

- Initiation of an erythropoiesis-stimulating agent is indicated for patients with anemia associated with chronic kidney disease who have hemoglobin levels less than 10 g/dL (100 g/L); however, other causes of anemia, including iron deficiency, hemoglobinopathies, vitamin B_{12} deficiency, and gastrointestinal blood loss, should be considered before beginning this therapy.

Bibliography

U.S. Food and Drug Administration. FDA modifies dosing recommendations for erythropoiesis-stimulating agents. FDA News & Events Web site. Available at www.fda.gov/NewsEvents/Newsroom/PressAnnouncements/ucm260670.htm. Updated June 24, 2011. Accessed July 23, 2012.

Item 9   Answer: A

Educational Objective: Manage metabolic alkalosis.

The addition of acetazolamide is indicated for this patient with significant metabolic alkalosis and hypervolemia. Metabolism of citrate contained in the blood products administered to this patient resulted in production of excess bicarbonate and metabolic alkalosis. Patients with normal kidney function and renal perfusion ordinarily can excrete excess bicarbonate, and the serum bicarbonate typically only increases by 1 to 2 meq/L (1-2 mmol/L), even with a very high filtered load of bicarbonate. Decreased renal blood flow in patients with cirrhosis, conversely, impairs kidney bicarbonate excretion because of increased proximal tubular reabsorption of filtered bicarbonate, leading to retention of the increased bicarbonate load and metabolic alkalosis. Acetazolamide promotes bicarbonate excretion and is the best therapeutic option for this patient with hypervolemia because it ameliorates both the metabolic alkalosis and sodium overload.

Furosemide facilitates sodium chloride but not bicarbonate excretion. Although this would result in increased sodium excretion, it might exacerbate the metabolic alkalosis if the patient becomes hypovolemic and develops further compromise of renal perfusion. This would lead to increased tubular bicarbonate reabsorption as well as enhanced bicarbonate generation in the cortical collecting duct.

Isotonic saline is unlikely to correct renal hypoperfusion in patients with cirrhosis and ascites who have underlying renal vasoconstriction and renal sodium avidity and therefore would not promote excretion of the increased bicarbonate load. Most of the infused sodium chloride would be retained because of increased tubular sodium chloride reabsorption, thereby aggravating the ascites and fluid overload.

H CONT.

In patients with active variceal bleeding, splanchnic vasoconstrictors such as octreotide are commonly used as an adjunctive treatment to endoscopic therapy. Infusions are typically continued for 3 to 5 days. Despite widespread use, octreotide is not associated with decreased mortality. This agent is not associated with metabolic alkalosis, and discontinuation of octreotide will not correct this patient's metabolic alkalosis.

KEY POINT

- **Acetazolamide promotes bicarbonate excretion and can be used to ameliorate metabolic alkalosis in patients with hypervolemia and sodium overload.**

Bibliography

Galla JH. Metabolic alkalosis. J Am Soc Nephrol. 2000;11(2):369-375. [PMID: 10665945]

Item 10   Answer: B

Educational Objective: Diagnose cytomegalovirus infection in a kidney transplant recipient.

The most likely diagnosis is cytomegalovirus (CMV) infection. Despite advances in immunosuppressive therapy and infection prophylaxis, more than 50% of kidney transplant recipients develop at least one infection during the first year after transplantation. CMV infection is particularly common in these patients. CMV infection is often suspected when patients have leukopenia and fevers during the posttransplant period. Viremia is best detected by polymerase chain reaction (PCR), a fast, sensitive, and reliable technique compared with serology, culture, or early antigen or CMV antigenemia detection. CMV infection can result in CMV disease, with organ involvement manifesting as retinitis, pneumonia, encephalitis, hepatitis, and gastrointestinal tract ulceration.

This patient underwent kidney transplantation 7 months ago and discontinued his CMV prophylaxis therapy 1 month ago as per standard protocol. Kidney transplantation from a donor who is seropositive for CMV to a recipient who is seronegative for this virus places the recipient at high risk for developing this condition. Furthermore, this patient's fever, leukopenia, and diarrhea are consistent with CMV infection, and his elevated liver chemistry studies raise suspicion for CMV-related hepatitis. Diagnosis of CMV infection is confirmed with a positive serum PCR test for viremia, and disease is confirmed by the presence of mucosal ulcers or erosion and CMV inclusion bodies seen on a biopsy specimen from the wall of the bowel obtained during colonoscopy.

Clostridium difficile infection may cause diarrhea and fever but does not explain this patient's leukopenia or elevated aminotransferase levels.

Mycophenolate mofetil can cause diarrhea and leukopenia but is rarely associated with elevated liver chemistry studies and does not explain this patient's fever. In addition, toxicity associated with mycophenolate mofetil usually occurs after a recent dosage change.

Tacrolimus toxicity can cause diarrhea but does not manifest as fever, leukopenia, or abnormal findings on liver chemistry studies.

KEY POINT

- **Cytomegalovirus infection is particularly common in kidney transplant recipients and may manifest as fever, leukopenia, and diarrhea.**

Bibliography

Helanterä I, Lautenschlager I, Koskinen P. The risk of cytomegalovirus recurrence after kidney transplantation. Transpl Int. 2011;24(12):1170-1178. [PMID: 21902725]

Item 11   Answer: D

Educational Objective: Diagnose multiple myeloma as a cause of acute kidney injury.

Serum and urine electrophoresis are indicated for this patient with probable multiple myeloma. Multiple myeloma, a plasma cell neoplasm resulting in the production of abnormal immunoglobulin (paraprotein), can present with bone pain, anemia, hypercalcemia, and kidney injury. Multiple mechanisms of kidney injury are involved in multiple myeloma, with kidney injury usually resulting from precipitation of paraproteins in the kidney. A clinical clue to the diagnosis is the presence of an elevated total urine protein, which quantifies both the albumin and non-albumin protein (paraprotein) present, when a urine dipstick (which measures only albumin) indicates only small amounts or no protein present. Similarly, the addition of sulfosalicylic acid to the urine in a patient with a urinary paraprotein will precipitate the proteins present with an increase in turbidity, while the urine dipstick shows minimal or no proteinuria. Serum and urine electrophoresis can identify the presence of the paraprotein in the blood and urine and can indicate the need for a bone marrow biopsy to confirm the hematologic diagnosis.

ANCA vasculitis can cause an elevated serum creatinine level, anemia, and fatigue, and it often occurs in patients over 60 years old. Anemia with vasculitis can be severe, particularly with lung hemorrhage. However, the urine sediment associated with vasculitis is active, with significant hematuria and dipstick-positive proteinuria, which is not present in this patient.

Kidney biopsy is indicated when there is kidney injury of unclear etiology. Kidney biopsy is not required for a diagnosis of multiple myeloma and is not indicated initially in the evaluation of this patient's acute kidney injury.

Although this patient has hypercalcemia, hyperparathyroidism does not adequately explain his degree of kidney injury; therefore, measurement of the parathyroid hormone level is not a useful diagnostic study in the context of myeloma-related hypercalcemia.

Answers and Critiques

KEY POINT

- Kidney injury commonly accompanies multiple myeloma and may be associated with a discrepancy between the measured and urine dipstick protein quantifications.

Bibliography

Palumbo A, Anderson K. Multiple myeloma. N Engl J Med. 2011;364(11):1046-1060. [PMID: 21410373]

Item 12　　Answer: A

Educational Objective: Diagnose resistant hypertension.

Ambulatory blood pressure monitoring is the most appropriate next step in management. This patient meets the diagnostic criteria for resistant hypertension, which is defined as blood pressure that remains above goal despite treatment with the optimal dosages of three antihypertensive agents of different classes, including a diuretic. Patient characteristics more likely to be associated with resistant hypertension include older age, BMI greater than 30, higher baseline blood pressure, diabetes mellitus, and black race. However, before this diagnosis is made, it is necessary to establish that this patient's blood pressure is truly high outside of the office. Ambulatory blood pressure monitoring can differentiate true resistant hypertension from a white coat effect that misleadingly suggests resistance to therapy. Once resistant hypertension is verified, a search for identifiable factors that may be modified is appropriate, including high salt intake, concurrent use of drugs such as NSAIDs, and the presence of other potentially exacerbating medical conditions such as obstructive sleep apnea.

Although potentially useful in assessing this patient's murmur or other suspected structural heart disease, echocardiography is not specifically indicated for evaluation of her hypertension.

The addition of another antihypertensive agent may be required for adequate blood pressure control but should be initiated only after resistant hypertension is diagnosed and other complicating factors are excluded.

In patients with resistant hypertension, consideration of possible secondary causes, such as assessment for catecholamine excess, may be indicated, but only after documentation that the diagnosis of resistant hypertension has been confirmed.

KEY POINT

- Resistant hypertension is defined as blood pressure that remains above goal despite treatment with the optimal dosages of three antihypertensive agents of different classes, including a diuretic.

Bibliography

Calhoun DA, Jones D, Textor S, et al. Resistant hypertension: diagnosis, evaluation, and treatment. A scientific statement from the American Heart Association Professional Education Committee of

Item 13　　Answer: D

Educational Objective: Manage asymptomatic hyponatremia.

At this time, the most appropriate management for this patient's hyponatremia is fluid restriction. The absence of neurologic findings suggests that this patient's hyponatremia is chronic, and rapid correction is therefore not indicated. Asymptomatic hyponatremia in patients with cirrhosis is a poor prognostic marker, and the benefits of correcting hyponatremia in asymptomatic patients who are not candidates for imminent liver transplantation are not clear. Thus, ongoing observation of the serum sodium concentration and mental status while implementing fluid restriction is indicated. Some experts recommend implementing fluid restriction only when the serum sodium level is less than 120 meq/L (120 mmol/L) or as a component of therapy in patients with neurologic symptoms attributed to hyponatremia.

Hypertonic (3%) saline is only indicated in the presence of neurologic symptoms or for correction of hyponatremia when the serum sodium level is less than 130 meq/L (130 mmol/L) immediately preceding liver transplantation; however, care should be taken to avoid increasing the serum sodium level above 8 to 10 meq/L (8-10 mmol/L) per day given the increased risk for osmotic demyelination syndrome.

Conivaptan blocks both the V_2 and V_{1a} receptors, the latter of which can decrease blood pressure and increase the risk of variceal bleeding in patients with cirrhosis and is therefore relatively contraindicated in this group.

Demeclocycline can be used to manage asymptomatic hyponatremia due to the syndrome of inappropriate antidiuretic hormone secretion (SIADH). This patient does not have SIADH, as indicated by the presence of edema, ascites, and low urine sodium concentration. Furthermore, demeclocycline exhibits increased nephrotoxicity in those with underlying liver disease and is contraindicated in these patients.

KEY POINT

- Fluid restriction is indicated for the management of asymptomatic hyponatremia in patients with cirrhosis when the serum sodium level is less than 120 meq/L (120 mmol/L) or as a component of therapy in patients with neurologic symptoms attributed to hyponatremia.

Bibliography

Ginès P, Guevara M. Hyponatremia in cirrhosis: pathogenesis, clinical significance, and management. Hepatology. 2008;48(3):1002-1010. [PMID: 18671303]

Item 14   Answer: B

Educational Objective: Assess the risk of pregnancy outcome in a patient with reduced kidney function.

Serum creatinine level measurement is indicated for this patient with IgA nephropathy who is considering pregnancy. The degree of baseline kidney injury, as estimated by the glomerular filtration rate (GFR) or serum creatinine level, is most useful in assessing risk for subsequent pregnancy outcome. Women with chronic kidney disease (CKD) have a greater risk of complications of the pregnancy and adverse outcomes for the fetus. Reduced kidney function imparts a greater risk for eclampsia and preeclampsia and also a possible irreversible decline in kidney function during pregnancy, intrapartum, or after delivery. When serum creatinine is used to estimate kidney function in women, a normal value is nearly always less than 1.0 mg/dL (88.4 micromoles/L) (although many laboratories may report a higher normal range) because women have less muscle mass than men, and serum creatinine is a breakdown product of muscle. When the serum creatinine value for a woman is more than 1.4 mg/dL (124 micromoles/L), this correlates with an estimated GFR of less than 60 mL/min/1.73 m^2, and the patient has CKD stage 3 or higher. In women with kidney dysfunction at this stage or higher, there is an increased risk for fetal growth restriction, preeclampsia, preterm delivery, and perinatal death, as well as for loss of more than 25% of existing kidney function in the mother. Women who have milder impairments in kidney function or proteinuria may be at greater risk for complications from pregnancy than healthy women but are less likely to have significant kidney impairment as a consequence of pregnancy. Proteinuria associated with CKD may worsen with pregnancy, but the degree of proteinuria present at the time of pregnancy does not predict the risk for pregnancy-associated complications.

Although abnormal glycosylations of IgA may play an important role in the pathogenesis of IgA nephropathy, measurement of IgA levels plays no role in the management of IgA nephropathy nor does it have any implications for pregnancy.

Hypertension associated with CKD is an important factor in pregnancy in women with CKD and needs to be carefully controlled during pregnancy, although the presence of hypertension alone is not predictive of pregnancy outcome. This patient has prehypertension but does not need a 24-hour ambulatory blood pressure determination to further assess the risk of pregnancy.

Pregnancy complications and outcome appear similar with kidney disease of different causes, although the need to actively treat an underlying medical illness associated with the kidney disease may be a contributing factor in pregnancy outcome. Nevertheless, the patient's diagnosis is known, and a repeat kidney biopsy to assess for histologic progression is unnecessary and potentially dangerous.

Bibliography

Williams D, Davison J. Chronic kidney disease in pregnancy. BMJ. 2008;336(7637):211-215. [PMID: 18219043]

Item 15   Answer: A

Educational Objective: Diagnose acute interstitial nephritis.

This patient most likely has acute interstitial nephritis (AIN), which is typically caused by a hypersensitivity reaction to a medication. The clinical presentation of AIN is variable and in part dependent on the precipitating medication. The classic presentation of AIN is fever, rash, and eosinophilia in a patient with an elevated serum creatinine level, but this presentation is found in only 10% of cases. Diagnosis is most often made by a history of exposure to a drug that has a high likelihood of causing AIN. AIN usually occurs after 7 to 10 days of drug exposure; however, prior exposure to a drug may result in a more sudden onset. Urinalysis may show leukocytes and leukocyte casts with negative urine cultures (sterile pyuria) and/or erythrocytes. The mainstay of AIN treatment is discontinuation of the offending agent. This patient has leukocytes in the urine and takes the proton pump inhibitor (PPI) omeprazole, which most likely induced the AIN because PPI-induced AIN often has a subacute presentation.

This patient is taking a bisphosphonate, which can cause acute tubular necrosis (ATN). Bisphosphonate-induced ATN occurs mainly with intravenous administration. The urine sediment in this case is also more consistent with AIN than ATN, which is associated with muddy brown casts but not leukocytes.

Giant cell arteritis typically affects large blood vessels, not the small blood vessels in the kidney. Although small-vessel vasculitis can affect the kidneys and large vessels, this patient's urine sediment is not consistent with a glomerulonephritis (dysmorphic erythrocytes, erythrocyte casts, and proteinuria).

Numerous medications can cause thrombotic thrombocytopenic purpura (TTP), including cancer chemotherapeutic agents, cyclosporine, tacrolimus, quinine, and ticlopidine but not prednisone, omeprazole, or risedronate. Manifestations of the thrombotic microangiopathies include acute kidney injury that is usually accompanied by microangiopathic hemolytic anemia and thrombocytopenia. This patient's normal lactate dehydrogenase level and urine sediment with leukocytes are not consistent with TTP.

KEY POINT

- Diagnosis of acute interstitial nephritis (AIN) is most often made by a history of exposure to a drug that has a high likelihood of causing AIN and a urinalysis that typically shows leukocytes, leukocyte casts, and erythrocytes.

Bibliography

Praga M, González E. Acute interstitial nephritis. Kidney Int. 2010;77(11):956-961. [PMID: 20336051]

Item 16   Answer: A

Educational Objective: Diagnose focal segmental glomerulosclerosis.

The most likely diagnosis is focal segmental glomerulosclerosis (FSGS). This condition is the most common cause of idiopathic nephrotic syndrome in adults and the most common cause of the nephrotic syndrome in black adults. FSGS also is the most common primary glomerular disease that causes end-stage kidney disease in the United States. Patients with primary (idiopathic) FSGS usually present with microscopic hematuria, hypertension, and kidney disease. Secondary FSGS results from other disease processes that cause glomerular hypertrophy and hyperfiltration and is also associated with some infections, toxin exposures, or atheroembolic disease. These patients have minimal edema and rarely have the full spectrum of the nephrotic syndrome. This patient's presentation of the full spectrum of the nephrotic syndrome (nephrotic-range proteinuria, hypoalbuminemia, severe edema, and hyperlipidemia) is most consistent with primary FSGS. Diagnosis of primary FSGS is confirmed by kidney biopsy, with light microscopy showing scarring or sclerosis involving some (focal) glomeruli, which are affected only in a portion of the glomerular capillary bundle (segmental).

IgA nephropathy has a predilection to develop in men who are white or Asian and is very uncommon in black persons. Patients with IgA nephropathy may present after an upper respiratory tract infection and may have microscopic or frequently gross hematuria. Proteinuria is typically mild, and rapid progression to kidney failure is uncommon. IgA nephropathy is characterized by deposits of IgA primarily in the mesangium on immunofluorescence on kidney biopsy.

Systemic lupus erythematosus (SLE) may cause various kidney disorders, primarily due to immune complex deposition. Lupus nephritis has a predilection for young women, and this patient has no clinical or serologic evidence of SLE.

Postinfectious glomerulonephritis usually presents as the nephritic syndrome and results from immune complex deposition in the kidney after streptococcal or staphylococcal infections. This patient has no history of a preceding infection.

KEY POINT

- Patients with primary focal segmental glomerulosclerosis typically present with the nephrotic syndrome, microscopic hematuria, hypertension, and kidney disease.

Bibliography

Swaminathan S, Leung N, Lager DJ, et al. Changing incidence of glomerular disease in Olmsted County, Minnesota: a 30-year renal biopsy study. Clin J Am Soc Nephrol. 2006;1(3):483-487. [PMID: 17699249]

Item 17   Answer: B

Educational Objective: Diagnose hypokalemic distal (type 1) renal tubular acidosis.

This patient most likely has hypokalemic distal (type 1) renal tubular acidosis (RTA), a disorder characterized by normal anion gap metabolic acidosis and hypokalemia. Causes of hypokalemic distal RTA include autoimmune disorders such as Sjögren syndrome, systemic lupus erythematosus, or rheumatoid arthritis; drugs such as lithium or amphotericin B; hypercalciuria; and hyperglobulinemia. The kidney's ability to excrete hydrogen ions in response to acidemia in hypokalemic distal RTA is impaired, resulting in an inappropriately alkali pH of the urine in the presence of a systemic acidosis. The persistently increased pH encourages the development of kidney stones. Therefore, the pH above 6.0 in the setting of acidemia and the presence of nephrocalcinosis in this patient support the diagnosis of hypokalemic distal RTA.

Gitelman syndrome is an autosomal recessive syndrome characterized by hypokalemic metabolic alkalosis, not acidosis as noted in this patient. Blood pressure is normal to low, and hypomagnesemia is common. The defect is due to inactivating mutations in the gene for the thiazide-sensitive sodium chloride cotransporter in the distal convoluted tubule, and the electrolyte profile is analogous to that induced by thiazide diuretics.

Laxative abuse may also present with a hypokalemic normal anion gap metabolic acidosis. Patients with increased gastrointestinal losses of bicarbonate and potassium have intact kidney tubular function resulting in a compensatory increase in urine ammonium production, indicating increased acid secretion by the kidney. Urine ammonium may be estimated by calculating the urine anion gap, with a negative urine anion gap suggesting increased acid secretion and a positive urine anion gap indicating decreased acid secretion. This patient's urine anion gap is positive and is therefore not consistent with laxative abuse.

Proximal (type 2) RTA, a defect in regenerating bicarbonate in the proximal tubule, is characterized by a normal anion gap metabolic acidosis, hypokalemia, glycosuria (in the setting of normal plasma glucose), low-molecular-weight proteinuria, and renal phosphate wasting.

However, distal urinary acidification mechanisms are intact, and the urine pH is less than 5.5 in the absence of alkali therapy. Proximal RTA is not associated with nephrocalcinosis or nephrolithiasis. This patient's normal urinalysis, high urine pH, and nephrocalcinosis are inconsistent with proximal RTA.

> **KEY POINT**
>
> • Hypokalemic distal (type 1) renal tubular acidosis is characterized by normal anion gap metabolic acidosis, hypokalemia, a urine pH greater than 6.0, and nephrocalcinosis.

Bibliography

Comer DM, Droogan AG, Young IS, Maxwell AP. Hypokalaemic paralysis precipitated by distal renal tubular acidosis secondary to Sjögren's syndrome. Ann Clin Biochem. 2008;45(Pt 2):221-225. [PMID: 18325192]

Item 18   Answer: C
Educational Objective: Diagnose hematuria.

A repeat urinalysis is appropriate for this low-risk patient with possible hematuria. Evaluation should ensure that a patient does not have any of the known risk factors, including a smoking history, occupational exposure to chemicals or dyes, history of gross hematuria, age older than 40 years, history of a urologic disorder, history of irritative voiding symptoms, history of urinary tract infection, analgesic abuse, or pelvic irradiation. In a patient under 40 years old, more than 3 erythrocytes/hpf on two or more occasions constitutes hematuria and is a common finding on urinalysis. A single episode in older patients or those at risk should initiate a full evaluation of the upper and lower urinary tract. This patient has had hematuria documented on one occasion; thus, urinalysis should be repeated before further evaluation, despite his family history. A family history of bladder cancer does not increase the patient's risk of developing a malignancy unless both family members have been exposed to similar toxins.

If hematuria is established after the repeat urinalysis, this patient should then be evaluated for its cause. Bleeding in patients with persistent hematuria may originate anywhere along the genitourinary tract, and the location of the bleeding must be identified in order to determine the next steps in evaluation. Therefore, differentiating between glomerular and nonglomerular hematuria by urine microscopy is important. Glomerular hematuria is characterized by the presence of dysmorphic erythrocytes or acanthocytes on urine microscopy, and hematuria associated with the presence of erythrocyte casts is specifically indicative of glomerulonephritis. Nonglomerular hematuria refers to blood in the urine that originates outside of the glomerulus. This condition is associated with isomorphic erythrocytes that usually appear normal on urine microscopy. The most common causes of asymptomatic nonglomerular hematuria are urinary tract infections and

kidney stones. Renal or bladder cancer may also cause non-glomerular hematuria. An appropriate evaluation for persistent nonglomerular hematuria in this patient may begin with upper urinary tract imaging. The American Urological Association recommends CT, ultrasonography, or intravenous urography and notes that CT urography is the best choice if available. This should be followed by cystoscopy and possibly urine cytology.

Urine culture is unlikely to be helpful in this patient in the absence of dysuria or voiding symptoms and no leukocytes on urinalysis.

> **KEY POINT**
>
> • In patients younger than 40 years, the finding of more than 3 erythrocytes/hpf on urinalysis should be confirmed on two or more occasions to establish the diagnosis of hematuria.

Bibliography

Margulis V, Sagalowsky AI. Assessment of hematuria. Med Clin North Am. 2011;95(1):153-159. [PMID: 21095418]

Item 19   Answer: A
Educational Objective: Evaluate a patient for malignancy before kidney transplantation.

CT with contrast is indicated to exclude malignancy in this patient before kidney transplantation. Imaging with contrast is often needed to definitively characterize a renal lesion. In this patient with minimal residual kidney function who is on hemodialysis, CT with contrast will provide the most conclusive imaging with the least risk to the patient. Although she still produces urine, it is a minimal amount and is not likely contributing significantly to the clearance she is obtaining with hemodialysis. Avoidance of nephrotoxins is preferred in patients with chronic kidney disease who are not on dialysis and in dialysis patients with significant kidney function. However, in this patient with minimal residual kidney function who is on dialysis, the benefits of using contrast outweigh the risk of additional nephrotoxicity.

Intravenous pyelography outlines the anatomy of the urinary collecting system. Although it may demonstrate a filling defect indicative of a mass, intravenous pyelography does not help differentiate malignant from nonmalignant lesions and is also associated with a significant dose of contrast.

The use of gadolinium in MRI should be avoided in patients with a glomerular filtration rate of less than 30 mL/min/1.73 m². Nephrogenic systemic fibrosis (NSF) is a fibrosing skin disease caused by an inflammatory reaction to gadolinium that accumulates in the body due to kidney failure. NSF usually occurs within a few months of gadolinium exposure and typically presents with edema and thickened skin in the extremities that ultimately limits mobility and can be associated with pruritus and pain. NSF is progressive and can affect visceral organs and lead to death.

There are no effective treatments for NSF; prevention is the best course of action.

Positron emission tomography (PET) shows metabolic activity of tissue. Because of the high level of baseline metabolic activity in the kidney, PET cannot definitively exclude malignancy.

KEY POINT

- **Contrast imaging should be avoided in patients with chronic kidney disease when possible; however, iodinated contrast can be given with less risk from nephrotoxicity in patients with minimal residual kidney function who are on dialysis.**

Bibliography
Krajewski KM, Giardino AA, Zukotynski K, Van den Abbeele AD, Pedrosa I. Imaging in renal cell carcinoma. Hematol Oncol Clin North Am. 2011;25(4):687-715. [PMID: 21763963]

Item 20   Answer: B
Educational Objective: Diagnose hepatitis C virus–associated glomerulonephritis.

The most likely cause of this patient's kidney findings is hepatitis C virus–associated glomerulonephritis (HCV-GN). This immune complex disease can occur in as many as 21% of patients with HCV infection. HCV-GN usually manifests as the nephritic syndrome. Other manifestations may include combined nephrotic-nephritic syndrome, isolated proteinuria with hematuria, rapidly progressive glomerulonephritis, and acute and chronic kidney failure. HCV-GN can also be a component of a systemic cryoglobulinemic vasculitis with involvement of the skin, peripheral nerves, and musculoskeletal system. Most patients with HCV-GN have low complement levels, particularly C4, and a positive rheumatoid factor. Mildly positive antinuclear antibodies can also be seen. Diagnosis is confirmed by kidney biopsy, which demonstrates the pattern of membranoproliferative glomerulonephritis with or without capillary cryoglobulin deposition on light microscopy. This patient has mixed cryoglobulinemia associated with HCV infection: palpable purpura, arthralgia, peripheral neuropathy, hypocomplementemia, a positive rheumatoid factor, and the typical biopsy pattern of membranoproliferative glomerulonephritis with cryoglobulin deposition associated with HCV-GN.

Immune complex glomerulonephritis can be associated with hepatitis B virus infection. This patient shows evidence of previous hepatitis B virus exposure but not active infection, making this an unlikely cause of his kidney disease.

Polyarteritis nodosa is a systemic necrotizing vasculitis that primarily affects medium-sized arteries and is commonly associated with hepatitis B virus infection. It may be associated with HCV infection, affect the kidneys, and involve other organ systems. However, kidney biopsy results typically show evidence of vasculitis without immune complex deposition in the glomeruli.

Thrombotic microangiopathy is characterized by microangiopathic anemia and thrombocytopenia. Additionally, the deposition of immunoglobulins and/or complement components associated with HCV-GN on biopsy is not seen in thrombotic microangiopathy.

KEY POINT

- **Diagnosis of hepatitis C virus–associated glomerulonephritis is confirmed by kidney biopsy, which demonstrates the pattern of membranoproliferative glomerulonephritis with or without capillary cryoglobulin deposition on light microscopy.**

Bibliography
Roccatello D, Fornasieri A, Giachino O, et al. Multicenter study on hepatitis C virus-related cryoglobulinemic glomerulonephritis. Am J Kidney Dis. 2007;49(1):69-82. [PMID: 17185147]

Item 21   Answer: E
Educational Objective: Evaluate a patient with probable kidney stones using noncontrast abdominal helical CT.

The most appropriate test to perform next in this patient is a noncontrast abdominal helical CT. This patient has new-onset gradual abdominal and flank pain and a urinalysis revealing hematuria with low-grade pyuria, all of which are associated with kidney stones. Most kidney stones are radiopaque and are easily visualized on abdominal radiography of the kidneys, ureters, and bladder (KUB), which is inexpensive, noninvasive, and widely available. However, false-negative results may occur in patients with small stones, radiolucent stones that are composed of uric acid or related to use of indinavir, and interference of the overlying bowel. Noncontrast abdominal helical CT is the gold standard for diagnosing kidney stones. This study reveals urinary tract obstruction with hydronephrosis, detects stones as small as 1 mm in diameter, and helps evaluate other potential causes of abdominal pain and hematuria. However, noncontrast abdominal helical CT is expensive and has a higher radiation exposure than other imaging studies.

MRI does not visualize stones; therefore, a negative study cannot exclude the diagnosis of nephrolithiasis.

KUB can be used to follow stone burden but should not be used diagnostically because of possible false-negative results.

Intravenous pyelography has a high sensitivity and specificity in the diagnosis of kidney stones. However, this study requires bowel preparation and the use of intravenous iodinated contrast agents, which are contraindicated in patients with acute kidney injury and chronic kidney disease.

Kidney ultrasonography is often available when other modalities are not and is less expensive than CT; it can show both radiolucent and radiopaque stones but is best for visualizing the kidney and renal pelvis. However, its lower sensitivity and specificity are often associated with the need for additional confirmatory imaging studies that may negate any cost savings.

> **KEY POINT**
>
> - **Noncontrast abdominal helical CT is the gold standard for diagnosing kidney stones.**

Bibliography
Goldfarb DS. In the clinic. Nephrolithiasis. Ann Intern Med. 2009;151(3):ITC2. [PMID: 19652185]

Item 22   Answer: C

Educational Objective: Manage metabolic acidosis in a patient with chronic kidney disease.

The addition of sodium bicarbonate therapy is indicated to treat metabolic acidosis in this patient with chronic kidney disease (CKD). Derangements in laboratory study results are common in patients with progressive CKD. As the estimated glomerular filtration rate (GFR) declines, more frequent assessment is needed to adjust medications and limit consequences of CKD. The metabolic acidosis that results from CKD is a common complication and typically develops when the GFR is less than 25 mL/min/1.73 m^2. Chronic metabolic acidosis has several adverse consequences, including exacerbation of bone disease as bone serves to buffer the pH. Chronic metabolic acidosis may also have adverse effects that impact thyroid hormone, growth hormone, muscle strength, and cardiovascular disease. Management of metabolic acidosis with oral sodium bicarbonate has been found to slow progression of CKD.

High uric acid levels have been associated with CKD progression, and there is increasing interest in the use of allopurinol to slow CKD progression; however, to date, there has not been conclusive evidence to support widespread use of allopurinol in patients without other indications for its use.

Noncalcium-containing phosphate binders such as sevelamer or lanthanum carbonate have been promoted to treat hyperphosphatemia without increasing the calcium phosphate product. The treatment of hyperphosphatemia is recommended in the management of secondary hyperparathyroidism. This strategy helps limit renal osteodystrophy, but it has not been proved to slow progression of CKD and is not indicated in this patient with a phosphorus level within the normal range.

Sodium polystyrene can be used to treat significant hyperkalemia in patients with CKD when other strategies such as dietary restriction, cessation of agents that block the renin-angiotensin system, or diuretics have failed. Sodium polystyrene, however, plays no role in halting progression of CKD and is otherwise not indicated in this patient with a potassium level of 4.8 meq/L (4.8 mmol/L).

> **KEY POINT**
>
> - **Management of metabolic acidosis with oral sodium bicarbonate therapy has been found to slow progression of chronic kidney disease.**

Bibliography
De Brito-Ahurst I, Varagunam M, Raftery MJ, Yaqoob MM. Bicarbonate supplementation slows progression of CKD and improves nutritional status. J Am Soc Neph. 2009;20(9):2075-2084. [PMID: 1960873]

Item 23   Answer: A

Educational Objective: Manage white coat hypertension.

This patient has white coat hypertension with no evidence of target organ damage and should therefore continue home blood pressure measurements and return for a follow-up visit in 6 months. White coat hypertension is characterized by at least three separate office blood pressure measurements above 140/90 mm Hg and at least two sets of measurements below 140/90 mm Hg obtained outside the office, accompanied by the absence of target organ damage. Ambulatory blood pressure monitoring is considered the gold standard for diagnosing this condition. Patients with white coat hypertension have a lower risk for cardiovascular events compared with those with sustained hypertension but also have a greater risk for developing sustained hypertension than those without this condition and should be carefully monitored, including with home blood pressure measurements.

Pharmacologic treatment of white coat hypertension has not been shown to reduce morbid events or produce cardiovascular benefit and is therefore inappropriate for this patient.

This patient has normal laboratory test results and a normal electrocardiogram and therefore is at low cardiovascular risk; ordering further tests such as echocardiography or a spot urine albumin–creatinine ratio to screen for microalbuminuria is not necessary at this time.

A plasma aldosterone-plasma renin activity ratio would be appropriate if primary hyperaldosteronism were a consideration. This patient is not hypertensive, and this test is not indicated at this time.

> **KEY POINT**
>
> - **Patients with white coat hypertension are at higher risk for developing sustained hypertension and should be carefully monitored.**

Bibliography
Verdecchia P, Angeli F. The natural history of white-coat hypertension in the long term. Blood Press Monit. 2005;10(2):65-66. [PMID: 15812252]

Item 24   Answer: D

Educational Objective: Diagnose acute kidney injury in a patient with HIV infection.

The most likely cause of acute kidney injury (AKI) in this patient with HIV infection is tenofovir-induced toxicity. Patients with HIV infection have an increased risk of AKI, and medications used to treat HIV infection can cause AKI. In this patient, medication toxicity from the antiretroviral agent tenofovir is the most likely cause of her elevated serum creatinine level. Tenofovir is associated with nephrotoxicity thought to be due to mitochondrial damage to renal tubular cells. It may cause changes similar to those seen in the Fanconi syndrome: glycosuria despite a normal plasma glucose level, mild proteinuria consistent with proximal tubular damage, and a low serum bicarbonate level without an elevated anion gap. Phosphaturia can also cause a low serum phosphorus level. When identified, tenofovir kidney injury is treated by discontinuing the drug. Most patients show recovery in kidney function over weeks to months, although permanent injury is possible.

Hepatitis C virus–associated kidney disease is an immune complex disorder that occurs in association with active hepatitis C virus infection and leads to the development of glomerulonephritis. This disorder typically manifests as the nephritic syndrome and is associated with significant hematuria and proteinuria, neither of which is found in this patient.

HIV infection is associated with some parenchymal diseases (HIV-associated nephropathy, interstitial/infiltrative diseases, immune complex–mediated nephritis), with a collapsing form of focal segmental glomerulosclerosis (FSGS) being the most common. This form of kidney disease typically presents in patients with a high HIV viral load and is characterized by the nephrotic syndrome with high levels of urine protein, which is not present in this patient.

Although the antiretroviral agent atazanavir is associated with kidney stones, this patient has no symptoms of urinary obstruction, and the urinalysis is more consistent with proximal tubular damage.

KEY POINT

- **Although patients with HIV infection are at increased risk for acute kidney injury (AKI) from a number of causes, medications are a leading etiology of AKI in this patient population.**

Bibliography

Izzedine H, Harris M, Perazella MA. The nephrotoxic effects of HAART. Nat Rev Nephrol. 2009;5(10):563-573. [PMID: 19776778]

Item 25   Answer: C

Educational Objective: Manage rhabdomyolysis.

Treatment using rapid infusion of intravenous 0.9% saline is indicated for this patient with rhabdomyolysis. Rhabdomyolysis develops when muscle injury leads to the release of myoglobin and other intracellular muscle contents into the circulation. Rhabdomyolysis most commonly develops after exposure to myotoxic drugs, infection, excessive exertion, or prolonged immobilization. Diagnosis should be considered in patients with a serum creatine kinase level above 5000 units/L who demonstrate blood on urine dipstick testing in the absence of significant hematuria. Complications of rhabdomyolysis include hypocalcemia, hyperphosphatemia, hyperuricemia, metabolic acidosis, acute muscle compartment syndrome, and limb ischemia.

Although dialysis may ultimately be necessary if this patient does not respond to intravenous saline, there are no acute hemodialysis needs at this time. Although he is hyperkalemic, he has no electrocardiogram changes, and increasing sodium delivery with intravenous fluids through the renal tubules should help renal potassium excretion. If the potassium does not improve after a trial of intravenous fluids or the patient develops volume overload, dialysis may need to be initiated.

Although mannitol may promote renal tubular flow, it might also lead to further hypovolemia and has not been shown superior to hydration in the treatment of rhabdomyolysis.

This patient's hypernatremia indicates a free water deficit, and his history and examination suggest a hypovolemic hypernatremia. Rapid infusion of 5% glucose in water will help correct this patient's water deficit but will not expand the patient's volume and promote urine flow as effectively as sodium-containing intravenous fluid.

KEY POINT

- **Intravenous fluid with saline is the treatment of choice for rhabdomyolysis.**

Bibliography

Better OS, Abassi ZA. Early fluid resuscitation in patients with rhabdomyolysis. Nat Rev Nephrol. 2011;7(7):416-422. [PMID: 21587227]

Item 26   Answer: A

Educational Objective: Diagnose central diabetes insipidus.

The most likely diagnosis is central diabetes insipidus. A urine osmolality of less than 200 mosm/kg H_2O in the setting of increased effective plasma osmolality and polyuria is compatible with a diagnosis of diabetes insipidus. This patient has risk factors for both central (cytomegalovirus encephalitis) and nephrogenic (foscarnet therapy) diabetes insipidus. The only way to distinguish these disorders is through observation of the response to desmopressin. Urine osmolality will increase above 600 mosm/kg H_2O after administration of desmopressin in patients with central diabetes insipidus, indicative of the normal tubular response to the antidiuretic hormone (ADH) analog. Conversely, the urine osmolality will remain below 300 mosm/kg H_2O in patients with nephrogenic diabetes insipidus. The observed increase in urine osmolality to 614 mosm/kg H_2O in this patient establishes the diagnosis of central diabetes insipidus.

Cerebral salt wasting may give rise to sodium depletion, hyponatremia, and hypovolemia but usually does not cause hypernatremia or polyuria. Hypovolemia causes non-osmotic release of ADH, leading to a concentrated urine, retention of ingested or intravenously administered water, and hyponatremia. The initial urine osmolality below 200 mosm/kg H_2O, absence of hypovolemia on physical examination, and high serum sodium level in this patient are not consistent with cerebral salt wasting.

The urine osmolality should be greater than 300 mosm/kg H_2O in patients undergoing an osmotic diuresis. The urine osmolality in this patient was consistently less than 200 mosm/kg H_2O, thus excluding this diagnosis.

KEY POINT

- Distinguishing between central diabetes insipidus and nephrogenic diabetes insipidus involves observation of the patient's response to desmopressin.

Bibliography

Loh JA, Verbalis JG. Disorders of water and salt metabolism associated with pituitary disease. Endocrinol Metab Clin North Am. 2008;37(1):213-234. [PMID: 18226738]

Item 27   Answer: B

Educational Objective: Identify the cause of hypotonic hyponatremia.

This patient has hypotonic hyponatremia due to low solute intake. Her history of anorexia and weight loss, in conjunction with clinical euvolemia and both low plasma and low urine osmolality and sodium, supports this diagnosis. Because some solute excretion by the kidney is required for urinary water excretion, this patient's low solute intake is limiting her ability to excrete free water, leading to hypotonic hyponatremia as her water intake exceeds her ability to excrete urinary water.

The absence of physical examination findings suggesting hypovolemia, including postural changes in blood pressure and pulse, decreases the likelihood of hypovolemic hyponatremia in this patient. In patients with hypovolemia, urine osmolality typically exceeds 400 mosm/kg H_2O, which reflects increased tubular water resorption under the influence of antidiuretic hormone.

Pseudohyponatremia is characterized by a low serum sodium concentration due to measurement in a falsely large volume; an interfering substance displaces the liquid component of the sample, similar to ice cubes in a pitcher. The most common space-occupying substances are lipids and paraproteins. Measured plasma osmolality is normal in pseudohyponatremia and cannot be accounted for by increases in other solutes such as glucose, urea, or alcohols. The low measured plasma osmolality and the absence of an osmolal gap are consistent with hypotonic hyponatremia and exclude the diagnosis of pseudohyponatremia.

Hyponatremia is found in most patients with primary adrenal insufficiency, reflecting both mineralocorticoid deficiency and increased vasopressin secretion caused by cortisol deficiency. The absence of hypotension, hypovolemia, hyperkalemia, and a relatively high morning serum cortisol level does not support a diagnosis of primary adrenal insufficiency.

KEY POINT

- Low solute intake can cause hypotonic hyponatremia.

Bibliography

Berl T. Impact of solute intake on urine flow and water excretion. J Am Soc Nephrol. 2008;19(6):1076-1078. [PMID: 18337482]

Item 28   Answer: B

Educational Objective: Estimate the glomerular filtration rate in a low-risk, healthy person.

Estimation of the glomerular filtration rate (GFR) using the Chronic Kidney Disease Epidemiology Collaboration (CKD-EPI) equation is indicated. The Modification of Diet in Renal Disease (MDRD) study equation underestimates GFR at higher (normal) values. Thus, when the value of this equation is >60 mL/min/1.73 m^2, the recommendation is to report it as such, rather than the exact value. The MDRD study included patients with CKD who had lower muscle mass than the general population; therefore, this equation may underestimate GFR in healthy, low-risk persons who have a normal or increased muscle mass. The CKD-EPI equation has reduced this bias, which was shown in the NHANES study, in which median estimated GFR was 94.5 mL/min/1.73 m^2 using the CKD-EPI equation versus 85 mL/min/1.73 m^2 using the MDRD study equation. Additionally, in large cohort studies, patients reclassified from stage 3 CKD via the MDRD study equation to no CKD via the CKD-EPI equation were at similar risk for cardiovascular events as those not classified as having CKD. This patient has stage 3 CKD according to the MDRD study equation but does not have CKD when using the CKD-EPI equation (estimated GFR of 61 mL/min/1.73 m^2). Although this value is still low, it is likely more accurate. The patient should be counseled to continue maintaining a healthy lifestyle, minimizing cardiovascular risk factors. Many Web sites (such as www.nephron.com) are available that allow physicians to easily calculate these values.

The Cockcroft-Gault method of assessing kidney function also tends to underestimate GFR at higher values and would not be expected to yield more accurate information than the MDRD study equation compared with the CKD-EPI equation.

Experts now recommend use of either a 24-hour urine collection for creatinine clearance or radionuclide kidney clearance scanning to obtain a precise estimation of kidney function, which is needed in circumstances such as the evaluation of living donor kidney transplant candidates. Properly collecting a 24-hour urine specimen is difficult, and over- or undercollection of a sample provides an inaccurate estimation of the GFR. Radionuclide kidney clearance scanning is more invasive and more expensive than an estimated GFR. This patient does not require a precise measurement of her kidney function because such a measurement is unlikely to change prognosis or treatment.

KEY POINT

- **The Chronic Kidney Disease Epidemiology Collaboration equation performs better at higher (normal) values of glomerular filtration rate.**

Bibliography

Levey AS, Stevens LA. Estimating GFR using the CKD Epidemiology Collaboration (CKD-EPI) creatinine equation: more accurate GFR estimates, lower CKD prevalence estimates, and better risk predictions. Am J Kidney Dis. 2010;55(4):622-627. [PMID: 20338463]

Item 29   Answer: A

Educational Objective: Manage hypertension in a patient with type 2 diabetes mellitus.

The addition of the calcium channel blocker diltiazem is indicated to manage hypertension in this patient who also has type 2 diabetes mellitus. Patients with diabetes and hypertension are at substantial cardiovascular risk. Managing high blood pressure is an effective way to reduce this risk, but debate exists regarding goal blood pressure levels. The American Diabetes Association and the National Kidney Foundation currently consider a target blood pressure goal of less than 130/80 mm Hg to be appropriate for most patients with diabetes, regardless of age, although modifications to this goal are reasonable based on individual patient characteristics and tolerance and side effects of antihypertensive treatment. This patient's blood pressure is substantially above this target; therefore, the use of diltiazem or a β-blocker is reasonable.

Thiazide diuretics are not effective in patients with an estimated glomerular filtration rate of less than 30 mL/min/1.73 m^2; these patients require a loop diuretic such as furosemide for effective volume control. This patient has no indication for a loop diuretic either on the basis of kidney function or signs of volume overload.

In most patients with hypertension in the absence of microalbuminuria, combined therapy with an ACE inhibitor and an angiotensin receptor blocker is not indicated because the risk of hyperkalemia and decreased kidney function outweighs the benefit. A calcium channel blocker such as diltiazem will be equally effective in controlling the blood pressure without the added risk.

Spironolactone is useful in patients who remain hypertensive despite three-drug therapy at optimal dosages. This patient does not meet this criterion. Furthermore, spironolactone can cause an increase in the serum potassium level, which is undesirable in this patient whose potassium level is near the upper limit of the normal range.

KEY POINT

- **The target blood pressure goal for most patients with hypertension and diabetes mellitus is less than 130/80 mm Hg; this goal may need to be appropriately modified based on patient characteristics and response to therapy.**

Bibliography

The American Diabetes Association. Standards of Medical Care–2012. Diabetes Care. 2012;35(suppl 1):S11-S63. [PMID: 22187469]

Item 30   Answer: B

Educational Objective: Manage hypercalciuria in a patient with nephrolithiasis.

In addition to recommending adequate fluid intake, treatment with a thiazide diuretic such as chlorthalidone is indicated for this patient with hypercalciuria and probable calcium oxalate nephrolithiasis. Hypercalciuria, defined as a urine calcium level greater than 300 mg/24 h (7.5 mmol/24 h), is the most common metabolic factor associated with calcium oxalate kidney stones. This patient has low urine volume and idiopathic hypercalciuria, which occurs in the setting of a normal serum calcium level and no other clear cause. Idiopathic hypercalciuria is associated with a family history of nephrolithiasis, as noted by this patient who also recently passed kidney stones. Imaging was performed in this patient to assess the stone burden or stones that have already formed within the kidney before the onset of treatment. This imaging strategy, appropriately done with plain radiography for radiopaque calcium oxalate stones, is important because if symptoms of nephrolithiasis develop during treatment, physicians can then determine whether these are related to stones that were present before therapy or new stones that developed despite treatment. The mainstay of therapy is a thiazide diuretic such as chlorthalidone, which can promote distal reabsorption of calcium.

A calcium-restricted diet is not advised for this patient; paradoxically, a low calcium diet is associated with an increase in nephrolithiasis. In addition, chronically limiting calcium intake may have long-term implications on bone mineral density and eventual fracture risk.

Potassium supplements may be needed to offset potassium loss caused by thiazide diuretics, although this is not a primary treatment for calcium oxalate nephrolithiasis. If potassium supplementation is needed, potassium citrate, rather than potassium chloride, would be preferable because the citrate also serves to chelate calcium and limit crystallization.

Alkalinization of the urine may help increase the solubility of calcium oxalate; however, potassium citrate is usually prescribed rather than sodium citrate. Sodium increases urine calcium and may exacerbate this patient's tendency to hypercalciuria. Also, significant alkalinization may lead to calcium phosphate stones because these are less soluble in an alkaline pH.

KEY POINT

- **The mainstay of therapy for idiopathic hypercalciuria is a thiazide diuretic.**

Bibliography

Worcester EM, Coe FL. Clinical practice. Calcium kidney stones. N Engl J Med. 2010;363(10):954-963. [PMID: 20818905]

Item 31   Answer: A

Educational Objective: Diagnose lead nephrotoxicity.

Chelation mobilization testing is the most appropriate next diagnostic study for this patient. Lead may be the cause of this patient's kidney injury based on his exposure history and other clinical and laboratory findings consistent with lead toxicity (hypertension and gout). Chronic kidney disease (CKD) resulting from lead typically occurs from chronic lead exposure, often in industrial settings, resulting in high blood levels. However, because more than 90% of the total body lead burden resides in the bones, blood levels may not be an adequate indicator of lead exposure over time, particularly if the acute exposure has been discontinued, as in this patient. Therefore, his normal blood lead level does not exclude lead as a potential cause of his CKD. Administration of the chelating agent calcium disodium ethylenediaminetetraacetic acid (EDTA), which mobilizes lead deposited in the tissues, is measured in the urine and can be used to assess for previous lead exposure. If this study reveals a high degree of lead excretion, chelation can then be used as therapy. Lead nephrotoxicity causes a chronic tubulointerstitial nephritis resulting in low-grade proteinuria, with rare leukocytes and erythrocytes in the urine sediment. Other kidney findings result in a Fanconi-like syndrome, with glycosuria in the setting of normoglycemia, hyperuricemia, hypophosphatemia, and aminoaciduria.

Erythrocyte protoporphyrin levels increase with active lead exposure but do not reflect the total body lead burden and are not helpful in detecting significant past lead exposure.

Lead lines seen on long bone radiographs are caused by increased density of the metaphysis of growing bones because of lead exposure and are therefore seen primarily in growing children exposed to high levels of lead; this testing is not effective in diagnosing lead exposure in adults.

The finding of basophilic stippling of erythrocytes on a peripheral blood smear is seen in lead toxicity. However, this finding is also seen in other conditions, such as megaloblastic anemia, and is not adequately specific for use in diagnosing lead toxicity.

KEY POINT

- **In patients with suspected lead nephrotoxicity, chelation mobilization testing may be required in those with normal blood lead levels.**

Bibliography

Ekong EB, Jaar BG, Weaver VM. Lead-related nephrotoxicity: a review of the epidemiologic evidence. Kidney Int. 2006;70(12):2074. [PMID: 17063179]

Item 32   Answer: C

Educational Objective: Recognize risk factors for damaging veins in patients with chronic kidney disease.

An attempt should be made to continue the use of peripheral intravenous access for antibiotic administration in this patient. In patients with chronic kidney disease who may eventually require hemodialysis, preservation of the patency of the central venous system is an important consideration in medical management. Stenosis of the central veins may render a patient's arm unsuitable for placement of a temporary dialysis catheter or an arteriovenous fistula or graft, which is the preferred access for long-term hemodialysis. Central vein stenosis most commonly results from endothelial damage due to mechanical trauma associated with centrally placed venous catheters.

There is currently no indication for placement of a temporary dialysis catheter in this patient given his stable kidney function; they also impart a significantly increased risk of central vein injury. Additionally, it is preferable to use a dedicated hemodialysis catheter for kidney replacement therapy and not for other interventions such as infusion of intravenous fluids or antibiotics.

Rates of stenosis depend on the type and location of the central catheter being used and the duration it is in place. Catheters in the subclavian position may have stenosis rates as high as 50%, whereas those in the right internal jugular position tend to have the lowest rate of stenosis (10%) because their anatomic location leads to less mechanical trauma. If central access is necessary in a high-risk patient, use of the right internal jugular vein is preferred.

Although they are inserted peripherally, peripherally inserted central catheter (PICC) lines may also cause central vein stenosis as well as thrombosis and occlusion of the peripheral veins, which may complicate the placement of long-term hemodialysis access. If a PICC line is used, it should only be placed after a multidisciplinary discussion between the nephrologist and access team in order to choose a site that will best preserve future dialysis access sites.

Bibliography

Hoggard J, Saad T, Schon D, Vesely TM, Royer T; American Society of Diagnostic and Interventional Nephrology, Clinical Practice Committee; Association for Vascular Access. Guidelines for venous access in patients with chronic kidney disease. A Position Statement from the American Society of Diagnostic and Interventional Nephrology, Clinical Practice Committee and the Association for Vascular Access [erratum in Semin Dial. 2009;22(2):221-222]. Semin Dial. 2008;21(2):186-191. [PMID: 18364015]

Item 33   Answer: B

Educational Objective: Evaluate a patient with high blood pressure.

Electrocardiography is the most appropriate next step for this patient with high blood pressure. The evaluation of a patient with high blood pressure is directed toward determining if the blood pressure is elevated as a primary phenomenon or is secondary to another cause, if there are other cardiovascular risk factors present, and if there is evidence of target organ damage. Electrocardiography is a means of assessing for the presence of cardiac effects of sustained blood pressure elevation. On electrocardiogram, cardiac damage from hypertension is manifested by the presence of left ventricular hypertrophy and possibly Q waves. These findings also indicate high risk for cardiovascular events. Measures of kidney function are also used to evaluate for possible end-organ damage due to sustained hypertension. The European Society of Hypertension guidelines also recommend evaluation for microalbuminuria, but guidelines from the Seventh Report of the Joint National Committee on Prevention, Detection, Evaluation, and Treatment of High Blood Pressure (JNC 7) advocate that this testing remain optional. Measurement of lipids is useful in assessing for other cardiovascular risks.

Drug treatment is recommended when blood pressure remains above 140/90 mm Hg in patients younger than 80 years of age. However, β-blockers such as atenolol are no longer universally recommended as first-line agents in the absence of a compelling indication. JNC 7, the European Society of Hypertension, and the World Health Organization/International Society of Hypertension guidelines continue to recommend these agents for patients with a history of myocardial infarction and heart failure.

Home blood pressure monitoring is reasonable if white coat hypertension is suspected; however, it is more important to finish the initial evaluation of this patient, which lacks an electrocardiography. This patient's retinal arteriolar changes support target organ effect of blood pressure, particularly in this patient who is young, making white coat hypertension less likely.

Secondary hypertension should be considered in patients with hypertension who have atypical clinical features (onset at a young age, absent family history, severe hypertension) and are resistant to antihypertensive therapy. Spontaneous hypokalemia is strongly suggestive of primary hyperaldosteronism, and the plasma aldosterone-plasma renin activity ratio (ARR) is a screening test for primary hyperaldosteronism. This patient has no features suggestive of a secondary cause of hypertension, including hypokalemia, and screening with an ARR is not needed.

Bibliography

American College of Physicians. In the clinic. Hypertension. Ann Intern Med. 2008;149(11):ITC6(1-15). [PMID: 19047024]

Item 34   Answer: B

Educational Objective: Treat a patient who has uric acid stones.

Allopurinol is indicated for this patient who has recurrent uric acid stones despite alkalinization of the urine. Patients who develop uric acid stones typically have low urine volume or hyperuricosuria. The latter may result from a high protein diet (as in this patient) or rapid purine metabolism as in tumor lysis syndrome. Other risk factors include gout, conditions associated with uric acid overproduction, diabetes mellitus, the metabolic syndrome, and chronic diarrhea. This patient also has inconsistent fluid intake, a relatively high urine uric acid level, and low urine volume, all of which are significant risk factors for development of uric acid nephrolithiasis. Treatment with potassium citrate to alkalinize the urine is often sufficient to decrease the risk for recurrent stones, with the goal of increasing the urine pH to greater than 6.0. This patient continues to have recurrent uric acid nephrolithiasis despite his urine pH being appropriately alkaline. In addition to encouraging more aggressive daily oral hydration and a diet with limited animal protein, seafood, and yeast, the next appropriate step in management is to begin a xanthine oxidase inhibitor to lower uric acid production and urine excretion.

Acetazolamide can alkalinize the urine, but chronic use may lead to a metabolic acidosis and is therefore not typically used for this purpose. Instead, efforts at increasing the urine alkalinization, if necessary, would focus on the dose and frequency of potassium citrate.

Calcium carbonate is often utilized for high urine oxalate excretion from enteric hyperoxaluria, which is not seen in this patient.

A thiazide diuretic such as chlorthalidone is not appropriate for this patient, because thiazide diuretics tend to increase the serum uric acid level and could increase his propensity to develop gout.

KEY POINT

- **In addition to urine alkalinization, treatment with allopurinol is indicated for patients who have recurrent uric acid stones.**

Bibliography

Goldfarb DS. In the clinic. Nephrolithiasis. Ann Intern Med. 2009;151(3):ITC2. [PMID: 19652185]

Item 35   Answer: A

Educational Objective: Diagnose AL amyloidosis.

The most likely diagnosis is AL amyloidosis, which most frequently affects the kidneys and the heart. Kidney involvement usually is manifested by the nephrotic syndrome with progressive worsening of kidney function. Amyloid deposition in the heart results in rapidly progressive heart failure caused by restrictive cardiomyopathy. Hepatomegaly commonly occurs and is caused by congestion from right-sided heart failure or by amyloid infiltration. A painful, bilateral, symmetric, distal, sensory neuropathy that progresses to motor neuropathy is the usual neurologic manifestation in AL amyloidosis. Amyloidosis is classified according to the type of protein deposited. AL amyloidosis is the most common type of systemic amyloidosis in the United States. The precursor protein is a monoclonal light chain, usually of the lambda isotype. In patients with suspected amyloidosis, a fat pad aspirate with Congo red staining is a minimally invasive and high-value diagnostic test. A rectal biopsy is another diagnostic option, and kidney biopsy should be considered if these studies are nondiagnostic. Serum and urine protein electrophoresis with immunoelectrophoresis is used to detect the monoclonal light chain in this disease. Up to 20% of patients with AL amyloidosis also have a coexisting multiple myeloma or other lymphoproliferative disease.

Although diabetes mellitus may lead to proteinuria and decreased kidney function, this patient does not have evidence of underlying diabetes, and this diagnosis would not explain his other clinical findings.

Patients with polyarteritis nodosa typically present with fever, abdominal pain, arthralgia, and weight loss that develop over days to months. Two thirds of these patients have mononeuritis multiplex, and one third have hypertension, testicular pain, and cutaneous involvement, including nodules, ulcers, purpura, and livedo reticularis. Polyarteritis nodosa is not associated with heart failure, hepatomegaly, macroglossia, or the nephrotic syndrome.

Although primary membranous glomerulopathy is more common than AL amyloidosis, only the latter manifests as a systemic disease. Macroglossia, systolic heart failure, peripheral neuropathy, and elevated serum total protein levels are not seen in primary membranous glomerulopathy.

KEY POINT

- **AL amyloidosis most frequently affects the kidneys and the heart; kidney involvement usually is manifested by the nephrotic syndrome with progressive worsening of kidney function.**

Bibliography

Zhu X, Liu F, Liu Y, et al. Analysis of clinical and pathological characteristics of 28 cases with renal amyloidosis. Clin Lab. 2011;57(11-12):947-952. [PMID: 22239026]

Item 36   Answer: A

Educational Objective: Diagnose Liddle syndrome.

The most likely diagnosis is Liddle syndrome, a rare autosomal dominant disorder that presents with early-onset hypertension often accompanied by metabolic alkalosis and hypokalemia. The syndrome results from an activating mutation of the epithelial sodium channel in the cortical collecting duct. The findings of hypertension, hypokalemia, metabolic alkalosis, and suppressed renin and aldosterone levels are consistent with a syndrome of apparent mineralocorticoid excess. 24-Hour urine free cortisol is normal in this patient, which excludes familial syndrome of apparent mineralocorticoid excess, congenital adrenal hyperplasia, Cushing syndrome, and 5-reductase deficiency. Patients with Liddle syndrome are treated with amiloride or triamterene, which directly inhibits sodium uptake through the epithelial sodium channel.

The absence of headaches, sweating, and palpitations in this patient with findings consistent with a syndrome of apparent mineralocorticoid excess argues against the diagnosis of pheochromocytoma.

Primary hyperaldosteronism is unlikely because the serum aldosterone level is suppressed as a result of the primary kidney sodium retention and expansion of the extracellular fluid volume.

Renin and aldosterone levels are elevated in patients with renovascular hypertension, which is defined as hypertension caused by narrowing of one or more of the renal arteries. Underperfusion and ischemia of the kidneys lead to stimulation of the renin-angiotensin system. This patient does not have the findings associated with renovascular hypertension.

- Liddle syndrome is a rare autosomal dominant disorder that presents with early-onset hypertension and is often accompanied by metabolic alkalosis, hypokalemia, and suppressed renin and aldosterone levels.

Bibliography
Lin SH, Yang SS, Chau T. A practical approach to genetic hypokalemia. Electrolyte Blood Press. 2010;8(1):38-50. [PMID: 21468196]

Item 37   Answer: B

Educational Objective: Manage overcorrection of hypotonic hyponatremia.

The most appropriate treatment for this patient is 5% dextrose in water. This patient has hypotonic hyponatremia associated with altered mentation, which typically warrants prompt correction with 3% saline. However, the increase in her serum sodium level following treatment exceeds the recommended initial target of 4 to 6 meq/L (4-6 mmol/L) over the first 24 hours. The high urine volume and decreasing urine osmolality following hypertonic saline administration reflect a rapid water diuresis and suggest that the serum sodium level will likely continue to increase, placing the patient at increased risk for osmotic demyelination syndrome (ODS). Therefore, hypotonic solutions such as 5% dextrose in water should be administered with close follow-up of the serum sodium level, with the goal of maintaining the serum sodium level in the range of 114 to 116 meq/L (114-116 mmol/L) in the first 24 hours.

Administration of 0.9% saline would result in continued increases in the serum sodium level in this patient undergoing a water diuresis, thereby placing her at risk for ODS.

Fluid restriction is indicated to manage hyponatremia due to the syndrome of inappropriate antidiuretic hormone secretion but would exacerbate overly rapid correction of the serum sodium level in this patient who is undergoing a water diuresis and has a rapidly rising serum sodium level.

Tolvaptan, a V_2 receptor antagonist, inhibits the activity of the antidiuretic hormone, thereby decreasing water uptake in the collecting ducts and promoting a water diuresis. This agent would augment the increase in the serum sodium level, exacerbating overcorrection of hyponatremia in this patient.

- When overcorrection of the sodium concentration has occurred in the management of euvolemic hypotonic hyponatremia, administration of 5% dextrose in water is appropriate to lower the serum sodium level.

Bibliography
Sterns RH, Hix JK. Overcorrection of hyponatremia is a medical emergency. Kidney Int. 2009;76(6):587-589. [PMID: 19721422]

Item 38   Answer: B

Educational Objective: Manage cardiorenal syndrome.

Initiation of intravenous furosemide is appropriate for this patient with cardiorenal syndrome. There is intricate physiologic interaction that occurs between the heart and the kidneys, and the term cardiorenal syndrome is used when one organ system dysfunction affects another. This patient's cardiorenal syndrome was likely precipitated by the intravenous fluid therapy given during his 3-day hospitalization. In the setting of baseline chronic kidney disease and heart failure, sodium excretion is impaired, and patients have difficulty managing the increased sodium load effectively, even if only maintenance rates of normal saline are administered. Impaired sodium excretion can lead to volume overload that, in turn, leads to decreased cardiac output based on the limited ability of the heart to compensate for an increase in preload. Treatment to enhance sodium excretion by the kidneys should be initiated, and an intravenous loop diuretic is appropriate for this patient. Although there is often some hesitancy to give diuretics to patients with a rising serum creatinine level, intravenous furosemide is appropriate in this setting of volume overload.

Administering more intravenous fluid is often a reflexive response to a rising serum creatinine level. However, in the setting of volume overload, this treatment may worsen this patient's medical condition.

Although ACE inhibitors are useful in managing chronic heart failure, increasing the lisinopril dose at this time will not immediately address the volume overload, which is precipitating this patient's symptoms.

Increasing the metoprolol dose would address a heart rate that is high for chronic heart failure; however, a β-blocker should not be increased in acute decompensated heart failure. It also would not address the underlying issue of volume overload, which is driving this patient's pathophysiology and increased pulse rate.

- Diuretics may be indicated in the setting of a rising serum creatinine level for patients with cardiorenal syndrome.

Bibliography
Ronco C, Haapio M, House AA, Anavekar N, Bellomo R. Cardiorenal syndrome. J Am Coll Cardiol. 2008;52(19):1527-1539. [PMID: 19007588]

Item 39   Answer: D

Educational Objective: Manage hypertension in a patient with chronic kidney disease.

Switching from hydrochlorothiazide to furosemide is indicated to manage resistant hypertension in this patient with chronic kidney disease (CKD). Resistant hypertension is defined as blood pressure that remains above goal despite treatment with the optimal dosages of three antihypertensive agents of different classes, including a diuretic. If a patient has CKD and uncontrolled blood pressure on hydrochlorothiazide, switching to a loop diuretic should be a first consideration. Although this patient takes antihypertensive medications from four different classes, his blood pressure measurements remain high. Hydrochlorothiazide is likely ineffective in this patient with an estimated glomerular filtration rate (GFR) of less than 30 mL/min/1.73 m². Therefore, changing hydrochlorothiazide to the loop diuretic furosemide dosed twice daily is appropriate. His edema on examination as well as his high blood pressure and lack of orthostasis indicate he is not hypovolemic and may be hypervolemic. Adding a loop diuretic has the added benefit of keeping the serum potassium level low because hyperkalemia is often a complication in patients with CKD.

Most patients with CKD and hypertension are hypervolemic, and a diuretic should be added to multidrug regimens in order to control hypertension. Adding a diuretic is preferred to adding drugs from other classes because the addition of an effective diuretic is likely to be more efficacious, associated with fewer side effects, and offers the convenience of single or twice daily dosing compared with other options, including hydralazine and clonidine.

Adding the angiotensin receptor blocker valsartan to an ACE inhibitor such as lisinopril may increase the chance of hyperkalemia and has not been shown to improve outcomes. In fact, the incidence of hyperkalemia and need for dialysis due to hyperkalemia may be higher in patients on both ACE inhibitors and angiotensin receptor blockers.

> **KEY POINT**
>
> - Thiazide diuretics are less effective antihypertensive agents than loop diuretics in patients with an estimated glomerular filtration rate of less than 30 mL/min/1.73 m².

Bibliography
Sarafidis PA, Bakris GL. Resistant hypertension: an overview of evaluation and treatment. J Am Coll Cardiol. 2008;52(22):1749-1757. [PMID: 19022154]

Item 40   Answer: D
Educational Objective: Diagnose glomerular hematuria.

The most appropriate diagnostic tests to perform next are a urine protein–creatinine ratio and a serum creatinine measurement to determine the degree of proteinuria and level of kidney function. This patient has microscopic hematuria that appears glomerular in origin. Glomerular hematuria on urine microscopy is characterized by the presence of dysmorphic erythrocytes or acanthocytes, which are erythrocytes that retain a ring shape but have "blebs" protruding from their membrane, giving them a characteristic shape (compared with acanthocytes in the blood, in which the

membrane protrusions appear to have a "spiked" shape). Significant hematuria may also be associated with the presence of erythrocyte casts. These findings are highly associated with a glomerular etiology of bleeding and are specifically suggestive of glomerulonephritis. Urine microscopy in patients with glomerular disease also may detect intact erythrocytes; however, these are less specific for glomerular disease.

After determining this patient's degree of proteinuria and level of kidney function, a further evaluation for glomerular disease may include complement levels, a hepatitis panel, and blood cultures as well as testing for antinuclear antibodies, ANCA, anti–glomerular basement membrane antibodies, and antistreptolysin O antibodies. Depending on the serologic test results, this patient may undergo a kidney biopsy to determine the cause of the glomerulonephritis.

If this patient's asymptomatic microscopic hematuria were nonglomerular in origin, ultrasonography would be appropriate; she will likely not require a cystoscopy.

There is no indication that this patient has a urinary tract infection (negative leukocyte esterase and absent leukocytes on microscopic urinalysis); therefore, a urine culture is not indicated.

> **KEY POINT**
>
> - Glomerular hematuria on urine microscopy is characterized by the presence of dysmorphic erythrocytes or acanthocytes, and significant hematuria may also be associated with the presence of erythrocyte casts; these findings are specifically suggestive of glomerulonephritis.

Bibliography
Cohen RA, Brown RS. Microscopic hematuria. N Engl J Med. 2003;348(23):2330-2338. [PMID: 12788998]

Item 41   Answer: D
Educational Objective: Screen for chronic kidney disease.

This patient should be screened for chronic kidney disease (CKD) with a serum creatinine measurement, estimated glomerular filtration rate (GFR), and urinalysis. Recognizing patients at risk for CKD is imperative in a disease that can be asymptomatic. Certain medical history, including diabetes mellitus and hypertension, and predisposing risk factors should prompt screening for CKD. In particular, evaluation for diseases that can damage the kidneys directly (such as scleroderma) or can cause damage through their treatment (such as cisplatin) is indicated. A family history of CKD is a risk factor, as more evidence points to an inherited predisposition to CKD. A history of acute kidney injury (AKI) is recognized as a risk for future AKI and CKD. Various genitourinary abnormalities also can cause CKD. Screening for CKD includes measurement of the serum creatinine level and estimation of GFR as well as urinalysis to evaluate for blood, protein, and casts. Although evidence is lacking that targeted screening improves clinical outcomes, the National Kidney Foundation guidelines recommend targeted screening for CKD. Guidelines, however, do not support screening of the general population for kidney disease.

A 24-hour urine collection for creatinine clearance is generally used to obtain a precise estimation of kidney function, which is needed in circumstances such as the evaluation of living donor kidney transplant candidates. It is not a screening test for CKD because of the difficulty in obtaining the specimen correctly and its inconvenience.

Kidney imaging (usually ultrasonography) should be considered if the serum creatinine level or urinalysis is abnormal. Except for patients with a family history of polycystic kidney disease, it is not an initial screening study for CKD.

Radionuclide kidney clearance scanning is considered the gold standard for estimating GFR in healthy persons and in those with AKI. However, use of these studies is limited because of cost, lack of widespread availability, and operator technical difficulties.

KEY POINT

- **Patients with a family history of chronic kidney disease should be screened for the disease.**

Bibliography

Drawz P, Rahman M. In the clinic. Chronic kidney disease. Ann Intern Med. 2009;150(3):ITC2-1-ITC2-15. [PMID: 19189903]

Item 42   Answer: E

Educational Objective: Manage chronic kidney disease-mineral bone disorder.

This patient should maintain her current therapeutic regimen without changes. Use of bisphosphonates such as risedronate in patients with chronic kidney disease (CKD) is controversial for several reasons. Firstly, patients with reduced glomerular filtration rate (GFR) were excluded from most studies on the safety and efficacy of these agents. Also, because bisphosphonates adhere to bone mineral, they may lead to adynamic bone disease. Finally, bone disease is common in patients with CKD, but bone mineral density studies are not able to differentiate osteoporosis from other bone disorders that do not respond to treatment with a bisphosphonate. When administered, a significant percentage of bisphosphonates is taken up by bone and blocks osteoclast activity. The remainder is excreted unchanged by the kidney by both glomerular filtration and active secretion in the proximal tubule. For this reason, the dose must be reduced in patients with stage 3 CKD. When the GFR is less than 30 mL/min/1.73 m^2, most experts agree that these agents should be discontinued altogether unless there is a compelling indication or a

bone biopsy is performed that confirms the presence of osteoporosis and there are indications to treat with a bisphosphonate, such as a fracture.

Cinacalcet is a calcimimetic used to manage secondary hyperparathyroidism in patients who cannot tolerate vitamin D analogs because of a tendency to develop hypercalcemia. Currently, it is only FDA approved for patients who have end-stage kidney disease. This patient does not have significant secondary hyperparathyroidism. For patients with stage 4 CKD, the target for intact parathyroid hormone is to maintain the parathyroid hormone at the normal range; this patient's level is at the upper limit of normal at 65 pg/mL (65 ng/L).

Sevelamer is used to treat patients with kidney disease who have high serum phosphorus levels. This agent is not indicated at this point because the patient's serum phosphorus level is normal.

Data are lacking on the most appropriate dose of calcium supplementation. High doses should be avoided; however, this patient takes 1000 mg/d, which is within the recommendations to keep total dietary calcium, calcium supplements, or calcium-containing phosphate binders below 2 grams daily.

KEY POINT

- **Bisphosphonates generally should not be used in patients with an estimated glomerular filtration rate of less than 30 mL/min/1.73 m^2.**

Bibliography

Gordon PL, Frassetto LA. Management of osteoporosis in CKD stages 3 to 5. Am J Kidney Dis. 2010;55(5):941-956. [PMID: 20438987]

Item 43   Answer: C

Educational Objective: Manage renovascular hypertension.

Doppler ultrasonography of the renal arteries is indicated for this patient with probable renovascular hypertension. Underperfusion and ischemia of the kidneys lead to stimulation of the renin-angiotensin system, with sodium retention and increased volume contributing to hypertension. Identification of renal artery stenosis and subsequent renal revascularization only improves hypertension in patients with an anatomic lesion that is hemodynamically significant and sufficiently severe to activate the renin-angiotensin system. Therefore, evaluation of renal artery stenosis in patients with suspected atherosclerotic renovascular hypertension should only be considered in patients with accelerated, resistant hypertension and possibly in those with evidence of atherosclerosis whose serum creatinine levels acutely increase after treatment with renin-angiotensin system blockers. This patient has accelerated, drug-resistant hypertension (blood pressure that exceeds the target goal despite taking three antihypertensive drugs, one of which is a diuretic). Doppler ultrasonography of the renal arteries offers a noninvasive estimate of renal artery patency and kidney size.

The addition of an ACE inhibitor to this patient's medication regimen could increase her serum creatinine level if she has significant bilateral renovascular disease and is therefore not indicated.

Increasing the β-blocker dose is not warranted because this patient's pulse rate is 60/min, and such an increase may result in symptomatic bradycardia.

Kidney angiography is the gold standard for the diagnosis of renal artery stenosis but is invasive and associated with several risks, including a large load of contrast dye that may precipitate acute kidney injury in susceptible persons. In addition, in an atherosclerotic aorta, the angiography catheter may disrupt a plaque with subsequent release of cholesterol emboli.

KEY POINT

- Evaluation of renal artery stenosis in patients with suspected atherosclerotic renovascular hypertension should only be considered in patients with accelerated, resistant hypertension and possibly in those with evidence of atherosclerosis whose serum creatinine levels acutely increase after treatment with renin-angiotensin system blockers.

Bibliography

Dworkin LD, Cooper CJ. Clinical practice. Renal-artery stenosis. N Engl J Med. 2009;361(20):1972-1978. [PMID: 19907044]

Item 44   Answer: B

Educational Objective: Identify the cause of hyperkalemia.

Celecoxib toxicity is the most likely cause of this patient's hyperkalemia. Regulation of kidney potassium excretion is dependent upon the renin-angiotensin-aldosterone system. NSAIDs such as celecoxib are known to inhibit renin synthesis, resulting in hyporeninemic hypoaldosteronism, decreased potassium excretion, and hyperkalemia. The ability of the kidney to excrete potassium in hyperkalemic patients can be assessed by calculating the transtubular potassium gradient (TTKG), an index that estimates the ratio of potassium in the cortical collecting duct to that in the peritubular capillaries. The TTKG is calculated by the following equation:

$$\text{TTKG} = [\text{Urine Potassium} \div (\text{Urine Osmolality}/\text{Plasma Osmolality})] \div \text{Serum Potassium}$$

In general, the TTKG in a patient on a normal diet is 8 to 9 and should be greater than 10 in hyperkalemic states, reflecting excretion of excess potassium. This patient's TTKG of 2.5 is consistent with a defect in kidney potassium excretion in the presence of a high serum potassium level. The temporal relationship of starting celecoxib

in the postoperative period and documentation of impaired potassium excretion strongly supports celecoxib toxicity as the cause for this patient's impaired potassium excretion and hyperkalemia.

Patients with bilateral adrenal hemorrhage, which leads to adrenal insufficiency and loss of glucocorticoid and mineralocorticoid activity, typically present with other clinical features such as hypotension, flank pain, fever, or nausea, which are not present in this patient.

High potassium intake is a rare cause of hyperkalemia in patients with normal kidney function and an intact renin-angiotensin-aldosterone system. The TTKG would be expected to be above 10 when dietary intake is the only factor contributing to the hyperkalemia.

Thrombocytosis can induce pseudohyperkalemia, typically when the platelet count exceeds 400,000/microliters (400×10^9/L), but the electrocardiogram changes of hyperkalemia as noted in this patient exclude this diagnosis.

KEY POINT

- NSAIDs such as celecoxib are known to inhibit renin synthesis, resulting in hyporeninemic hypoaldosteronism, decreased potassium excretion, and hyperkalemia.

Bibliography

Nyirenda MJ, Tang JI, Padfield PL, Seckl JR. Hyperkalaemia. BMJ. 2009;339:b4114. [PMID: 19854840]

Item 45   Answer: C

Educational Objective: Identify laxative abuse as the cause of a normal anion gap metabolic acidosis.

This patient with normal kidney function has a normal anion gap metabolic acidosis most likely caused by laxative abuse. The cause of a normal anion gap metabolic acidosis may be characterized by assessing the kidney's ability to excrete an acid load. Excreted acid results in urine ammonium, although these levels are difficult to measure directly. However, urine ammonium excretion may be estimated through assessment of the urine osmolal gap, which is calculated using the following equation:

$$\text{Urine Ammonium Level (meq/L)} \cong \text{Urine Osmolal Gap (mosm/kg H}_2\text{O)}/2$$

$$\text{Urine Osmolal Gap} = \text{Measured Urine Osmolality} - \text{Calculated Urine Osmolality}$$

$$\text{Calculated Urine Osmolality (mosm/kg H}_2\text{O)} =$$
$$2\,(\text{Urine Sodium [meq/L]} + \text{Urine Potassium [meq/L]}) + \text{Urine Urea (mg/dL)}/2.8 + \text{Urine Glucose (mg/dL)}/18$$

Because urine ammonium is not directly measured, its presence in the urine represents excreted acid and will increase the measured urine osmolality, whereas the estimated urine osmolality will not reflect the presence of this cation. Patients with predominantly extrarenal losses of bicarbonate have urine ammonium levels above 80 meq/L, whereas those with a primary kidney defect have urine ammonium levels of less than 30 meq/L. This patient's urine osmolal gap is as follows: $290 - (2 \times (22 + 15) + 112/2.8 + 0/18) = 176$. Because the urine ammonium level is approximately one half the urine osmolal gap, or 88 meq/L, this value reflects an appropriate kidney response to the acidemia.

Laxative abuse can lead to chronic diarrhea, resulting in a normal anion gap metabolic acidosis. This occurs when colonic bicarbonate loss exceeds increased ammonium excretion stimulated by acidemia and potassium depletion. The increased urine ammonium excretion observed in this patient with hypokalemia is most consistent with laxative abuse. The urine ammonium level is usually greater than 80 meq/L in diarrheal acidosis unless there is concomitant hypovolemia.

Diuretic abuse and surreptitious vomiting can cause hypokalemic metabolic alkalosis, which is inconsistent with the hypokalemic metabolic acidosis observed in this patient.

Hypokalemic distal (type 1) renal tubular acidosis is associated with marked impairment of urine ammonium excretion due to tubular acidification defects. Unlike this patient, urine ammonium levels would be expected to be less than 30 meq/L despite systemic acidosis.

> **KEY POINT**
> - Laxative abuse can lead to chronic diarrhea, resulting in a normal anion gap metabolic acidosis.

Bibliography

Gennari FJ, Weise WJ. Acid-base disturbances in gastrointestinal disease. Clin J Am Soc Nephrol. 2008;3(6):1861-1868. [PMID: 18922984]

Item 46   Answer: A
Educational Objective: Diagnose masked hypertension.

The most appropriate next step in management is to obtain 24-hour ambulatory blood pressure monitoring. Masked hypertension is the most likely cause of this patient's unexplained left ventricular hypertrophy. Masked hypertension is characterized by a normal office blood pressure measurement and high ambulatory blood pressure measurement. This condition may affect up to 10 million persons in the United States. Patients with masked hypertension have a definite increased risk for cardiovascular events compared with patients with normal office and ambulatory blood pressure measurements. Suspicion for masked hypertension is usually raised when the physician is informed of discrepancies between office and home blood pressure readings or the discovery of unexplained findings such as left ventricular hypertrophy. Ambulatory blood pressure monitoring can be used to confirm this diagnosis.

If a diagnosis of hypertrophic cardiomyopathy is suspected despite nondiagnostic echocardiography, cardiac MRI can detect focal areas of ventricular hypertrophy and small areas of scarring, which would support the diagnosis. Echocardiographic findings of hypertrophic cardiomyopathy include asymmetric hypertrophy of the ventricle with preserved systolic function but abnormal diastolic function. This patient's echocardiographic findings are not compatible with hypertrophic cardiomyopathy, and cardiac MRI is not indicated.

There are no clinical trials addressing treatment of masked hypertension. However, treatment is indicated for patients with an elevated average 24-hour ambulatory blood pressure measurement. Initiation of chlorthalidone may be appropriate if masked hypertension is diagnosed with 24-hour ambulatory blood pressure measurement.

The coronary artery calcium (CAC) score correlates with cardiovascular risk but is not a direct measure of the severity of luminal coronary disease, and CAC scores are not indicated for routine screening. CAC measurement may be considered in asymptomatic patients with an intermediate risk of coronary artery disease (10%-20% 10-year risk) because a high CAC score (>400) is an indication for more intensive preventive medical treatment. This patient has no indication for CAC scoring, and it cannot explain the patient's left ventricular hypertrophy.

> **KEY POINT**
> - Masked hypertension is characterized by a normal office blood pressure measurement and high ambulatory blood pressure measurement.

Bibliography

Cuspidi C, Negri F, Sala C, Mancia G. Masked hypertension and echocardiographic left ventricular hypertrophy: an updated overview. Blood Press Monit. 2012;17(1):8-13. [PMID: 22183044]

Item 47   Answer: B
Educational Objective: Diagnose hemolytic uremic syndrome.

The most likely cause of this patient's acute kidney injury (AKI) is hemolytic uremic syndrome (HUS), which is caused by some strains of *Escherichia coli*, including the O157:H7 strain that produces Shiga-like toxin (also known as verotoxin). Shiga-like toxin is effective against small blood vessels such as those found in the digestive tract and the kidneys; one specific target for the toxin is the vascular endothelium of the glomerulus, causing cell death, breakdown of the endothelium, hemorrhage, and activation of platelets and inflammatory pathways resulting in intravascular thrombosis and hemolysis. In developing countries, enteric pathogen infections usually develop after ingesting contaminated food or water. This patient manifests the classic triad of microangiopathic hemolytic anemia (anemia, elevated reticulocyte count and lactate dehydrogenase level, low haptoglobin level, and schistocytes on the peripheral blood smear), thrombocytopenia, and AKI in the setting of dysentery caused by an enteric pathogen.

Acute tubular necrosis is an unlikely diagnosis in a patient with microangiopathic hemolytic anemia, thrombocytopenia, and evidence of glomerular damage (erythrocyte casts in the urine). Patients with acute tubular necrosis are more likely to present with muddy brown casts.

Postinfectious glomerulonephritis more commonly occurs after streptococcal and staphylococcal infections and characteristically has a latency period of 7 to 120 days before the onset of AKI. Postinfectious glomerulonephritis is not associated with microangiopathic hemolytic anemia.

Scleroderma renal crisis (SRC) occurs almost exclusively in patients with early diffuse cutaneous systemic sclerosis. This condition is characterized by the acute onset of severe hypertension, kidney failure, and microangiopathic hemolytic anemia. SRC is not associated with bloody diarrhea, and the absence of skin findings makes this diagnosis unlikely.

KEY POINT

- **Patients with hemolytic uremic syndrome typically present with the classic triad of microangiopathic hemolytic anemia, thrombocytopenia, and acute kidney injury.**

Bibliography

Zipfel PF, Heinen S, Skerka C. Thrombotic microangiopathies: new insights and new challenges. Curr Opin Nephrol Hypertens. 2010;19(4):372-378. [PMID: 20539230]

Item 48   Answer: C
Educational Objective: Diagnose orthostatic proteinuria.

A split urine collection is an appropriate initial evaluation for sustained, isolated proteinuria. Protein excretion may vary based on time of collection and, in a small percentage of children and young adults, with posture. Orthostatic (postural) proteinuria refers to protein excretion that increases during the day but decreases at night during recumbency. Diagnosis of orthostatic proteinuria is established by comparing the urine protein excretion during the day with findings from a separate urine collection obtained during the night. An 8-hour nighttime urine collection containing ≤50 mg of protein is required for diagnosis. Typically, urine protein excretion is less than 1 g/24 h but can rarely be greater than 3 g/24 h. Orthostatic proteinuria is benign and has not been associated with long-term kidney disease. Other benign causes of transient or isolated proteinuria include febrile illnesses and rigorous exercise. Transient or isolated proteinuria is typically benign and does not warrant further evaluation.

Kidney biopsy is recommended when histologic confirmation is needed to help diagnose kidney disease, implement medical therapy, or change medical treatment. Kidney biopsy is used predominantly in patients with glomerular disease, and the most common indications for kidney biopsy include the nephrotic syndrome, acute glomerulonephritis, or kidney transplant dysfunction. It is inappropriate to consider a kidney biopsy before excluding benign causes of proteinuria such as orthostatic proteinuria.

A repeat 24-hour urine collection for protein is unnecessary for this patient who already has a urine dipstick that is positive for albuminuria and a previous 24-hour urine collection (gold standard test) positive for proteinuria.

A spot urine protein–creatinine ratio does not necessarily add more information to an accurately collected 24-hour urine collection.

More than 95% of adults will excrete less than 130 mg/24 h of protein in the urine, and the normal value is defined as less than 150 mg/24 h. Reassurance in this case is incorrect because if orthostatic proteinuria is not established as the cause of the patient's proteinuria, this may be an indication of early kidney dysfunction.

KEY POINT

- **A split urine collection is an appropriate initial evaluation for sustained, isolated proteinuria.**

Bibliography

Naderi AS, Reilly RF. Primary care approach to proteinuria. J Am Board Fam Med. 2008;21(6):569-574. [PMID: 18988725]

Item 49   Answer: C
Educational Objective: Manage chronic kidney disease.

This patient's antihypertensive therapy should be increased to decrease his average blood pressure readings. Blood pressure control has been shown to delay chronic kidney disease (CKD) progression and reduces cardiovascular risk. Current recommended levels of blood pressure control in patients with CKD are less than 130/80 mm Hg. Sodium restriction is an effective means of controlling blood pressure in all patients with CKD and hypertension. Diuretics are reasonable initial therapy for hypertension in patients with nonproteinuric CKD, particularly if they have edema. Angiotensin blockade (ACE inhibitors or angiotensin receptor blockers) is particularly beneficial in patients with proteinuric CKD. Nondihydropyridine calcium channel blockers also have an antiproteinuric effect, although dihydropyridine calcium channel blockers may be more potent antihypertensives. Delaying CKD progression in patients without proteinuria should focus more on blood pressure control than on the specific agent. In this patient with nonproteinuric CKD, hypertension, and no edema, increasing either of his current antihypertensive agents is reasonable to achieve a desired blood pressure goal.

Administration of sodium bicarbonate has recently been shown to delay CKD progression in patients with stage 4 and 5 disease and initial serum bicarbonate levels of 15 to 20 meq/L (15-20 mmol/L). This patient has stage 3 CKD and a serum bicarbonate level of 22 meq/L (22 mmol/L).

Although this patient has evidence of secondary hyperparathyroidism with a slightly elevated parathyroid hormone (PTH) level, his calcium and phosphorus levels are within normal limits. It would be reasonable to start a 2- to 4-month trial of a low phosphate diet and repeat his laboratory studies. A phosphate binder can be considered if dietary modification does not help or if his phosphorus level increases. Initiating activated vitamin D therapy at this level of PTH is not indicated.

KEY POINT

- **Blood pressure control to a goal of less than 130/80 mm Hg is a key intervention for delaying progression of chronic kidney disease.**

Bibliography

de Galan BE, Perkovic V, Ninomiya T, et al; ADVANCE Collaborative Group. Lowering blood pressure reduces renal events in type 2 diabetes. J Am Soc Nephrol. 2009;20(4):883-892. [PMID: 19225038]

Item 50   Answer: D

Educational Objective: Identify the cause of hypophosphatemia.

This patient's hypophosphatemia is likely due to kidney phosphate wasting caused by proximal (type 2) renal tubular acidosis (RTA) due to ifosfamide nephrotoxicity. Ifosfamide, a synthetic analog of cyclophosphamide, is associated with considerable nephrotoxicity because of direct tubular injury. It commonly induces proximal RTA and other findings that resemble those seen in the Fanconi syndrome (glucosuria and renal phosphate, uric acid, and amino acid wasting) due to tubular dysfunction. Ifosfamide renal toxicity may be minimized primarily by limiting the cumulative dose, if possible. In most patients, tubular function returns to near normal with time after discontinuation of the drug, although in some patients there may be persistent tubular function defects requiring ongoing treatment.

Hypophosphatemia is defined as a serum phosphate concentration less than 2.5 mg/dL (0.81 mmol/L) and is most common in patients with a history of chronic alcohol use, critical illness, and malnutrition. When the cause of hypophosphatemia is uncertain, urine phosphate excretion can be assessed by calculating the fractional excretion of phosphate (FE_{PO4}) from a random urine specimen by the following formula:

$$FE_{PO4} = (\text{Urine Phosphate} \times \text{Serum Creatinine} \times 100) \div (\text{Serum Phosphate} \times \text{Urine Creatinine})$$

An FE_{PO4} of less than 5% suggests increased cellular uptake or extrarenal phosphate loss as the cause of the low serum phosphate, whereas a value greater than 5% is consistent with renal phosphate wasting, as seen in this patient, which is consistent with ifosfamide-induced nephrotoxicity.

This patient's history of nausea and anorexia raises the possibility of malnutrition as the cause of the hypophosphatemia; however, the FE_{PO4} should be less than 5% when there is inadequate intake.

Oncogenic osteomalacia is a form of acquired hypophosphatemia associated with kidney phosphate wasting usually seen in patients with small, slow-growing mesenchymal tumors usually located in the craniofacial extremities. Other manifestations of proximal tubular dysfunction, such as glycosuria as noted in this patient, are not characteristic of oncogenic osteomalacia, arguing against this diagnosis. Recent evidence has implicated the phosphaturic hormone fibroblast growth factor-23 (FGF-23) in the pathogenesis of this disorder.

Primary hyperparathyroidism, when severe, can induce hypophosphatemia by inhibiting proximal reabsorption of phosphate. Hypercalcemia generally precedes onset of hypophosphatemia in primary hyperparathyroidism, and glycosuria with normoglycemia as noted in this patient would not be present.

KEY POINT

- **A fractional excretion of phosphate greater than 5% in patients with hypophosphatemia is consistent with renal phosphate wasting.**

Bibliography

Liamis G, Milionis HJ, Elisaf M. Medication-induced hypophosphatemia: a review. QJM. 2010;103(7):449-459. [PMID: 20356849]

Item 51   Answer: B

Educational Objective: Diagnose IgA nephropathy.

The most likely cause of this patient's gross hematuria complicated with acute kidney injury (AKI) is IgA nephropathy. Gross hematuria associated with an episode of respiratory or gastrointestinal infection can be the first clinical presentation of primary IgA nephropathy, which can precipitate AKI. Infections activate mucosal defenses and the production of IgA antibodies, which are deposited in the glomeruli, causing injury and bleeding. The mechanism of AKI is thought to be the combination of several factors: acute tubular necrosis due to tubular obstruction by erythrocyte casts, free hemoglobin and/or iron direct toxicity to tubular epithelium mediated by lipid peroxidation and free radical formation, and hemoglobin being a scavenger of nitric oxide whose reduction results in vasoconstriction and decreased oxygen supply. Patients who have IgA nephropathy presenting with AKI associated with macroscopic hematuria commonly have a good prognosis, with spontaneous recovery after cessation of the hematuria; however, factors such as macroscopic hematuria for more than 10 days, age greater than 50 years, severely decreased glomerular filtration rate (GFR), and severity of tubular damage on kidney biopsy increase the risk of chronic kidney disease. The presence of glomerular crescents on kidney biopsy has also been linked to an unfavorable prognosis and requires the use of immunosuppressive agents in addition to supportive therapy.

NSAIDs, particularly when taken in high doses, may be associated with decreased kidney function and AKI. However, injury is typically not due to glomerular damage, and gross hematuria is an uncommon manifestation of analgesic kidney injury.

Patients with postinfectious glomerulonephritis (PIGN) secondary to streptococcal or staphylococcal infections can present with dark urine and AKI. In this case, this diagnosis is unlikely in the absence of a latency period between the infection and the onset of the kidney disease. Additionally, PIGN usually is accompanied by low complement levels and elevated antistreptolysin O antibodies when associated with streptococcal infections.

Rhabdomyolysis develops when muscle injury leads to the release of myoglobin and other intracellular muscle contents into the circulation, which may lead to AKI. Although this patient may have had muscle pain associated with his respiratory infection, his normal creatine kinase level and negative urine myoglobin exclude this diagnosis.

KEY POINT

- **Gross hematuria associated with an episode of respiratory or gastrointestinal infection can be the first clinical presentation of primary IgA nephropathy.**

Bibliography

Gutiérrez E, González E, Hernández E, et al. Factors that determine an incomplete recovery of renal function in macrohematuria-induced acute renal failure of IgA nephropathy. Clin J Am Soc Nephrol. 2007;2(1):51-57. [PMID: 17699387]

Item 52   Answer: A

Educational Objective: Identify colonic pseudo-obstruction as the cause of hypokalemia.

This patient's hypokalemia is most likely caused by colonic pseudo-obstruction. He has hypokalemia without an obvious concurrent acid-base disorder. Random values of urine potassium can be used to assess the kidney response to hypokalemia but must be corrected for the degree of urinary concentration. This can be achieved by calculating the urine potassium–creatinine ratio (meq/g), which is calculated as follows:

$$\text{Urine Potassium (meq/L)} \times 100 \; [(mg \times L)/(dL \times g)] \div \text{Urine Creatinine (mg/dL)}$$

A urine potassium–creatinine ratio above 20 meq/g is consistent with kidney potassium wasting, whereas a value below 15 meq/g suggests extrarenal potassium loss, cellular

redistribution, or decreased intake. This patient's urine potassium–creatinine ratio is 13 meq/g, thus indicating either extrarenal losses of potassium or redistribution. Colonic pseudo-obstruction is associated with up-regulation of potassium channels in the colon, resulting in secretory diarrhea, intestinal potassium loss, and hypokalemia.

Furosemide can cause hypokalemia through direct blockade of potassium uptake in the thick ascending loop of Henle as well as through induction of hypovolemia and secondary hyperaldosteronism. The urine potassium–creatinine ratio, however, should be greater than 20 meq/g, reflecting ongoing urine potassium loss, and not less than 15 meq/g as noted in this patient.

Vomiting and nasogastric suction can induce urine potassium losses by increasing delivery of sodium bicarbonate to the cortical collecting duct, as well as through secondary hyperaldosteronism when there is concurrent hypovolemia. Potassium levels are relatively low in gastric fluid (5-10 meq/L [5-10 mmol/L]), and potassium depletion in patients undergoing nasogastric suction is primarily due to urine potassium losses.

This patient's history does not suggest potassium redistribution (shift of potassium from the extracellular to the intracellular space), and the serum bicarbonate level of 28 meq/L (28 mmol/L) would not be predicted to cause alkalemia to a degree sufficient to shift potassium into cells and cause severe hypokalemia.

KEY POINT

- **Colonic pseudo-obstruction is associated with up-regulation of potassium channels in the colon, resulting in secretory diarrhea, intestinal potassium loss, and hypokalemia.**

Bibliography

Sandle GI, Hunter M. Apical potassium (BK) channels and enhanced potassium secretion in human colon. QJM. 2010;103(2):85-89. [PMID: 19892809]

Item 53   Answer: E

Educational Objective: Manage poststreptococcal glomerulonephritis.

The most appropriate treatment for this patient with poststreptococcal glomerulonephritis is supportive care with antihypertensive agents and diuretics for his hypertension and fluid retention. Poststreptococcal glomerulonephritis, a form of postinfectious glomerulonephritis, is an immunologic disease triggered by an infection, which is followed by the release of immunoglobulins and activation of complement proteins that are deposited in the glomeruli, activating cytokine inflammatory pathways. Acute nephritic syndrome is the typical manifestation of postinfectious glomerulonephritis, regardless of the offending organism, and is characterized by rapid onset of edema, hypertension, oliguria with low urine sodium, and erythrocyte casts in the urine sediment. Most patients with a typical presentation for poststreptococcal glomerulonephritis do not require a kidney biopsy to establish the diagnosis. A biopsy should be considered if the course or findings are atypical for poststreptococcal glomerulonephritis or if there is no clear history or documentation of a prior streptococcal infection. Early treatment of bacterial infections with appropriate antibiotics can prevent or lessen the severity of postinfectious glomerulonephritis. Management of established postinfectious glomerulonephritis is supportive, aiming to control the manifestations of the disease, particularly volume overload with diuretics, antihypertensives, and, if necessary, dialysis.

Less commonly, postinfectious glomerulonephritis can manifest as rapidly progressive glomerulonephritis (RPGN) or as persistent nephritic-nephrotic syndrome that may progress to advanced chronic kidney disease. The management of postinfectious glomerulonephritis presenting as RPGN or persistent nephritic-nephrotic syndrome can require intravenous pulse methylprednisolone, prednisone, cyclophosphamide, cyclosporine, and/or plasmapheresis. However, this patient is in the early course of the disease, and it is premature to consider these aggressive measures for a condition that will most likely resolve spontaneously.

KEY POINT

- **Management of poststreptococcal glomerulonephritis is primarily supportive, with attention to blood pressure and volume control.**

Bibliography

Nadasdy T, Hebert LA. Infection-related glomerulonephritis: understanding mechanisms. Semin Nephrol. 2011;31(4):369-375. [PMID: 21839370]

Item 54   Answer: D

Educational Objective: Diagnose primary membranous glomerulopathy in a patient with long-standing diabetes mellitus.

This patient most likely has primary membranous glomerulopathy, which usually manifests as the nephrotic syndrome, although some patients may have asymptomatic proteinuria. Microscopic hematuria and an absence of erythrocyte casts are common. Factors such as the baseline serum creatinine level and degree of proteinuria determine the rate of disease progression. Membranous glomerulopathy is usually primary but may occur secondary to conditions such as hepatitis B or C virus infection, malaria, syphilis, systemic lupus erythematosus, diabetes mellitus, or rheumatoid arthritis; use of drugs such as NSAIDs, captopril, or penicillamine; and malignancies of the breast, colon, stomach, kidney, or lung. Membranous glomerulopathy is confirmed by kidney biopsy showing characteristic diffuse glomerular membrane thickening without cellular infiltration, and coarsely granular deposits of IgG and C3 along the capillary loops by immunofluorescence microscopy. Electron microscopy shows moderate podocyte foot

process effacement consistent with changes leading to protein leakage from the glomerulus.

It is unlikely to see sudden onset of the nephrotic syndrome as the first manifestation of diabetic nephropathy, and this patient has well-controlled diabetes and no prior evidence of microalbuminuria or microvascular complications such as retinopathy or neuropathy.

Membranous lupus nephritis is unlikely without the diagnosis of lupus, a disease that is more commonly seen in younger women and shows a different pattern of immune complex deposition than in membranous glomerulopathy.

Minimal change glomerulopathy is more common in children and is not an immune complex glomerulonephritis. Minimal change glomerulopathy is characterized by normal light and immunofluorescence microscopies but with effacement of podocyte foot processes on electron microscopy.

KEY POINT

- **Primary membranous glomerulopathy typically manifests as the nephrotic syndrome, and diagnosis is confirmed by kidney biopsy.**

Bibliography

Tarrass F, Anabi A, Zamd M, et al. Idiopathic membranous glomerulonephritis in patients with type 2 diabetes mellitus. Hong Kong J Nephrol. 2005;7(1):34-37.

Item 55   Answer: A

Educational Objective: Manage chronic tubulointerstitial nephritis associated with lithium use.

Amiloride is appropriate for this patient. Long-term lithium exposure can result in chronic tubulointerstitial nephritis. High chronic lithium levels and repeated episodes of lithium toxicity can result in worsening dysfunction. Specific kidney manifestations include a decreased glomerular filtration rate and incomplete distal renal tubular acidosis. Lithium often causes a partial nephrogenic diabetes insipidus, resulting in high urine output and an inability to concentrate the urine. Lithium is reabsorbed along the nephron at sites where sodium is reabsorbed, accumulating in renal tubular cells. In patients with lithium-associated nephrotoxicity, this agent should be discontinued and another appropriate medication used in its place. However, this patient has been unable to do so. In such patients, medication levels should be followed closely so that they are maintained in the therapeutic range. If the agent must be continued, other steps should be considered to mitigate the ongoing damage by the medication. Amiloride directly blocks the epithelial sodium channel and decreases lithium uptake, resulting in less long-term damage.

Restricting water intake will only result in a free water deficit and possible hypernatremia, rather than a decrease in urine output or improvement in kidney function and is therefore not indicated for this patient.

The chronic damage that occurs with lithium is not improved with prednisone, which may be used for patients with acute tubulointerstitial nephritis if there is no improvement after discontinuation of the offending/inciting agent.

Indications for tolvaptan include hypervolemic or euvolemic hyponatremia, chronic heart failure, cirrhosis, and the syndrome of inappropriate antidiuretic hormone secretion. This medication is not used to treat partial nephrogenic diabetes insipidus.

KEY POINT

- **Long-term lithium exposure can result in chronic tubulointerstitial nephritis; if lithium cannot be discontinued, amiloride is indicated to decrease lithium uptake, resulting in less long-term damage.**

Bibliography

Grünfeld JP, Rossier BC. Lithium nephrotoxicity revisited. Nat Rev Nephrol. 2009;5(5):270-276. [PMID: 19384328]

Item 56   Answer: B

Educational Objective: Treat a patient who has hyperkalemia.

In addition to intravenous calcium and insulin-dextrose, hemodialysis is appropriate for this patient who has significant hyperkalemia with evidence of cardiac conduction abnormalities, which warrants emergency treatment. Hyperkalemia is defined as a serum potassium concentration greater than 5 meq/L (5 mmol/L). Risk factors include underlying acute or chronic kidney disease and decreased renin-angiotensin-aldosterone activity. Clinical manifestations include ascending muscle weakness, electrocardiographic changes, and life-threatening cardiac arrhythmias and paralysis when the hyperkalemia is severe. Intravenous calcium and insulin-dextrose are temporizing measures to decrease the arrhythmogenic effect of excessive potassium on the myocardium, and definitive therapy ultimately requires potassium removal. The presence of concurrent acute kidney injury (AKI) and recent gastrointestinal surgery in this patient favors use of hemodialysis.

The efficacy of furosemide in promoting a kaliuresis would likely be impaired in this patient with AKI and low urine output and is not considered a reliable method to address this degree of life-threatening hyperkalemia.

Sodium bicarbonate has limited efficacy in the management of hyperkalemia in the setting of end-stage kidney disease or severe AKI. In these populations, the hypokalemic response is often minimal and delayed by several hours, insufficient to bring about a clinically meaningful decrease in the serum potassium level. Conversely, patients with hyperkalemia, hypovolemia, and metabolic acidosis usually respond well to hydration with sodium bicarbonate.

Use of the cation exchange resin sodium polystyrene sulfonate is contraindicated in those who have had recent bowel surgery because these patients are at risk for intestinal necrosis. The risk of this complication appears to be increased in preparations formulated with sorbitol.

KEY POINT

- **Sodium polystyrene sulfonate is contraindicated in the treatment of hyperkalemia in patients with recent bowel surgery.**

Bibliography

Elliott MJ, Ronksley PE, Clase CM, Ahmed SB, Hemmelgarn BR. Management of patients with acute hyperkalemia. CMAJ. 2010;182(15):1631-1635. [PMID: 20855477]

Item 57   Answer: C

Educational Objective: Diagnose salicylate toxicity.

This patient most likely has salicylate toxicity. The differential diagnosis of combined increased anion gap metabolic acidosis and respiratory alkalosis includes salicylate toxicity, liver disease, and sepsis. Although intentional or accidental ingestion of aspirin is the most common route of salicylate exposure, toxicity may also occur with cutaneous exposure to salicylate-containing compounds such as oil of wintergreen, which is the most likely source of exposure in this case. Symptoms may include mental status changes, nausea, fever, vomiting, and tinnitus. Pulmonary edema is more common in chronic intoxication, particularly in the elderly population. The anion gap is slightly increased at 14 in this patient, likely reflecting increased serum levels of salicylate. The diagnosis is confirmed by measuring the serum salicylate level.

Metformin toxicity can cause severe lactic acidosis in patients with acute kidney injury on chronic therapy who have an estimated glomerular filtration rate less than 30 mL/min/1.73 m^2, particularly in the setting of critical illness or following acute overdose. This patient's normal serum lactate level excludes this diagnosis.

Methanol poisoning typically presents with an increased anion gap metabolic acidosis and concomitantly increased osmolal gap but does not cause a primary respiratory alkalosis. The osmolal gap, normally less than 10 mosm/kg H_2O, is calculated using the following equation:

$$\text{Osmolal Gap} = \text{Measured Plasma Osmolality} - \text{Calculated Plasma Osmolality, where}$$

$$\text{Plasma Osmolality (mosm/kg } H_2O) = 2 \times \text{Serum Sodium (meq/L)} + \text{Plasma Glucose (mg/dL)}/18 + \text{Blood Urea Nitrogen (mg/dL)}/2.8$$

The osmolal gap in this patient is less than 10 (308 – [(145 × 2) + 158/18 + 15/2.8] = 4), making this diagnosis much less likely.

Sepsis is less likely in this patient given the absence of other features of sepsis such as leukocytosis, lactic acidosis, or hypotension.

KEY POINT

- Although ingestion of aspirin is the most common route of salicylate exposure, toxicity may also occur with cutaneous exposure to salicylate-containing compounds such as oil of wintergreen.

Bibliography

Pearlman BL, Gambhir R. Salicylate intoxication: a clinical review. Postgrad Med. 2009;121(4):162-168. [PMID: 19641282]

Item 58   Answer: C

Educational Objective: Manage renovascular hypertension secondary to fibromuscular dysplasia.

Percutaneous transluminal kidney angioplasty is indicated for this patient with renovascular hypertension secondary to fibromuscular dysplasia, a nonatherosclerotic, noninflammatory renovascular disease. Renovascular hypertension due to fibromuscular dysplasia is most commonly caused by medial fibroplasia of the renal artery. On angiogram, the characteristic finding of fibromuscular dysplasia is the "string of beads" appearance of the involved artery, which is apparent in this patient's angiogram. Fibromuscular dysplasia is a disease of unknown cause and most commonly involves the renal and carotid arteries. Hypertension caused by fibromuscular dysplasia is more common in women and usually affects patients between 15 and 30 years of age. Catheter-based kidney angiography is the most accurate method to diagnose this condition. This study is indicated for patients whose clinical presentation raises strong suspicion for fibromuscular disease–related hypertension, such as those with severe resistant hypertension and high plasma renin activity. Revascularization with kidney angioplasty may be performed at the same time as diagnostic angiography. The young age of many patients with fibromuscular dysplasia, such as this 27-year-old woman, reduces the risk of complications from this procedure.

The high likelihood of both technical success and meaningful blood pressure improvement from kidney angioplasty makes drug therapy in this young patient unnecessary at this time.

Surgical revascularization is not first-line treatment for this patient given the higher morbidity. Surgery should be reserved for patients who do not respond to kidney angioplasty or who have arterial anatomy too complex for kidney angioplasty.

KEY POINT

- Management of renovascular hypertension secondary to fibromuscular dysplasia may involve revascularization with kidney angioplasty.

Bibliography

Olin JW, Sealove BA. Diagnosis, management, and future developments of fibromuscular dysplasia. J Vasc Surg. 2011;53(3):826-836.e1. [PMID: 21236620]

Item 59   Answer: C

Educational Objective: Manage end-stage kidney disease and Alport syndrome.

Evaluation for kidney transplantation is appropriate for this patient. He has end-stage kidney disease (ESKD) based on his estimated glomerular filtration rate (GFR) of 13 mL/min/1.73 m². He also has Alport syndrome, an X-linked disease affecting basement membranes due to a collagen protein synthesis defect. Clinical disease is characterized by sensorineural hearing loss, ocular abnormalities, and a family history of kidney disease and deafness. Patients with this disease can have proteinuria and hematuria, leading to ESKD in the second or third decade. There are no specific therapies for Alport syndrome. Kidney transplantation is the treatment of choice for patients with Alport syndrome and ESKD because the underlying disease does not recur in the transplanted kidney, and patients are relatively young at the time when kidney replacement therapy is indicated.

Everolimus is a derivative of sirolimus that is used as an immunosuppressant and also has a role in the treatment of several types of malignancies. It also has been shown to slow cyst progression in patients with autosomal dominant polycystic kidney disease and possibly slow tumor growth in patients with tuberous sclerosis complex. However, it has no known benefit in Alport syndrome.

Although this patient has ESKD with a very low GFR, he has no clear uremic signs or symptoms; therefore, hemodialysis should not be initiated at this time.

There is some evidence suggesting that angiotensin blockade with either an angiotensin receptor blocker (ARB) or ACE inhibitor may decrease protein excretion and slow the progression of kidney disease in Alport syndrome. This patient is already being treated with an ARB, and there would be no benefit of changing this to an ACE inhibitor such as lisinopril.

KEY POINT

- Kidney transplantation is the treatment of choice for patients with Alport syndrome and end-stage kidney disease because the underlying disease does not recur in the transplanted kidney.

Bibliography

Gubler MC. Inherited diseases of the glomerular basement membrane. Nat Clin Pract Nephrol. 2008;4(1):24-37. [PMID: 18094725]

Item 60   Answer: C

Educational Objective: Diagnose postinfectious glomerulonephritis.

The most likely cause of this patient's acute kidney injury (AKI) is postinfectious glomerulonephritis (PIGN). PIGN presents with acute nephritic syndrome characterized by rapid onset of edema, hypertension, oliguria, and erythrocyte casts in the urine sediment. Less commonly, PIGN can manifest as rapidly progressive glomerulonephritis or as persistent nephritic-nephrotic syndrome that may progress to advanced chronic kidney disease (CKD). Diagnosis of PIGN is confirmed when at least three of the following criteria are fulfilled: clinical or laboratory evidence of infection preceding the onset of the disease; low serum complement levels; an exudative-proliferative glomerulonephritis pattern by light microscopy; C3-dominant or co-dominant glomerular staining by immunofluorescence microscopy; and subepithelial humps by electron microscopy. This patient had a documented stable baseline serum creatinine level of 1.4 mg/dL (123.8 micromoles/L) within the first 2 weeks of the infectious event onset before the onset of AKI 2 weeks later accompanied by hypocomplementemia due to activation of both the classic and alternative pathways. PIGN is confirmed by characteristic findings on kidney biopsy.

Diabetic nephropathy alone does not explain the onset of this patient's AKI. The natural history of progressive diabetic nephropathy in patients with type 2 diabetes mellitus is predictable, and decline of the glomerular filtration rate is no greater than 12 to 16 mL/min/1.73 m^2 per year.

Patients with IgA nephropathy may present with an episode of AKI and macroscopic or gross hematuria concomitantly with an infectious episode. However, there is no latency period between the infection and the AKI in IgA nephropathy. IgA deposition can be seen in PIGN associated with staphylococcal infections in which enterotoxins can act as superantigens, initiating an immunologic response.

Adult patients with primary membranous glomerulopathy frequently present with the nephrotic syndrome: timed urine protein collection of more than 3.5 g/24 h, edema, hypoalbuminemia, and hyperlipidemia. Another 30% to 40% of patients present with asymptomatic proteinuria, usually in the subnephrotic range. The urine sediment can reveal erythrocytes and granular casts, but erythrocyte casts are not a feature. Furthermore, complement levels are always normal.

KEY POINT

- **The typical manifestation of postinfectious glomerulonephritis is a preceding infection associated with an acute nephritic syndrome, which is characterized by rapid onset of edema, hypertension, oliguria, and erythrocyte casts in the urine sediment.**

Bibliography
Nasr SH, Share DS, Vargas MT, D'Agati VD, Markowitz GS. Acute poststaphylococcal glomerulonephritis superimposed on diabetic glomerulosclerosis. Kidney Int. 2007;71(12):1317-1321. [PMID: 17311069]

Item 61   Answer: D
Educational Objective: Identify hypertension as a contraindication to kidney biopsy.

Uncontrolled hypertension is a contraindication to kidney biopsy in this patient. She has systemic lupus erythematosus (SLE) and hypertension and is planning to undergo a kidney biopsy for suspected rapidly progressive glomerular disease. In patients with SLE, rapidly progressive glomerular disease left untreated can result in end-stage kidney disease. Thus, it is important to obtain an accurate tissue diagnosis as quickly as possible. However, severe hypertension can lead to increased rates of complications, such as post-biopsy hemorrhage. Although specific outcomes data establishing the optimal level of blood pressure control before kidney biopsy are not available, a measurement of less than 160/95 mm Hg is considered an appropriate level before proceeding to biopsy. Hypertension can be managed relatively quickly if present. Before the biopsy, the patient should be counseled to take all prescribed antihypertensive medications. All over-the-counter medications that may cause hypertension should be avoided, including certain cold remedies such as those containing phenylephrine. Patients can be prescribed a mild sedative (such as lorazepam) before the biopsy if they are anxious, which can also raise blood pressure. At the time of biopsy, if blood pressure is elevated, short-acting β-blockers (such as metoprolol) or centrally acting α-agonists (such as clonidine) can be prescribed. Blood pressure should be closely monitored before, during, and after the procedure.

Other contraindications to kidney biopsy include coagulopathy, thrombocytopenia, hydronephrosis, atrophic kidney, numerous kidney cysts, and acute pyelonephritis. The presence of a solitary kidney is a relative contraindication to percutaneous kidney biopsy because of the risk for nephrectomy due to uncontrolled bleeding. However, percutaneous kidney biopsy may be performed in this setting under direct visualization by laparoscopy. Kidney masses or renal cell carcinomas also are relative contraindications to kidney biopsy because they are associated with an increased risk of bleeding and spread of malignant cells through the biopsy tract.

A slightly increased BMI, chronic prednisone use, and mild anemia are not contraindications to kidney biopsy.

KEY POINT

- **Uncontrolled hypertension is a contraindication for kidney biopsy.**

Bibliography
Whittier WL, Korbet SM. Renal biopsy: update. Curr Opin Nephrol Hypertens. 2004;13(6):661-665. [PMID: 15483458]

Item 62   Answer: D

Educational Objective: Diagnose aldosterone excess in a patient with resistant hypertension.

Obtaining a plasma aldosterone-plasma renin activity ratio (ARR) is indicated for this patient. He has resistant hypertension, which is defined as blood pressure that remains above goal despite the administration of three antihypertensive drugs, one of which is a diuretic. A high proportion of patients with resistant hypertension have secondary hypertension due to primary hyperaldosteronism or renovascular hypertension; therefore, these conditions should be excluded in patients with resistant hypertension. Primary hyperaldosteronism is inconsistently associated with hypokalemia, and its absence in a patient with resistant hypertension should not influence the decision to screen for this condition. The ARR is a screening test for primary hyperaldosteronism. The normal range varies among institutions because renin and aldosterone assays may differ, but an ARR above 25 is generally considered abnormal. An elevated ARR alone is not diagnostic of primary hyperaldosteronism unless nonsuppressible or autonomous aldosterone excess is demonstrated by the presence of a urine aldosterone excretion of 12 micrograms/24 h (33.2 nmol/24 h) or higher obtained after correction of hypokalemia and adherence to a high-sodium diet for 3 days. In some patients, administering an intravenous saline infusion also may demonstrate nonsuppressible serum aldosterone levels. Both medical and surgical management have proved effective in the treatment of aldosterone excess.

The substitution of a loop diuretic such as furosemide for a thiazide diuretic is recommended in patients with difficult to control hypertension and chronic kidney disease or hypervolemic states. This patient has normal kidney function and no evidence of hypervolemia; therefore, the substitution is unlikely to affect his blood pressure.

Aliskiren is not a more effective antihypertensive agent than lisinopril. More importantly, evaluating for potential secondary causes of resistant hypertension is a more effective long-term strategy to control this patient's blood pressure than is switching to a new drug.

Atherosclerotic renovascular disease is usually associated with widespread atherosclerosis, peripheral vascular disease, cardiovascular disease, and ischemic target organ damage. This patient has no risk factors for renovascular hypertension; therefore, kidney Doppler ultrasonography is not warranted at this time.

KEY POINT

- A high proportion of patients with resistant hypertension have secondary hypertension due to primary hyperaldosteronism or renovascular hypertension.

Bibliography

Rossi GP. Diagnosis and treatment of primary aldosteronism. Rev Endocr Metab Disord. 2011;12(1):27-36. [PMID: 21369868]

Item 63   Answer: D

Educational Objective: Diagnose pigment nephropathy from rhabdomyolysis.

The most likely diagnosis is pigment nephropathy from rhabdomyolysis, which develops when muscle injury leads to the release of myoglobin and other intracellular muscle contents into the circulation. Nephrotoxicity results from kidney ischemia and tubular obstruction. Rhabdomyolysis most commonly develops after exposure to myotoxic drugs, infection, excessive exertion, or prolonged immobilization. Diagnosis should be considered in patients with a serum creatine kinase level above 5000 units/L. Another clue is heme positivity on urine dipstick testing in the absence of significant hematuria. The dipstick heme assay detects the presence of myoglobin. This patient presented with bruises and lacerations from a fight, and he was found immobile after consuming alcohol, all of which are risk factors for muscle damage and rhabdomyolysis. His high urine sodium and granular casts suggests intrinsic renal damage.

Patients with acute interstitial nephritis should have a suspicious medication exposure, which is not part of this patient's history.

Hepatorenal syndrome is associated with a significant history of liver disease and a low urine sodium, neither of which is seen in this patient.

Patients with intra-abdominal compartment syndrome usually have had surgery or massive volume resuscitation as well as a tense abdomen on physical examination, usually in a critical care setting.

KEY POINT

- **Rhabdomyolysis is a cause of intrinsic renal disease associated with high urine sodium, high fractional excretion of sodium, pigmented casts, and a history suggestive of muscle damage.**

Bibliography

Bosch X, Poch E, Grau JM. Rhabdomyolysis and acute kidney injury [erratum in N Engl J Med. 2011;364(20):1982]. N Engl J Med. 2009;361(1):62-72. [PMID: 19571284]

Item 64   Answer: A

Educational Objective: Manage primary membranous glomerulopathy.

The most appropriate treatment for this patient is an ACE inhibitor to control blood pressure and to reduce proteinuria as well as a statin to manage hyperlipidemia. This patient has primary membranous glomerulopathy, which frequently presents as the nephrotic syndrome and can be accompanied by hematuria, hypertension, kidney failure, and thromboembolic events. Observational studies have identified male gender, age older than 50 years, elevated serum creatinine level or low glomerular filtration rate (GFR), hypertension, secondary glomerulosclerosis, and chronic tubulointerstitial changes observed on biopsy at the time of diagnosis as risk factors associated with progressive chronic kidney disease (CKD). During follow-up or monitoring of kidney function, persistent proteinuria of ≥4 g/24 h for longer than 6 months and a decline in GFR over time are the most important risk factors associated with progression of primary membranous glomerulopathy to advanced CKD. In untreated primary membranous glomerulopathy, approximately two thirds of patients undergo spontaneous complete or partial remission, and only one third of patients have a persistent and/or progressive disease that may result in end-stage kidney disease within 10 years of onset. This patient has a low risk for disease progression, but she requires an ACE inhibitor to manage hypertension and proteinuria as well as a statin to manage hyperlipidemia. ACE inhibitors should be used cautiously in women of childbearing age, because these agents can be associated with severe congenital malformations.

Because of the potential toxicity of immunosuppressive therapies and the high rate of spontaneous remission of this disease, the clinical features and risk for disease progression should determine the most appropriate management in patients with primary membranous glomerulopathy. This patient has a low risk for CKD, and immunosuppressive agents should be initially avoided.

KEY POINT

- Low-risk primary membranous glomerulopathy is managed with an ACE inhibitor and a statin.

Bibliography
Cattran D. Management of membranous nephropathy: when and what for treatment. J Am Soc Nephrol. 2005;16(5):1188-1194. [PMID: 15800117]

Item 65   Answer: B
Educational Objective: Diagnose propofol-related infusion syndrome.

This patient most likely has propofol-related infusion syndrome, which is characterized by type B lactic acidosis, hypertriglyceridemia, rhabdomyolysis, and myocardial abnormalities seen as J-point elevation or a Brugada-like pattern on electrocardiogram. This rare syndrome occurs in approximately 1% of critically ill patients receiving propofol and most commonly occurs in those receiving doses above 4 mg/kg/h administered for more than 48 hours. The proposed mechanism involves the uncoupling of oxidative phosphorylation and energy production in mitochondria by propofol, coupled with the normal stress response to critical illness, to cause the characteristic findings of the syndrome. The findings of urine dipstick positivity for blood in the absence of hematuria consistent with rhabdomyolysis, lipemic serum, and unexplained anion gap acidosis in this critically ill patient receiving propofol support the diagnosis of propofol-related infusion syndrome. Treatment consists of discontinuing propofol and continued supportive care.

Fosphenytoin is not associated with significant metabolic abnormalities or an increased anion gap metabolic acidosis when appropriately dosed for kidney failure and potential drug interactions.

Propylene glycol is a solvent used in preparations of intravenous benzodiazepines (such as lorazepam and diazepam), and a lactic acidosis with an increased anion gap may occur in patients being treated with high doses of these medications, although the other findings in this patient are not associated with propylene glycol toxicity.

Pyroglutamic acidosis is usually observed in patients receiving therapeutic doses of acetaminophen in the setting of critical illness. Increased oxidative stress in patients receiving acetaminophen leads to depletion of glutathione stores, which disrupts the γ-glutamyl cycle and results in accumulation of pyroglutamic acid.

KEY POINT

- Propofol-related infusion syndrome is characterized by lactic acidosis, rhabdomyolysis, hypertriglyceridemia, and myocardial abnormalities on electrocardiogram.

Bibliography
Roberts RJ, Barletta JF, Fong JJ, et al. Incidence of propofol-related infusion syndrome in critically ill adults: a prospective, multicenter study. Crit Care. 2009;13(5):R169. [PMID: 19874582]

Item 66   Answer: D
Educational Objective: Treat a patient who has salicylate toxicity.

Sodium bicarbonate infusion is indicated for this patient with salicylate toxicity. Salicylate toxicity commonly presents with abnormalities in acid-base balance, the most common in adults being respiratory alkalosis, which occurs in response to stimulation of the medullary respiratory center. With more severe intoxication, increased anion gap metabolic acidosis develops both as a result of the salicylate anion and concomitant lactic and ketoacidosis. Early manifestations include tinnitus, confusion, tachypnea, and, occasionally, low-grade fever. Nausea and vomiting develop as a result of direct gastric mucosal toxicity. Management of salicylate poisoning depends on the magnitude of the serum salicylate level, the severity of clinical manifestations, and whether there is underlying kidney dysfunction. Alkalinization of the arterial pH to 7.5 to 7.6 is indicated to decrease intracellular uptake and toxicity of salicylic acid. Hydration and urine alkalinization to a pH of 7.5 to 8.0 will promote salicylate excretion. Follow-up serum salicylate levels, serum electrolyte levels, and acid-base parameters should be obtained at least every 2 hours to document improving clinical status. Hypokalemia, when present, should be corrected to prevent increased salicylate absorption in the distal tubule. Patients with impaired mentation warrant supplemental intravenous glucose to attenuate salicylate-induced neuroglycopenia.

H CONT.

Although acetazolamide increases urine pH by decreasing proximal bicarbonate reabsorption, the use of this medication in salicylate toxicity is contraindicated because of the associated decrease in systemic pH, which promotes intracellular uptake of salicylic acid and toxicity.

Hemodialysis is indicated in patients with serum salicylate levels that exceed 80 mg/dL (5.8 mmol/L), altered mentation, pulmonary edema, advanced kidney disease, or when the clinical status worsens despite optimal medical therapy, none of which is present in this patient.

In the absence of absolute indications, mechanical ventilation should be avoided in patients with salicylate poisoning to avoid decreasing the systemic pH, thereby promoting intracellular uptake of salicylate and associated toxicity.

KEY POINT

- **Management of salicylate toxicity depends on the magnitude of the serum salicylate level, the severity of clinical manifestations, and whether there is underlying kidney dysfunction.**

Bibliography

Bora K, Aaron C. Pitfalls in salicylate toxicity. Am J Emerg Med. 2010;28(3):383-384. [PMID: 20223401]

H **Item 67   Answer: D**

Educational Objective: Diagnose prerenal azotemia.

This patient most likely has prerenal azotemia. Prerenal azotemia generally occurs in patients with a mean arterial pressure below 60 mm Hg but may occur at higher pressures in patients with chronic kidney disease or in those who take medications, such as NSAIDs, that can alter glomerular hemodynamics. Patients with prerenal azotemia may have a history of decreased fluid intake accompanied by examination findings consistent with volume depletion. This patient was exposed to the sun for a prolonged period of time and took ibuprofen before going to the emergency department. She also takes hydrochlorothiazide daily for hypertension. Although her fractional excretion of sodium (FE_{Na}) is more than 1%, she is on a diuretic, which can increase the FE_{Na} even with prerenal azotemia. Because the fractional excretion of urea is less influenced by diuretics, it can be helpful in patients on diuretic therapy. It is calculated similarly to the FE_{Na} using the serum and urine urea levels. In prerenal azotemia, the fractional excretion of urea is below 35%, as in this patient. Finally, her urinalysis is concentrated, with hyaline casts and a high urine specific gravity.

Acute interstitial nephritis is most commonly caused by a hypersensitivity reaction to a medication. Urinalysis findings include leukocyte casts and eosinophils, neither of which is seen in this patient.

Acute tubular necrosis (ATN) is characterized by damage to the renal tubule due to a physiologic insult to the kidney such as hypoxia, toxins, or prolonged hypoperfusion. Kidney failure tends to be rapid, and the urine traditionally shows muddy brown casts. Although ATN may result from prolonged prerenal azotemia, this patient's clinical presentation and urinalysis are not consistent with this diagnosis.

This patient's lupus does not appear to be active, her urine is unremarkable for an active sediment (no dysmorphic erythrocytes or erythrocyte casts), and her urine protein is low in the setting of a concentrated urine, making lupus nephritis an unlikely diagnosis.

KEY POINT

- **Patients with prerenal azotemia may have a history of decreased fluid intake accompanied by examination findings consistent with volume depletion.**

Bibliography

Lameire N, Van Biesen W, Vanholder R. Acute renal failure. Lancet. 2005;365(9457):417-430. [PMID: 15680458]

Item 68   Answer: B

Educational Objective: Identify Balkan nephropathy as a cause of chronic tubulointerstitial nephritis.

The most likely diagnosis is Balkan nephropathy, a chronic tubulointerstitial condition of unclear cause found in patients from southeastern Europe (the Balkan region). It is thought to be caused by aristolochic acid, a plant alkaloid found in that region. Diagnostic criteria include epidemiologic criteria, decreased glomerular filtration rate, urine protein excretion of less than 1 g/24 h, and exclusion of other kidney diseases. There is an increased risk of urothelial cancers in these patients; therefore, physicians should have a high index of suspicion for these cancers. This patient has chronic kidney disease (CKD), minimal proteinuria, and a relatively benign urine sediment consistent with chronic tubulointerstitial disease. She is from Romania, which has areas with a very high incidence of Balkan nephropathy. She also has a cousin who has CKD and is possibly from the same area.

Analgesic nephropathy can result from exposure to large quantities of particular analgesics over years. This patient reports no history of high-dose exposure and is unlikely to have accumulated enough to result in analgesic nephropathy.

Hypertensive nephropathy can result after a long history of poorly controlled hypertension. Given her diagnosis of hypertension at the time of her CKD diagnosis, it is unlikely that her hypertension was poorly controlled for a prolonged period of time and is unlikely to be the cause of her CKD.

Patients with IgA nephropathy at this later stage of kidney disease are unlikely to exhibit no hematuria and only trace protein.

> **KEY POINT**
>
> - Balkan nephropathy is a chronic tubulointerstitial condition found in patients from southeastern Europe (the Balkan region) that is thought to be caused by aristolochic acid.

Bibliography

Stefanović V, Polenaković M. Fifty years of research in Balkan endemic nephropathy: where are we now? Nephron Clin Pract. 2009;112(2):c51-c56. [PMID: 19390202]

Item 69   Answer: B

Educational Objective: Treat a patient who has symptomatic hyponatremia.

This patient has symptomatic hypotonic hyponatremia, and a rapid increase in the serum sodium level using 3% saline infusion is indicated. The low plasma osmolality associated with a urine sodium level exceeding 40 meq/L (40 mmol/L) and urine osmolality greater than 200 mosm/kg H_2O in this patient without evidence of hypovolemia is most consistent with the syndrome of inappropriate antidiuretic hormone secretion (SIADH) as the cause of her hyponatremia. Infusion of 3% saline is used to treat patients who have SIADH with symptomatic hyponatremia because infusion of 0.9% (normal) saline can result in excretion of most of the infused sodium and retention of a significant portion of the infused water, leading to positive water balance and worsening hyponatremia. Because of its hypertonicity, 3% saline rapidly increases the serum sodium level but must be used with great caution to avoid overcorrection and the risk of central nervous system damage resulting from changes in plasma osmolality. Recent evidence suggests than an increase in the serum sodium level by approximately 4 to 6 meq/L (4-6 mmol/L) over the first 24 hours is sufficient in symptomatic patients. If the extracellular fluid osmolality rapidly normalizes in a patient with chronic hyponatremia, cell shrinkage may occur and can precipitate osmotic demyelination syndrome. Correction that exceeds the maximal limits of 10 meq/L (10 mmol/L) in the first 24 hours and/or 18 meq/L (18 mmol/L) in the first 48 hours should therefore be reversed with infusion of hypotonic intravenous solutions such as 5% dextrose in water and possibly concurrent administration of intravenous subcutaneous desmopressin.

Furosemide can be used as adjunctive management of hyponatremia caused by SIADH because this agent interferes with urinary concentration, thus increasing water excretion. However, the rapidity of correction expected with furosemide alone is insufficient to increase the serum sodium to an appropriate level in a symptomatic patient. Furosemide may be of benefit to patients with chronic asymptomatic hyponatremia due to SIADH, particularly when the urine osmolality exceeds 400 mosm/kg H_2O, by causing excretion of a more dilute urine.

Tolvaptan, an oral V_2 receptor vasopressin antagonist, is approved to treat patients with asymptomatic euvolemic and hypervolemic hyponatremia. However, the safety of this agent in the management of symptomatic hyponatremia has yet to be established, and too rapid correction and overcorrection of the serum sodium level have been reported.

> **KEY POINT**
>
> - Patients with symptomatic hyponatremia due to the syndrome of inappropriate antidiuretic hormone secretion require a rapid increase in the serum sodium level using 3% saline infusion.

Bibliography

Sterns RH, Hix JK, Silver S. Treating profound hyponatremia: a strategy for controlled correction. Am J Kidney Dis. 2010;56(4):774-779. [PMID: 20709440]

Item 70   Answer: B

Educational Objective: Manage hypertension in a woman of childbearing age.

This patient has essential hypertension and should be switched from lisinopril to labetalol before pregnancy. Exposure to ACE inhibitors such as lisinopril during the first trimester has been associated with fetal cardiac abnormalities, and exposure during the second and third trimesters has been associated with neonatal kidney failure and death. Angiotensin receptor antagonists such as losartan have been associated with similar fetal toxicity as ACE inhibitors, most likely because of the dependence of the fetal kidney on the renin-angiotensin system. Therefore, both of these agents are pregnancy category X drugs and are contraindicated throughout pregnancy and in women planning to conceive.

Labetalol is a pregnancy risk category C drug and is commonly used during pregnancy owing to its combined α- and β-blocking properties and because it does not compromise uteroplacental blood flow. Methyldopa also is used extensively in pregnancy and is one of the only agents in which long-term follow-up of infants exposed in utero has proved to be safe. Furthermore, methyldopa is the only agent classified as a pregnancy category B drug. However, controlling blood pressure with single-agent methyldopa is often difficult, and many women are bothered by its sedating properties.

Cessation of antihypertensive therapy in a patient with hypertension is not recommended before pregnancy.

Aldosterone antagonists such as spironolactone have an antiandrogenic effect on the fetus when exposure occurs during the first trimester and should be avoided in women planning to conceive.

Bibliography

Cooper WO, Hernandez-Diaz S, Arbogast PG, et al. Major congenital malformations after first-trimester exposure to ACE inhibitors. N Engl J Med. 2006;354(23):2443-2451. [PMID: 16760444]

Item 71   Answer: A

Educational Objective: Prevent diabetic nephropathy in a patient with type 2 diabetes mellitus and hypertension.

An ACE inhibitor is indicated for this patient with type 2 diabetes mellitus who has hypertension and normal urine albumin excretion. Because of the increased risk of cardiovascular and kidney disease associated with diabetes, control of hypertension is essential in the management of patients with diabetes. Although the benefit of treatment of hypertension with ACE inhibitors has been well established in diabetic patients with albuminuria by preventing progression of proteinuria and subsequent decline in glomerular filtration rate, there is also evidence that interruption of the renin-angiotensin system may decrease the risk of developing microalbuminuria in hypertensive, type 2 diabetic patients. This effect of treating hypertension with an ACE inhibitor (or angiotensin receptor blocker [ARB]) in these patients with normal urine albumin excretion appears to be independent of the achieved blood pressure compared with similar hypertension control with other antihypertensive agents. In diabetes, glomerular hyperfiltration mediated by the renin-angiotensin-aldosterone system is very important in the pathogenesis and progression of diabetic nephropathy. The use of ACE inhibitors or ARBs reduces the glomerular hyperfiltration. This patient's blood pressure is greater than 140/90 mm Hg, and he is unlikely to reach his goal with lifestyle modifications alone. Therefore, he requires pharmacologic treatment, preferentially with an ACE inhibitor or ARB, for his hypertension until he reaches the American Diabetes Association recommended blood pressure goal of less than 130/80 mm Hg for patients with diabetes.

Other antihypertensives such as β-blockers, calcium channel blockers, and diuretics lower blood pressure but do not affect the glomerular hyperfiltration. Therefore, these antihypertensive classes are not first-line agents but may be considered for combination use if patients do not achieve their blood pressure goal with ACE inhibitor or ARB monotherapy or if they do not tolerate ACE inhibitors or ARBs.

Bibliography

American Diabetes Association. Standards of medical care in diabetes–2012. Diabetes Care. 2012;35(suppl 1):S11-S63. [PMID: 22187469]

Item 72   Answer: D

Educational Objective: Manage polyoma BK virus–associated nephropathy in a kidney transplant recipient.

A decrease in immunosuppression is indicated for this patient with evidence of polyoma BK virus–associated nephropathy. This patient is a recent kidney transplant recipient and now has a decline in kidney function. Polyoma BK virus is an increasingly recognized cause of graft nephropathy. Although infection is asymptomatic in most persons, it often causes clinical disease in immunosuppressed patients. As the virus infects uroepithelial cells, viral activity in immunosuppressed kidney transplant patients is particularly problematic. Screening with polymerase chain reaction testing and urine cytology is recommended in the first year following transplantation and when there is a decline in kidney function. This patient is positive for polyoma BK virus, and his urinalysis is abnormal with erythrocytes, leukocytes, and some leukocyte casts, which is suggestive of interstitial nephritis. Kidney transplant biopsy provides the definitive diagnosis and shows evidence of polyoma BK virus–associated nephropathy with inflammation of the tubules and viral inclusions in the tubular epithelial cells. Initial treatment is directed at decreasing the immunosuppression. This patient's immunosuppression should be lowered by reducing the dose of either or both of his antirejection medications to as great a degree as possible without jeopardizing graft survival. This intervention may be adequate to control the activity of the infection.

If decreased immunosuppression is not effective, several agents show activity against polyoma BK virus, including fluoroquinolones, leflunomide, and cidofovir (off-label use). Most common antiviral agents, including ganciclovir and acyclovir, appear to have little activity against this virus.

Muromonab-CD3, a monoclonal antibody against the CD3 receptor on lymphocytes, acts to deplete lymphocytes and increase immunosuppression, which would likely exacerbate the infection rather than control it.

KEY POINT

- Screening for polyoma BK virus is recommended in kidney transplant recipients in the first year after transplantation and when there is a decline in kidney function.

Bibliography

Barraclough KA, Isbel NM, Staatz CE, Johnson DW. BK virus in kidney transplant recipients: the influence of immunosuppression. J Transplant. 2011;2011:750836. [PMID: 21766009]

Item 73   Answer: C

Educational Objective: Screen for chronic kidney disease in a patient with diabetes mellitus.

A spot urine albumin–creatinine ratio is indicated to evaluate this patient for chronic kidney disease (CKD). She has type 2 diabetes mellitus, a population that is at risk for CKD, and testing for microalbuminuria is appropriate. The National Kidney Foundation and the American Diabetes Association recommend annual testing to assess urine albumin excretion in patients with type 1 diabetes of 5 years' duration and in all patients with type 2 diabetes starting at the time of diagnosis by measuring the albumin–creatinine ratio. Microalbuminuria is defined as an albumin–creatinine ratio of 30 to 300 mg/g; diagnosis requires an elevated albumin–creatinine ratio on two of three random samples obtained over 6 months. Patients with diabetes and microalbuminuria are at increased risk for progression of CKD and cardiovascular disease. Use of ACE inhibitors or angiotensin receptor blockers delays progression in patients with proteinuric kidney disease or in patients with diabetes and microalbuminuria, underscoring the importance of early detection.

The gold standard for measuring urine protein excretion is a 24-hour urine collection. However, this test is cumbersome and unreliable if not collected correctly. Patients have a difficult time accurately collecting urine for 24 hours, in addition to keeping it on ice. Therefore, the National Kidney Foundation Kidney Disease Outcomes Quality Initiative (NKF KDOQI) recommends use of urinary ratios on random urine samples as an alternative method of estimating proteinuria in the clinical assessment of kidney disease. Furthermore, a 24-hour urine collection may not diagnose low-grade microalbuminuria.

Kidney ultrasonography can be performed once a diagnosis of CKD is made but should not be used to screen for CKD.

Although this patient has an estimated glomerular filtration rate of >60 mL/min/1.73 m² and normal urinalysis results, she has diabetes and should therefore be evaluated for CKD.

KEY POINT

- The National Kidney Foundation and the American Diabetes Association recommend annual testing to assess urine albumin excretion in patients with type 1 diabetes mellitus of 5 years' duration and in all patients with type 2 diabetes starting at the time of diagnosis by measuring the albumin–creatinine ratio.

Bibliography

KDOQI. KDOQI clinical practice guidelines and clinical practice recommendations for diabetes and chronic kidney disease. Am J Kidney Dis. 2007;49(2 suppl 2):S12-S154. [PMID: 17276798]

Item 74   Answer: D

Educational Objective: Manage hyperkalemia and hypertension in a patient with chronic kidney disease.

Increasing the furosemide dose is appropriate to manage hypertension and hyperkalemia in this patient with chronic kidney disease (CKD). Managing hypertension is indicated for all patients with kidney disease and is critical in the management of CKD regardless of the underlying etiology. Controlling blood pressure helps to decrease cardiovascular risk and may help to prevent progression to end-stage kidney disease. ACE inhibitors (such as lisinopril) or angiotensin receptor blockers (ARBs) are the preferred antihypertensive agents in patients with CKD, especially in those with proteinuria. ACE inhibitors and ARBs reduce efferent arteriolar resistance and lower intraglomerular pressure. The lower intraglomerular pressure is thought to be protective for the kidney but may be associated with a slight increase in the serum creatinine level. An increase in the serum creatinine of up to 30% after initiation of ACE inhibitors or ARBs is acceptable. Use of these agents also may cause hyperkalemia. Management of hyperkalemia using diuretics is preferred, especially in patients with hypertension. Diuretics are effective agents for blood pressure control in patients with CKD and are also useful in those with edema. Patients with CKD usually require higher diuretic doses to be effective. This patient remains hypertensive despite the increase in lisinopril dose. Increasing the furosemide dose should reduce intravascular volume, a common contributor to hypertension in patients with CKD and lower blood pressure.

Sodium polystyrene sulfonate can lower the serum potassium level but would have minimal effect on blood pressure and also causes gastrointestinal side effects.

Although spironolactone may help improve blood pressure control, its mechanism of aldosterone blockade will decrease urine potassium loss and may result in worsening hyperkalemia. Because of this, spironolactone should be used with caution in patients with CKD and in those on medications that may increase the serum potassium, and only with close monitoring of the serum potassium level.

Although discontinuing or lowering the ACE inhibitor (lisinopril) dose should help lower this patient's serum potassium level, these actions do not address the high blood pressure and likely would result in higher blood pressure.

> **KEY POINT**
>
> - In patients with chronic kidney disease, adding a diuretic, particularly a loop diuretic such as furosemide, can enhance the antihypertensive and antiproteinuric effects of antihypertensive agents and lower serum potassium concentration.

Bibliography

Ernst ME, Gordon JA. Diuretic therapy: key aspects in hypertension and renal disease. J Nephrol. 2010;23(5):487-493. [PMID: 20677164]

Item 75   Answer: C

Educational Objective: Diagnose nephrolithiasis using noncontrast abdominal helical CT.

Noncontrast abdominal helical CT is indicated for this patient with symptoms of renal colic. Distal ureteral stones may cause pain that radiates to the testicle in men or to the labia majora in women because the pain is referred from the ilioinguinal or genitofemoral nerves. A detailed physical examination, including that of the genitals, is appropriate. Noncontrast abdominal helical CT is the gold standard for diagnosing nephrolithiasis. This study can identify all types of kidney stones along the urinary tract with a sensitivity of more than 95% and is also able to detect associated urinary tract obstruction, if present.

Abdominal radiography of the kidneys, ureters, and bladder (KUB) is sometimes useful in the chronic management of patients with calcium-containing kidney stones. KUB can be used to follow the stone burden or to help with planning for surgical interventions. In the acute setting, KUB is not sufficiently sensitive or specific to guide management; patients may have bowel gas, extrarenal calcifications, or radiolucent stones that limit characterization.

Intravenous pyelography had previously been the standard imaging modality for nephrolithiasis, which utilizes intravenous contrast to characterize the anatomy, site, and size of stones, if present. However, this modality is rarely used currently because of the superiority of the images obtained by CT and the need for contrast exposure. It is also a more labor-intensive test that may require multiple delayed images.

Testicular ultrasonography is beneficial if testicular torsion is suspected and can identify other anatomic abnormalities of the testes, including tumors, hernia, abscess, or testicular rupture from trauma. However, the typical age range for testicular torsion is 12 to 18 years, and this patient's testicular examination is normal.

> **KEY POINT**
>
> - Noncontrast abdominal helical CT is the gold standard for diagnosing nephrolithiasis.

Bibliography

Coursey CA, Casalino DD, Remer EM, et al; Expert Panel on Urologic Imaging. ACR Appropriateness Criteria® acute onset flank pain–suspicion of stone disease. Guideline Summary. U.S. Department of Health and Human Services Web site. Available at www.guidelines.gov/content.aspx?id=32639&search=kidney+stone#Section420. Accessed July 24, 2012.

Item 76   Answer: A

Educational Objective: Manage proximal (type 2) renal tubular acidosis.

Discontinuation of tenofovir is appropriate. This patient has proximal (type 2) renal tubular acidosis (RTA) most likely related to tenofovir therapy for HIV infection. Her urine pH is less than 5.5, indicating preserved distal tubular function and urine acidification. Glycosuria in a patient with a normal glucose level, tubular-range proteinuria, and hypophosphatemia consequent to decreased proximal tubular reabsorption of phosphate, as observed in this patient, is most consistent with proximal RTA. The response to alkali therapy can serve as an important clue to the diagnosis. Patients with proximal RTA often require 10 to 15 meq/kg/d to correct the acidosis, whereas patients with distal RTA usually require only 1 to 2 meq/kg/d. The mechanism of kidney injury due to tenofovir is believed to be drug-related damage to mitochondrial DNA, noted most significantly in the renal tubules and causing tubular dysfunction. Patients taking tenofovir should therefore be monitored closely for evidence of kidney injury while on treatment. Drug withdrawal is indicated if nephrotoxicity is present; most patients show improvement in kidney function over weeks to months after stopping the medication, although permanent tubulointerstitial damage is possible.

The trimethoprim component of trimethoprim-sulfamethoxazole tends to cause hyperkalemia but not hypokalemia as noted in this patient. Trimethoprim, particularly in acid urine, blocks the epithelial sodium channel in the cortical collecting duct, leading to increased lumen positive potential, impaired potassium and proton secretion, hyperkalemia, and metabolic acidosis. This effect is more common with high doses of parenteral trimethoprim-sulfamethoxazole or when there is concomitant blockade of the renin-angiotensin-aldosterone system. Trimethoprim can also decrease the tubular secretion of creatinine, leading to a reversible increase in the serum creatinine level (usually up to approximately 0.5 mg/dL [44.2 micromoles/L]) that does not reflect a true decrease in glomerular filtration rate.

Lactic acid is a normal by-product of cellular metabolism, but when elevated due to overproduction or decreased metabolism, it causes an increased anion gap metabolic acidosis. Because the metabolic acidosis in this patient is associated with a normal anion gap, lactic acidosis as a cause of her acid-base disturbance is not likely.

Laxative abuse can cause normal anion gap metabolic acidosis when bicarbonate losses exceed hypokalemic-induced enhanced ammoniagenesis. This does not explain the glycosuria and hypophosphatemia consistent with proximal RTA seen in this patient.

KEY POINT

- Medications such as tenofovir can cause proximal (type 2) renal tubular acidosis, and discontinuation of the offending agent is indicated.

Bibliography

Unwin RJ, Luft FC, Shirley DG. Pathophysiology and management of hypokalemia: a clinical perspective. Nat Rev Nephrol. 2011;7(2):75-84. [PMID: 21278718]

Item 77   Answer: A

Educational Objective: Diagnose abdominal compartment syndrome.

This patient has abdominal compartment syndrome (ACS), which is defined by new organ dysfunction in the setting of a sustained, abnormal increase in the intra-abdominal pressure. Intra-abdominal pressure is normally between 0 and 5 mm Hg and is usually maintained in that range by the significant compliance of the abdominal wall. However, when a pathologic process (such as massive ascites, volume overload, or intra-abdominal or retroperitoneal hemorrhage) is present, the pressure may exceed the ability of the abdominal wall to compensate. Intra-abdominal hypertension is defined by sustained intra-abdominal pressures greater than 12 mm Hg; ACS occurs when the pressure exceeds 20 mm Hg and is accompanied by new organ dysfunction. The exact pathophysiology of ACS is uncertain, but high intra-abdominal pressure may adversely affect kidney function. Patients with a distended abdomen in the setting of aggressive fluid resuscitation and recent abdominal surgery should be evaluated for ACS. Measurement of the intravesicular pressure through a bladder catheter is the most common method for assessing the intra-abdominal pressure; although this value may not be identical to a directly measured intra-abdominal pressure, bladder pressure measurement appears to correlate adequately to be used in clinical decision making. Surgical decompression of the abdomen is often necessary to definitively treat ACS.

Aminoglycosides are well-known nephrotoxins. However, a single dose of tobramycin makes this a less likely cause of acute kidney injury (AKI), and aminoglycoside nephrotoxicity cannot account for this patient's increased intra-abdominal pressure.

Although kidney injury from ACS may appear prerenal because it is often associated with low blood pressures, the isosthenuric urine with a fractional excretion of sodium greater than 1% and the patient's unresponsiveness to fluids make this diagnosis less likely.

Although obstruction may have similar pathophysiology to ACS, the presence of an indwelling bladder catheter and lack of hydronephrosis on ultrasound suggest a different etiology of the AKI.

KEY POINT

- Abdominal compartment syndrome occurs when intra-abdominal pressure exceeds 20 mm Hg and is accompanied by new organ dysfunction.

Bibliography

De Waele JJ, De Laet I, Kirkpatrick AW, Hoste E. Intra-abdominal hypertension and abdominal compartment syndrome. Am J Kidney Dis. 2011;57(1):159-169. [PMID: 21184922]

Item 78   Answer: D

Educational Objective: Diagnose minimal change glomerulopathy.

Minimal change glomerulopathy (MCG) associated with lithium use is the cause of the nephrotic syndrome in this patient. MCG is usually idiopathic, but it also can be associated with atopic diseases; infections such as mononucleosis; malignancies such as Hodgkin lymphoma or carcinomas; and the use of NSAIDS, lithium, or rifampin. MCG usually presents as the nephrotic syndrome and may be accompanied by acute kidney injury, hematuria, and hypertension. Diagnosis is confirmed with kidney biopsy that reveals diffuse fusion and effacement of podocyte foot processes on electron microscopy with normal glomeruli by light and immunofluorescence microscopies. Lithium potentiates tumor necrosis factor– and interleukin-1–induced cytokines and cytokine receptor expression in T-cell hybridomas. It also accelerates interleukin-2 production in human T cells. These effects may have a role in podocyte toxicity and may explain why some patients develop massive proteinuria.

Lupus nephritis is unlikely in the absence of other findings associated with systemic lupus erythematosus and a negative antinuclear antibody titer.

Hepatitis C virus–associated glomerulonephritis, lupus nephritis, and membranous glomerulopathy always exhibit immune complex deposition on immunofluorescence microscopy.

KEY POINT

- Minimal change glomerulopathy is usually idiopathic, but it also can be associated with atopic diseases; infections such as mononucleosis; malignancies such as Hodgkin lymphoma or carcinomas; and the use of NSAIDS, lithium, or rifampin.

Bibliography

Jefferson JA, Nelson PJ, Najafian B, Shankland SJ. Podocyte disorders: Core Curriculum 2011. Am J Kidney Dis. 2011;58(4):666-677. [PMID: 21868143]

Item 79   Answer: D
Educational Objective: Treat a patient who has a kidney stone.

Treatment with tamsulosin is indicated for this patient who has a kidney stone that became symptomatic several days ago. The stone is of moderate size at 4 mm. Ninety percent of stones less than 5 mm pass spontaneously. In contrast, stones that are more than 10 mm are unlikely to pass without intervention. Although several days have passed, there is still a significant chance that he will pass the stone without surgical intervention. To increase the chance of stone passage, medical expulsive therapy using the α-blocker tamsulosin or a calcium channel blocker such as nifedipine should be employed. Tamsulosin is a very well-tolerated drug with mild side effects such as dizziness or rhinitis. This agent causes very little of the postural hypotension seen with other α_1-adrenergic antagonists and is generally better tolerated than a calcium channel blocker. Utilization of these agents for the facilitation of kidney stone passage is off label but common practice for stones less than 10 mm and well-controlled symptoms and is recommended by the American Urological Association and the European Association of Urology.

24-Hour urine collections are essential to identify specific abnormalities in urine composition and to tailor therapy for patients with a propensity to nephrolithiasis. Collections should be performed several weeks after stone passage when the patient is consuming his or her regular diet.

Patients who do not have an urgent indication for urologic intervention may still require intervention if the stone does not pass after a period of observation. The choice of intervention may depend on characteristics of the stone and practice of the particular center. Extracorporeal shock wave lithotripsy is a widely used, noninvasive strategy used to treat symptomatic calculi located in the proximal ureter or within the kidney.

Repeat imaging by noncontrast CT would expose the patient to more radiation without providing additional important diagnostic or prognostic information and is not indicated at this time.

Stones located in the distal ureter are usually accessible by directed therapy guided by ureteroscopy. During ureteroscopy, "intracorporeal" lithotripsy can be performed using lasers, ultrasonography, or other techniques. However, this intervention is premature at this time.

KEY POINT

- **Medical expulsive therapy using the α-blocker tamsulosin or a calcium channel blocker such as nifedipine is appropriate to increase the chance of passage of kidney stones less than 10 mm in patients with well-controlled symptoms.**

Bibliography

Parsons JK, Hergan LA, Sakamoto K, Lakin C. Efficacy of alpha-blockers for the treatment of ureteral stones. J Urol. 2007;177(3):983-987. [PMID: 17296392]

Item 80   Answer: C   H
Educational Objective: Diagnose normotensive ischemic acute kidney injury.

This patient most likely has normotensive ischemic acute kidney injury (AKI), which results when a patient with vascular risk factors and hypertension attains a blood pressure lower than usual measurements. If the new blood pressure is lower than the patient's range of renal autoregulation, an increased serum creatinine level due to renal hypoperfusion may result. This patient's medical history suggests underlying chronic kidney and vascular disease, which increase his risk for a normotensive ischemic insult. His lower blood pressure in the hospital may be the result of his infection, better adherence to medications, and/or diet. The findings of an elevated fractional excretion of sodium, fractional excretion of urea, granular casts on urinalysis, and normal kidney ultrasound are all consistent with this diagnosis.

Acute interstitial nephritis, which is most often caused by a hypersensitivity reaction to a medication, usually occurs after 1 week of exposure to the offending agent. This patient's lack of rash, fever, and leukocytes or erythrocytes on urinalysis also argues against this diagnosis.

Cholesterol crystal embolization may cause AKI in patients with aortic atherosclerotic plaques. This condition may occur spontaneously but most often develops after coronary or kidney angiography or aortic surgery. Anticoagulation with heparin, warfarin, or thrombolytic agents is believed to help incite this condition. It is associated with cutaneous and extrarenal manifestations and a bland urine sediment. Although this patient likely has underlying vascular disease, he has not had an invasive procedure or anticoagulation and lacks any of the associated skin or extrarenal manifestations of the syndrome, making this diagnosis less likely.

Patients with prerenal azotemia may have a history of fluid losses and decreased fluid intake accompanied by physical examination findings consistent with extracellular fluid volume depletion. Two findings make prerenal azotemia unlikely in this patient: fractional excretion of sodium above 2% and fractional excretion of urea above 50% (more reliable than fractional excretion of sodium for patients on diuretics). These findings are more consistent with acute tubular necrosis.

KEY POINT

- **Normotensive ischemic acute kidney injury can occur when patients with vascular risk factors and hypertension attain a blood pressure lower than their usual measurements.**

Bibliography

Abuelo JG. Normotensive ischemic acute renal failure. N Engl J Med. 2007;357(8):797-805. [PMID: 17715412]

Item 81   Answer: A

Educational Objective: Manage enteric hyperoxaluria in a patient who has a calcium oxalate stone.

Calcium carbonate supplements are indicated for this patient. Following gastric bypass surgery, she has developed kidney stones most likely caused by enteric hyperoxaluria. Her urinalysis shows the presence of characteristic calcium oxalate crystals in the urine sediment and a high specific gravity, which suggest that the urine is very concentrated. She also has a low urine volume of 1300 mL/24 h; patients with kidney stones should aim for at least 2000 mL of urine daily. Fatty acid malabsorption may occur following gastric bypass surgery and other causes of enteric hyperoxaluria. In this patient, oxalate absorption is increased because calcium, which normally binds to oxalate in the gut and limits oxalate absorption, binds to fatty acids. At the same time, the colon is exposed to insoluble bile salts and fatty acids, which increase the permeability to small molecules such as oxalate. Management of enteric hyperoxaluria includes a low fat diet and calcium carbonate supplementation to decrease oxalate absorption and excretion in the urine, coupled with aggressive oral hydration to decrease the concentration of the urine, both of which encourage stone formation.

Thiazide diuretics are useful to manage hypercalciuria because these agents promote reabsorption of urine calcium in the distal tubule. However, this patient's urine calcium level is normal.

Potassium citrate is useful in treating patients who have low urine citrate, which serves as an important inhibitor of crystallization by chelating urine calcium. Potassium citrate also is essential for treating patients with uric acid stones. This patient has both a normal urine citrate and uric acid excretion.

The α-blocker tamsulosin can be used to promote the movement of a stone along the ureter but will not affect the tendency to develop new stones.

KEY POINT

- **Management of enteric hyperoxaluria includes a low fat diet, calcium carbonate supplementation, and aggressive oral hydration.**

Bibliography

Kumar R, Lieske JC, Collazo-Clavell ML, et al. Fat malabsorption and increased intestinal oxalate absorption are common after Roux-en-Y gastric bypass surgery. Surgery. 2011;149(5):654-661. [PMID: 21295813]

Item 82   Answer: C

Educational Objective: Identify over-the-counter medication use as a cause of elevated blood pressure.

This patient should discontinue his over-the-counter medications and his blood pressure should be rechecked. He has chronic kidney disease (CKD) and may be taking an over-the-counter sinus decongestant, which often contains pseudoephedrine or phenylephrine, and/or an NSAID, medications that can elevate blood pressure. In the clinical setting of elevated blood pressure in a patient with previously well-controlled hypertension, exogenous factors such as new medications should be considered. Any suspicious medications should be stopped and the blood pressure followed for resolution.

The combination of an ACE inhibitor and an angiotensin receptor blocker (ARB) such as losartan to decrease the degree of proteinuria in patients with CKD is associated with significant adverse effects and unclear effects on kidney disease outcome. However, using combination therapy in patients with IgA nephropathy has not been studied extensively, and some clinicians use this intervention if the level of proteinuria and blood pressure are not adequately controlled with monotherapy. Dual treatment is not indicated in this patient, given his otherwise stable kidney function and lower level proteinuria.

Although an upper respiratory infection suggests a possible link to IgA nephropathy, the patient's urine studies do not support an exacerbation of IgA nephropathy. His serum creatinine level, microscopic hematuria, and proteinuria are at baseline; therefore, his increased blood pressure is not likely associated with worsening of his IgA nephropathy, and treatment with immunosuppression is not indicated.

ACE inhibitor or ARB therapy is a primary intervention to treat the proteinuria and hypertension frequently associated with IgA nephropathy. Increasing this patient's lisinopril dose may be appropriate if his blood pressure remains elevated, although exclusion of other causes of worsening blood pressure is important before making any dose adjustment, particularly given his previously effective blood pressure control and stable proteinuria.

KEY POINT

- **Over-the-counter medications can contribute to hypertension in patients with chronic kidney disease.**

Bibliography

Spence JD. Physiologic tailoring of treatment in resistant hypertension. Curr Cardiol Rev. 2010;6(2):119-123. [PMID: 21532778]

Item 83   Answer: D

Educational Objective: Diagnose rapidly progressive glomerulonephritis.

This patient most likely has rapidly progressive glomerulonephritis (RPGN), a clinical syndrome characterized by urine findings consistent with glomerular disease and rapid loss of kidney function over a period of days, weeks, or months. RPGN is most typically due to either anti–glomerular basement membrane antibody disease, immune complex deposition (for example, lupus nephritis),

H
CONT.

or an ANCA-positive vasculitis. Glomerulonephritis is characterized by hematuria, oliguria, hypertension, and kidney insufficiency caused by glomerular inflammation. Urinalysis usually reveals hematuria as well as cellular and granular casts, and proteinuria is typically present. This patient is subacutely ill with generalized symptoms of decline, poorly controlled hypertension, and periorbital and lower extremity edema. These findings, along with the presence of erythrocyte casts on urinalysis, make the diagnosis of RPGN most likely in this patient.

Acute interstitial nephritis may present with hematuria but more predominantly with pyuria and leukocyte casts. Furthermore, poorly controlled hypertension and periorbital edema are not in the typical constellation of symptoms associated with this disorder.

Acute tubular necrosis (ATN) is a common form of intrarenal disease that usually occurs after a sustained period of ischemia or exposure to nephrotoxic agents. More than 70% of patients with ATN have muddy brown casts in the urine. This patient's rapid clinical course, absence of risk factors for ATN, and presence of erythrocyte casts are inconsistent with ATN.

Polyarteritis nodosa is a vasculitis of medium-sized vessels. Clinical features include hypertension, variable kidney insufficiency, and, occasionally, kidney infarction bleeding caused by renal artery microaneurysm rupture. Urinalysis may show hematuria and subnephrotic proteinuria; however, because there is no inflammation or necrosis of glomeruli, erythrocyte casts are not seen.

KEY POINT

- **Rapidly progressive glomerulonephritis is characterized by hematuria, oliguria, hypertension, and kidney injury caused by glomerular inflammation.**

Bibliography

Mukhtyar C, Guillevin L, Cid MC, et al; European Vasculitis Study Group. EULAR recommendations for the management of primary small and medium vessel vasculitis. Ann Rheum Dis. 2009;68(3):310-317. [PMID: 18413444]

Item 84   Answer: D

Educational Objective: Identify the cause of a patient's change in blood pressure.

A repeat blood pressure measurement is indicated for this patient to ensure proper technique. Poor technique in measuring blood pressure is a common cause of apparent fluctuations in blood pressure, particularly in the ambulatory setting. The American Heart Association recommendations require 5 minutes of rest, bladder empty, back supported with feet on the floor (not in the supine position on an examination table), and proper cuff size, with the cuff bladder encircling at least 80% of the arm. In general, blood pressure also should not be measured through clothing and coats because this may lead to inaccuracies. In a hurried

situation, several of the requirements for blood pressure measurement can be violated, leading to errors in readings, as noted in this patient. Despite its critical importance as a vital sign, surprisingly few health care workers receive formal training in proper blood pressure measurement. Errors in positioning the patient, incorrect cuff size relative to arm circumference, intercurrent conversation, and interferences such as recent caffeine intake or cigarette smoking contribute to variability in blood pressure measurement. The increasing use of devices that allow patients to have repeated blood pressure measurements without a health care worker (physician or nurse) in the room may obviate some of this controversy, although these may also be associated with different forms of technical error.

It is important to make adjustments to a patient's antihypertensive regimen, regardless of setting, only if the blood pressure measurements on which those adjustments are being made are accurate and reflect evidence of sustained, inadequate control.

Ambulatory blood pressure monitoring is used to diagnose white coat hypertension and masked hypertension and to determine whether treatment of hypertension is adequate outside the office or hospital setting. However, it is not indicated in this patient with generally well-controlled blood pressure and a single abnormal determination.

KEY POINT

- **Errors in positioning the patient, incorrect cuff size relative to arm circumference, intercurrent conversation, and interferences such as recent caffeine intake or cigarette smoking contribute to variability in blood pressure measurement.**

Bibliography

Chobanian AV, Bakris GL, Black HR, et al; National Heart, Lung, and Blood Institute Joint National Committee on Prevention, Detection, Evaluation, and Treatment of High Blood Pressure; National High Blood Pressure Education Program Coordinating Committee. The Seventh Report of the Joint National Committee on Prevention, Detection, Evaluation, and Treatment of High Blood Pressure: the JNC 7 report. JAMA. 2003;289(19):2560-2572. [PMID: 12748199]

Item 85   Answer: A

Educational Objective: Prevent preeclampsia.

Low-dose aspirin (75 to 150 mg/d) is associated with a 10% to 15% relative risk reduction in preventing preeclampsia and reducing adverse maternal and fetal outcomes. Preeclampsia is defined as a systolic blood pressure ≥140 mm Hg or a diastolic blood pressure ≥90 mm Hg and a 24-hour urine protein excretion greater than 300 mg/24 h after the 20th week of gestation in a woman who did not have hypertension or proteinuria earlier in pregnancy. Clinical manifestations of preeclampsia may include headache, visual disturbances, liver dysfunction, and fetal growth restriction. The HELLP (hemolysis, elevated liver enzymes, low platelets) syndrome is a variant of preeclampsia. Several factors are associated with an increased risk of preeclampsia, including a personal history of preeclampsia, chronic hypertension, chronic kidney disease, and a family history of preeclampsia. This patient is at risk for preeclampsia because of her family history of preeclampsia, the fact that she is primiparous, and her personal history of borderline hypertension. Currently, only low-dose aspirin has been shown to modestly decrease the risk of preeclampsia, and most experts recommend this agent to women at risk.

Methyldopa is a first-line agent in the treatment of hypertension in the setting of pregnancy but has not been shown to decrease the risk of preeclampsia from chronic hypertension.

Calcium supplements reduce hypertension and preeclampsia modestly only in women consuming a baseline low-calcium diet.

Intravenous magnesium sulfate is used as an anticonvulsant to prevent eclampsia, but oral formulations of magnesium have not been shown to prevent either preeclampsia or eclampsia.

Reducing blood pressure to less than 120/80 mm Hg has not been shown to decrease the risk of preeclampsia. Instead, blood pressure goals are less stringent than those used for nonpregnant persons and are aimed primarily at limiting maternal end-organ damage during this finite period. Specific targets vary somewhat by professional society but generally aim for less than 150/100 mm Hg.

KEY POINT

- **Low-dose aspirin (75 to 150 mg/d) is associated with a 10% to 15% relative risk reduction in preventing preeclampsia and reducing adverse maternal and fetal outcomes.**

Bibliography

American College of Obstetricians and Gynecologists. ACOG Practice Bulletin No. 125: chronic hypertension in pregnancy. Obstet Gynecol. 2012;119(2 Pt 1):396-407. [PMID: 22270315]

Item 86   Answer: C

Educational Objective: Manage hypertension in a black patient with chronic kidney disease.

The addition of the ACE inhibitor ramipril is indicated for this black patient with hypertension, stage 3 chronic kidney disease (CKD), and proteinuria. Black patients tend to experience enhanced target organ damage at any level of blood pressure compared with most other groups, particularly white patients. Cardiovascular complications are also more frequent in black patients, and black patients are approximately fourfold more likely to experience end-stage kidney disease compared with white patients. These findings emphasize the need for aggressive blood pressure control in black patients, although the optimal level of control relative to other patient groups is unclear. Recommendations for high blood pressure management in black patients were released in the International Society on Hypertension

in Blacks (ISHIB) consensus statement. ISHIB defines treatment goals in black patients based on either the absence of target organ damage (primary prevention), in which the blood pressure goal is less than 135/85 mm Hg, or the presence of target organ damage (secondary prevention), in which the blood pressure goal is less than 130/80 mm Hg. In hypertensive patients with proteinuria, treatment with a renin-angiotensin system inhibitor (an ACE inhibitor or angiotensin receptor blocker) has been shown to decrease proteinuria and slow the progression of kidney disease. Despite the finding that black patients do not respond well to an ACE inhibitor as monotherapy for hypertension without proteinuria, the African American Study of Kidney Disease and Hypertension (AASK), performed in patients with long-standing hypertension and mild proteinuria, demonstrated that the ACE inhibitor ramipril slowed kidney disease progression in black patients with impaired kidney function caused by hypertension and is therefore an appropriate addition to this patient's treatment regimen.

In this same study, both metoprolol and amlodipine were inferior to ramipril for progression of kidney disease and are therefore not preferable agents to add to this patient's regimen.

The benefit of an ACE inhibitor in mitigating progression of kidney disease is due to hemodynamic changes within the glomerulus and other effects due to renin-angiotensin system blockade, in addition to treating systemic hypertension. While increasing this patient's dose of diuretic might successfully lower his blood pressure, he would not benefit from the treatment of his proteinuria associated with ramipril.

KEY POINT

- **In black patients with hypertensive kidney disease and proteinuria, treatment with the ACE inhibitor ramipril is appropriate for blood pressure control and to decrease kidney disease progression.**

Bibliography

Flack JM, Sica DA, Bakris G, et al; International Society on Hypertension in Blacks. Management of high blood pressure in blacks: an update of the International Society on Hypertension in Blacks consensus statement. Hypertension. 2010;56(5):780-800. [PMID: 20921433]

Item 87   Answer: D

Educational Objective: Manage severe ANCA vasculitis.

The most appropriate treatment for this patient with severe ANCA vasculitis is induction therapy with plasmapheresis, cyclophosphamide, and corticosteroids, followed by maintenance therapy with azathioprine and corticosteroids. Severe small-vessel vasculitis presenting as rapidly progressive glomerulonephritis (RPGN) is an emergency, and its

CONT.

early recognition is often missed. This patient had a progressive rise of the serum creatinine level to 6.7 mg/dL (592 micromoles/L), accompanied by respiratory manifestations for 4 months prior to hospitalization. Among the glomerular diseases that can manifest as RPGN, small-vessel vasculitis with ANCA positivity is the most frequent, occurring in 60% of patients with this disease. In patients with severe small-vessel vasculitis, induction therapy with plasmapheresis, cyclophosphamide, and corticosteroids, followed by maintenance therapy with azathioprine and corticosteroids, reduces the risk of end-stage kidney disease or mortality to 31% from the expected risk of 51%. Infection must be excluded before initiating the immunosuppressive therapy.

Induction therapy with cyclophosphamide and corticosteroids without plasmapheresis, followed by maintenance therapy with azathioprine and corticosteroids, is reserved for patients with moderately active vasculitis. Moderately active vasculitis usually manifests with a lesser degree of kidney disease (rise of serum creatinine to ≤5.8 mg/dL [513 micromoles/L] and/or no need for dialysis) without pulmonary hemorrhage.

Induction therapy with mycophenolate mofetil and corticosteroids, followed by maintenance therapy with mycophenolate mofetil and corticosteroids, has not been demonstrated to be effective in adequately designed trials.

The use of plasmapheresis alone to rapidly remove ANCAs can lead to a rebound production of these antibodies if cyclophosphamide with corticosteroids is not used.

KEY POINT

- **Induction therapy for severe ANCA vasculitis includes plasmapheresis, cyclophosphamide, and corticosteroids.**

Bibliography

Jayne DR, Gaskin G, Rasmussen N, et al; European Vasculitis Study Group. Randomized trial of plasma exchange or high-dosage methylprednisolone as adjunctive therapy for severe renal vasculitis. J Am Soc Nephrol. 2007;18(7):2180-2188. [PMID: 17582159]

Item 88   Answer: D

Educational Objective: **Diagnose tuberous sclerosis complex.**

This patient has a possible family history of kidney disease and a bilateral kidney cystic disorder, which most likely is tuberous sclerosis complex (TSC). TSC is most commonly manifested by angiomyolipomas or tubers of the skin, retina, kidneys, and other organs. Cognitive impairment, decreased visual acuity, and cystic lesions in the kidney can also be manifestations of the disease. Diagnostic criteria require either the presence of at least two major features or one major feature and two minor features. Major criteria include facial angiofibromas, three or more hypomelanotic macules (ash leaf spots), kidney angiomyolipomas, and

retinal hamartomas. Minor criteria include nonrenal hamartomas, multiple kidney cysts, and various dental abnormalities such as pits on dental enamel or gingival fibromas. This patient exhibits one major criterion (the presence of three or more hypomelanotic macules) and two minor criteria (dental enamel pits and possible gingival fibromas), making TSC a definitive diagnosis. Patients should have kidney ultrasonography at the time of diagnosis with repeat testing every 1 to 3 years if kidney lesions are found. In patients with TSC, 1% to 2% of adults can develop renal cell carcinoma and other concerning lesions that can result in hemorrhage. Some patients with TSC also have autosomal dominant polycystic kidney disease (ADPKD) because one of the TSC mutations is found on chromosome 16p (*TSC2*) that is immediately adjacent to the gene for ADPKD (*PKD1*).

The most common inherited cystic disease of the kidney is ADPKD; however, this patient's findings are most consistent with TSC. The number of kidney cysts seen on ultrasound that are required to establish a diagnosis of ADPKD varies based on the patient's age, PKD genotype, and whether a family history of ADPKD is present.

Tubular dilatation is the hallmark of autosomal recessive polycystic kidney disease and is associated with massive kidney enlargement at birth, abdominal masses, and respiratory distress. Difficult-to-control hypertension and growth retardation also are common.

Fabry disease is an X-linked disorder caused by deficiency of the α-galactosidase A enzyme and is not a cystic disease. Clinical manifestations include mild nephrotic-range proteinuria, slow deterioration in kidney function, cutaneous angiokeratomas, painful paresthesias of the hands, and premature coronary artery disease.

KEY POINT

- **Tuberous sclerosis complex is most commonly manifested by angiomyolipomas or tubers of the skin, retina, kidneys, and other organs.**

Bibliography

Curatolo P, Bombardieri R, Jozwiak S. Tuberous sclerosis. Lancet. 2008;372(9639):657-668. [PMID: 18722871]

Item 89   Answer: C

Educational Objective: **Evaluate a patient for early diabetic nephropathy.**

A urine albumin–creatinine ratio now is indicated to screen for diabetic nephropathy in this patient with newly diagnosed type 2 diabetes mellitus. Diabetic nephropathy is the most common glomerular disease and develops in approximately 35% of patients with type 1 and 2 diabetes. The American Diabetes Association guidelines specifically recommend annual measurement of the urine albumin excretion for patients who have had type 1 diabetes for 5 years or more and for all patients with type 2 diabetes beginning at the time of diagnosis. Screening for microalbuminuria usually involves obtaining a urine albumin–creatinine ratio on a first morning void urine sample, a random sample, or a timed urine collection. Microalbuminuria is confirmed when two of three samples obtained within a 6-month period reveal a urine albumin–creatinine ratio between 30 and 300 mg/g. Microalbuminuria is the first easily detectable sign of diabetic nephropathy and usually occurs 5 to 15 years after the diagnosis of diabetes. Approximately 10 to 15 years after the diagnosis of diabetes, macroalbuminuria (urine albumin–creatinine ratio above 300 mg/g) can be detected on urine dipstick and is accompanied by decreasing kidney function and increased blood pressure. Preventive measures in managing microalbuminuria include early initiation of an ACE inhibitor and/or angiotensin receptor blocker, adequate blood pressure control, blood glucose and lipid control, and smoking cessation, which reduce the risk of end-stage kidney disease and cardiovascular events.

The Modification of Diet in Renal Disease (MDRD) study equation was developed for patients with chronic kidney disease and has not been shown to accurately estimate kidney function in healthy persons or in diabetic patients with preserved glomerular filtration.

Waiting 5 years to screen for microalbuminuria is not appropriate in patients with type 2 diabetes because many patients may have diabetes for years before diagnosis, and earlier onset of diabetic nephropathy and faster progression of its clinical stages are common compared with type 1 diabetes.

The urine protein–creatinine ratio can be used in patients with overt proteinuria or later stages of diabetic nephropathy, neither of which is seen in this patient at this time.

KEY POINT

- **A urine albumin–creatinine ratio is indicated to screen for diabetic nephropathy in patients with newly diagnosed type 2 diabetes mellitus.**

Bibliography

Johnson SL, Tierney EF, Onyemere KU, et al. Who is tested for diabetic kidney disease and who initiates treatment? The Translating Research into Action for Diabetes (TRIAD) study. Diabetes Care. 2006;29(8):1733-1738. [PMID: 16873772]

Item 90   Answer: C

Educational Objective: Evaluate a patient with chronic kidney disease using ultrasonography.

Kidney ultrasonography is indicated for this patient with stage 3 chronic kidney disease (CKD), based on an estimated glomerular filtration rate (GFR) of 37 mL/min/1.73 m². He has not yet been evaluated for the cause of his CKD, which may have implications for therapy, including future transplantation. The patient's mother had known CKD, raising the possibility that there is a genetic

component to this patient's CKD. Kidney ultrasonography is often the first imaging choice to assess kidney disease because it is safe, not dependent upon kidney function, noninvasive, and relatively inexpensive. Because it does not require contrast dye, ultrasonography does not place patients at risk for contrast-induced nephropathy. Kidney ultrasonography can show small echogenic kidneys, elements of obstruction, or other chronic entities such as autosomal dominant polycystic kidney disease.

Abdominal CT can reveal information regarding causes of CKD and may be used for patients who are not suitable for ultrasonography (for example, unable to image because of obesity or large amounts of intestinal gas). However, CT is more costly than ultrasonography, exposes patients to additional radiation, and may involve use of intravenous iodinated contrast agents, which are associated with a risk for contrast-induced nephropathy in patients with an estimated GFR of less than 60 mL/min/1.73 m². Experts therefore recommend against the use of these agents in this population group.

Kidney biopsy is predominantly used in patients with glomerular disease. The most common indications for kidney biopsy include the nephrotic syndrome, acute glomerulonephritis, and kidney transplant dysfunction. None of these indications is present in this patient.

Radionuclide kidney clearance scanning can calculate GFR and renal plasma flow very accurately. However, its use is limited because of cost, lack of widespread availability, and operator technical difficulties. Estimating equations for GFR are reasonably accurate in patients with stage 3 CKD such as in this case; these equations can be calculated without the need for invasive studies and are generally preferred to radionuclide kidney clearance scanning.

KEY POINT

- **Kidney ultrasonography is often the first imaging choice to assess kidney disease because it is safe, not dependent upon kidney function, noninvasive, and relatively inexpensive.**

Bibliography

Drawz P, Rahman M. In the clinic. Chronic kidney disease. Ann Intern Med. 2009;150(3):ITC2-1-ITC2-15. [PMID: 19189903]

Item 91   Answer: A

Educational Objective: Identify the cause of kidney function decline in a patient with hypertension.

The increase in this patient's serum creatinine level is likely due to treatment with an angiotensin receptor blocker (ARB) for his essential hypertension. He has target organ damage to the kidneys that was present when treatment was initiated. A significant increase in serum creatinine occurs in some patients when an ARB is started, and similar changes are frequently noted with ACE inhibitors. Because of their mechanism of action, these medications tend to decrease the glomerular filtration rate and cause an increase in serum creatinine in patients with disorders in which intra-renal perfusion pressure is maintained by increased angiotensin, including hypertensive kidney disease, chronic kidney disease, heart failure, and renovascular disease. The rise in serum creatinine may be more pronounced in patients who have preexisting but unrecognized kidney injury before treatment is started, with the medication uncovering underlying kidney failure. However, these same effects may be protective against progression of kidney failure, and their use in these conditions may be beneficial if kidney function remains stable and there are no other complications of treatment, such as hyperkalemia.

The magnitude of proteinuria and otherwise unremarkable urine sediment on urinalysis do not suggest the presence of primary glomerular disease and are consistent with findings typically seen in patients with hypertensive kidney disease.

The patient's current level of blood pressure control appears adequate, and his increased serum creatinine level over the past 3 years likely does not reflect inadequate current blood pressure control.

Although this patient has several risk factors for vascular disease, he has no evidence of existing atherosclerotic disease by history or on examination, making renovascular causes of his kidney failure less likely.

KEY POINT

- **Angiotensin receptor blockers and ACE inhibitors may lead to an increase in the serum creatinine level and may uncover previously undetected kidney dysfunction.**

Bibliography

Taylor AA, Siragy H, Nesbitt S. Angiotensin receptor blockers: pharmacology, efficacy, and safety. J Clin Hypertens (Greenwich). 2011;13(9):677-686. [PMID: 21896150]

Item 92   Answer: C
Educational Objective: Diagnose polyarteritis nodosa.

This patient most likely has polyarteritis nodosa, a necrotizing vasculitis of the medium-sized arteries. The affected vessels are characterized by necrosis and inflammation in a patchy distribution. Approximately 50% of cases of polyarteritis nodosa are associated with hepatitis B virus infection, usually of recent acquisition; ANCA assays are almost always negative, particularly in patients with concomitant hepatitis B virus infection. Patients with polyarteritis nodosa typically present with fever, abdominal pain, arthralgia, and weight loss that develop over days to months. Two thirds of these patients have mononeuritis multiplex, and one third have hypertension, testicular pain, and cutaneous involvement, including nodules, ulcers, purpura, and livedo reticularis. In patients with a compatible clinical presentation, diagnosis is often confirmed by a biopsy from the skin

or a sural nerve. Radiographic imaging of the mesenteric or renal arteries can also be used to establish a definitive diagnosis of polyarteritis nodosa. Characteristic findings of this condition include aneurysms and stenoses of the medium-sized vessels.

Giant cell arteritis is a granulomatous vasculitis that most commonly affects the large and medium-sized arteries of the head and neck, including the temporal, ophthalmic, and posterior ciliary arteries. Subclinical involvement of the proximal and distal aorta also is common. Kidney involvement is not typical.

Granulomatosis with polyangiitis (also known as Wegener granulomatosis) is a necrotizing vasculitis that typically affects the respiratory tract and the kidneys. More than 70% of patients present with upper airway symptoms, particularly sinusitis. Kidney biopsy specimens reveal a pauci-immune crescentic glomerulonephritis; medium-sized artery aneurysms and stenosis are not found.

Takayasu arteritis is a large-vessel vasculitis associated with fever, arthralgia, myalgia, malaise, weight loss, and eventual vascular insufficiency. Diagnosis is made by demonstrating great-vessel narrowing visible on imaging studies, typically most marked at branch points in the aorta. This patient's short clinical course and involvement of medium-sized arteries is not compatible with Takayasu arteritis.

KEY POINT

- **Characteristic angiographic findings of polyarteritis nodosa include aneurysms and stenoses of the medium-sized vessels.**

Bibliography

Henegar C, Pagnoux C, Puéchal X, et al; French Vasculitis Study Group. A paradigm of diagnostic criteria for polyarteritis nodosa: analysis of a series of 949 patients with vasculitides. Arthritis Rheum. 2008;58(5):1528-1538. [PMID: 18438816]

Item 93   Answer: D
Educational Objective: Diagnose type B lactic acidosis.

The most likely diagnosis is type B lactic acidosis caused by linezolid toxicity. This patient has an anion gap metabolic acidosis associated with an increased serum lactate level. Type A lactic acidosis is associated with tissue hypoperfusion and hypoxia. The absence of shock or hypoxia in this patient is consistent with type B lactic acidosis. Type B lactic acidosis is often due to medication or toxin exposure and may also occur in patients with advanced malignancy, liver disease, or glucose-6-phosphate dehydrogenase deficiency. Linezolid is known to induce type B lactic acidosis by interfering with activity of the mitochondrial respiratory complex. Other medications known to induce type B lactic acidosis include acetaminophen overdose, metformin, the nucleoside reverse transcriptase inhibitors stavudine and didanosine, propofol, and salicylates. Lactic acidosis due to linezolid toxicity most commonly occurs after several weeks of therapy, although one third of reported cases occur within the first 2 weeks of therapy. Polymorphisms of mitochondrial DNA have been identified in affected persons. Onset of type B lactic acidosis warrants discontinuation of the offending agent (linezolid in this case), which leads to resolution of lactic acidosis in most patients. Those with end-stage kidney disease may benefit from intensification of dialysis to promote linezolid clearance.

Diabetic ketoacidosis presents with ketonemia, increased anion gap metabolic acidosis, and hyperglycemia with plasma glucose levels that usually exceed 300 mg/dL (16.7 mmol/L). This patient's modest degree of hyperglycemia and absence of detectable serum ketones argues against this diagnosis.

Pyroglutamic acidosis usually occurs in critically ill patients receiving therapeutic doses of acetaminophen. Patients present with unexplained increased anion gap metabolic acidosis due to the accumulation of pyroglutamic acid (also known as 5-oxoproline) as a consequence of impaired glutathione regeneration. Lactic acidosis is not a feature of pyroglutamic acidosis.

Although sepsis should always be considered in patients with lactic acidosis, the absence of leukocytosis, fever, tachycardia, and hypotension makes this diagnosis unlikely.

KEY POINT

- **Type B lactic acidosis is often due to medication or toxin exposure and may also occur in patients with advanced malignancy, liver disease, or glucose-6-phosphate dehydrogenase deficiency.**

Bibliography

Velez JC, Janech MG. A case of lactic acidosis induced by linezolid. Nat Rev Nephrol. 2010;6(4):236-242. [PMID: 20348931]

Item 94   Answer: C

Educational Objective: Evaluate a patient who has hypokalemic metabolic alkalosis.

Measurement of the urine chloride level is the most appropriate test to determine the cause of this patient's hypokalemic metabolic alkalosis. Metabolic alkalosis is caused by the net loss of acid or the retention of bicarbonate. The diagnostic evaluation of metabolic alkalosis begins with the clinical assessment of the volume status and blood pressure. Metabolic alkalosis that is associated with hypovolemia will correct with the administration of isotonic saline and volume expansion and is thus noted to be saline-responsive. When the metabolic alkalosis is associated with increased extracellular fluid volume and hypertension, it will not respond to isotonic saline and is termed saline-resistant. In this patient who does not have hypertension and has a normal or slightly decreased effective arterial blood

volume, the urine sodium and chloride levels can help distinguish the various causes of metabolic alkalosis. Patients with low urine chloride levels (<15 meq/L [15 mmol/L]; normal for men, 25-371 meq/L [25-371 mmol/L]) are usually either vomiting or have a decreased effective arterial blood volume from various causes, including prior use of diuretics or low cardiac output. Patients with high urine chloride levels (>15 meq/L [15 mmol/L]) most commonly are receiving active therapy with diuretics or, more rarely, may have a genetically based tubular disorder such as Bartter or Gitelman syndrome.

Plasma aldosterone and renin levels are most helpful in the diagnostic evaluation of metabolic alkalosis if there is associated hypertension. A plasma aldosterone-plasma renin activity ratio of 20 to 30 when the plasma aldosterone level is greater than 15 ng/dL (414 pmol/L) is highly suggestive of primary hyperaldosteronism, whereas suppression of both renin and aldosterone is consistent with syndromes of apparent mineralocorticoid excess. Plasma aldosterone and renin levels are elevated in patients with malignant hypertension, renin-secreting tumors, and renovascular hypertension.

Hypomagnesemia can lead to urine magnesium wasting and metabolic alkalosis and can be observed in patients with Bartter or Gitelman syndrome. However, serum magnesium measurement is not as helpful as the urine chloride value in distinguishing between the various causes of hypokalemic metabolic alkalosis.

The urine osmolal gap is a method of estimating urine ammonium excretion and is useful in the evaluation of normal anion gap metabolic acidosis. Ammonium excretion is variable in metabolic alkalosis and depends on numerous factors, including the magnitude of potassium depletion, protein intake, and volume status.

KEY POINT

- **The diagnostic evaluation of metabolic alkalosis begins with the clinical assessment of the volume status and blood pressure; urine sodium and chloride levels can help distinguish the various causes.**

Bibliography

Shin HS. Value of the measurement of urinary chloride in hypokalaemic metabolic alkalosis. Nephrology. 2010;15(1):133. [PMID: 20377781]

Item 95   Answer: A

Educational Objective: Assess the risk of contrast-induced nephropathy in a patient with chronic kidney disease.

Hydration with isotonic saline is indicated to decrease this patient's risk for contrast-induced nephropathy (CIN) associated with her cardiac catheterization. Patients with underlying kidney injury are particularly susceptible to additional kidney injury due to exposure of the renal tubule to

CONT.

nephrotoxic contrast media. Thus, avoidance of exposure to contrast in high-risk patients is preferable. However, in those who require contrast studies, use of low osmolar contrast agents and hydration to promote urine flow and avoid volume contraction has been shown to decrease the risk for CIN. There is some evidence that isotonic saline is preferable to hypotonic solutions for periprocedural hydration. Multiple studies have evaluated normal saline or intravenous fluids containing isotonic sodium bicarbonate as the prophylactic fluid. At this time, neither formulation appears significantly more effective than the other.

Although given to increase urine flow, diuresis with mannitol or a loop diuretic has not been shown to decrease the risk for CIN and may even increase the risk.

Oral hydration, with or without sodium loading, has not been shown to be more effective, and may be less effective, than intravenous hydration with isotonic saline.

Prophylactic hemodialysis has been evaluated as a method for removing nephrotoxic contrast agents in patients with existing kidney failure. No benefit has been shown, with possibly poorer outcomes, than with medical therapy.

KEY POINT

- **Risk factors for contrast-induced nephropathy include poor baseline glomerular filtration rate and heart failure.**

Bibliography

Solomon R, Dauerman HL. Contrast-induced acute kidney injury. Circulation. 2010;122(23):2451-2455. [PMID: 21135373]

Item 96   Answer: C

Educational Objective: Manage cardiovascular risk in a patient with chronic kidney disease.

An increase in the atorvastatin dose to lower the cholesterol level is indicated in this patient with chronic kidney disease (CKD). Besides therapies to delay CKD progression, treatment also includes managing the complications of CKD. Patients with CKD are at high risk for cardiovascular events, and the presence of CKD is considered a coronary heart disease equivalent in assessing risk and for guiding treatment. Although data about treatment of dyslipidemia with statins suggest no benefit in dialysis patients, statin therapy has been shown to reduce all-cause and cardiovascular deaths in patients with kidney disease not on dialysis. Statins may also reduce proteinuria and have beneficial anti-inflammatory and vascular effects. The goal for LDL cholesterol levels in patients with CKD is similar to those with significant coronary disease risk factors or known coronary artery disease, with a target of less than 100 mg/dL (2.59 mmol/L), and preferably less than 70 mg/dL (1.81 mmol/L).

Although treating secondary hyperparathyroidism is a management objective for patients with CKD, this patient's parathyroid hormone level is not far from a goal level for a patient with stage 3 CKD. Lowering parathyroid hormone levels has not been shown to improve mortality in patients with CKD.

The metabolic acidosis associated with CKD may have adverse effects, including worsening of bone disease. Sodium bicarbonate replacement therapy, typically to maintain a serum bicarbonate level ≥23 meq/L (23 mmol/L), is used in patients with CKD to treat kidney injury–associated metabolic acidosis and may delay kidney disease progression. It has not yet been shown to reduce mortality. Furthermore, this patient's serum bicarbonate level is adequate, and therapy is not indicated.

Increasing the ACE inhibitor dose in this patient with a blood pressure at target and a low level of proteinuria is unlikely to provide as much cardiovascular benefit as increasing the statin therapy.

KEY POINT

- **Chronic kidney disease represents a cardiovascular risk factor, and management of dyslipidemia with statins can reduce cardiovascular risk in patients with chronic kidney disease.**

Bibliography

Navaneethan SD, Pansini F, Perkovic V, et al. HMG CoA reductase inhibitors (statins) for people with chronic kidney disease not requiring dialysis. Cochrane Database Syst Rev. 2009;(2): CD007784. [PMID: 19370693]

Item 97   Answer: D

Educational Objective: Manage chronic hypertension in a pregnant patient.

For this pregnant patient with chronic hypertension, continuation of her current medication regimen is appropriate. Prior to conception, her medication was changed to labetalol, which is considered first-line therapy for the management of hypertension during pregnancy. This patient has a normal serum creatinine level but has proteinuria. She previously had been on an ACE inhibitor, which decreases proteinuria. Proteinuria is typically increased during pregnancy in patients with preexisting proteinuria. There is an increase in the glomerular filtration rate (GFR) related to the increase in plasma volume, yet this increase in GFR is not matched by an increase in tubular absorption of proteins; therefore, an increase in proteinuria follows. If this patient were not pregnant, strict blood pressure goals would be applied with blockade of the renin-angiotensin-aldosterone system. In contrast, blood pressure goals in pregnancy have not been rigorously tested; instead, management is focused on avoiding end-organ damage in the mother during this finite period. Although there are slight differences in the antihypertensive goals from various professional societies, most agree that the blood pressure should be less than 150/100 mm Hg. Currently, this patient's blood pressure is well within the target for management of chronic hypertension during pregnancy. Therefore, close monitoring and follow-up are indicated.

Although methyldopa is an acceptable medication with an established safety history for use in pregnancy, it frequently has a sedating effect and often needs to be given three times daily for an adequate antihypertensive effect. Furthermore, because this patient has achieved a reasonable blood pressure goal, there is no indication for add-on therapy at present.

Exposure to ACE inhibitors or angiotensin receptor blockers such as losartan during the first trimester has been associated with fetal cardiac abnormalities; exposure during the second and third trimesters has been associated with neonatal kidney failure and death. These agents are considered pregnancy category X drugs and should be held until after delivery.

There is no reason to increase the labetalol at this time because she is at a reasonable blood pressure goal and is tolerating the current dose well.

KEY POINT

- Close monitoring and follow-up are indicated for pregnant patients who have chronic hypertension with blood pressure measurements within target goals.

Bibliography

Seely EW, Ecker J. Clinical practice. Chronic hypertension in pregnancy. N Engl J Med. 2011;365(5):439-446. [PMID: 21812673]

Item 98   Answer: D

Educational Objective: Manage hypertension in a patient who is over the age of 80 years.

No change in management is required at this time. This 82-year-old woman has hypertension and currently takes indapamide and an ACE inhibitor; her blood pressure measurements have been less than 150 mm Hg systolic. The pattern of blood pressure elevation in older patients is typically characterized by a prominent systolic blood pressure. This relates in large part to the significant role of vascular stiffness in the blood pressure increases of older patients, which in addition to raising systolic pressure, also leads to a decline in the diastolic pressure. In the past, these physiologic changes were thought to be normal, and elevated blood pressures in older patients were not treated. However, it has been shown that treatment of blood pressure in aging patients does lead to improved cardiovascular outcomes. Although a target blood pressure of 140/90 mm Hg is generally accepted for most patients with hypertension, there are less data on patients over the age of 80 years to guide therapy. The Hypertension in the Very Elderly Trial (HYVET) enrolled patients at least 80 years of age and used a target systolic blood pressure of 150 mm Hg, which is assumed to be a reasonable goal for this population. HYVET also provided evidence affirming that treatment of

older patients with hypertension leads to fewer deaths and less heart failure with active drug therapy. This older patient with target blood pressure measurements does not require additional treatment, and a follow-up visit in 4 months is appropriate.

Adding an additional antihypertensive agent such as amlodipine or metoprolol to this patient's regimen is not appropriate because reducing the systolic value to less than 140 mm Hg in older patients has not been shown to be beneficial. Furthermore, an additional agent with a different mechanism of action may cause adverse effects in older patients who may not be able to compensate effectively for the physiologic changes induced by multiple medications.

This patient's current regimen of the diuretic indapamide and an ACE inhibitor appears to be reasonably effective; therefore, a diuretic substitution is unnecessary.

KEY POINT

- Treating hypertension in older patients has been shown to be effective in reducing death and adverse cardiovascular outcomes, although reducing the systolic blood pressure to less than 140 mm Hg has not been shown to be beneficial in this population.

Bibliography

Beckett NS, Peters R, Fletcher AE, et al; HYVET Study Group. Treatment of hypertension in patients 80 years of age or older. N Engl J Med. 2008;358(18):1887-1898. [PMID: 18378519]

Item 99   Answer: D

Educational Objective: Recognize the increased risk of cardiovascular disease in the setting of chronic kidney disease.

This patient should be sent promptly to the emergency department for evaluation and treatment of unstable angina. Patients with chronic kidney disease (CKD) who have acute coronary disease are less likely to have chest pain but are more likely to have atypical symptoms such as dyspnea or nausea. Recent evidence suggests that acute coronary disease is underrecognized and undertreated in patients with CKD. Although this patient is relatively young and has never smoked, the presence of both CKD and proteinuria are serious risk factors for cardiovascular disease. Even with well-controlled blood pressure and lipids, patients with CKD have a greater incidence of cardiovascular events and cardiovascular mortality compared with those with similar comorbid conditions. This finding has led many to consider nontraditional risk factors for cardiovascular disease that may play a role such as abnormal vascular calcification, inflammation, hyperhomocysteinemia, or neurohumoral activation. Because these nonconventional factors are poorly understood, efforts to manage traditional risk factors are of paramount importance.

Starting albuterol before establishing a cause of the patient's dyspnea is not appropriate.

Although patients with CKD may experience dyspnea due to volume overload, and a diuretic may be helpful in relieving symptoms, the patient's physical examination findings are not supportive of this diagnosis. More importantly, because exertional dyspnea can be an anginal equivalent in patients with CKD, this diagnosis should be evaluated before any other diagnosis is considered or treatment is undertaken.

If the patient's dyspnea is not due to coronary artery disease–related left ventricular dysfunction, a pulmonary evaluation that includes spirometry would be reasonable.

KEY POINT

- **Patients with chronic kidney disease have a greater incidence of cardiovascular events and cardiovascular mortality compared with those with similar comorbid conditions.**

Bibliography

Hage FG, Venkataraman R, Zoghbi GJ, Perry GJ, DeMattos AM, Iskandrian AE. The scope of coronary heart disease in patients with chronic kidney disease. J Am Coll Cardiol. 2009;53(23):2129-2140. [PMID: 19497438]

Item 100   Answer: B

Educational Objective: Screen for intracranial cerebral aneurysms in a patient with autosomal dominant polycystic kidney disease.

MR angiography of the cerebral arteries is appropriate for this patient with autosomal dominant polycystic kidney disease (ADPKD) and a family history of potential cerebral aneurysm rupture. Intracranial cerebral aneurysms occur in approximately 8% of patients with ADPKD. The most important risk factor for the development of an intracranial cerebral aneurysm is a family member with a known intracranial aneurysm, particularly in a first-degree relative with a previously ruptured aneurysm. Therefore, imaging to assess for the presence of an intracranial cerebral aneurysm is appropriate in this patient with ADPKD who has a family history of potential intracranial cerebral aneurysm rupture. MR angiography and high-resolution CT angiography are imaging options, having supplanted cerebral arteriography because of its invasiveness and risk of stroke associated with the procedure. MR angiography is adequately sensitive for detecting clinically significant aneurysms, although the use of gadolinium-based contrast agents in patients with moderate to severe kidney disease is contraindicated because of the risk of nephrogenic systemic fibrosis. The role of screening patients with ADPKD and no family history of cerebral aneurysm as well as the frequency of follow-up for high-risk screened patients without a cerebral aneurysm remain unclear.

This patient's laboratory studies already include a urine protein–creatinine ratio, which is a reasonable proxy for a 24-hour urine measurement of protein. Therefore, a 24-hour urine collection would not provide additional information relevant to long-term management.

Genotype testing is not routinely performed as part of the evaluation of ADPKD because it is expensive, difficult to obtain, and would not influence the initial management of this patient.

Abdominal CT is not necessary to confirm the diagnosis of ADPKD if the patient already has documentation of ADPKD by other imaging such as ultrasound.

KEY POINT

- **Screening for intracranial aneurysms is recommended for patients with autosomal dominant polycystic kidney disease who have a family history of potential intracranial cerebral aneurysm rupture.**

Bibliography

Pirson Y. Extrarenal manifestations of autosomal dominant polycystic kidney disease. Adv Chronic Kidney Dis. 2010;17(2):173-180. [PMID: 20219620]

Item 101   Answer: C

Educational Objective: Manage secondary hyperparathyroidism in a patient with chronic kidney disease.

The addition of cholecalciferol (vitamin D_3) is indicated for this patient with chronic kidney disease (CKD) who has vitamin D insufficiency. An elevation in the parathyroid hormone level is often the first detectable change associated with chronic kidney disease mineral bone disorder (CKD-MBD), which may occur very early in the course of CKD; therefore, the Kidney Disease Improving Global Outcomes (KDIGO) guidelines recommend testing for MBD beginning with stage 3 CKD. This evaluation typically begins with measurement of serum parathyroid hormone levels, vitamin D levels, and calcium and phosphorus concentrations. This patient's intact parathyroid hormone level is elevated, but there is evidence of vitamin D insufficiency. There is ongoing debate on the definition of vitamin D deficiency; nevertheless, suboptimal levels can contribute to secondary hyperparathyroidism. Before beginning a course of more expensive vitamin D analogs, it is appropriate to treat with the inactive forms of vitamin D, cholecalciferol or ergocalciferol, which may improve or correct the secondary hyperparathyroidism due to vitamin D insufficiency or deficiency.

If the intact parathyroid hormone level is elevated but the 25-hydroxy vitamin D level is more than 30 ng/mL (75 nmol/L), then an active oral vitamin D sterol such as calcitriol, alfacalcidol, or doxercalciferol should be utilized. Use of these agents requires careful monitoring to avoid hypercalcemia, vascular calcifications, or oversuppression of parathyroid hormone.

In the absence of vitamin D insufficiency or deficiency, calcium salts such as calcium carbonate can bind phosphorus in the gut and help control hyperphosphatemia of CKD.

Sevelamer is indicated to manage phosphate retention in patients with CKD who are unable to control hyperphosphatemia with oral calcium salts, cannot tolerate oral calcium, or develop hypercalcemia using calcium as a phosphate binder. However, this patient's serum phosphorus level is normal and does not require treatment with sevelamer.

KEY POINT

- Underlying vitamin D insufficiency/deficiency can cause secondary hyperparathyroidism in patients with chronic kidney disease.

Bibliography

Sprague SM, Coyne D. Control of secondary hyperparathyroidism by vitamin D receptor agonists in chronic kidney disease. Clin J Am Soc Nephrol. 2010;5(3):512-518. [PMID: 20133492]

Item 102   Answer: C
Educational Objective: Diagnose prehypertension.

This patient has prehypertension. Classification of hypertension is based on an average of two or more seated blood pressure readings obtained more than 1 minute apart at two or more visits. The prehypertension category established by the Seventh Report of the Joint National Committee on Prevention, Detection, Evaluation, and Treatment of High Blood Pressure (JNC 7) designates a group at high risk for progression to hypertension in whom lifestyle modifications may be preemptive. The JNC 7 definition of prehypertension is an average blood pressure reading of 120 to 139 mm Hg systolic or 80 to 89 mm Hg diastolic. Studies such as the Trial of Preventing Hypertension (TROPHY) have shown that about two thirds of patients diagnosed as prehypertensive will develop stage 1 hypertension during 4 years of follow-up.

Masked hypertension is characterized by blood pressure that is higher at home than in the office setting. Suspicion for masked hypertension is usually raised when the physician is informed of discrepancies between office and home blood pressure readings or findings that suggest the presence of undiagnosed hypertension such as left ventricular hypertrophy. Ambulatory blood pressure monitoring can be used to confirm this diagnosis.

Normotension is defined as a blood pressure measurement of less than 120/80 mm Hg.

White coat hypertension is characterized by at least three separate office blood pressure measurements above 140/90 mm Hg with at least two sets of measurements below 140/90 mm Hg obtained outside the office, accompanied by the absence of target organ damage. Ambulatory blood pressure monitoring is considered the gold standard for diagnosing this condition. This patient does not fit the criteria for the diagnosis of white coat hypertension.

KEY POINT

- Patients with prehypertension (defined as an average blood pressure reading of 120 to 139 mm Hg systolic or 80 to 89 mm Hg diastolic) are at high risk for progression to hypertension, and lifestyle modifications in this patient population may be preemptive.

Bibliography

Chobanian AV, Bakris GL, Black HR, et al; Joint National Committee on Prevention, Detection, Evaluation, and Treatment of High Blood Pressure; National Heart, Lung, and Blood Institute; National High Blood Pressure Education Program Coordinating Committee. Seventh report of the Joint National Committee on Prevention, Detection, Evaluation, and Treatment of High Blood Pressure. Hypertension. 2003;42(6):1206-1252. [PMID: 14656957]

Item 103   Answer: A
Educational Objective: Diagnose underlying chronic kidney disease and hypertension in a pregnant patient.

This patient is at 17 weeks' gestation and has underlying chronic kidney disease and hypertension. Because baseline proteinuria typically increases during pregnancy and edema is commonly seen during pregnancy, it is often difficult to determine whether a patient has an exacerbation of underlying kidney disease or a disorder associated with pregnancy. This patient describes hypertension complicating her first pregnancy. Currently, her blood pressure is elevated. During pregnancy, blood pressure levels typically decrease early in the first trimester and may remain lower than nonpregnant levels until term; therefore, when hypertension is present before 20 weeks' gestation, this represents chronic hypertension rather than a hypertensive disorder of pregnancy (gestational hypertension or preeclampsia). In addition, her serum creatinine level is elevated. The serum creatinine level typically falls during pregnancy because the increased plasma volume leads to an increase in glomerular filtration rate. She also has proteinuria noted on urine dipstick and confirmed by the urine protein–creatinine ratio. These findings suggest that the patient has chronic kidney disease and hypertension, which now complicate her second pregnancy.

Gestational hypertension refers to hypertension that develops after 20 weeks' gestation in the absence of proteinuria or other maternal end-organ damage. Up to 45% of women initially diagnosed with gestational hypertension develop preeclampsia, and the risk is greatest if the hypertension develops remote from term.

The nephrotic syndrome is characterized by a urine protein–creatinine ratio greater than 3.5 mg/mg, hypoalbuminemia, hyperlipidemia, lipiduria, edema, and hypercoagulability. This patient's urinalysis results show 1+ protein, which is likely to fall below the nephrotic range, and her urine protein–creatinine ratio suggests that the protein is less than 1 g/24 h.

Preeclampsia is characterized by new-onset hypertension accompanied by the development of proteinuria. This condition can develop any time after 20 weeks of pregnancy but usually occurs close to term.

KEY POINT

- **Hypertension that occurs before 20 weeks' gestation suggests the presence of chronic hypertension and not a hypertensive disorder of pregnancy.**

Bibliography

Yoder SR, Thornburg LL, Bisognano JD. Hypertension in pregnancy and women of childbearing age. Am J Medicine. 2009;122(10):890-895. [PMID: 19786154]

Item 104   Answer: A

Educational Objective: Identify gentamicin as the cause of hypokalemic metabolic alkalosis.

This patient's hypokalemic metabolic alkalosis is most likely caused by gentamicin toxicity. The differential diagnosis of hypokalemic metabolic alkalosis and normal to low extracellular fluid volume status includes diuretics, gastric fluid loss through vomiting or nasogastric suction, gentamicin toxicity, the inherited tubulopathies Gitelman and Bartter syndromes, and high-dose penicillin therapy. Exposure to greater than 1.2 grams of gentamicin is known to induce a Bartter-like syndrome. Aminoglycosides are divalent cations that can activate the calcium-sensing receptor in the thick ascending limb. Activation of the calcium-sensing receptor inhibits the sodium-potassium-chloride cotransporter in the thick ascending limb, mimicking the effect of loop diuretics and leading to hypokalemic metabolic alkalosis. The urine potassium–creatinine ratio of 50 meq/g is consistent with urine potassium losses due to tubular dysfunction caused by gentamicin toxicity.

This patient's elevated urine sodium, chloride, and potassium levels are consistent with primary hyperaldosteronism. However, the absence of hypertension as well as the acute onset of hypokalemic metabolic alkalosis temporally associated with gentamicin therapy makes this diagnosis unlikely.

Exposure to supratherapeutic doses of quetiapine has been reported to induce redistribution of potassium into the intracellular space and hypokalemia. The urine potassium–creatinine ratio should be less than 15 meq/g in this circumstance, and metabolic alkalosis is not an associated feature.

Vancomycin is associated with nephrotoxicity but is not known to induce hypokalemic metabolic alkalosis. Vancomycin-associated tubular injury most commonly results in hyperkalemia rather than hypokalemia.

KEY POINT

- **Exposure to greater than 1.2 grams of gentamicin is known to induce a Bartter-like syndrome, which is associated with hypokalemic metabolic alkalosis.**

Bibliography

Zietse R, Zoutendijk R, Hoorn EJ. Fluid, electrolyte and acid-base disorders associated with antibiotic therapy. Nat Rev Nephrol. 2009;5(4):193-202. [PMID: 19322184]

Item 105   Answer: D

Educational Objective: Diagnose anemia in chronic kidney disease.

Measurement of serum iron and ferritin concentrations and total iron-binding capacity (TIBC) to assess this patient's iron stores is indicated. She has normochromic normocytic anemia. Anemia is common in patients with chronic kidney disease (CKD) because of relative deficiency of erythropoietin, erythropoietin resistance, and shortened erythrocyte survival. The anemia of CKD is usually normochromic and normocytic with a low reticulocyte count. Anemia often occurs earlier in the course of kidney disease in patients with diabetic nephropathy compared with other kidney diseases. Before attributing anemia to CKD, it is important to exclude other etiologies. Iron deficiency is common in patients with CKD. Although most do not have an identifiable cause, patients with CKD are prone to ulcer disease and angiodysplasia-induced gastrointestinal blood loss, resulting in iron deficiency and eventually the development of microcytosis.

Patients with anemia should be evaluated for iron deficiency by serum iron and ferritin concentrations and TIBC. The serum iron concentration, a poor reflection of iron stores, is usually low in patients with iron deficiency; the TIBC is high; the percentage of transferrin saturation (iron/TIBC) is low; and the serum ferritin concentration is low. Because the serum ferritin concentration can increase in inflammatory states, ferritin may be normal or elevated in patients with iron deficiency, but a ferritin concentration of greater than 100 ng/mL (100 micrograms/L) excludes iron deficiency, and a ferritin level of less than 15 ng/mL (15 micrograms/L) confirms iron deficiency. If the results suggest iron deficiency, patients should be evaluated for blood loss, and iron should be prescribed.

ACE inhibitors can contribute to anemia in patients with marginal erythropoietin production; however, the benefit of ACE inhibitors in slowing progression of diabetic kidney disease outweighs this concern. Therefore, lisinopril should not be discontinued in this patient.

Initiation of erythropoiesis-stimulating agents should only be considered after patients have been evaluated for other causes of anemia and iron stores are adequate (ferritin >100 ng/mL [100 micrograms/L] and transferrin saturation >20%).

In patients with CKD, measurement of the serum erythropoietin level does not help to discriminate among other causes of anemia or to guide treatment decisions because CKD may be associated with reduced production of erythropoietin or erythropoietin resistance.

KEY POINT

- The anemia of chronic kidney disease is a diagnosis of exclusion.

Bibliography

National Kidney Foundation. KDOQI clinical practice guidelines and clinical practice recommendations for anemia in chronic kidney disease (2006). Available at www.kidney.org/professionals/KDOQI/guidelines_anemia/index.htm. Accessed July 24, 2012.

Item 106   Answer: C
Educational Objective: Diagnose obstructive acute kidney injury.

Kidney ultrasonography is indicated for this patient with acute kidney injury (AKI) most likely caused by urinary obstruction. Because relief of obstruction can reverse kidney injury and prevent chronic damage, timely diagnosis is essential. Urinary obstruction can be asymptomatic and can be associated with no noted change in urine output. Because of the lack of definitive symptoms on presentation, kidney imaging, typically ultrasonography, should be considered in all patients with AKI, particularly when risk factors for obstruction are present. Medical history findings, including pelvic tumors or irradiation, congenital urinary abnormalities, kidney stones, genitourinary infections, procedures or surgeries, and prostatic enlargement, should increase suspicion for obstruction. Bladder ultrasonography can be done as a quick bedside procedure and may also diagnose bladder obstruction; however, it will not reveal hydronephrosis or kidney anatomy.

In obstruction, the urinalysis is bland. Urine electrolytes are variable; in early obstruction, the urine sodium and fractional excretion of sodium (FE_{Na}) may be low, but in late obstruction, the urine sodium and FE_{Na} may be high, indicative of tubular damage. Because of impaired kidney excretion of potassium, acid, and water, hyperkalemic metabolic acidosis and hyponatremia can be present. The FE_{Na} is not helpful in obstruction, and the clinical information provided does not suggest a prerenal etiology of AKI should be entertained.

Kidney biopsy is performed to evaluate for kidney injury of unknown cause. In this patient with a history suggestive of obstruction, imaging to exclude obstruction should be done first.

Rhabdomyolysis is associated with an increased serum creatine kinase level and can cause elevated serum creatinine and potassium levels; however, the patient has no risk factors for rhabdomyolysis (crush injury, muscle pain, or medications known to cause rhabdomyolysis).

KEY POINT

- Kidney imaging, typically ultrasonography, should be considered in all patients with acute kidney injury, particularly when risk factors for obstruction are present.

Bibliography

Licurse A, Kim MC, Dziura J, et al. Renal ultrasonography in the evaluation of acute kidney injury: developing a risk stratification framework. Arch Intern Med. 2010;170(21):1900-1907. [PMID: 21098348]

Item 107   Answer: C
Educational Objective: Diagnose pheochromocytoma.

Measurement of this patient's plasma metanephrine level is appropriate. The surge in this patient's blood pressure noted during anesthesia induction could reflect a stimulus to catecholamine release from a tumor such as a pheochromocytoma. Pheochromocytomas are relatively rare tumors composed of chromaffin cells derived from the neural crest that occur in 0.1% to 0.6% of persons with hypertension. Most pheochromocytomas predominantly secrete norepinephrine, which results in sustained or episodic hypertension. Major symptoms include diaphoresis, pallor, palpitations, and headaches; the classic triad of sudden severe headache, diaphoresis, and palpitations is highly suggestive of pheochromocytoma. Other symptoms may include weight loss and dyspnea. Clinical manifestations are variable, with hypertension (episodic or sustained) observed in more than 90% of patients. Other manifestations include arrhythmias (atrial and ventricular fibrillation) and catecholamine-induced cardiomyopathy. Diagnosis requires a high degree of suspicion, with confirmation of excess catecholamine production either by 24-hour urine collection for catecholamine and metanephrine excretion or by measurement of plasma metanephrine; the latter is easier to obtain and has good sensitivity and specificity. Definitive therapy for these tumors is surgical removal.

Elevated catecholamines typically prompt a tumor search by conventional imaging of the adrenal glands (such as CT or MRI) or the use of specialized nuclear scans such as iodine-131–metaiodobenzylguanidine (^{131}I-MIBG). CT or MRI should be obtained only after the diagnosis of pheochromocytoma is biochemically confirmed and is therefore not appropriate for this patient at this time.

Catheter-based kidney angiography can be harmful for this patient because pheochromocytomas occasionally secrete catecholamines in response to the iodinated contrast. Furthermore, severe hypertension associated with anesthesia induction is most compatible with pheochromocytoma, not renal artery stenosis.

Transthoracic echocardiography has many indications, most commonly for evaluating heart murmurs and left ventricular function. This patient has no obvious

CONT.

indication for transthoracic echocardiography, and this test will not be helpful in the evaluation of her recent episode of hypertension.

> **KEY POINT**
>
> - Pheochromocytoma can cause sustained or paroxysmal hypertension, diaphoresis, headache, and anxiety.

Bibliography

Prejbisz A, Lenders JW, Eisenhofer G, Januszewicz A. Cardiovascular manifestations of phaeochromocytoma. J Hypertens. 2011;29(11):2049-2060. [PMID: 21826022]

Item 108   Answer: B
Educational Objective: Manage hypernatremia.

The presence of significant hypernatremia indicates a relative deficit of water to sodium, and correction of the water deficit with 5% dextrose in water is indicated for this patient. The urine osmolality greater than 300 mosm/kg H_2O in this patient with polyuria is consistent with an osmotic diuresis. The diuresis that follows relief of urinary tract obstruction is predominantly due to excretion of retained solute. Urinary tract obstruction can lead to tubular injury and an associated concentrating defect. There is little evidence to guide the optimal rate of correction of hypernatremia, but a correction rate of 6 to 10 meq/L (6-10 mmol/L) per day is reasonable.

The presence of edema and hypernatremia in this patient is indicative of excess total body sodium; therefore, 0.45% sodium chloride is not indicated.

Desmopressin is indicated to treat patients with central diabetes insipidus and can also be employed as an adjunct in the management of nephrogenic diabetes insipidus, but the relatively high urine osmolality and high urine volume are most consistent with a solute diuresis.

Urine osmolality is generally less than 200 mosm/kg H_2O in patients with diabetes insipidus. A water deprivation test, which poses a risk of worsening hypernatremia, is therefore not indicated.

> **KEY POINT**
>
> - Correction of the water deficit using 5% dextrose in water is appropriate in patients with significant hypernatremia without evidence of hypovolemia or sodium depletion.

Bibliography

Pokaharel M, Block CA. Dysnatremia in the ICU. Curr Opin Crit Care. 2011;17(6):581-593. [PMID: 22027406]

Answers and Critiques

Index

Note: Page numbers followed by f and t denote figures and tables, respectively. Test questions are indicated by Q.

A · NAME AND ADDRESS (Please complete.)

Last Name   First Name   Middle Initial

Address

Address cont.

City   State   ZIP Code

Country

Email address

ACP
AMERICAN COLLEGE OF PHYSICIANS
INTERNAL MEDICINE | Doctors for Adults

Medical Knowledge Self-Assessment Program® 16

TO EARN *AMA PRA CATEGORY 1 CREDITS*™ YOU MUST:

1. Answer all questions.
2. Score a minimum of 50% correct.

- -

TO EARN *FREE* SAME-DAY *AMA PRA CATEGORY 1 CREDITS*™ ONLINE:

1. Answer all of your questions.
2. Go to **mksap.acponline.org** and access the appropriate answer sheet.
3. Transcribe your answers and submit for CME credits.
4. You can also enter your answers directly at **mksap.acponline.org** without first using this answer sheet.

To Submit Your Answer Sheet by Mail or FAX for a $10 Administrative Fee per Answer Sheet:

1. Answer all of your questions and calculate your score.
2. Complete boxes A–F.
3. Complete payment information.
4. Send the answer sheet and payment information to ACP, using the FAX number/address listed below.

B · Order Number

(Use the Order Number on your MKSAP materials packing slip.)

C · ACP ID Number

(Refer to packing slip in your MKSAP materials for your ACP ID Number.)

COMPLETE FORM BELOW ONLY IF YOU SUBMIT BY MAIL OR FAX

Last Name   First Name   MI

Payment Information. Must remit in US funds, drawn on a US bank.

The processing fee for each paper answer sheet is $10.

☐ Check, made payable to ACP, enclosed

Charge to ☐ **VISA** ☐ **Master** ☐ **AMERICAN EXPRESS** ☐ **DISCOVER**

Card Number _____

Expiration Date _____ / _____
            MM   YY

Security code (3 or 4 digit #s) _____

Signature _____

Fax to: 215-351-2799

Questions?
Go to **mskap.acponline.org** or email **custserv@acponline.org**

Mail to:
Member and Customer Service
American College of Physicians
190 N. Independence Mall West
Philadelphia, PA 19106-1572

D

TEST TYPE

Test Type	Maximum Number of CME Credits
○ Cardiovascular Medicine	18
○ Dermatology	10
○ Gastroenterology and Hepatology	14
○ Hematology and Oncology	20
○ Neurology	14
○ Rheumatology	14
○ Endocrinology and Metabolism	12
○ General Internal Medicine	24
○ Infectious Disease	16
○ Nephrology	16
○ Pulmonary and Critical Care Medicine	16

E

CREDITS CLAIMED ON SECTION
(1 hour = 1 credit)

Enter the number of credits earned on the test to the nearest quarter hour. Physicians should claim only the credit commensurate with the extent of their participation in the activity.

F

Enter your score here.

Instructions for calculating your own score are found in front of the self-assessment test in each book.

You must receive a minimum score of 50% correct.

_____ %

Credit Submission Date: _____

1 Ⓐ Ⓑ Ⓒ Ⓓ Ⓔ
2 Ⓐ Ⓑ Ⓒ Ⓓ Ⓔ
3 Ⓐ Ⓑ Ⓒ Ⓓ Ⓔ
4 Ⓐ Ⓑ Ⓒ Ⓓ Ⓔ
5 Ⓐ Ⓑ Ⓒ Ⓓ Ⓔ
6 Ⓐ Ⓑ Ⓒ Ⓓ Ⓔ
7 Ⓐ Ⓑ Ⓒ Ⓓ Ⓔ
8 Ⓐ Ⓑ Ⓒ Ⓓ Ⓔ
9 Ⓐ Ⓑ Ⓒ Ⓓ Ⓔ
10 Ⓐ Ⓑ Ⓒ Ⓓ Ⓔ
11 Ⓐ Ⓑ Ⓒ Ⓓ Ⓔ
12 Ⓐ Ⓑ Ⓒ Ⓓ Ⓔ
13 Ⓐ Ⓑ Ⓒ Ⓓ Ⓔ
14 Ⓐ Ⓑ Ⓒ Ⓓ Ⓔ
15 Ⓐ Ⓑ Ⓒ Ⓓ Ⓔ
16 Ⓐ Ⓑ Ⓒ Ⓓ Ⓔ
17 Ⓐ Ⓑ Ⓒ Ⓓ Ⓔ
18 Ⓐ Ⓑ Ⓒ Ⓓ Ⓔ
19 Ⓐ Ⓑ Ⓒ Ⓓ Ⓔ
20 Ⓐ Ⓑ Ⓒ Ⓓ Ⓔ
21 Ⓐ Ⓑ Ⓒ Ⓓ Ⓔ
22 Ⓐ Ⓑ Ⓒ Ⓓ Ⓔ
23 Ⓐ Ⓑ Ⓒ Ⓓ Ⓔ
24 Ⓐ Ⓑ Ⓒ Ⓓ Ⓔ
25 Ⓐ Ⓑ Ⓒ Ⓓ Ⓔ
26 Ⓐ Ⓑ Ⓒ Ⓓ Ⓔ
27 Ⓐ Ⓑ Ⓒ Ⓓ Ⓔ
28 Ⓐ Ⓑ Ⓒ Ⓓ Ⓔ
29 Ⓐ Ⓑ Ⓒ Ⓓ Ⓔ
30 Ⓐ Ⓑ Ⓒ Ⓓ Ⓔ
31 Ⓐ Ⓑ Ⓒ Ⓓ Ⓔ
32 Ⓐ Ⓑ Ⓒ Ⓓ Ⓔ
33 Ⓐ Ⓑ Ⓒ Ⓓ Ⓔ
34 Ⓐ Ⓑ Ⓒ Ⓓ Ⓔ
35 Ⓐ Ⓑ Ⓒ Ⓓ Ⓔ
36 Ⓐ Ⓑ Ⓒ Ⓓ Ⓔ
37 Ⓐ Ⓑ Ⓒ Ⓓ Ⓔ
38 Ⓐ Ⓑ Ⓒ Ⓓ Ⓔ
39 Ⓐ Ⓑ Ⓒ Ⓓ Ⓔ
40 Ⓐ Ⓑ Ⓒ Ⓓ Ⓔ
41 Ⓐ Ⓑ Ⓒ Ⓓ Ⓔ
42 Ⓐ Ⓑ Ⓒ Ⓓ Ⓔ
43 Ⓐ Ⓑ Ⓒ Ⓓ Ⓔ
44 Ⓐ Ⓑ Ⓒ Ⓓ Ⓔ
45 Ⓐ Ⓑ Ⓒ Ⓓ Ⓔ

46 Ⓐ Ⓑ Ⓒ Ⓓ Ⓔ
47 Ⓐ Ⓑ Ⓒ Ⓓ Ⓔ
48 Ⓐ Ⓑ Ⓒ Ⓓ Ⓔ
49 Ⓐ Ⓑ Ⓒ Ⓓ Ⓔ
50 Ⓐ Ⓑ Ⓒ Ⓓ Ⓔ
51 Ⓐ Ⓑ Ⓒ Ⓓ Ⓔ
52 Ⓐ Ⓑ Ⓒ Ⓓ Ⓔ
53 Ⓐ Ⓑ Ⓒ Ⓓ Ⓔ
54 Ⓐ Ⓑ Ⓒ Ⓓ Ⓔ
55 Ⓐ Ⓑ Ⓒ Ⓓ Ⓔ
56 Ⓐ Ⓑ Ⓒ Ⓓ Ⓔ
57 Ⓐ Ⓑ Ⓒ Ⓓ Ⓔ
58 Ⓐ Ⓑ Ⓒ Ⓓ Ⓔ
59 Ⓐ Ⓑ Ⓒ Ⓓ Ⓔ
60 Ⓐ Ⓑ Ⓒ Ⓓ Ⓔ
61 Ⓐ Ⓑ Ⓒ Ⓓ Ⓔ
62 Ⓐ Ⓑ Ⓒ Ⓓ Ⓔ
63 Ⓐ Ⓑ Ⓒ Ⓓ Ⓔ
64 Ⓐ Ⓑ Ⓒ Ⓓ Ⓔ
65 Ⓐ Ⓑ Ⓒ Ⓓ Ⓔ
66 Ⓐ Ⓑ Ⓒ Ⓓ Ⓔ
67 Ⓐ Ⓑ Ⓒ Ⓓ Ⓔ
68 Ⓐ Ⓑ Ⓒ Ⓓ Ⓔ
69 Ⓐ Ⓑ Ⓒ Ⓓ Ⓔ
70 Ⓐ Ⓑ Ⓒ Ⓓ Ⓔ
71 Ⓐ Ⓑ Ⓒ Ⓓ Ⓔ
72 Ⓐ Ⓑ Ⓒ Ⓓ Ⓔ
73 Ⓐ Ⓑ Ⓒ Ⓓ Ⓔ
74 Ⓐ Ⓑ Ⓒ Ⓓ Ⓔ
75 Ⓐ Ⓑ Ⓒ Ⓓ Ⓔ
76 Ⓐ Ⓑ Ⓒ Ⓓ Ⓔ
77 Ⓐ Ⓑ Ⓒ Ⓓ Ⓔ
78 Ⓐ Ⓑ Ⓒ Ⓓ Ⓔ
79 Ⓐ Ⓑ Ⓒ Ⓓ Ⓔ
80 Ⓐ Ⓑ Ⓒ Ⓓ Ⓔ
81 Ⓐ Ⓑ Ⓒ Ⓓ Ⓔ
82 Ⓐ Ⓑ Ⓒ Ⓓ Ⓔ
83 Ⓐ Ⓑ Ⓒ Ⓓ Ⓔ
84 Ⓐ Ⓑ Ⓒ Ⓓ Ⓔ
85 Ⓐ Ⓑ Ⓒ Ⓓ Ⓔ
86 Ⓐ Ⓑ Ⓒ Ⓓ Ⓔ
87 Ⓐ Ⓑ Ⓒ Ⓓ Ⓔ
88 Ⓐ Ⓑ Ⓒ Ⓓ Ⓔ
89 Ⓐ Ⓑ Ⓒ Ⓓ Ⓔ
90 Ⓐ Ⓑ Ⓒ Ⓓ Ⓔ

91 Ⓐ Ⓑ Ⓒ Ⓓ Ⓔ
92 Ⓐ Ⓑ Ⓒ Ⓓ Ⓔ
93 Ⓐ Ⓑ Ⓒ Ⓓ Ⓔ
94 Ⓐ Ⓑ Ⓒ Ⓓ Ⓔ
95 Ⓐ Ⓑ Ⓒ Ⓓ Ⓔ
96 Ⓐ Ⓑ Ⓒ Ⓓ Ⓔ
97 Ⓐ Ⓑ Ⓒ Ⓓ Ⓔ
98 Ⓐ Ⓑ Ⓒ Ⓓ Ⓔ
99 Ⓐ Ⓑ Ⓒ Ⓓ Ⓔ
100 Ⓐ Ⓑ Ⓒ Ⓓ Ⓔ
101 Ⓐ Ⓑ Ⓒ Ⓓ Ⓔ
102 Ⓐ Ⓑ Ⓒ Ⓓ Ⓔ
103 Ⓐ Ⓑ Ⓒ Ⓓ Ⓔ
104 Ⓐ Ⓑ Ⓒ Ⓓ Ⓔ
105 Ⓐ Ⓑ Ⓒ Ⓓ Ⓔ
106 Ⓐ Ⓑ Ⓒ Ⓓ Ⓔ
107 Ⓐ Ⓑ Ⓒ Ⓓ Ⓔ
108 Ⓐ Ⓑ Ⓒ Ⓓ Ⓔ
109 Ⓐ Ⓑ Ⓒ Ⓓ Ⓔ
110 Ⓐ Ⓑ Ⓒ Ⓓ Ⓔ
111 Ⓐ Ⓑ Ⓒ Ⓓ Ⓔ
112 Ⓐ Ⓑ Ⓒ Ⓓ Ⓔ
113 Ⓐ Ⓑ Ⓒ Ⓓ Ⓔ
114 Ⓐ Ⓑ Ⓒ Ⓓ Ⓔ
115 Ⓐ Ⓑ Ⓒ Ⓓ Ⓔ
116 Ⓐ Ⓑ Ⓒ Ⓓ Ⓔ
117 Ⓐ Ⓑ Ⓒ Ⓓ Ⓔ
118 Ⓐ Ⓑ Ⓒ Ⓓ Ⓔ
119 Ⓐ Ⓑ Ⓒ Ⓓ Ⓔ
120 Ⓐ Ⓑ Ⓒ Ⓓ Ⓔ
121 Ⓐ Ⓑ Ⓒ Ⓓ Ⓔ
122 Ⓐ Ⓑ Ⓒ Ⓓ Ⓔ
123 Ⓐ Ⓑ Ⓒ Ⓓ Ⓔ
124 Ⓐ Ⓑ Ⓒ Ⓓ Ⓔ
125 Ⓐ Ⓑ Ⓒ Ⓓ Ⓔ
126 Ⓐ Ⓑ Ⓒ Ⓓ Ⓔ
127 Ⓐ Ⓑ Ⓒ Ⓓ Ⓔ
128 Ⓐ Ⓑ Ⓒ Ⓓ Ⓔ
129 Ⓐ Ⓑ Ⓒ Ⓓ Ⓔ
130 Ⓐ Ⓑ Ⓒ Ⓓ Ⓔ
131 Ⓐ Ⓑ Ⓒ Ⓓ Ⓔ
132 Ⓐ Ⓑ Ⓒ Ⓓ Ⓔ
133 Ⓐ Ⓑ Ⓒ Ⓓ Ⓔ
134 Ⓐ Ⓑ Ⓒ Ⓓ Ⓔ
135 Ⓐ Ⓑ Ⓒ Ⓓ Ⓔ

136 Ⓐ Ⓑ Ⓒ Ⓓ Ⓔ
137 Ⓐ Ⓑ Ⓒ Ⓓ Ⓔ
138 Ⓐ Ⓑ Ⓒ Ⓓ Ⓔ
139 Ⓐ Ⓑ Ⓒ Ⓓ Ⓔ
140 Ⓐ Ⓑ Ⓒ Ⓓ Ⓔ
141 Ⓐ Ⓑ Ⓒ Ⓓ Ⓔ
142 Ⓐ Ⓑ Ⓒ Ⓓ Ⓔ
143 Ⓐ Ⓑ Ⓒ Ⓓ Ⓔ
144 Ⓐ Ⓑ Ⓒ Ⓓ Ⓔ
145 Ⓐ Ⓑ Ⓒ Ⓓ Ⓔ
146 Ⓐ Ⓑ Ⓒ Ⓓ Ⓔ
147 Ⓐ Ⓑ Ⓒ Ⓓ Ⓔ
148 Ⓐ Ⓑ Ⓒ Ⓓ Ⓔ
149 Ⓐ Ⓑ Ⓒ Ⓓ Ⓔ
150 Ⓐ Ⓑ Ⓒ Ⓓ Ⓔ
151 Ⓐ Ⓑ Ⓒ Ⓓ Ⓔ
152 Ⓐ Ⓑ Ⓒ Ⓓ Ⓔ
153 Ⓐ Ⓑ Ⓒ Ⓓ Ⓔ
154 Ⓐ Ⓑ Ⓒ Ⓓ Ⓔ
155 Ⓐ Ⓑ Ⓒ Ⓓ Ⓔ
156 Ⓐ Ⓑ Ⓒ Ⓓ Ⓔ
157 Ⓐ Ⓑ Ⓒ Ⓓ Ⓔ
158 Ⓐ Ⓑ Ⓒ Ⓓ Ⓔ
159 Ⓐ Ⓑ Ⓒ Ⓓ Ⓔ
160 Ⓐ Ⓑ Ⓒ Ⓓ Ⓔ
161 Ⓐ Ⓑ Ⓒ Ⓓ Ⓔ
162 Ⓐ Ⓑ Ⓒ Ⓓ Ⓔ
163 Ⓐ Ⓑ Ⓒ Ⓓ Ⓔ
164 Ⓐ Ⓑ Ⓒ Ⓓ Ⓔ
165 Ⓐ Ⓑ Ⓒ Ⓓ Ⓔ
166 Ⓐ Ⓑ Ⓒ Ⓓ Ⓔ
167 Ⓐ Ⓑ Ⓒ Ⓓ Ⓔ
168 Ⓐ Ⓑ Ⓒ Ⓓ Ⓔ
169 Ⓐ Ⓑ Ⓒ Ⓓ Ⓔ
170 Ⓐ Ⓑ Ⓒ Ⓓ Ⓔ
171 Ⓐ Ⓑ Ⓒ Ⓓ Ⓔ
172 Ⓐ Ⓑ Ⓒ Ⓓ Ⓔ
173 Ⓐ Ⓑ Ⓒ Ⓓ Ⓔ
174 Ⓐ Ⓑ Ⓒ Ⓓ Ⓔ
175 Ⓐ Ⓑ Ⓒ Ⓓ Ⓔ
176 Ⓐ Ⓑ Ⓒ Ⓓ Ⓔ
177 Ⓐ Ⓑ Ⓒ Ⓓ Ⓔ
178 Ⓐ Ⓑ Ⓒ Ⓓ Ⓔ
179 Ⓐ Ⓑ Ⓒ Ⓓ Ⓔ
180 Ⓐ Ⓑ Ⓒ Ⓓ Ⓔ

MK1